Red and Hot

RED AND HOT

*The Fate of Jazz
in the Soviet Union
1917–1980*

S. FREDERICK STARR

New York   Oxford
OXFORD UNIVERSITY PRESS
1983

Copyright © 1983 by Oxford University Press, Inc.

Library of Congress Cataloging in Publication Data
Starr, S. Frederick.
Red and hot.
Includes index.
1. Jazz music—Soviet Union—History
and criticism. I. Title.
ML3509.S7S7   1983   785.42'0947   82–14506
ISBN 0–19–503163–6

Printing (last digit): 9 8 7 6 5 4 3 2 1

Printed in the United States of America

Dedicated to my fellow
jazz musicians in the USSR

Forsan et haec olim
meminisse juvabit . . .
Virgil, *Aeneid* I, 203

Acknowledgments

This book is a long answer to a simple question frequently posed to me by friends: Is there any relationship between two of my principal interests, the Soviet Union and jazz? For years my standard reply was that there was not, that Russians considered jazz to be a particularly decadent manifestation of dying capitalism. And there the matter rested, until I noticed that this reply raised eyebrows among persons more knowledgeable than myself. Marie Ciliberti and Willis Conover of the Voice of America assigned themselves the task of educating me. Along with David Burns of the International Communication Agency, they introduced me to Alexei Batashev's fine monograph *Sovetskii dzhaz*. The idea of translating this study immediately came to mind.

But the project soon ran into difficulties. Many things had to be explained for Western readers; important events not touched on in the book had to be filled in, and the entire story brought up to date. Most important, valuable new materials had to be exploited and the entire story retold from the standpoint of its significance to the history of Soviet culture as a whole. Soon a new book was born. Nonetheless, I wish to acknowledge my indebtedness to Mr. Batashev, and also to the many other Soviet authors whose published work I have drawn on. I am honored to claim them as colleagues, fellow musicians, and friends. But they are in no way responsible for any interpretations or views expressed in this book. Indeed, I would expect that they might frequently wish to set me straight.

The gathering of documentary information on Soviet jazz required the collaboration of many people. Kevin Hendzel, a promising young Sovietologist from Georgetown University, has been particularly helpful over several years and has added his own astute judgments at several important points. Al Starck of Neenah, Wisconsin, generously shared his splendid collection of Soviet jazz recordings, and John Bowlt, director of the Institute of Modern Russian Culture at Blue Lagoon, had made available rare printed sheet music. Others who have provided timely assistance or criticism include George Avakian, Professor Sheila Fitzpatrick of the University of Texas, Professor Alma H. Law of the City University of New York, Professor Richard Stites of Georgetown University, Dr. John Steiner of Milwaukee, Valentin Berezhkov of the Academy of Sciences of the USSR, New Orleans's jazz chronicler Al Rose, and especially my father, Stephen Z. Starr. Thanks to the Woodrow Wilson International Center for Scholars and its director, James H. Billington, it was possible to exploit the unparalleled resources of the Library of Congress.

Finally, I wish to express my enormous gratitude to Mrs. Wynona Hebert Burmaster of Harvey, Louisiana, who prepared the manuscript at several stages. Her combination of Cajun cheer and redbeans-and-rice practicality helped to bring the project to completion.

This book draws heavily on oral interviews and rare printed sources preserved only in private collections. My gratitude to the following people who permitted themselves to be interviewed is enormous, and far beyond my capacity to thank them here: Vassily Aksyonov; Nina Berberova; Igor Berukshtis; Jurgis Blekaitis; Harold Boxer; Mikhail Brantsberg; Vladimir Brovkin; Gigi Cavicchioli; George Costakis; James Critchlow; Ruth Dreyfous; Vera S. Dunham; Ambassador Eldridge Durbrow; Vladimir Feuertag; Leo

Feigin; Maurice Friedberg; Vladimir Frumkin; John Garvey; Anatole Gerasimov; Daniil Granin; Lev Grozovski; Juri Jelagin; Ruth Turkow Kaminska; Ambassador and Mrs. George F. Kennan; Kenneth Kerst; Leonid Khotin; Alexander Kofman; Vadim Konson; Roman Kunsman; Mikhail Lantsman; Alexander Lehrman; Nathan Leites; Boris Ludmer; Igor Lundstrem; Louis Markowitz; Zbigniew Namyslowski; Valter Ojakäär; Stella Ogonkova; Mikhail Oleinikov; Valery Ponomarev; Bronis Raila; Francis Ronald; Felix Roven; Andre Rusanoff; Harrison Salisbury; Igor Saulsky; Mrs. Frances Schillinger; Vladimir Sermakashev; Arkadi Shabashov; Mr. and Mrs. Henry Shapiro; Konstantin Simis; Josef Skvorecky; Arthur Stoyanov; Vladimir Stoyanov; Kurt Strobel; Ilya Suslov; Vladimir Tkalich; Valentin Tsonev; Hans A. Tuck; Yuri Valov; Vadim Vyadro; Igor Vysotski; Igor Yahilevich; Ilkhonen Yoffe; Lev Zabeginsky; Sergei Zamashchikov.

New Orleans, Louisiana   S.F.S.
October 1982

A Note on Transliteration

Any system of transliteration from the Russian runs one of two risks. Either it follows commonly accepted English usage, in which case many Russian words become indecipherable to the experts. Or it adheres to one of the linguistically more precise systems, in which case the common reader is forced to discover the name of the composer of *Swan Lake* in *Chaikovskii* or, worse, *Čaikovskij*.

To resolve this problem, all Russian words appearing in footnotes are transliterated according to the Library of Congress system, except that soft signs are not indicated. But in the text, common English usage is followed throughout, e.g., *Tchaikovsky* rather than *Chaikovskii*; *Alexander* rather than *Aleksandr*, etc.

It is hoped that this dual system will satisfy both generalists and specialists.

Contents

Red and Hot

I
The Two Revolutions
of 1917

But in abandoning our ancestors' social state and throwing
their institutions, ideas, and mores pell-mell behind us, what
have we to put in their place?

Alexis de Tocqueville, 1835

Europe's nineteenth century ended not in 1900 but in 1914 with
the outbreak of the War To End All Wars. Before the carnage was
over, the empires of Germany and Austria-Hungary had crashed to
pieces. Great Britain and France, the nominal victors, paid such a
price in lives and resources that henceforth their greatest hope was
simply to hold on to the overseas territories they possessed, rather
than add to them. In Russia, the war so weakened the Romanov
dynasty, which had just celebrated its tricentennial in 1913, that it
was easily toppled by a *coup d'état* on March 12, 1917.

Maurice Ravel (who was later influenced by jazz)[1] created a musical memorial to the demise of old Europe in "La Valse." For the
century that began with the "dancing congress" of Vienna in 1815,
this ballroom dance had epitomized the fragile balance of form and
freedom, bourgeois refinement and peasant sensuality that the economic and political elite of post-Napoleonic Europe regarded so
highly. Wherever European civilization held sway, there was the
waltz. Leaders of the Meiji Restoration in Japan donned frock coats
to dance it, and when the Mexican army's band traveled the countryside, it brought along such three-quarter-time favorites as Juven-

tino Rojas's "Sobre las olas." Jewish orchestras in Odessa featured waltzes in their programs, as did black and Creole orchestras in New Orleans.[2] In "La Valse" the lilting dance melody breaks down into screaming cacophony. Even without Ravel's heavy symbolism, music lovers and politicians everywhere realized that an established order had collapsed.

What would replace the political system the war had destroyed? Alternatives were posed almost immediately. Disillusioned young men in Italy and Germany began dreaming of a restoration of their countries' might along rigorously nationalist and populist lines rather than on the liberal or conservative models that had long held sway. More enduring in the long run than this nascent fascism were the political ideals epitomized by Woodrow Wilson and Vladimir Ilich Lenin. By strange coincidence, April 16, 1917, marked a major milestone in the lives of both men as well as the beginning of their momentous impact on the future of the world. On that day, President Wilson announced that the United States would enter the war against Germany and Lenin arrived at the Finland Station in the Russian capital to lead his Bolshevik party's effort to take power from the temporary government that had been formed after the successful coup against Tsar Nicholas II. Each man was impelled by the messianic conviction that the new Europe would best be constructed on the basis of his own political program. From one fringe of the European world, Wilson brought the ideal of constitutional democracy, which he worked vigorously to implant in the new states carved out of the ruins of the Austro-Hungarian and Russian empires. From the other fringe of the European world, Lenin espoused the cause of proletarian dictatorship and announced to his surprised comrades that the time was ripe to seize power from the Provisional Government and then ignite all Europe with the flame of Bolshevik revolution.

If the collapse of the nineteenth-century order called for new ideals in politics, still more did it cause a vacuum in the realm of culture. Members of the prosperous upper and middle classes who had waltzed through the nineteenth century had also revelled in the ideals of rationalism, nationalism, romanticism, and progress. They disseminated these ideals wherever they extended their political sway, and dedicated academies, opera houses, and libraries to them. Not everyone accepted the program of the establishment, however. Youth rejected cold rationalism, socialists abjured nationalism, feminists opposed the chivalric trappings of romanticism, and a diverse band of decadents denied that history was moving forward.[3] Together, these dissidents constituted a kind of motley counterculture barely held in check by official values. The dam finally burst in World War I, allowing free rein to these and other discordant voices. In Russia, Germany, and elsewhere, the stresses of war and defeat destroyed orthodoxies and opened the way for the prewar rebels to take over. The rush to define and embrace new values was on.

The Bolsheviks' Mobilization of Culture

The Bolsheviks who seized power in Petrograd had no doubt that their revolution would create a totally new culture, one that would eventually permeate every aspect of life and art. Never before had a government come to power with more grandiose expectations. The French Revolution had given rise to great hopes, but the methods of mass communication open to the Jacobins were insignificant in comparison with those made possible in the industrialized twentieth century. The Bolsheviks by contrast had gained control over the eighth industrial power on earth and could reasonably expect to build up modern media of communications. The film and recording industries were placed at the disposal of the proletarian dictatorship and were used to the hilt. Over the years after 1917 it gradually became apparent that there had never been a government more willing to use the full weight of its power to implant its cultural ideals in every area of human endeavor, using every means available to do so, including force.

Beyond this, the Bolsheviks were agreed that the new culture they would create would eventually cross all national frontiers and be embraced by working people everywhere. They marched to the "Internationale," and under a banner emblazoned with Marx's slogan, "Workers of the World Unite." From the outset, Bolshevik pronouncements on culture and the arts were addressed to the entire world. According to their scenario, laboring people would unite politically and then lay claim to the first truly popular culture of the secular masses.

There was serious disagreement among Bolshevik leaders as to how the new culture would be forged. For over a decade before 1917 the party had been split between rival advocates of two very different approaches. One faction, more activist, held that a "proletarian culture" should be created at once and implanted in society by governmental action. The second faction, with which Lenin sided, principally for pragmatic reasons, held that the government should concentrate its attention on building a socialist economy and let the cultural "superstructure" arise naturally from the new conditions. The chasm between these two approaches was deep and gave rise to heated polemics that crackled in the years before 1917.

In practice, the activist approach accorded better with the Bolshevik mentality than did the more evolutionary, and hence passive, approach. Having rushed Marx's timetable by seizing power in a relatively backward part of Europe, the Bolsheviks were tempted now to force the pace of change in the cultural sphere by governmental intervention. Their goal was to create the New Soviet Man in Russia even before a state of socialism, let alone communism, had been reached. The argument for such a cultural revolution "from above" flew in the face of the writings of Marx and Engels but became more attractive simply because such a tactic might actually succeed. The history of Soviet culture between 1917 and the unleashing of Stalin's Cultural Revolution in 1928 is the story of the triumph of this interventionist approach.

None of the separate components of Bolshevik cultural politics was new in 1917. The notion of a culture of the proletarian masses, the idea of internationalism and the vigorous use of state power to implant it, all had ample precedents in both the radical and the conservative traditions of Europe. Even the exploitation of modern technology to disseminate official ideals had been pioneered by the European powers, most notably in the propaganda campaigns mounted to whip up support for the Great War. The Bolsheviks strove to develop these inherited methods further than anyone before them, and their experience was closely studied elsewhere. The widespread willingness to shape mass attitudes "from above" is one of the truly revolutionary legacies of the World War I era in general and of the Bolshevik victory in particular.

What was to be the content of the official mass culture patronized by the Bolshevik state? No clear answer existed in 1917, or even by the time of the tenth anniversary of the October Revolution in 1927. Indeed, skeptics might wonder whether any adequate answer has even been put forward. One early and provocative intimation of what Russia's new proletarian culture might be like, at least in the conception of an avant-garde elite, was provided by an effervescent group of innovators in art, music, and literature. The avant-gardists struggled to demonstrate the compatibility of abstract and nonobjective art with political revolution. The new Bolshevik establishment saw matters differently, however. Having seized power as a minority, the Bolsheviks regarded maintaining control as their first objective. To do so, it was absolutely essential that they demonstrate to the population at large that they could rebuild the shattered economy, construct new factories, and impose order in the countryside and tranquility in the cities. Is it surprising that they should have turned their backs on purely abstract art and that civic themes dominated every mode of expression patronized by the new Bolshevik regime? The country desperately needed work done, so the dignity of labor was everywhere trumpeted. It was hoped that a less austere life would eventually be possible, once Russia had passed into socialism and thence to pure communism. Meanwhile, however, the theme of honest toil was endlessly repeated in the realistic paintings of the Association of Artists of the Russian Revolution,[4] in the words to hundreds of officially commissioned popular songs, in the librettos of operas, and in the numerous architectural competitions for designs for workers' clubs and factory kitchens. Leisure was not completely ignored. But the playing fields, cinema theaters, and vacation facilities that were constructed had as their explicit purpose the mobilization of labor for the task of national reconstruction.

The Americans' Cultural Revolution

Meanwhile, a very different cultural ideal was bursting through the crust of middle-class European life. Gaining momentum with astounding speed, it rushed into the spiritual vacuum created by a disastrous war, the same vacuum, of course, that Bolshevism intended to fill. No less revolutionary in its message than the Soviet ideology, this new wave also swept into the European world from its periphery, in this instance from the United States. American popular culture, taken for granted at home, became a powerful force abroad.

As a land of immigrants of diverse origins, America could claim no indigenous and broadly accepted folk culture. The localized folk life—and there was a great deal of it—was either condemned to provincial obscurity or quickly picked up and transformed by a host of small and independent business enterprises dedicated to detecting and serving the mass taste of the highly diversified American public. Traveling circuses, music publishers, mail order houses and chain stores, mass-circulation magazines, movie makers, and clothing manufacturers contributed to the formation of a mass culture. Backing up these myriad industries were energetic advertising agents who, in turn, were served by market researchers. By the early twentieth century, Americans could boast of a mass culture that was truly popular and, equally important, in no way beholden to the state for its creation or maintenance. Indeed, in no other major nation was the government less in a position to alter public taste than in the United States. No major European country had so thin a superstructure of "high culture" or so few official organs dedicated to its preservation and maintenance. With no generalized folk culture to fall back on, Americans at all levels of society devoted relatively more time and interest to the ever-changing world of popular culture than did Europeans. To a degree that Americans themselves seem incapable of appreciating, their society became, by the early twentieth century, the world's leading laboratory for the creation and dissemination of a consumer-oriented popular culture "from below."

If the collapse of the nineteenth-century European order opened the way for the rise of the Bolshevik ideal of a mass culture defined "from above," it equally cleared the way for America's multinational popular culture to penetrate back to the many nations from which the population of the United States was originally drawn. The various forms of popular culture pioneered in the United States were to change Europeans' lives far more than the new economic and political order introduced by Lenin.

American popular culture manifests itself in a bewildering range of forms and media. To single out one as the sun around which the others revolve is grossly to understate the diversity and richness of the autonomous public imagination. Yet in the twentieth century there does exist one form of expression—jazz—that has far outstripped the others in its impact upon social life, private relations, and practically every other field of the arts. This form crystallized so completely the values of the times that the post-World War I era became known as the "Jazz Age."

What is jazz? Critics and musicologists have squabbled for years over a satisfactory definition. Quite reasonably, they have concentrated on such musical traits as synocopation, improvisation, and the use of "blue" notes. As the list is extended, and as the discussion plunges deeper and deeper into the arcana of polyphony and contrapuntal rhythmic formations, the essence of the music is easily lost from view. To performers and audience alike, the glory or baseness of jazz at its inception was its raucousness and utter indifference to the niceties of nineteenth-century musical etiquette. This was a music in which horn players deliberately bent notes off pitch, in which drummers played at once whole sets of noisemakers including cymbals and Chinese tom-toms, in which the newly popular slide trombone was permitted to smear notes together in guttural glissandos, and in which—and this was the worst of all—that obnoxiously nasal misfit, the saxophone, was actually received as an equal partner. You could growl into your cornet or stick your fingers into its bell, you could hum or spit into your clarinet like a Kurdish tribesman, or you could hold a toilet plunger in front of your trombone—and be praised for it! A generation of young people the world over were to escape from the tedious ritual of compulsory musical instruction through jazz.

Jazz, then, appeared to the world of 1917 as aggressively anarchistic, a slap in the face of "cultivated" taste, the antithesis of the virtues of proficiency and technical mastery that had built European civilization in the nineteenth century. It was no less aggressively individualistic. In retrospect, we might be impressed by the close coordination among performers necessary to produce the tight New Orleans ensemble style that conquered the public in 1917. At the time, however, it was the exuberant individualism of the new music that aroused comment. Every player seemed to fend for himself. Gone was the enlightened despotism of the director, without whose permission you could play neither loud nor soft in a classical orchestra. In jazz you could do just as you liked, or so it seemed to critics and the countless young musicians who flocked to the bold new idiom. Not only that but it all worked out in the end to produce an unprecedented and exciting music. Unlike the old societies that had been discredited by the Armageddon of World War I, the "society" of the jazz band offered unlimited freedom to the individual, and yet the community as a whole—the "sound"—was still greater than the sum of its parts. Thus, the jazz band solved the great conundrum of nineteenth-century social theory and romantic aesthetics. It reconciled the individual and society, giving each a new freedom and direction that was inconceivable even to the most utopian dreamers of the world that had died.

A second line of definition of jazz, equally valid, concentrates on its social role. F. Scott Fitzgerald, who gave the Jazz Age its name, offered this:

> The word "jazz," in its progress toward respectability, has meant first sex, then dancing, then music. It is associated with a state of nervous stimulation, not unlike that of big cities behind the lines of war.[5]

The New Orleans *Times-Picayune*, whose editors had to confront jazz long before most writers had the opportunity, said much the same thing, in high dudgeon, in June 1917:

> To uncertain natures, wild sound and meaningless noise have an exciting, almost an intoxicating effect, like crude colors and strong perfume, the sight of flesh or the sadistic pleasure in blood. To such as these, the jass [*sic*] is a delight. A dance to the unstable bray of the sackbut is a sensual delight more intense and quite different from the languor of a Viennese waltz or the refined sentiment and respectful emotion of the eighteenth century minuet.[6]

Hundreds of newspaper articles around the world were to echo this complaint over the succeeding decades. They correctly, if malevolently, identified the passions that suffused the world of jazz and contrasted them with the more decorous feelings that had been considered acceptable in nineteenth-century middle-class society.

Those seeking the genealogy of jazz have frequently focused on Storyville, New Orleans's notorious red-light district established in 1897. Something akin to jazz was already being played on New Orleans streets and at public gatherings well before alderman Sidney Story applied the idea of concentrating prostitution in the twenty-square-block area. But even if jazz was not born in Story's "District," it thrived in that lusty sporting-house environment and, more important, carried the aura of that milieu wherever it went, like the smell of cigar smoke in the clothes of an old-time politician. Pious and well-intentioned campaigns by do-gooders to clean up the image of jazz either failed outright or had precisely the opposite effect that their promoters intended.

The gradual demise of Storyville after 1905 attests to the breakup of nineteenth-century repressiveness. As one Storyville bawd put it, the girls out at the country club carried on so much that they were ruining business in the District.[7] The migration of freewheeling social and sexual mores from Storyville to the country club in the years before 1914 is the first step in a process that was to sweep jazz around the world. Everywhere jazz carried with it a message of social and sexual emancipation. Everywhere it thrust that message before the public at large, without respect for rank or education. Jazz, with its link to unrestrained physical motion and exuberant dance, became the premier symbol of the liberation of the human body. If the Bolshevik ideal of mass culture pertained most directly to the harnessing of collective man's physical energy through work, the message of American jazz spoke to the individual's free use of his bodily powers on his own time. If the emancipation movement embodied in the October Revolution and the culture it spawned was directed to the perfection of society in some utopian future, jazz epitomized the desire of each human being to express all the passions of the imperfect present—sadness, laughter, love, hate—through a Dionysian blend of rhythm, melody, and dance. No less than the dream of political revolution, jazz promised liberation from what the World War I era English poet Rupert Brooke described as "a world grown old and cold and weary."

The possible link between American jazz music and this fundamental shift in Western values in the twentieth century was pointed out almost as soon as the audience for the new music began to expand. Many who noted the connection were as appalled by jazz as they were by the morals they associated with it. Others viewed the matter more positively. One of the earliest, and certainly the most expansive, writers on the subject was a European, the German critic Georg Barthelme, who regaled readers of the *Kölnische Zeitung* with these words in 1919:

> Jazz is a philosophy of the world, and therefore to be taken seriously. Jazz is the expression of a *Kultur* epoch. . . . Jazz is a musical revelation, a religion, a philosophy of the world, just like Expressionism and Impressionism. Jazz is the logical development and completion of an idea that is called to introduce a new and better age. . . . There is nothing higher, nothing beyond![8]

That a European had been exposed to American jazz by 1919 attests to the intimate tie between that art form and the rapidly evolving technology of sound recording. To modern ears, the acoustical recordings of the teens and twenties offer little more than scratchy metallic inklings of the actual sound, which is lost. For those earlier in our century, who had encountered sound reproduction only through player pianos, the same acoustical recordings came as a revelation. With an investment of only a few francs or rubles for equipment, a listener in Paris or Moscow could eavesdrop on a studio in Chicago or New York. By 1914 over 500,000 phonographs were being produced each year in America alone; by 1919 the figure had soared to two and one quarter million. The number of individual records manufactured annually in America passed 50 million in 1914 and reached 100 million by 1921.[9]

Not everyone greeted sound recordings with equal enthusiasm. John Philip Sousa, for one, had vented his spleen against the new technology in an article in *Appleton's Magazine* as early as 1906. As the king of American march music saw it, recordings would bring about "a marked deterioration in American music and musical taste, an interruption in the musical development of the country and a host of other injuries to music in its artistic manifestations. . . ."[10] Sousa's trepidations were not without foundation. He was, after all, a composer and conductor, not an instrumentalist. His great achievement was to have welded four score individual bandsmen into what was virtually a single instrument controlled solely by his baton and dedicated to performing his own compositions. Sound recording shifted the spotlight from the conductor and composer to the performer and soloist. The poor conductor or arranger was invisible to the phonograph audience and even his best efforts paled beside those of the musicians whose performances were mysteriously re-created in the front parlors of the Western world.

A second source of Sousa's agitation was purely commercial. How would a composer realize financial gain from recordings of his works? Only in 1909 did American copyright law extend its protection to composers, and royalties for performance did not appear until after the foundation of the American Society of Composers, Authors, and Publishers (ASCAP) in 1914. Even then, it was above all the performer who benefited from the new technology. Enrico Caruso proved this beyond doubt when he used the humble vehicle of Italian folk songs to become a millionaire through recordings made before 1914.

By its nature, jazz could embrace the new technology with a vengeance. In its early days at least, jazz music had few jealous composers to protect. The authorship of many of the most popular works of classic jazz remains to this day a subject of lively contention among specialists. In cases where authorship was known, the "composer" was usually a performer as well, so that the tension between composer and performer was virtually nonexistent. Jazz, as a performer's music, welcomed the phonograph's emphasis on performance.

With the phonograph, the individuality of each performer could be communicated to the invisible audience. That the earliest jazz was contrapuntal, with several horns playing separate rhythmic lines at once, was all the better. Acoustical recording techniques were far better at picking up the sharply individuated sounds of distinct instruments in jazz than the smooth ensemble sound beloved by romantic symphonic orchestras and bands.

Yet another aspect of sound recording that made it peculiarly appropriate to jazz was its capacity to capture the spontaneity of the moment and render it repeatable.[11] Jazz in its essence is tentative, experimental. A tune of the early 1920s like "London Blues" was recorded by a whole series of classic New Orleans bands, but never played the same way twice. The twelve-bar blues form is as standarized as the Model T Ford, but its development in thousands of recorded performances has fully warranted the hundreds of names it has been given by musicians and record company executives. This experimental and spontaneous essence of jazz performance could be captured by recording, preserved, and transmitted to listeners half a world away. No longer was a direct and personal laying on of hands necessary in order for a popular art form to spread from one audience to the next.

Many of the greatest musicians in jazz were first introduced to the new music through recordings. Bix Beiderbecke, the cornetist from Davenport, Iowa, whose innovations set jazz on a new course in the mid-1920s, studied the new music in his middle-class home. So did Edward ("Duke") Ellington, whose proper Washington parents had no use for the earthy jazz music, and William ("Count") Basie, who had scant opportunity to hear live music of any kind in his native Red Bank, New Jersey. Never in history had an innovation in art been communicated more broadly and with greater speed than was jazz, thanks to the phonograph. Through this new technology, jazz, with all its overtones of social emancipation and individual expression, was transformed from a local fad into a thoroughly cosmopolitan movement.

Contact

The steps by which jazz came to the ears first of the American public and then of the entire European world can be retraced with some precision. For several years before 1917 both black and white bands from New Orleans had begun fanning out across the country in a diaspora that was to bring the new syncopated music to circus and theater-circuit audiences from coast to coast. One group of white musicians, Stein's Dixie Jass Band, scored a notable success at Schiller's Café on Chicago's South Side in the late spring of 1916. Drummer Johnny Stein's group gained notoriety when the Anti-Saloon League raided Schiller's on April 29. The mounting wave of publicity the following winter swept the five-piece band to New York, where it emerged as the Original Dixieland Jazz Band. An advertisement in the *New York Times* on February 2, 1917, ballyhooed the opening of the "400 Room" in the New Reisenweber Building at Eighth Avenue and Fifty-eighth Street. The strange new word "jazz" reached a mass audience for the first time in its now-standard spelling.[12] Meanwhile, the mounting strain of America's neutrality in the ever-expanding Great War found release in the frantic dancing at the "400 Room" and other dancing palaces throughout the country. Seizing the moment, the Victor Talking Machine Company invited the Original Dixieland Jazz Band to its studio in Camden, New Jersey, where two tunes, the "Livery Stable Blues" and the "Original Dixieland Jass Band One-Step," were recorded on February 26, 1917.[13]

These epochal recordings, the first issued by any jazz band, were released to the public on March 7, just five days before the *coup d'état* in the Russian capital of Petrograd, formerly St. Petersburg. The record was a smashing success, with reissues following in rapid succession. Before the end of 1917 a lawsuit was instituted over the authorship of tunes that no one had bothered to claim only eight months earlier. By the end of 1917, too, the Original Dixieland Jazz Band had accepted an invitation to tour England the following spring. Even before Irving Berlin wrote "Send a Lot of Jazz Bands Over There," the Original Dixieland Jazz Band was spreading the new music abroad through live performances and records issued in Great Britain.

On November 7, the Russian battleship *Aurora*, formerly of the tsar's navy but now controlled by the Bolsheviks, turned its guns on the Winter Palace and scared the Provisional Government into capitulation. Five days after this Storyville was finally closed down, under pressure from the U.S. Navy. With their local markets temporarily in eclipse and a rapidly expanding national and international market open to them, a number of New Orleans musicians took to the road, following the trail blazed by the Original Dixieland Jazz Band and, earlier, by such pioneer black groups as Bill Johnson's Original Creole Orchestra. By the end of 1917 the various itinerant New Orleanians and the recordings of the Original Dixieland Jazz Band had inspired scores of imitators.

Thus, at precisely the moment the proletarian dictatorship was being established in Russia and its cultural programs first proclaimed, another revolution in popular culture had burst out in America and was spreading rapidly. Both cultural explosions being thoroughly cosmopolitan, it was inevitable that they should eventually touch one another.

In the United States, their contact was limited, and was to remain so until the appearance of a generation of politically radical black jazz musicians in the 1960s. As F. Scott Fitzgerald observed, "It was characteristic of the Jazz Age that it had no interest in politics at all." [14] In contrast to such folk musicians as Woody Guthrie, America's jazz musicians for the most part took no active interest in political causes. Some, like saxophonist Bud Freeman, were sympathetic to the arguments of American Communists but did not personally trust the political activists. But in general, the American jazz world neither supported nor condemned the ideal of mass cul-

ture being propounded in Moscow. The most intense contact between the two cultural ideals occurred in the Soviet Union.

The raucous new American music first reached Russia on discs
of shellac, courtesy of those venturesome engineers in Camden. The
architects of the new Soviet state expressed their views on jazz
practically from the day of their first encounter with it. Some condemned it outright and with a ferocity that recalls the eleventh-
century Kievan monk Isaac, who excoriated the Devil for appearing to him in his cell in the form of a demon playing loudly on
flutes and tambourines.[15] Others, like Karl Radek, the editor of
Pravda and later an author of Stalin's 1936 Constitution, were so
eloquent in their enthusiasm for jazz as to cause anxiety among the
more spartan Communists at home and abroad. Soviet musicians
and composers were to be similarly polarized by a type of music
that symbolized all they liked or feared in the world beyond their
borders. Most important, Soviet officials and "legitimate" musicians were confronted by the public's unabashed fascination with
the new music. Those seeking to establish a distinctively Soviet form
of mass culture had to contend with the reality of mass taste. Official actions may have been based on the proposition that public
taste is infinitely malleable, but nobody realized better than Soviet
officials themselves how much that proposition had to be qualified.

The exuberant American music that found its way to Russia during the 1920s became a kind of litmus test for Soviet principles and
practices in music and, by extension, in the cultural area as a whole.
At one level, its reception reveals the purely musical judgments of
trained performers and critics. At another, it lays bare the attitudes
of Soviet officialdom and of the public at large toward the West,
the United States in particular. Whether Russians and other Soviet
peoples have really been as insular and xenophobic as they have
sometimes been portrayed is clearly tested in their reaction to jazz
and in the efforts to play jazz in their own country. At still another
level, the reception of jazz in Russia reflects the way in which social
structure affects taste, the phenomenon that Van Wyck Brooks (in
an essay of 1914) dubbed "Highbrow" and "Lowbrow."[16] Most of
all, this litmus test provides insights on the reception in Russia of

that second revolution in 1917 that sought to liberate the individual from social tyranny rather than society from the tyranny of individuals and classes.

The curious tale of jazz in Russia pales before the grandiose and brutal saga of social and economic upheaval that Soviet orators call "Socialist construction." But the life of any society presents an infinite variety of microscopic concerns, any one of which, like a cell, is coded with the defining characteristics of the entire social organism. The phenomenon of Soviet jazz is one such concern.

The interaction of Russians with America's most distinctive art form has taken place on many planes, not all of them pertinent to our inquiry. It is interesting but not germane that the legendary Gene Goldkette, leader of a star-studded group of the big band era, was educated in Russia, and that the swing era jam tune "Bei mir bist du schön," an old Russian-Jewish folk tune, was written down and copyrighted by a Russian-Jewish immigrant in New York and then exported back to Soviet jazzmen.

Such examples of Russian-American intercourse attest to the fact, so easily forgotten in the twentieth century, that Russia and America have interacted closely since the mid-eighteenth century.[17] The mutual influences are constant and reciprocal. In the arts, Russia's contribution to American life has generally been focused on the realm of high culture, the young Henry James's infatuation with the novels of Ivan Turgenev being a typical case in point. The composers Glinka and Mussorgsky were no strangers to American concertgoers, and both Rubinstein and Tchaikovsky actually toured the United States. By contrast, American contributions to Russian cultural life have been concentrated in the more popular arts and sciences. Mayne Reid, Jack London, Mark Twain, and James Fenimore Cooper were familiar names in every Russian classroom by 1900, as were Ben Franklin and Thomas Edison.

However greatly the commodities of cultural trade might have differed, Russian-American contact was sufficiently extensive by the early twentieth century that the educated public in each country could be sure of learning quickly of the latest developments in the other. Detailed information on the Bolshevik Revolution reached the United States almost instantly, thanks to telegraphed reports from Petrograd by John Reed and other American correspondents. Alluring intimations of the new directions in American popular culture reached the Russian heartland through equally well-established channels. The impact of the Bolshevik Revolution on American politics, diplomacy, and literature has been the object of much study. The impact in Russia of America's democratic and liberationist upheaval in popular culture remains *terra incognita*.

2

The "Low Sweet Fever"
Under Tsar Nicholas II

... orchestras set the rhythm of the year, summing up the
sadness and suggestiveness of life in new tunes.

F. Scott Fitzgerald, *The Great Gatsby*

On August 12, 1914, Maurice Paléologue, France's keenly literate
ambassador to the Russian court at St. Petersburg, observed the
tsar's army marching through the capital to entrain for Russia's
endangered western border:

> All day long, on Nevsky Prospekt and on the Liteiny and Sado-
> vaia Boulevards I encountered regiments moving towards the
> Warsaw Station. The men—robust, well-equipped, a serious and
> resolute look on their faces, and marching in a firm and ca-
> denced step—impressed me most. Looking at them, I imagined
> large numbers of them already to be marked for death.[1]

In retrospect, Paléologue's description presents a final tableau of
Russia under the old regime. *Exeunt omnes*, and on their heels let
the new forces march onto the stage. In actuality, however, the old
world and the new in Russia were inexorably intermingled. The
handsome regiments may have evoked images from Tolstoy's *War
and Peace* in the mind of the French ambassador, but the life of the
officers had already changed beyond recognition. Was Paléologue
aware that the brass band of the dashingly attired Sumskoi Hussar
Regiment had only recently issued a hit recording of Irving Berlin's
"Alexander's Ragtime Band"? Or that the orchestra of the tsar's

own Volhynia Life Guards Regiment had delighted the public with its recording of "At a Georgia Camp Meeting" and other two-steps and cakewalks? Probably not. These facts would have shattered the glass-plate image of an old Russia populated by fabulous aristocrats in court dress, long-suffering peasants in bast shoes, a few intellectuals and colorless nihilists for good measure, and the sinister figure of the mad monk Rasputin lurking in the wings. The reality was different.

To be sure, there was a Rasputin, and he was indeed murdered on the night of December 29, 1916, by Prince Felix Yusupov, scion of an ancient aristocratic family, and several of his friends. But times had changed. The Yusupovs had maintained a private orchestra since the eighteenth century, when their serf musicians regularly mounted operas in the gem-like theater of the family's palace on the Moika Canal in St. Petersburg. Now, however, alongside the violins and cellos was a six-man saxophone section—the largest in Europe at the time. Even before the Yusupovs' bold decision to introduce this newfangled hybrid into St. Petersburg society, it had gained notoriety as the ill-bred harbinger of new social mores. Young Prince Felix and his wife moved in a fast set. They insisted on dancing the two-step in the long ballroom of their palace, beneath the ancestral portraits. And on the night of December 29, when Felix finally poisoned the monk who had dared meddle in imperial politics, he did so to the accompaniment of American popular music. "As we entered [our] house," he recalled, "I could hear my friends talking while the gramophone played 'Yankee Doodle Went to Town.'"[2]

It is unlikely that troopers in the Sumskoi Hussars ever heard their regimental band's popular recordings, or that many Russians outside of Prince Yusupov's high-spending circle had the opportunity to hear cakewalks performed by the Yusupovs' orchestra. The new American fashions in music and dance were slow to percolate down in society. But they did so nevertheless. The currents in Russian popular culture that are the object of our concern made their first tentative entry into Russian society at the top, in the waning years of Nicholas II's reign. Only later, as Stalin was rising to power, did they reach the public at large and thereby become a potent force in the cultural life of the Russian cities.

It is far less surprising that American popular culture first penetrated tsarist Russia at elite levels than that it managed to gain a toehold in that country at all. It is not easy for citizens of a democratic society to appreciate the polarization of culture that existed in Russia under the old regime. Russia was by no means lacking in a middle class in 1914, but with respect to its cultural values it was pulled between waning but still deep-rooted folk traditions on the one hand and the sophisticated world of highbrow values on the other. Thus, in the years after 1900 the bold young innovators who grouped around the impresario Sergei Diaghilev fostered both the new music of Igor Stravinsky and Arnold Schoenberg and the peasantry's traditional music as performed by Mitrofan Piatnitsky's folk chorus. When the dignified Society for Natural Science, Anthropology, and Ethnography decided to patronize public concerts, it juxtaposed the most advanced orchestral modernists and primitive folk performers on the same stage.[3]

So strong was the gravitational pull of the sophisticated tradition of high culture in Russia that it was capable of channeling the latest communication technologies into its own well-established patterns, as the reception of the phonograph demonstrates with particular clarity. The phonograph industry began commercial recordings in America in 1890. In that year, the Columbia Talking Machine Company began to produce bulky cylinders that packaged two minutes of sound, mostly for consumption in coin-in-the-slot machines leased to amusement parks and cafés. The extremely limited acoustical possibilities of the new invention, combined with the unpretentious tastes of the American middle-class buying public, drove the new technology at first in the direction of decidedly lowbrow entertainment. Russell Hunting, a star of the 1890s, recorded outrageous Irish lampoons for the New England Phonograph Company, John Y. AtLee amused Columbia's audiences with his artistic whistling, while a host of "Descriptive" records in all major categories featured animal sounds, crashes, and castanets, all to marginally musical accompaniments.

The progress in Europe of the phonograph (or, more accurately, gramophone) was no less dramatic but very different in character. Edison's wax-cylinder apparatus were being sold in England and on the Continent by 1890. In 1894 Charles and Emile Pathé bought an Edison machine to enliven their Bar Américain just off the boisterous Place Pigalle in Paris.[4] Soon they were producing cylinders patterned after Edison's. As the technology rapidly improved, the possibility of reproducing more sophisticated performances increased. In Europe this new frontier was exploited most fully. The European market turned out to be greatly receptive to classical music, and particularly to operatic arias. Instead of whistlers, minstrels, and vaudeville Irishmen, the Pathé brothers focused their attention on singers from the nearby Paris Opera. The same focus proved profitable at the Pathé's branch office in Milan, where the young Caruso was first recorded. This rich diet was relieved by folk songs but relatively few examples of the raucous exotica that American listeners relished. Only when the price of equipment and of cylinders declined did European manufacturers tap the substantial market for songs by music-hall entertainers.

The first records manufactured in Russia were produced in 1899 by a St. Petersburg branch of Deutsche Grammophon A.G., which was in turn a division of the Berliner Gramophone Company of Philadelphia. Edison had already established a permanent office in the Russian capital and another in Moscow by this time, and Pathé cylinders were readily available in major cities throughout the empire.[5] The journal *Grammofon i fonograf* (*Gramophone and Phonograph*) was founded in 1903, *Svet i zvuk* (*Light and Sound*) in 1905, and *Novosti grammofona* (*News of the Gramophone*) in 1907, by which year a half-million machines had been imported.

By American standards, the Russian buying public's taste in music was awesomely highbrow. In fact, pre-revolutionary Russia's great contribution to the industry—the Red Seal records—reflects that society's keen respect for the received tradition in classical music. A St. Petersburg entrepreneur named Rappaport opened a record emporium on the fashionable Nevsky Prospect shortly after the turn of the century. His was a palace of the record, with handsome woodwork, potted palms, and Oriental carpets on the floor. The chic clientele he lured onto the premises had little use for vaudeville songs and gypsy ballads, so Rappaport pleaded with the English Gramophone Company (Berliner's London branch) to sign up stars from the Imperial Opera and issue their performances on long-playing ten-inch discs. The Gramophone Company agreed and also accepted Rappaport's suggestion that the new deluxe series be distinguished by red labels. Thus was born what later became the Victor Red Seal line, records of unprecedented fidelity featuring performances by the greatest classical musicians of the era. By 1905 the line had revolutionized the record industry, opening it to horizons that had been all but invisible to the more populist American society in which the technology had been born.

The same predilection for the traditional forms of European elite culture that guided Rappaport proved to be the single most powerful source of opposition to jazz in Russia. It was reinforced by nearly the entire educational system. It was crystallized in an institutional network embracing philharmonic societies, conservatories, journals devoted to the arts, and, later, radio stations. Aristocratic in nature, this bias was so pervasive that it penetrated even to nominally anti-aristocratic circles of avant-garde musicians and artists, and aggressively anti-aristocratic movements such as the radical political parties. Russia's future Bolshevik leaders were raised in this tradition. Most were from the middle and upper middle classes, the very bourgeoisie that the Revolution set out to destroy. Lenin professed adoration for the music of Beethoven and patronizingly accepted folk music. But neither he nor most of his followers viewed with sympathy the commerically reproduced cultural forms of their own class.

American jazz eventually found a welcome reception in Russia not because "serious" music had lost its dominant position, but because popular music in the decades before the Revolution managed to carve a niche for itself between symphonic and operatic music on the one hand and folk music on the other. Urban vernacular culture expanded at the expense both of folk life and of traditional upper-class culture. This process corresponds exactly to the emergence of an urban populace whose members were neither peasants nor noblemen nor officials.

Tsarist Pop

The chief components of this new vernacular musical culture had existed for generations in Russia's cities. Vaudeville, for example, had flourished since the first third of the nineteenth century in Moscow and St. Petersburg. Originally based on French comic operas of the eighteenth century, vaudeville in Russia eventually developed several features that were pertinent to jazz. In addition to the usual comedy routines, Russian vaudeville linked the latest popular music with the most recent fads in dancing. As Chekhov's favorite theatrical director, Konstantin Stanislavsky, put it, "The vaudeville personage lives in his special world, where it is accepted to express one's feelings and thoughts not only in words and actions but also by singing and dancing."[6] Moreover, Russian vaudeville did not insist that musicians read music. In the town of Poltava, the director of the local vaudeville troupe overcame this potential difficulty by teaching each musician his part individually. Under the circumstances it is not surprising that improvisation was common.[7]

Far less respectable even than vaudeville (or *Muzik-Khol*, as it later came to be called, after the English) was the earthy musical *demi-monde* of bars and drinking gardens. For centuries these odoriferous establishments had served as focal points for male social life in Russian villages and towns. Well into the nineteenth century, Western tourists expressed surprise at the antique ways preserved at such watering holes. With the growth of cities in the late nineteenth century things began to change, however. The Danish literary critic Georg Brandes found women in the pubs and reported that many of the guests were dancing boisterously to music produced by large mechanical hand organs.[8]

The first gypsy choir had been organized in the 1780s by the grandee Alexei Orlov. By the early nineteenth century they were fixtures of every bar and drinking garden on the outskirts of Moscow.[9] Embellished by Pushkin and Tolstoy with an aura of Oriental exoticism, the gypsy establishments actually combined music, dancing, and sex in about the same proportions as in Storyville. The gradual decline of gypsy restaurants in the early twentieth century attests to the same change of taste in music and relaxation of morals that took New Orleans jazz from Storyville to the country club.

With the rapid growth of the middle class in Russia's cities before 1914 and its gradual turn away from the cultural style of the aristocracy, a substantial infrastructure of businesses supporting popular culture came into being. For the first time it became possible to buy sheet music for the latest popular songs in cheap editions. Many of the new publishers were linked with firms abroad, principally in Leipzig, so they could disseminate quickly the latest popular songs in inexpensive and simple adaptations for piano. Russians had no word for a popular "hit," so they adopted the German term *Schlager*. The Russian hit parade was thoroughly cosmopolitan by the 1890s, such Tin Pan Alley tearjerkers as "The Little Lost Child" (1894) being in particular favor.[10] The very fact that musically conservative Russian entrepreneurs were slow to subject popular music to the mass production of Tin Pan Alley's "song factories" made Tsar Nicholas II's realm more receptive to influences from abroad.

Nor was the record industry untouched by the rise of popular music. Independent of such posh international establishments as Rappaport's in St. Petersburg, a number of Russian factories—some branches of West European firms—sprang up to meet the large but less sophisticated demand. Competition among firms such as Florofon and Zonofon made them aggressive in testing local markets. Humor, burlesque, and even prayers were pressed in shellac, although the latter were banned by the Holy Synod in 1912.[11]

In a move that anticipated the propaganda songs of the 1930s, the tsarist government began pushing patriotic songs during its disastrous war against Japan in 1905. The virtual disappearance of such potboilers once the war was over suggests that taste was no more readily manipulated in Russia than anywhere else. When the public wanted to hear the composer Petr Nevsky's hit "The Dan-

ube" or a burlesque by the clown Bim-Bom, it was not to be put
off with patriotic bombast.

Another crucial link in the chain of organizations supporting
popular music was the movie theaters that sprang up after 1900.
Film production in Russia began only a few years later than in
Western Europe and America, but movies from abroad were overwhelming favorites with Russian audiences. Even during the 1920s,
when avant-garde Soviet directors were in their glory, the backbone
of the industry consisted of Hollywood tearjerkers and comedies
imported from America.[12] Russian directors could not compete with
Douglas Fairbanks or Mary Pickford, and they soon learned it was
best not to try. Unimpeded by language barriers, the world of silent
films was far more cosmopolitan than that of the later "talkies."
Acknowledging as much, pre-revolutionary Russian theater owners
endowed their movie palaces with names such as the "Parisiana"
or the "Piccadilly" in St. Petersburg. Various attempts were made
to Russify the cinema by adding recorded dialogues. Two theaters
in the capital invested in expensive "Grammophysioscopophones,"
but this sound device was as primitive as it was pretentious.[13]

Most owners of movie palaces in Russia were content to use player
pianos or orchestras. Some theater ensembles, such as the Yarchuka-
Kucherenko group at the Lux in Odessa, stuck doggedly to folk or
classical selections. Most attempted to catch the mood of the film.
The predominance of imported films made movie theaters ideal
conduits for popular songs from abroad. Many future Soviet musicians, including Dmitri Shostakovich, were to try their hand at
American ragtime or jazz while toiling before the flickering screen.

Through mounting competition among music publishers, recording companies, and film studios, tsarist Russia on the eve of World
War I acquired a popular culture that was neither folksy nor "cultivated." Fashions in popular entertainment succeeded each other
with accelerating speed. Music merchandisers strained to ferret out
each shift in the public temper and to concoct words and melodies
that mirrored it. These rapid changes reflected the quickening pulse
of urban life in the decade before 1917. The urban populace had
grown over the previous decade, and its qualitative change was

even more dramatic. Nearly all male employees in the 15 to 35 age group could claim basic literacy, notwithstanding that millions of these same men had only recently immigrated from the country-side.[14] The university population also soared; on the eve of World War I tsarist Russia was second only to the United States in the number of its students in college.[15]

Such changes drew attention to the roles of women and youth. A suffragette movement swelled during and immediately after the aborted Revolution of 1905. A number of the most politically radical women of the capital had come athwart the law, and in the process, had proven that, as one St. Petersburg prison official put it, "Women, in terms of criminality, ability, and possession of the urge to escape, are hardly distinguishable from men."[16]

The emancipation of Russian women touched every aspect of their lives. Billowing Victorian gowns were sent to the attic, re-placed by the unimpeding and svelte dresses by the fashionable fashion designer Lamanova and her legion of imitators. Divorce laws were eased in response to feminine demands for freedom of choice in marriage. As the French ambassador wryly observed, "Today, Anna [Karenina] would immediately have obtained a di-vorce in order to marry Vronsky, and there the novel would end."[17]

Women and youth encountered much greater resistance to re-form in the more rigid society of Prussia. For twenty years before 1914 the urban youth of Germany had been in open rebellion against the bureaucratic state schools and the authoritarian family. Damn-ing their elders, they sought to create a distinctive "youth culture" (*Jugendkultur*) by withdrawing into their own world and rejecting urban life and all its cultural trappings, including hit songs, alco-hol, and even the piano, that ungainly beast crouching in every bourgeois parlor. They turned instead to the German past, and to folk songs sung to the accompaniment of guitar or lute.[18] Russian youth before 1917 were also in ferment. But far from rejecting modern urban life, they embraced it with enthusiasm, criticizing their elders who adhered to sentimental notions of the patriarchal countryside. Precisely because Russia's economy was relatively backward compared to Germany's or America's, Russian youth wanted to catch up and were open to whatever fashions from abroad captured the aura of modern life. Their new religion was pantheistic, embracing simultaneously the gods of women's liberation, social reform, sports, technical education, and freer sexual mores. In this charged atmosphere of urbanism, youth, feminist activism, and cosmopolitanism the dance craze of the early twentieth century exploded.

Dancemania

Rumblings of the new excitement had been audible across the European continent for years.[19] By 1910 dancemania raged in full fever. Hesitation waltzes, two-steps, and even "animal dances" crossed oceans and continents like epidemics. Clothing was cut looser to accommodate it. As hemlines rose, high starched collars were thrown aside in favor of softer ones that permitted the agitated movement demanded by the new dances. Record sales soared. An English chronicler of the age recalled that "All things danceable—even Redskin tomtom records—were proving popular!"[20]

In the years following the collapse of the Revolution of 1905, urban Russia embraced the new sensation of "liberated" dancing with a vengeance. Dance pavilions and halls proliferated, especially in the port cities. By 1910 three orchestras were needed to meet dancers' demand at the gardens on Nikolaevsky Boulevard in Odessa.[21] Even at inland Kiev the Palais Royal had trouble keeping up with the dancers' appetite. Sergei Diaghilev raised eyebrows by clothing Nijinsky in nothing but tights for a Bacchic performance at the Imperial Theater. Isadora Duncan, already an ardent Russophile, imported Russian children to her school of free dance outside Paris.[22]

New dances arrived from all corners of the globe. The tango, born in Buenos Aires, hit New York, London, and Paris almost simultaneously. St. Petersburg felt the boom by 1914.[23] Thus the Latin craze that influenced W. C. Handy when he wrote the tango chorus of "St. Louis Blues" gripped Russia's dancers and musicians only a few years later. So popular was the tango in Russia by World

War I that government propagandists tried to capitalize on it by pushing "[Kaiser] Wilhelm's Bloody Tango" as a pop tune.[24]

While Russia's dance craze was fed by many nations, the most popular new dances and music came from the United States. The link between urban Russians and American popular culture that has survived to the present day was forged by the dance craze after 1910 and was achieved without the slightest encouragement from either government. The spread of American popular culture in Russia, in fact, coincided exactly with a wave of anti-Americanism promoted by the tsarist government.

This hostility was fed by diplomatic, economic, and ideological differences. Though Theodore Roosevelt had helped to extricate the tsar from his disastrous war with Japan, he received scant gratitude from Russian nationalists. Reactionary politicians in Russia saw America's emerging power as a threat to Russian interests in both Europe and the Far East. The rapid expansion of American industry was also perceived as a threat, although a few sober minds in St. Petersburg counseled Nicholas's government to learn from the example of America's industrialization.[25] Finally, America's decision to champion Russia's Jewish minority against officially sponsored anti-Semitism rankled Russian nationalists. After heated exchanges of several years, the 1832 Treaty of Navigation and Commerce between Russia and the United States was abrogated in 1911—precisely when American popular music was sweeping into the realm of Nicholas II.

Two forces that helped to neutralize popular (if not official) hostility toward the United States were ragtime music and the cakewalk. The appearance of these phenomena in Russian urban life gave form to many of the new values and prepared the way for the later introduction of jazz and jazz dancing. The cakewalk originated in the efforts of newly urbanized Florida blacks to ape and parody the formal ballroom dances of the 1880s. The exuberant satire in this high-stepping dance assured its popularity wherever people were growing bored with quadrilles, schottisches, and waltzes. Ragtime picked up the slow march tempos and multistrain format of the cakewalk and gave it definitive form as syncopated music.

Pioneered in Sedalia and St. Louis, Missouri, in the early 1890s, ragtime music for the first time enabled even moderately competent parlor pianists to accompany the new dances. Scott Joplin and other pioneers wrote out their ragtime scores and discouraged improvisation, which allowed the music to be accurately transmitted through the traditional medium of printed sheet music. Well before the new century, ragtime had established itself as a musical safety valve for Americans' restless energies.

The impact of ragtime music on England and Western Europe was more sudden and deep than that of any previous current in American culture. It hit London in the 1890s like a tornado, sweeping the record and sheet music industry into its vortex and swamping the homegrown music-hall tradition with syncopated imports. The discography of English ragtime before 1920 fills a whole volume.[26] Why did Britain's indigenous popular music fall so easily? asks Ian Whitcomb, the student of British dance music.[27] Whitcomb's answer: British migrants to the cities left their folk music in Wales and the Scottish highlands. Also, London's Tin Pan Alley simply didn't have the talent or organization of New York's, and English music-hall songs were engaging but parochial. The Cambridge poet Rupert Brooke took party after party to performances of the revue *Hello Ragtime*. Clearly, he found an antidote both to Victorian bleakness and music-hall blandness in the boisterous new music.[28]

The impact of ragtime and the cakewalk was no less strong in Germany after 1900.[29] Local editions of recordings and sheet music issued by branches of American firms or local houses allowed the new fad to reach the public in Berlin and Hamburg only months after London. France also fell in quick order. French composers, more than other European musicians, immediately recognized the musical potential of the new idiom. By 1913 Debussy had written "Gollywog's Cakewalk," "Minstrels" and "General Lavine Eccentric"; a few years later Igor Stravinsky, then living in France, included a "ragtime" movement in his *Histoire du soldat*. The new popular culture had begun its assault on the musical Parnassus!

The same wave that carried ragtime music to Germany and France hit Russia's shore in 1910. In that year the wealthy merchant Kara-

tet Ilich Nazarov and his wife Gaiana enrolled in a school of modern dance (of which there were several in St. Petersburg) in order
to learn the cakewalk. The instructor and instructress were both
Negroes, the man dressed in tails and top hat and the woman decked
out in a flashy gown daringly slit to the knee. Though Gaiana was
taller than her husband, the pair mastered the new steps and decided to unveil them at a large party in their home. After a warm-
up show featuring clowns and musicians, the Nazarovs disappeared and returned with their instructors to perform a raucous
cakewalk. A black "tickler" (*tapyor* in Russian, from the English
"tapper," meaning pianist) provided music, and the Nazarovs gri-
maced behind black masks with red lips. Karatet and Gaiana scored
a risqué triumph.[30]

Within a year the music prompted by the Nazarovs' bold sally
had won general acceptance, at least in the *haut monde*. In 1911
the Moscow publisher S. I. Yambor began issuing a whole series of
American dance tunes. His first release was "Très Moutard," a "new
American dance" (written, to be sure, by an Englishman, Cecil
Macklin) that Yambor touted as a "colossal success" in the United
States and Europe. Hard on the heels of the cakewalk came the one-
step, the Boston, and finally the fox-trot, which was making its way
into St. Petersburg (by then renamed Petrograd) society on the very
eve of the fall of tsardom in February 1917.

Not everyone was so fortunate as the Nazarovs, who had native
American instructors. Nor was it necessary. Russians could study
the latest dances at the movies, to appropriate piano accompaniment. In St. Petersburg they could go to the Variété theater, where
the new steps were strutted on stage. For years Russian stenographers and dancers had been detailed to London to learn the new
dances and to steal lines from music-hall performers there, often
bribing their English sources with gold rubles to speed the trans-
fer.[31] Those in the provinces with no access to the popular theaters
could buy teach-yourself booklets on the cakewalk and fox-trot or
could unravel the steps from diagrams conveniently included on
sheet music issued by the firms of Gutheil in Moscow or Schmidt
in St. Petersburg. These aids, coupled with a few of the countless

"Kek-Voks" records listed in every number of the journal *Grammofon (The Gramophone)* assured that the new dance craze penetrated to every corner of the country.

In Russia, cakewalks and ragtime music were inseparably linked with the public's fascination with black Americans. Down to the twentieth century their contact had been extremely limited. A Negro named Nelson had accompanied John Quincy Adams's family to Russia in 1809 and was allowed to join the tsar's service rather than return to America. The U.S. minister to Russia in 1894 was surprised to discover that another black American, from Tennessee, was a servant at the court of Nicholas II.[32] A handful of American Negroes managed to amass fortunes as jockeys in tsarist Russia; a black barman, Jim, mixed drinks at the L'Europe Hotel in St. Petersburg; and Emma Harris from Kentucky was lured from a touring theatrical troupe by a Russian grand duke and spent the rest of her life in Russia.[33] But, with rare exceptions, the black Americans best known to Russians were musicians or actors.[34]

All blacks were considered exotic. The actor Ira Aldridge had performed *Othello* in Odessa in the 1860s and was still being talked about a half-century later.[35] With the rise of ragtime and the general interest in exotica in the early twentieth century, curiosity about black Americans reached a new high. A Ukrainian orchestra performed a cakewalk entitled "A Negro's Dream" in 1912,[36] and the Schmidt publishing firm had in press cakewalks titled "The Creole Girl," "The Negro Dance," and "The Holiday of the Negroes." A St. Petersburg confectioner exploited the notion of ragtime as black music by issuing the latest hits on records pressed into discs of hard baker's chocolate. Since none of these discographic gems has survived, it can be assumed that the listening public eagerly consumed them.[37]

Surveying the manner in which ragtime music and the new "Negro" dances were promoted in Russia, one cannot fail to be struck by the dissonance between image and reality. The image fostered by Russia's nascent popular music industry and embraced by the public presented the new idiom as exotic, earthy, and blatantly lascivious. Sheet music covers conjured up uninhibited savages wailing erotic melodies under a tropical moon. Yet the reality was a carefully structured written music developed by black and white Americans of the lower and middle classes and embraced by white Americans and Europeans of the middle and upper classes. Unlike the polka and the mazurka, which had existed as folk dances for generations before being invited into the parlor, the cakewalk and the fox-trot were both swept immediately into middle-class urban life, quickly losing whatever earthy and folkish origins they may have had. But Russians, like other Europeans and white Americans, seemed to wish the music to have an even more erotic and disreputable background than it had. In this wish can be sensed the breakup of nineteenth-century values.

Backlash

Nowhere did the shift of values occur without conflict. The assault on ragtime and the dance craze in America was launched as early as 1901, when the American Federation of Musicians condemned the music and urged its members to abstain from playing it.[38] Ragtime found a few defenders in the early years of the century but by 1912–13 a fresh assault had begun. One writer pointed out the "dangers that lie in ragtime" while another warned darkly of the "ragtime menace."[39] When in the spring of 1913 the respected journal *Musical America* dared to editorialize on "Ragtime as a Source of National Music,"[40] a New York highbrow unleashed a barrage that remains to this day the most comprehensive assault on the idiom. Significantly, the author was Russian, a recent émigré from the sophisticated environment of the St. Petersburg Conservatory. Because Ivan Narodny's vitriolic attack on popular culture anticipates so many of the arguments raised decades later in the Soviet Union, it is worth considering in detail.[41]

Narodny based his critique on a conception of folk song as being " . . . the product of a village atmosphere. It mirrors the joys and sorrows, hopes and passions of the country people. It is moulded under the blue sky, in sunshine and storm. . . . Like a fairy tale it exults sincerity, poetry, and an idea." A ragtime melody, by contrast, is urban and the product "of an individual whose idea is to make money with its composition. It exalts the noise, rush and vulgarity of the street. It suggests repulsive dance halls and restaurants." It is meant " . . . for the tired and materially bored mind. It shows the same stirring qualities as a sensational newspaper story does. It is essentially obvious, vulgar and yet strong. . . ."

Narodny, like countless later Soviet critics, tried to clinch his arguments by quoting expert opinion. He cited an American ragtime pianist's statement that "Ragtime is the real thing for America because it pays. And as long as money is the ideal of the country, ragtime will be its national music." Narodny then sewed up his case by presenting the report of a Mr. Ostrovsky, a St. Petersburg music critic, to whom Narodny had mailed a collection of ragtime compositions so that he might play them and test the reactions "not only in musical circles, but in the average public circles." Here is Ostrovsky's report:

> My experiment with your American ragtime compositions . . . proved that the circle of musicians—mostly people of established music convictions—found them interesting as studies of aesthetic sentiment in the New World. They all agreed—there were about fifty of them—that this American music expresses distinctly, in its peculiarly affected vigor and rhythm, the purposeless energy of never-tiring and always alert minds. But with our best will we could find no traces of any art, new or old, in it. As a whole, all were interested in the strange tunes that seemed to us imitations of Negro melodies.
>
> Following your advice, I arranged the compositions for performance in a couple of regular cabaret restaurants, places where mostly students and artists gather, and then at public concert halls for the working people and soldiers. There the effect was far more unfavorable than we had expected and than that produced in intelligent musical circles. The managers of all the places told me that such "novelties" would soon rid them of their regular customers. The audience expressed utter indifference or disgust.

A strange report, this! At a time when Tsar Nicholas II's own military bands were already playing ragtime, when the Russian public had created a highly lucrative market for ragtime music, when the cakewalk, fox-trot, and turkey-trot were being performed at the many new public dance halls, Ostrovsky managed to locate "a couple of regular cabaret restaurants" and "public concerts for the working people and soldiers" where ragtime music was greeted with indifference or hostility. Now, it is possible that Mr. Ostrovsky actually found such places and carried out the research he was charged to do, although he provides no concrete evidence of it. But Narodny's report of Ostrovsky's report on the Russian public's response to ragtime does not ring true. In its tone and method it resembles the later Stalinist denunciations of jazz, in which "typical Soviet workers" were paraded before Western newsmen to express their undying revulsion against the music.

We now know that most such representations of Soviet opinion were utterly false, Potemkin villages that masked a very different situation. And given what we know of Russian public attitudes toward ragtime music in 1913, it is evident that Narodny and his friend Ostrovsky were engaging in similar tactics—pioneering them, in fact—because they knew full well that what F. Scott Fitzgerald aptly termed "the low sweet fever" had already spread to Russia. Four years before the October Revolution, Russia's distinguished musical establishment had issued the first broadside against American popular music in a campaign that was to last a half-century.

3

Red, But Not Hot,
1917–1924

... for we were naive in those days and did not know that it
is far more difficult to change man than to change the system
of a country's government.

Ilya Ehrenburg

The musical shock wave generated by the Original Dixieland Jazz
Band at the Victor studio in 1917 hit Europe that same year, six
months before the band began a two-month London engagement
on April 19, 1918. The band's 1918 recordings in London reveal
them at their best, and the impact of their live performances on the
British public was explosive, almost violent. Londoners had danced
to ragtime orchestras for almost two decades. Suddenly such groups
seemed decorous and stiff. Here was something different. The horn-
men played standing up, waving their horns about and shocking
the audience with their carelessness and naughty *esprit*. The public
loved it.

Several groups of black musicians, mustered out of the American
Expeditionary Force during the war, had been working the Continent before the Original Dixieland Jazz Band hit London. One, led
by James Reese Europe, had impressed audiences with its rags and
dance tunes. Mr. Europe's musicians were well-behaved and definitely not hot. Nor were Louis Mitchell's Jazz Kings, who had stolen the march on the Original Dixieland Jazz Band with bookings
across England, Belgium, and France in 1917.[1] Mitchell misread
the signs of the times, at least briefly, when in 1919 he tried to

organize a fifty-man "orchestra." Realizing his mistake, he quickly reverted to the small-group format with which he began and gave free rein to his hotter instincts. The reconstituted Jazz Kings were a smashing success at the Casino de Paris and the Alhambra in Brussels. "It was the greatest emotion I had ever experienced," declared the Belgian critic Robert Goffin.[2] Meanwhile, Will Marion Cook's large Southern Syncopated Orchestra also gave way to a smaller, more informal ensemble in 1919. The Swiss conductor Ernest Ansermet was so thunderstruck by a London performance of this group that he used the occasion to pen the first serious appreciation of the new music in the *Revue Romande* in 1919.[3] Two of Cook's stars, clarinetist Sidney Bechet and trombonist Frank Withers, were to score similar successes in Russia in 1926.

Between 1919 and 1924 black and white jazz bands penetrated every major city in Western Europe, and then beyond to such far-flung centers as Istanbul and Shanghai. The money was good—far better than in Chicago—and the color line was smudged or nonexistent. As a result, Western Europe heard some fine jazz in those years. As in New York or Indianapolis, jazz meant dancing, entertainment. Groups such as Benny Peyton's orchestra, the Southern Rag-a-Jazz Band, the Original Orchestra, and Frank Guarente's Georgians forced jazz onto the consciousness of the European musical establishment. Paul Hindemith heard Sam Wooding's orchestra in Berlin in 1921 and found it a "revelation."[4] Evidence of his conversion (which proved temporary) can be found in the Shimmy and Foxtrot movements of his *Kammermusik*, Opus 24, No. 1, and in his 1924 *Suite for Piano*. In France, Darius Milhaud used jazz motifs in *La Creation du monde*, and Jean Wiener composed *Sonatine syncopée.*[5]

European musicians, even more than composers, were quick to take up the new idiom. Ted Heath, who later played an important role in British jazz, cut his teeth as a fill-in with the Southern Syncopated Orchestra in 1919. American groups performing in Brussels and Berlin, the Continent's leading markets for hot jazz, were finding they could turn to local talent whenever their own jazzmen exercised their unalienable right to be capricious. London remained the center, but homegrown European groups sprang up like mush-rooms wherever good American bands had prepared the soil.[6]

Resistance

Jazz did not reach Russia until 1922 and did not take root there until three years later. Why was a country that had been so quick to import ragtime music so slow to receive jazz? Looking back through the glass of Stalinism, the answer seems simple: because jazz was seen as decadent. But in 1917–19 the evidence was not clear, even in America. In Europe, strong outcries against the supposed depravity of jazz were not made until 1922, by which time the first jazz concert was already being staged in the Bolsheviks' new capital.

A more plausible explanation of the slow pace at which jazz penetrated Russia is that between 1918 and 1920 the country was embroiled in a bloody civil war. While the Red and White armies battled each other for control in the countryside, urban Russia starved and froze, for provisions and fuel were cut off. Russia's cities shrank to half their former size. The grim conditions gave an urgency to the struggle for survival and permitted little indulgence in music. So the argument goes. But Civil War Russia rang with music. Wherever the White Army was in control—Omsk, Vladivostok, Irkutsk, Odessa, Rostov-on-Don—a frantic nightlife flourished. Music was also to be heard in areas occupied by the Reds. Countless memoirs attest to this, and published schedules of programs and concerts document the great number of performances given.

The musical culture of peasant Russia is predominantly vocal, and the mass conscription of peasants into the Red and White armies brought that culture to the fore. Hundreds of military choirs sprang up to sing patriotic classics like "Variag" or new revolutionary tunes such as "The Red Army." Some of the repertoire, notably "The Little Apple" ("Iablochka"), which emerged from the rank and file of the Red Army in the Ukraine, achieved genuine popularity.

Bolsheviks had appreciated the power of mass voices at least since

1911, when they had begun organizing worker choirs in major factories.[7] These choirs had gained popularity among all who still had one foot in country life. Lenin's new government took great pains to ensure the ideological correctness of their repertoire. Music publishing houses, which were nationalized and combined into a single entity in 1918, spewed forth potboilers in a new genre of "agitational music," or "*agitmuzyk*" for short. Folk ditties (*chastushki*) were turned into political limericks set to music and became popular.[8]

The Bolshevik party did not speak with one voice on musical matters. During the decade before 1917 a split had emerged between the militants, who demanded the immediate establishment of a proletarian music, and those who were content with spreading the highest existing musical values among the populace at large. The former, devout believers in the possibility of cultural engineering, formed themselves into a "proletarian culture movement" (*Proletkult*) and campaigned against the entire musical heritage, not to mention modernism, with a tireless fanaticism throughout the Civil War. For political rather than cultural reasons, Lenin himself was never comfortable with this program. Proletkult demanded autonomy, so that it could work side by side with, rather than in subordination to, the Party. Lenin rejected this out of hand and stifled the movement at its All-Russian Congress in October 1920.[9] Having destroyed Proletkult as an independent entity, the Party was free to appropriate its program, which it eventually did with devastating effects during the Cultural Revolution of 1928–31.

In the meantime, the newly formed Commissariat of Public Enlightenment vigorously set about organizing scores of new orchestras and choirs and placing the country's formidable musical riches at the disposal of the working population. There is something appealing about Feodor Chaliapin singing operatic classics before tens of thousands of soldiers, workers, and peasants. But due to the government's monopoly of patronage, Chaliapin had no choice if he cared to eat. To their credit, the masses turned out in droves, eager to experience the refined delicacy that the tsarist elite had kept to itself. One is tempted to compare this to the sacking of the

wine cellars of the Winter Palace by Bolshevik troops after the seizure of power in 1917. But the musical nectar kept replenishing
itself, much to the benefit of the listening audience.

These circumstances alone do not suffice to explain the inability
of jazz to penetrate Russia in the early years after the Revolution.
There was, in addition, the profound isolation imposed on the
country by World War I and by the nominally internationalist revolution. In June 1916, the French ambassador had observed that
"The war has erected an impassable barrier between Russia and
Europe, a Wall of China." [10] This isolation took many forms. The
international links that had brought the latest recordings to Russia
were severed. The nationalized publishing industry turned its back
on Western *Schlagers*, which it would have been unable to purchase
even if it had wanted to on account of Russia's new unconvertible
currency. The few Western pop tunes that were issued, such as "A
Corner of Piccadilly" and "Guitars, Songs, and Wine," were five
years out of date. The currency problem and Russia's general isolation from the West also affected the record industry, and at a critical moment, at least from the standpoint of jazz. No fewer than
110 million records were produced in 1922 alone in the United
States and Western Europe, and much of that music was jazz. The
"industry of human happiness" boomed at precisely the time Russia was least able to participate in its growth. [11]

Government regulation of the popular or "light" music industry
further impeded change. In December 1919, the Centrotheater organization was established to mount variety shows and provide
censorship of cabaret theaters through licensing control. [12] In February 1920, the Moscow Council (*Soviet*) assumed control over all
concert life in the city. In a move that was to reverberate over the
next half-century, an "Artistic Control Commission" was set up
and empowered to issue permits for all local concerts. [13] Similar
bureaucratic entities were created in Petrograd and other leading
cities. No monopolist in the capitalist West ever enjoyed such control. With one stroke the doctrine of residual powers, so essential
to pluralistic societies, was set on its head. Henceforth, all initiative
not specifically entrusted to the public remained in the hands of the

government. Fortunately, it proved far easier to claim such grandiose powers than to exercise them. But, at the least, a formidable weapon of intimidation had entered the musical scene.

Even without these various hindrances, an aspiring jazz musician in Russia would have had great difficulty in the early 1920s. A jazz band, was, after all, an orchestra of new instruments as well as new techniques for playing them. Where could one find a banjo in Moscow? Or a bass drum struck by the newly invented pedal mechanism? Saxophones, the ultimate symbol of the Jazz Age, were as rare in Russia as balalaikas on Chicago's South Side. Bobbed hair, bell-bottom trousers, short skirts, and all the other accoutrements of a John Held, Jr., cartoon could be improvised, but jazz without a saxophone was inconceivable. The saxophone *was* jazz, its wail of abandon symbolizing the free style of life with which jazz was associated. Alexei Kozlov, who had preserved his tenor sax through the Civil War, formed a quintet that performed Western pop tunes in Petrograd in 1924. Kozlov knew how members of his audience viewed his silver horn and fulfilled their expectations by releasing flares and fireworks from its bell—no doubt reducing Russia's supply of saxophones by one.[14] The instrument's symbolism did not die. A decade later, the most popular Russian swing band was performing before a backdrop dominated by cardboard saxophones.

The scarcity of saxophones and other instruments was a genuine impediment to the spread of jazz in Russia. A pioneer Moscow saxophonist, Mikhail Lantsman, recalls that there were only three players in Moscow in 1931. After deciding to play the newfangled instrument, Lantsman scoured Moscow for a saxophone but to no avail. He had to travel to Kiev to buy one from an old tsarist military bandsman at the royal figure of 600 rubles.[15] The sax shortage endured for decades. More than thirty years later, in 1966, Mikhail Brantsberg, an aspiring Siberian saxophonist, traveled all the way to Central Asia to buy a fancy French Selmer instrument that had somehow fallen into the hands of a village bandsman near Tashkent![16]

Any one of these various economic and political difficulties could have thwarted the spread of jazz into Soviet-ruled Russia. As early as 1918, however, the first quasi-jazz band had been formed in newly independent Estonia, on Russia's very doorstep. Amidst the freedom that prevailed in this tiny new republic, three youths in the capital city of Tallinn had no difficulty getting together to imitate the popular music they had heard on American recordings. Led by drummer Kurt Strobel, the German-speaking gymnasium students rehearsed daily. Expanded to include drums, saxophone, banjo, violin, and cello, the group performed successfully at private parties and the local YMCA from 1919 on. By 1920 they had dubbed themselves "The Murphy Band." Over the next decade they achieved colossal success with arrangements pirated from Paul Whiteman, Vincent Lopez, and the English bands of Bert Ambrose and Jack Hylton. Long before jazz was played in most parts of the USSR, one could hear bouncy performances of the latest American pop tunes at the Café Marcelle or the Estonia Restaurant in Tallinn.[17]

The Eccentric Mr. Parnakh

The barriers to the free flow of new cultural forms into the Soviet Union in the 1920s were formidable but by no means insurmountable. In jazz, they could be overcome by anyone capable of developing a convincing explanation of why this outlandish music should be fostered under the new Communist regime and of somehow securing all the necessary instruments and music. The person who accomplished both these feats was the Russian Futurist poet, Dadaist, Surrealist, editor and dancer but non-musician, Valentin Parnakh.[18] Thanks to Parnakh, Russia had the distinction of being one of the few European countries—along with independent Estonia— in which jazz was first introduced by a native son, rather than by a touring American group.

Born to a Jewish family in the south of Russia, Parnakh followed the parade of pre-World War I émigrés to Europe and, after tossing about Spain for a while, arrived in Paris in 1913. He was a striking figure. Friends in Paris recall him being short and extremely frail, "like a jockey, like a leaf."[19] His slight frame was sustained largely by coffee which he imbibed in Paris cafés and at the small rue Callot apartment of the émigré painters Mikhail Larionov and Natalia Goncharova. A surviving sketch by Picasso depicts him as handsome, but contemporaries recall his head being too large and perched constantly at an unnatural angle. Memoirs devote far more attention to his strange dance movements than to his poetical work.

Parnakh's first exposure to jazz was a performance by Louis Mitchell's Jazz Kings at the Trocadero in Paris in July 1921.[20] Later that year he heard other touring American groups in Berlin. The café and dance-hall settings were important. For Parnakh, jazz was above all dance music, a vehicle for the fox-trot and the shimmy. In jazz, this ungainly poet found a physically liberating rhythm that could make the common man an artist and, in the process, drive decadent classical ballet from the stage. This is how Parnakh saw his mission in Russia.

Parnakh carefully laid the groundwork for a crusade on behalf of jazz before departing for Russia. He placed articles on "The New Dances" and "The Jazz Band" in *Veshch*, an avant-garde émigré journal that was well known and respected in Russia. The new American dances, he argued, embodied the spirit of postwar "detente" (he actually used the word) and translated the life of modern man into linear, mechanistic but free movement, just as the nineteenth century's unfocused yearnings had coalesced in the swimming movement of the waltz. "All these dances are therefore the expression of a jazz orchestra, of a music of dissonances, syncopations, crashes, soaring brasses, shrieking ratchets, whistles, howls, and alarm sirens all sounding like an alternating current of electricity," Parnakh explained in his essay on "The Jazz Band." However limited Parnakh's knowledge of music, he clearly knew less about electricity! In this same essay the word "jazz" appears in Russian for the first time.[21] But Parnakh did not dwell on its musical qualities. Instead, he stressed the visual aspects of the new music. the bass drum must be lighted with an electric light, and the horn players must gyrate with their instruments. When Mitchell's bandsmen performed a New Orleans-style second-line strut through the Trocadero, Parnakh was in ecstasy. A jazz band plays for dancing, but the band itself also dances: it is a "mimetic orchestra."

Parnakh arrived in Moscow in the summer of 1922 with a collection of the necessary instruments. Immediately, he began pressing his campaign in the Soviet press. In several fresh attacks he argued that jazz is a distillation of modern man's movements and manners. He compared the movements of Mitchell's pianist on his stool at the Elite Café with what he imagined Chopin's movements to have been, and praised the freedom of the former. The key to jazz dance and music, Parnakh argued, is its "eccentricity," the vibrant energy and motion released by the granting of boundless individual freedom to each participant.[22]

Why did Parnakh believe that Moscow was ready for his crusade of emancipation? Much had changed since the bleak Civil War years 1918–20. Lenin, realizing that the peasantry was solidly opposed to bolshevism and that the Bolsheviks themselves possessed neither the numbers nor the skills to manage the economy, took a giant step backward to state capitalism. The New Economic Policy (NEP), proclaimed in 1921, enabled the new regime to consolidate its control while permitting both entrepreneurs and labor unions to pursue their own interests, so long as they did not collide with those of the government. Exhausted by war, revolution, and civil strife, urban Russia breathed a sigh of relief. Olivier's Hermitage, a Moscow restaurant and garden famed for its variety shows and its mayonnaise, reopened in the autumn of 1921. Crooked Jimmy's, another cabaret theater that had survived the turmoil since 1918, expanded its programs.[23] And when the Aquarium Gardens reopened in Petrograd a sign at the door proclaimed "Everything as Before." In 1917 Russians had sung the "Marseillaise"; by 1922 they were crooning Yuri Miliutin's pop hit "The Sound of Nocturnal Marseilles."

Parnakh placed his propaganda pieces in highbrow journals, indicating that he was far more interested in winning over the cultural avant-garde than in seducing the public at large. He had grounds for optimism in 1922. After a half-decade of separation from the West, Russia's artists now worked diligently to make up for lost time. Each letter or visitor from abroad seemed to bear the same message: modernism is in the air. A new generation of modern architects was poised for its debut. In music, efforts were already underway in 1922 that were to give rise to the formation the following year of an Association of Contemporary Music and also a Quarter Tone Society. An acoustical engineer, Lev Thermin, had given Lenin a demonstration of the first electronic musical instrument, the "Therminovox,"[24] and the First Symphonic Ensemble (*Persimfans*) was successfully performing the entire classical repertoire without the aid of that anti-revolutionary authority figure, the conductor.[25] Attempts to incorporate the abrasive sounds of industry into music were also going forward, probably to the wide-eyed amazement of the few industrial workers exposed to it.[26]

Within this encouraging environment, the blond-haired poet set about organizing what became known as "The First Eccentric Orchestra of the Russian Soviet Federated Socialist Republic—Valentin Parnakh's Jazz Band." The ensemble consisted of a piano, banjo, drums, xylophone, and two violins. The first concert was announced for Sunday, October 1, 1922, in the auditorium of the State Institute for Theatrical Art in Moscow.

Every shred of evidence suggests that the first jazz concert in Russia was an event better read about than heard. In all likelihood Parnakh concentrated entirely on syncopated rhythms and the strange new sounds of trap drums, wood blocks, and banjo. It is not clear whether he succeeded in finding someone to play saxophone.[27] But enough people liked what they heard to encourage Parnakh almost immediately to announce a second performance for December 3. He promised this time "the newest numbers of 'jazz band literature'" to be performed by an expanded orchestra. As in the first concert, Parnakh led off with a report on "eccentric art," followed by readings of his "jazz poetry" and demonstrations of the latest American dance steps.[28] Then the orchestra performed eight numbers.

What did Russia's first jazz band sound like? Only a few tantalizing hints have survived. Parnakh himself speaks of the melodic line but makes no reference to polyphony. He speaks also of American melodies, suggesting that he had brought a few arrangements from Paris.[29] Improvisation, of course, was out of the question, and remained so in Russia for another decade. The entire stress was on the syncopated rhythms created by the drums, banjo, and xylophone. Parnakh also speaks of dissonances produced by the saxophone, suggesting bent notes. These must have sounded rather strange, since the handful of Russian sax players all used a tight, classical embouchure until the visit of Sidney Bechet in 1926, and hence could produce neither a convincing glissando nor a relaxed vibrato. Parnakh's "jazz," then, consisted of American popular songs accompanied by a syncopated rhythm band.

This was enough to stun the audience. The Petrograd conductor Nikolai Malko came away from the performance convinced that jazz would open up new areas of musical timbre for composers of the future.[30] The theater critic Vladimir Fedorov also judged the event a success and went so far as to declare that Parnakh's shimmy, fox-trot, and two-steps "might provide an excellent means of enlivening dance halls and organizing the free time of labor."[31]

Fedorov's mention of dance halls and workers is of particular interest. Up to this time Russians had viewed jazz as a manifestation of the urban "noise music" which the Italian Futurist artists had been calling for since 1913.[32] At Parnakh's second concert the jazz group had been juxtaposed to just such a "noise orchestra" organized by the composer N. N. Foregger and featuring artistic performances on bottles, sheet metal, sirens, whistles, and machines of various sorts. That such an arsenal might produce the music of the future became an article of faith among a handful of Russia's left-wing avant-gardists. Invented *for* the people rather than *by* them, it represented a kind of revolutionary elitism.

At least one critic came away from Parnakh's concerts convinced that noise music and jazz were one and the same. Jazz must be stopped, he wrote, "before it is too late."[33] The noise orchestra movement reached its apogee with the establishment of the First Experimental Synthetic Chamber Ensemble in 1923 by the pianist Leonid Varpakhovsky. As Varpakhovsky recalled to the Soviet jazz historian Alexei Batashev, the Ensemble consisted of nineteen players performing on no fewer than 124 noisemakers.[34] This was certainly no jazz group, but it did manage to render even the baroque classics on slide whistles and kazoos.[35]

Parnakh, thrown on the defensive, took pains to disassociate jazz from noise and novelty orchestras.[36] He based his case on the now familiar argument that jazz, far from being noise by and for the avant-garde, was popular dance music. But was Parnakh's band popular in Russia? The question is unfair, for Parnakh's jazz bore no more resemblance to the real thing than chop suey does to the haute cuisine of Peking; hence, the audience's reaction to it does not fairly reflect its response to jazz as such. Even Parnakh's syncopated rhythms were probably quite rudimentary. When the French pianist Jean Wiener performed in Moscow at this time he found Russian musicians interested in his jazz pieces but unable to master the rhythms.[37] Parnakh's audience, too, could not have been fully informed about or appreciative of his new music because neither recording studios nor radio broadcasts were open to jazz in Russia during the early and mid-twenties. Hence, the new music was not reinforced by the new media that were disseminating jazz in Western Europe and America. Denied these channels, jazz had to be spread through direct contact between performer and audience.

The audience remained small. A large number of itinerant, rich, and fun-loving foreigners in Moscow would have hastened the spread of jazz. Unfortunately, there were too few such people to swell audiences. Soviet Russia was off limits to Western café society. So few countries recognized the USSR that the diplomatic corps was minute; and the small number of tourists who made the eastward trek were either businessmen or earnest socialists eager to pay homage to the New Jerusalem.[38]

What jazz initially lacked in audience support it made up through backing from the Soviet government. *Glavlit*, the censorship organ within the Commissariat of Public Enlightenment, regularly approved Western fox-trots and "waltz-Bostons" for publication.[39] The Commissar of Agriculture hired Parnakh's group to perform at the 1923 "First All Union Exhibition of Agriculture and Cottage Industries,"[40] and the Communist International called on Parnakh to entertain foreign comrades as its congress on the occasion of the fifth anniversary of the Bolshevik Revolution in November 1922. A French Communist who attended the meeting described "a formidable band thundering away, crude and noisy."[41] Except for the Original Dixieland Jazz Band's performance at the 1918 London ball in honor of the forthcoming opening of peace negotiations at Versailles, this was probably the first appearance of a jazz band at any state occasion.

If Parnakh did not at first attract a large popular audience, did jazz then appeal to Russia's artists and intellectuals? The poet Sergei Esenin, whose doleful eyes had attracted a red-faced and overweight Isadora Duncan, summed up his impressions of Western culture during a tour of Western Europe in 1922:

> Apart from the fox-trot there is almost nothing here. [Western Europeans] gorge themselves on drink, and then fox-trot once more. I've not met one human being so far, and see no trace of one. Even if we are poor . . . we have a soul, which people here hire out to others as unwanted. . . .[42]

Vladimir Mayakovsky, self-styled "poet of the revolution" and, unlike Esenin, sympathetic to the industrial city, wrote in 1923 of Western cities where

> words're deafened by the one-step tempo,
> and again through the one-step tempo tremble:
> "What's all the merriment?
> Really?"[43]

The artist Alexander Rodchenko ornamented the publication of these lines with a poster combining the images of "Die Jazz-Band," flappers, dirigible-like cigars, liquor, caviar, and the "Jazz-Two-Step Fox-Trot und Shimmy." These were the years in which students at Walter Gropius's Bauhaus in Germany organized themselves into a jazz band.[44] By contrast, at the Higher Technical Workshops (*Vkhutemas*), Moscow's booming school for avant-garde crafts, such activity was unknown. Not that *agitmuzyk* was any more popular. Indeed, the Association of Proletarian Musicians, organized in 1923 to foster ideologically committed music, drew only yawns from educated youth.[45]

Eccentricity Invades the Stage

Russia's leading artists and intellectuals were slow to embrace jazz and the emancipated social life it embodied. Imbued with the self-aggrandizing notion of an avant-garde, they were, for the most part, far better disposed to welcome the many experimental composers who visited Russia in the 1920s—Milhaud, Berg, Hindemith, and others—than to link the words "popular" and "culture" in the same phrase. But there were exceptions, and Valentin Parnakh sparked their interest. The film director Sergei Eisenstein came away from Parnakh's second concert eager to learn the fox-trot. Parnakh obliged. The innovative theatrical director Vsevolod Meierhold went even further and decided to exploit jazz in his next production.

Meierhold broke new ground by placing a full jazz band on the Russian stage as early as 1922. Jazz bands were not to appear frequently even on the European stage until the late 1920s, although it is true that Kurt Weill's *Die Dreigroschenoper* of 1928 and Ernst Křenek's *Jonny spielt auf* culminated several years of those composers' experimentations with jazz and cabaret.[46] Meierhold's opportunity came with his production of Fernand Crommelynck's bedroom farce, *The Magnanimous Cuckold*, at the old Zon Theater in Moscow. The play was pure froth, and doubtless would have raised eyebrows among the left-wing intelligentsia had it not been for the innovative Constructivist sets by Liubov Popova. The only music was provided by a meek pianist. After several performances in the autumn of 1922, however, Meierhold dropped a bomb in the third act by unleasing Parnakh's full jazz band on stage. According to a musician who was present, the entire audience "stamped its feet and clapped in time with the music."[47]

Meierhold capitalized on the success of his bold stroke with an adaptation of Ilya Ehrenburg's propagandistic novel *The Trust D.E.*[48] Ehrenburg's story combined naiveté, absurdity, paranoia, and racism in equal measures. It depicts a sinister band of American monopolists who seek, through their "Give Us Europe [abbreviated to D.E. in Russian] Trust," to conquer all Europe, depopulate it, and colonize it with Africans. Fortunately, the heroic proletariat of the

Soviet Union is still around to save the day. Tunneling from Petrograd to New York (this drawn from Bernhard Kellermann's story *The Tunnel*) the proletarians pop up in Manhattan to destroy the D.E. Trust at its very *omphalos*. All this action is modestly described in the published program for the performance as "a sharp agitational weapon aimed against the bourgeoisie."[49] Germany, Austria, and France are saved in the nick of time; England is yanked from the edge of cannibalism; and the Red Army assures the success of revolution in America.

Meierhold's task as director was to contrast the decadent Americans with the vital and revolutionary Russians. He accomplished this masterfully, but quite differently than the author may have intended. Muscle-bound members of the proletariat perform acrobatics, play soccer, and strut around the stage to the accompaniment of march music performed on the harmonica. Is it any wonder that even *Izvestiia*, the government newspaper, declared such a depiction of Soviet life to be "pale and unconvincing"?[50] But there was nothing pale about Meierhold's bourgeoisie! In contrast to the dull naturalism of the Soviet heroes, the despised capitalists were dressed in elegant tuxedos and stepped out in racy cabarets with beautiful women. Parnakh's jazz band roared through eight numbers in the course of the cabaret-type revue, and sexy dancing girls in heavy makeup hoofed it up to "Dancing Honeymoon," "Dardanella," "Rose of the Rio Grande," "Japanese Sandman," and other pop-jazz hits.[51]

The Red Army may have won the war on stage, but Parnakh's jazz band clearly won the audience. After a rollicking debut at the Leningrad Conservatory on June 15, 1924, the show was moved to Moscow to entertain delegates to the Fifth Congress of the Communist International. The delegates, who had already heard Parnakh once in 1922, were ecstatic at his band's stage performance.[52] So were audiences at the newly opened Meierhold Theater, where every performance of *D.E.* was sold out for several years.[53]

Was Meierhold aware of what he had done? Beyond doubt. He had deliberately packed the production with jazz numbers and, as we shall see, missed no opportunity to promote the sinful allure of the jazz band. When the show toured to Kiev, the director himself ordered "Jazz-band" to be placed prominently on the poster. Again, the house was packed. Meierhold may have conceived the play as half circus and half propaganda but it was, more than either, a showcase for *le dernier cri* in the West. Within weeks the Java Tobacco factory was producing its fashionable new "D.E. cigarettes."

Meierhold's production of *D.E.* represents, as one critic has noted, "a crisis of revolutionary content, as well as of form."[54] It was a deliberately engineered crisis, however. Meierhold's sympathies lay clearly with the culture of jazz and the "fox-trotting West." It is significant that Soviet audiences demonstrably shared Meierhold's enthusiasm. But it is no less important for the future that jazz, in its Moscow debut five years after the 1917 revolution, was juxtaposed to bolshevism. This juxtaposition stuck in the Russian mentality for half a century.

In 1925, the tension was not yet acute. The tidal wave of American jazz crashed on Western Europe with great force, but its power was much reduced by the time it reached Russia. Indeed, because jazz did not rush into Russia with the fury with which it hit Western Europe, the Soviet Union was able to absorb a great deal of the apparently anarchistic new music before a strong reaction set in.

The comparative mildness of Russians' initial reaction to jazz deserves special emphasis. Because Soviet Russia was relatively isolated from international currents in popular culture, it took no real part in the great controversy over jazz that raged in the countries most deeply affected by it. In the United States judges railed against jazz and the dance craze and various persons called for legislation to ban them both.[55] The *Ladies' Home Journal* decried the "jazz path of degradation" and announced that "Unspeakable Jazz Must Go!" The stakes were high, for jazz represented the "triumph of the jungle."[56] In Wales and Scotland local magistrates imposed curfews to limit the spread of jazz. The situation was scarcely better in France, where in 1923 police broke up a jazz funeral on the grounds that mourners should not fox-trot, while in Italy various petitions were circulating against jazz.[57]

In the years to come, there were few charges leveled against jazz in the Soviet Union that had not already been tested in the West. But in the Western democracies, though German Foreign Minister Dr. Gustav Stresemann might opine that jazz is not music and Queen Mary of England might plead with a racetrack orchestra not to play jazz,[58] it was all but impossible to translate such feelings into enforceable laws. In Russia such splenetic outbursts could become the bases for governmental policies. This, as much as the negative feelings themselves, was what was to make the fate of jazz in Soviet Russia different.

The smooth entry of jazz into the Soviet Union between 1922 and 1925 was facilitated by the toleration fostered by Lenin's New Economic Policy. The survival of the NEP into 1928 was to provide three more crucial years for jazz to take root and thrive before facing its first major assault during the Cultural Revolution of 1928– 31. This breathing space was to prove vitally important in several respects. Both the quality and the quantity of jazz heard in Soviet Russia greatly increased. Russian critics for the first time were given a chance to assess real jazz, rather than wooden imitations. Most important, jazz in the years 1925–28 reached out beyond the audiences of highbrow theaters and confronted the Soviet urban public at large. So warmly was it received in the final years of the NEP that for the next half-century jazz in the USSR was saddled with the image of decadence and abandon which all true Stalinists applied to the NEP era as a whole.

4
Russia's Roaring Twenties, 1925–1928

Some men and some women, they care nothing for the
  gospel life,
Till the bell rings and the whistle blows, and the little
  black train's in sight
                    Rev. J. M. Gates, Vocalion Records, 1926

Toward the end of February 1926 a group of thirty-five black American dancers, singers, and jazz musicians disembarked at Moscow's Warsaw Station for a three-month tour of the Soviet Union. As they descended from the ample Russian-gauge sleeping cars they were met by eager and hospitable representatives of *Rosfil*, the Russian Philharmonic Society, which had booked the tour. They were to be royally paid, far more than the $400 per month they had been receiving for two years in Western Europe. The bandleader, Sam Wooding, had been assured a figure well in excess of his usual $1200 a month.[1] In spite of the hospitable welcome and the unheard-of salaries, members of the cast of *The Chocolate Kiddies* were uneasy. They had not wanted to go to Russia at all and had accepted Rosfil's extravagant offer only at the urging of the United States consul in Madrid, where they had played some months previously. The original drummer had been so apprehensive that he had refused to get on the train for Russia, leaving Wooding in the lurch. Fortunately, a replacement was found. The others left their families in Paris and Berlin. But their fears soon proved unfounded. "Much to our amazement," Wooding reported, "our Russian engagements were the best in all Europe."[2]

The band performed at the Moscow Circus and then at the Leningrad Music Hall, playing to packed audiences in both cities. Scores of prominent persons from the Soviet cultural elite turned out for what was advertised as a "Negro operetta." The posters by the avant-garde artists Georgi and Vladimir Stenberg recalled a turn-of-the-century American minstrel show. For three years Russians had fantasized over what a real jazz band would be like. Few records were available, and Soviet radio did not as yet consider jazz fitting musical fodder for proletarian tastes. So direct exposure to Sam Wooding's group was important. With Wooding's arrival at the Warsaw Station, Parnakh's heroic effort to introduce jazz in Russia with purely local talent came to an end. For the next three years the USSR was to participate more fully in world popular culture than would be possible for the next three decades.

Who were the Chocolate Kiddies and with what kind of program did they regale Moscow and Leningrad audiences? The entire production had been thrown together in 1924 for the European market, where demand was enormous. As a Scandinavian producer explained to the *New York Times*, "The jazz craze in Europe has gathered force so fast that musical shows throughout Europe, to be profitable, must engage American girls, adopt American costumes, or teach their performers to dance like American girls." [3] Curiously, an émigré Russian impresario had gone to Harlem to assemble a show to take back to Berlin with him. In New York he found that Eubie Blake and Noble Sissle's *Chocolate Dandies* had just closed and parts of the cast were available. Wooding's eleven-piece band had just moved from Atlantic City to the Club Alabam in Times Square and was all the rage. The reconstituted *Chocolate Dandies*, now called *The Chocolate Kiddies*, and Wooding's band sailed for Germany on June 22, 1924. After a successful stint in the uninhibited German capital, the Chocolate Kiddies were sent by their Russian manager on tour through France, Italy, Turkey, Czechoslovakia, Tunisia, and Spain. In Madrid Rosfil had caught up with them. [4]

Far from being a "Negro operetta," *The Chocolate Kiddies* was actually a variety revue in two acts. It began with the latest dances executed by high-stepping babes dressed in above-the-knee flapper skirts and their Harlem swells decked out in tuxedos. These were followed by singers and clowns who led into the second act, which was devoted exclusively to a jazz concert. Wooding's band was a formidable ensemble. A New Orleanian, Tommy Ladnier, led the three-man trumpet section, and Garvin Bushell on alto drove the sax section. The group worked largely from written arrangements, which came from the pen of Wooding.[5]

The sheer polish of a band that had kept nearly the same members for over two years guaranteed its high professionalism. But the visual impact and influence of the dancers and musicians was more important than the music. Dziga Vertov, the young cinematographer who chronicled the era of the New Economic Policy, was led to include a whole scene from the revue in his silent film of 1926, *A Sixth of the World*. Discussion of the visual aspect of jazz dominated the appreciative reviews by a pleiad of Russia's most distinguished theatrical producers, including Chekhov's old friend Konstantin Stanislavsky, Alexander Tairov, and Petr Kogan, president of the Academy of Artistic Sciences.[6] Not all the reviews were favorable, however. The *Red Press* fulminated against the dancers' blatant sexuality and concluded that jazz was an unwholesome import.[7] Hostile writers took pains to dismiss jazz as fitting only for circuses and variety shows.[8] Criticism in this vein was so common that one suspects at least part of the musical establishment feared jazz might invade its hallowed precincts.

Sam Wooding encouraged this anxiety. Born in Philadelphia to proper and ambitious parents, Wooding took pains to disassociate himself from jazz. He immodestly boasted of "knowing the classical repertoire and having played through tomes of Bach, Beethoven, Chopin, Schumann, and other masters."[9] And he made it known to all and sundry, in an act of transparent self-promotion, that he considered jazz a means of survival until he could "attain loftier ultimate aims." Throughout the Russian tour, he urged his men to attend symphony concerts, and he himself claimed to take special pleasure in hearing the cathedral choirs and in witnessing the conductorless Persimfans perform Stravinsky. All this gave rise to perplexity among the Russian critics, for it suggested that Wooding, despite his modest background and limited technical skill, wanted to be judged as a musician, and not simply as a jazz entertainer. It is not surprising that the strongest praise for Wooding came from writers and theater directors, not musicians. Perhaps he would have done better by sticking to the role of Negro primitive that was expected of him.

There were good musical reasons for the coolness of the musical establishment as well. The pretentious Wooding, far from loving the hard-driving Harlem style, actually favored the "symphonic" approach to jazz pioneered during the early 1920s by Paul Whiteman.[10] Wooding's 1925 Vox recordings of "By the Waters of the Minnetonka" and "Alabammy Bound" reveal an ensemble that was tight but tediously straight, sounding more like a ragtime orchestra than one of the harder jazz groups of the day. It is no wonder that Wooding's tendency to move away from jazz increased during his stay in Europe, especially as he had cut himself off from the boisterous dancing audiences that nurtured the new music at home. This was apparently Wooding's preference. Sidney Bechet, who later played briefly with the Wooding band in Europe, said:

> We didn't get no chance to play jazz. You see, we had some good musicians but Wooding only wanted to play them Sears Roebuck things. We wouldn't have got them jobs if we wasn't niggers. That's how it was in Europe. Still is.[11]

Jazz historian Al Rose, who knew Wooding in the 1930s, described his piano playing as "technically unimpressive and artistically vapid, built entirely on clichés."[12] A Frenchman who attended one of Wooding's performances in Moscow referred to "the failure of an ex-New York jazz band." Even *Izvestiia*'s reviewer found Wooding's performance to be in the vein of Anglo-German cabaret music and "not at all hot or eccentric."[13]

The Fast Life During the NEP

Three years after the Russians' first clumsy attempts to imitate jazz, the Soviet government's newspapers were criticizing a Harlem band for being insufficiently hot. Such published sentiments reveal the deep change in Russia since the Civil War. Through a stupendous reconstruction effort, Russians had gotten their economy back on the move. Prewar levels of production had been attained again in most industries, and cities had regained their vitality. Dramatic new buildings, some in the Constructivist style, were rising in Moscow and the partial renewal of international tourism gave the city a cosmopolitan air that had long been absent. Ideological zeal was decidedly out of fashion.

Lenin had died on January 21, 1924, after a prolonged illness. With the Father of the Revolution dead and embalmed, the younger generation could take its oedipal revenge. Nightclubs boomed, privately owned boutiques poured out flapper fashions, and in the workers' capital there appeared a breed of young people with seemingly nothing to do all day. A series of novels, beginning with Sergei Malashkin's *The Moon on the Right Side*, a literary *cause célèbre* in 1926, documented the degeneracy of youth in lurid detail.[14] The stories of members of *Komsomol* (the Young Communist League) engaging in orgies of alcohol and drugs were not far off the mark. Everyone knew that powerful marijuana from Central Asia was readily available at the Sukharevka Market,[15] and that the suspension in 1925 of the liquor prohibition law Nicholas II had foolishly introduced in 1914 had put vodka within easy reach of anyone with a ruble to spare.

The apparent idleness of youth bothered moralists and confounded sociologists. The country's leading pollster, Sergei Strumilin, surveyed high school and college students, as well as young factory workers, in order to find out how they spent their days. None reported more than a few hours of free time each week.[16] Yet to all appearances there were large numbers of young men and women with time on their hands.

By 1926 the desire to revert to the pre-revolutionary fashions in popular culture was dead. Nor did the Party's Civil War songs and *agitmuzyk* hold much attraction. Even the true believers' journal, *For Proletarian Music*, had to admit that young people and workers found the ideological potboilers "dull, deadly, and gray."[17] Earnest researchers attempted to elicit the true tastes of the nation's popular audiences. Their conclusion: neither folk songs nor the tired diet of hits from light operas satisfied anyone.[18]

The researchers needed only to have perused the sheet music ads of the State Press (*Giz*) to learn what the public wanted: Matvei Blanter's "John Gray," "Aero-Foxtrot," "I and Billy," or "Eccentric Dances"; M. Nikolaevsky's "Miss Evelyn Foxtrot"; Lev Drizo's "Yes! We Killed the Bottle"; "The Hypnosis Tango"; and Yuri Miliutin's fox-trot "Harry and Barry." Russia was fox-trotting to communism, and when the official publishers couldn't meet the demand for new fox-trot melodies, the writers published them on their own, often engaging the best designers to do the covers.[19] Even young Dmitri Shostakovich, the shining star of musical Leningrad, arranged Vincent Youmans's "Tea for Two" as a fox-trot for symphonic orchestra called "Tahiti Trot."[20]

The new music existed to enable people to dance the latest steps, which were in turn a means of celebrating publicly the new social values of post-Victorian Russia. These values spread with great rapidity. Visiting European leftists wrote much nonsense about the high-minded and austere values of Soviet youth during the late 1920s. The German publicist Klaus Mehnert, for example, would have had his readers believe that youths in Soviet Russia were so single-minded in their dedication to the building of communism that they had neither the time nor the inclination to flirt with the movement on behalf of individual liberation and expression that was sweeping the European world.[21] In practically the same year as Mehnert's visit, however, the director of New York's newly founded Museum of Modern Art attended a youth party at Herzen House (*Dom Gertsena*) in Moscow and found "bad jazz . . . , ostentatious Charlestoning, and good food."[22] The Leningrad painter Vladimir Lebedev documented similar scenes, scenes that could have come from Georg Grosz's Berlin or any black-and-tan nightspot in Harlem.

The Russians' interest in the latest wild dances was fed by improved communication links with Western Europe. The Charleston, which the dancer Ada Smith (known as "Bricktop") had introduced to Paris in the winter of 1925–26,[23] reached Moscow and

Leningrad only months later, thanks to the Chocolate Kiddies, as well as returning Soviet travelers. The generous provisions for private enterprise under the New Economic Policy enabled literally dozens of small-time entrepreneurs to open dance studios in their living rooms, where members of the new Soviet fast set could brush up their steps before going public.[24]

The latest "American dances" also invaded the popular stage after 1925. Elsa Krüger and her partner "Mack" picked up the gestures of the exotic prewar Tango of Death and gave them new life by performing them to a strong jazz beat. Another popular prerevolutionary figure who successfully adapted to the times was Nikolai Alexandrov. A frequent traveler to Western Europe, Alexandrov and his partner, Nina Boyarskaia, had gradually abandoned the Ukrainian folk dances of their earlier days and devoted themselves nearly full time to dances of the Jazz Age. They were quick to pick up both the Charleston and the black bottom and were touted on posters as "the best dancers in the USSR" as they dazzled audiences across the country with their alluring performances.[25] Alexandrov and Boyarskaia accumulated substantial fortunes, not least because they served as living fashion magazines. To be sure, not every Soviet woman could expect to own a peacock feather blouse ornamented with diamonds, as Boyarskaia flaunted, but their squires could reasonably hope to buy or borrow a tuxedo (*smoking* in Russian) cut to Alexandrov's up-to-date pattern.[26]

By the late 1920s the Soviet popular stage was seething and writhing with erotica. Elsa Krüger's solo "Amazon Dance" bore little relationship to the regime's sectarian strictures on the equality of the sexes. Still less did the "Apache Dances" that had appeared by mid-decade. Performed to fox-trots, tangos, and Charleston rhythms, these provocative numbers paired frightened, submissive females with cruelly masterful males. The fact that Apache Dances were branded "decadent" by the few reviewers who bothered to write about them in no way reduced their huge popularity.

Such terpsichorean erotica might readily be dismissed if it had merely been a depraved holdover from the bourgeois past, as later ideologists were to claim. But how, then, to account for the phenomenal popularity of Lydia Iver and Arcadi Nelson, both of whom began their careers in 1919 but achieved genuine popularity only after 1925, thanks to the enthusiasm of a new generation whose members had scarcely entered their teens in 1917?[27] Their melo-dramatic presentation of the new dance steps contrasted sharply with the coldly controlled manner of such pre-revolutionary idols as Komnen and Iving. Lydia Iver would burst on the stage in a velvet cape, then throw it off to reveal bobbed hair, high-heeled tap shoes, and the scantiest flapper dress. High style indeed, and a per-fect juxtaposition to the urban tough and prostitute image of the Apache Dances.

Writing of such popular dances in Germany, Kurt Weill observed:

> Unlike art music, dance music does not reflect towering person-
> alities standing above time, but rather the instincts of the masses.
> And a glance into the dance halls of all continents demonstrates
> that jazz is just as precisely the outward expression of our time
> as the waltz was of the outgoing nineteenth century.[28]

This state of affairs was bound to bring Soviet Mrs. Grundys out of their corner. The first was one Anna Zelenko of Moscow. In a 1927 volume published for the propaganda office *Agitprop* by the "Worker of Enlightenment" press, Zelenko staged a rearguard campaign in behalf of "healthy, hygienic, and pretty amusement for youth."[29] How dreadful that youth wanted only the new dances—the tango, Boston, fox-trot, Charleston, etc.—and what a relief that at least some directors of workers' clubs were banning them since, as a reviewer put it, "the sexual element dominates in them all." Zelenko's solution? To create a new "mass dance" that would en-able every couple to vent energy in free improvisation but within a morally and ideologically acceptable context.

The measure of the failure of such efforts between 1925 and 1929 can be found in the history of the Blue Blouse movement, a clever attempt to combine Communist ideology with variety theater.[30] The founder of the movement, Boris Yuzhanin, intended his small musical-theatrical companies to be "living newspapers," which would pre-sent the events of the day in proper ideological perspective through the media of music, mime, poetry, and acrobatics. Stated differently, the Blue Blouses offered sugar-coated propaganda through dance and song. To be effective, such a program had to accept and build on the tastes of the working public. In this sense, Yuzhanin was a lineal descendent of Martin Luther, who adapted boisterous German drinking songs to the praise of God. The numerous Blue Blouse troupes employed folk songs, music-hall tunes, and variety hits in their early years. By 1926 they had bowed to the inevitable and were playing jazz tunes, often with kazoos, slide whistles, and washboards.[31] Parnakh's example in Meierhold's *The Magnanimous Cuckold* and *D.E.* had confirmed them in this shift to jazz.[32] Only jazz rhythms and dances, it turned out, could attract and hold the attention of Soviet audiences in teahouses and workers' cafés.

New Orleans Touches Moscow

The rapid penetration of jazz dances into Soviet cities goes far toward explaining the qualified success of Sam Wooding's jazz band in the spring of 1926. "Anybody can play for dancing," he later wrote, "but not anybody can give a concert."[33] Wooding, infatuated with the notion of a dignified symphonic jazz, did not condescend to satisfy the desire of his Moscow and Leningrad audiences for hot, danceable jazz.

Nothing more vividly illustrates the direction in which popular taste had moved than the enthusiastic, even frenzied, reception accorded to Benny Peyton's Jazz Kings, who swept into Moscow only days before Wooding and the Chocolate Kiddies and stayed on in Russia several months after Wooding left. This seven-piece band of New Orleans-style improvisers bewitched audiences in Moscow, Kharkov, Odessa, and Kiev. Until the arrival of rock groups such as the Nitty Gritty Dirt Band in the 1970s, Peyton's band was arguably the most uproariously Western ensemble to tour the Soviet circuit.

The group consisted of old cronies drawn largely from Will Marion Cook's Southern Syncopated Orchestra—the same outfit which in 1919 had inspired Ernest Ansermet to pen his prophetic comment on the new medium for *Revue Romande*. When part of Cook's team had been lost in a ship at sea in 1921, Peyton, the drummer, had set out on his own with a seven-piece band, the Jazz Kings. Frank Withers was billed as the King of the Trombone. He and New Orleans-born clarinetist Sidney Bechet joined the group between stints with Josephine Baker's *La Revue Nègre*.[34] The seven-piece format effectively killed the possibility of pretentious symphonic jazz and ensured spontaneity.

It could not have been otherwise with the exuberant and mischievous Bechet on hand. In London in 1919 he had had a nasty scrap with a bobby over a prostitute. "All I could hear was rape, rape, rape," he recalled. Later, he had lived the life of Riley in Paris as part of the revue that introduced the Charleston to Europe. "That really started something," Bechet acknowledged.[35] Bechet took his free-wheeling style to Russia—he later had to extend his visa several weeks in order to recuperate from the effects of too much vodka.

It is a pity that the 1920 recordings made by Bechet, Peyton, and several other members of the group that later toured Russia were never released. Their sound must be deduced from the comments of critics. One would have expected that Bechet, with his commanding musical presence, would have completely dominated Russians' impression of the group. But he did not, and at least one reviewer dwelt instead on the (to him) utter novelty of the pianist's and drummer's techniques.[36] Other critics, including Dmitri Shostakovich's close friend, Leningrad conductor Nikolai Malko, concentrated on the ensemble as a whole:

> So sharply does their musical culture differ from that of Europe that they are, for us, an entirely new phenomenon. . . . The ensemble executed some dozen pieces beginning with "Greetings to Moscow" (their own composition) and ending with songs and dance music. The corpus of music demonstrated by the Negroes is not great in its content, nor does it call forth great interest. It is not the content but the performance of their music that counts. Their execution truly stunned the listeners and not just with clever effects, which were few. . . . The players actually *play* rather than triumph over difficulties. A transition to new tempos

and rhythms is not done according to any written music. . . . It
is *played*, subordinated to the freely developing sense of the tune.
It is an ideal ensemble and has no need for any visual signals, as
in any orchestra, with its conductor.[37]

Malko was not alone in sensing that jazz embodies new notions
of individual expression through movement and dance. Osip Brik,
one of the capital's most astute left-wing art critics, realized that
"A jazz band is not suited to being received in isolation; it must be
heard and felt. A jazz band presupposes not a sitting audience but
an undulating crowd, whether at a dance or at another form of
public merrymaking." Brik also perceived that jazz was a form
of mass art, and, as such, "is for us a new and necessary form of
musical culture."[38] Similar reviews followed the band throughout
its tour.[39]

The surroundings in which Peyton's musicians performed doubtless helped to reinforce the image of jazz as the embodiment of
modern informality. True, they held forth in the House of Writers
and even at the Great Hall of the Moscow Conservatory. But their
real base of operation in the Soviet capital was the movie theater
Malaia Dmitrovka. This palace of the silver screen was a staging
ground for the American infection. A new Hollywood film opened
there each week before packed audiences, and profits on ticket sales
for American films were so large that they helped to cover the costs
of producing the ideologically "correct" Soviet films which the public
generally ignored. Whenever Peyton's group performed at the Malaia Dmitrovka, the theater was packed hours before the first note
sounded. Couples took to the aisles and wiggled in the Charleston
style.[40] The scene was reenacted in every city the band visited. Such
luminaries as Commissar of Public Enlightenment Anatoli Lunacharsky dropped in, often forming negative opinions of the dancing
that were to surface publicly only after a lapse of several years.
More important, young musicians turned out in numbers. Mikhail
Lantsman, later a prominent Moscow saxophonist, first heard jazz
when Peyton and Bechet performed at the Malaia Dmitrovka. "It
was a sensation. I couldn't tear myself away," he recalled.[41]

The total impact of Sam Wooding's and Benny Peyton's jazz bands in the USSR was enormous. Scarcely had they departed than the Muztorg publishing house in Moscow issued its first "American Blues," a Handy-esque melody by Yuri Grin titled "Guyana." Leo Asher issued a series of "American dances," all bearing the censor's seal of approval.[42] The *jeunesse dorée* took jazz to its heart, seeing in the uninhibited behavior of Peyton's bandsmen in particular a living model for elegant rebellion.[43] To satisfy the growing demand, numerous small orchestras, which played at restaurants like The Roof in Moscow, began affecting the style of American jazzmen. The change was superficial, of course, because the music remained strange and exotic to all but a handful of Russians. But even advocates of *agitmuzyk* began to give in to public pressure. Hard rhythm, it turned out, was not only acceptable to the ideological zealots but was actually preferred by them over what they considered the placid decadence of the modernists.[44]

Acknowledging the huge success of these two American jazz bands in Russia, one cannot help but be struck by the difference in their receptions. Wooding's symphonic approach and more European demeanor struck the public as less exotic and hence less exciting than Peyton's band, but it also rendered his band more accessible to Russian musicians and critics. They debated furiously over the merits of his jazz, with both partisans and critics sharing an elitist perspective, whether conservative or avant-garde. Peyton's group, by contrast, won the public's heart but, with the exception of a few astute observers like Malko, failed to reach the musical establishment. And, really, why would a conservatory-trained critic lurk about dance palaces and movie houses to cover the howlings of besotted bordello entertainers?

Still, in the aftermath of the Wooding and Peyton tours it was not immediately clear whether the hot or symphonic style would triumph in Russia. The first group that capitalized on the new jazz market definitely inclined toward the hot style, although without a trace of improvisation. The AMA Jazz Band (*Amadzhaz*) was the brainchild of the Association of Moscow Authors, a privately organized music publishing house. The idea was simple. The Association hoped to cash in on the jazz market and needed a band to push its hits. By the same process that had put many American ragtime pianists on publishers' payrolls, the AMA Jazz Band earned its salary as an instrument of advertising. An eight-piece outfit, the band reigned supreme at the Hermitage Gardens in Moscow and, later, at the Casino Restaurant. The Soviet Union finally had acquired an authentic commercial jazz group dedicated to serving a market of dancers, drinkers, and listeners, rather than to creating an audience *ex nihilo*.[45] The AMA Jazz Band and its director, Alexander Tsfasman, established so many "firsts" in Russian jazz that we will return to it later.

Research in Philadelphia

The Chocolate Kiddies had scarcely left Leningrad in 1926 than young Leningrad pianist Leopold Teplitsky set sail for America to study the new music in its native habitat. Teplitsky's mission was to master the techniques of American jazz, buy up stock arrangements and all the necessary musical instruments, and then put all this to use in a new jazz orchestra for the city of Lenin's Revolution. Tsar Peter I had brought modern shipbuilding to Russia in much the same way, and later Soviet officials were to import computer software from the West after initially denouncing it, too, as "bourgeois." The parallel is appropriate because Teplitsky was sent to America by none other than the Commissariat of Public Enlightenment and its chief, Lunacharsky.[46]

Teplitsky went to Philadelphia. Lunacharsky's choice of city can only be explained by the fact that Sam Wooding had talked of his hometown when he met the commissar. Teplitsky had been chosen for the mission because through his own exertions he had mastered the art of ragtime piano. One can only speculate what his teacher, the composer Glazunov, thought of Teplitsky's self-study of Scott Joplin, if indeed he knew of it at all!

Arriving in America early in 1926, Teplitsky promptly bought himself a sleek roadster, joined a five-piece combo playing at a Philadelphia bar, and laid seige to Paul Whiteman for copies of his arrangements. Again, the turn to Whiteman might be traced to Wooding's influence, since Wooding himself had come under the spell of the walrus-shaped "King of Jazz" from Denver.

Because "Pops" Whiteman was a mediocre conductor, wore elegantly tailored suits, and made good money, he has had terrible press among purists. By scrubbing up jazz and washing the smell of the speakeasy from its clothing, Whiteman, it is said, founded the "sweet" tradition that culminated in the syrupy non-jazz of Guy Lombardo, Lawrence Welk, and others. He is unfairly charged. Whiteman was, in fact, a symphonic musician who had achieved national fame even before jazz came on the scene. He was the first to adapt jazz to anything other than its accustomed functions and milieu. Through his role as George Gershwin's patron for *Rhapsody in Blue* (1923) he invaded the sanctuary of classical music. His orchestra also pioneered the application of jazz to the entire light-music industry, and he encouraged more young jazz talent than anyone before him. So successful was Whiteman that his achievement was taken for granted everywhere in the United States by the time of Teplitsky's arrival in 1926.[47]

Purists who cavil at Whiteman's success at introducing jazz into the concert hall conveniently forget that, to a far greater extent, he enticed fundamentally hostile audiences to take jazz seriously. At the same time, he devised a style of jazz capable of luring burghers and professional folk who would have otherwise refused to dance to flapper music. Whiteman earned general's rank in the army of musicians who were assaulting the bastions of musical Victorianism. Whiteman's mission had direct relevance to Europe, where the tradition of light orchestral music was far stronger than in America, and especially to Russia, where the schism between high and popular styles was so great. On both sides of the Atlantic, Whiteman was a force for change, not stability, in the 1920s. Knowing this, the English journal *Musical Opinion* proposed in 1923 that he be banned from the country.[48]

Only when the audiences had fully accepted the more uninhibited style of performance, usually as a result of dancing, did Whiteman and Whiteman-style bands receive a cool reception. There was some evidence that this was Sam Wooding's fate in 1926. It was certainly the undoing of Teplitsky's efforts in 1927.

Teplitsky returned to Leningrad in February 1927, armed with several trunks of recordings, more than a score of Whiteman arrangements, and over forty musical instruments.[49] The Commissariat of Public Enlightenment had obviously provided him with an ample expense account. He immediately organized the First Concert Jazz Band, a fourteen-piece ensemble consisting of six different instruments for the three saxophonists, two of the fashionable new American-made piston-valve trumpets, a bass trombone, tuba, two violins, piano, drums, and—here the Whiteman touch—an oboe. Because his bandsmen were culled from the best Leningrad orchestras and the Leningrad conservatory faculty, Teplitsky called them "my professors."[50] After two months of rehearsals, the band announced its first concert for Thursday, April 28, 1927. Assaulting the very pinnacle of Parnassus, Teplitsky managed to schedule his group at the elegant State Academic Capella, formerly the concert hall for the tsar's court choir.

It must have been a long evening. The published program lists works by George Gershwin and Irving Berlin, including "Fascinating Rhythm" and "In the Middle of the Night." Several hotter numbers, including "Yes, Sir, That's My Baby" and James P. Johnson's "Charleston," livened up the proceedings. Mixed in were a number of adaptations of classical themes drawn from Gounod, Liszt, Rubinstein, Verdi, and Rimsky-Korsakov. Jazzing up the classics was all the rage at the time, and printed scores were readily available. Whiteman had perfected this practice, but it had been common even among the New Orleans pioneers. It was a dreadful mistake in Leningrad, however. Rimsky-Korsakov's son, a critic, was sitting in the audience, his pen poised for the kill. "What is jazz?" he asked his readers the next day. It is an addiction of "fashionable" (*feshene-blnoe*) society, who gather at a dancing room (*densingrum*) and, between the fifth and sixth courses, dance the fox-trot "for their digestion." People who are total strangers to one another combine for five minutes in a cold hug and writhe to "barbarous harmonies, which sound as if they have been worked over with a hammer." Jazz, Rimsky-Korsakov, Jr., concluded, is a "senseless parody of melody and chords," a vulgar music suitable only for theater foyers. Slightly sweetening his bitter pill, he ended his review by admitting that "The First Concert Jazz Band scored a success with the public and did not play badly."[51]

Professor Boris Wohlmann, Teplitsky's pianist, was even less generous in his reminiscences. He admitted that "the public interest in our performances was great, but to tell the truth the orchestra had no sense of true jazz. The venerable musicians, accustomed to a completely different style of playing, could do no more than conscientiously play the printed notes. Improvisation and any creative initiative by the performers was out of the question."[52]

Leningrad professionals had their reservations about Teplitsky's efforts, too, but the public was enthusiastic nonetheless. On May 9, 1927, the First Concert Jazz Band was warmly received at the Red Putilov Factory, the Leningrad steel mill whose workers had been among the most ardent supporters of the Bolsheviks ten years earlier. The band played Moscow and then took off for three months in the provinces. Everywhere posters announced that the group would play "the latest American music," and that "American dances" would be demonstrated by that daringly chic couple, Iver and Nelson. Teplitsky, obviously loving his role, billed himself as an American.[53] His antics, however, were directly responsible for his arrest and exile during an official campaign against jazz four years later.[54]

The schizophrenic character of Teplitsky's programs, their great leaps from the Charleston to jazzed-up Gounod, can be accounted for by the tension that had emerged between those who defended or attacked jazz from an elite perspective and those who judged it as a mass phenomenon connected with dancing and the new urban social values. In America, urban popular culture had long since secured itself a niche between refined European culture and the more folkish modes of expression of the countryside. In Russia, the split between elite culture and mass urban culture early assumed the proportions of a geological fault. The music of other Leningrad musicians who capitalized on Teplitsky's success revealed the same schism. With them, however, it was, for the first time, also reflected in the nature of the patronage they received.

In his short career, Boris Krupyshev combined popular music and private patronage. Krupyshev put together a twelve-piece band early in 1928 and opted entirely for the American pop repertoire. From Teplitsky or another source, he obtained the scores of hit tunes by Walter Donaldson, Sam Coslow, Irving Berlin, and others. The band's advertising flyers announced that it was the first Soviet group to play blues. Unlike Teplitsky, with his official patronage, or Tsfasman in Moscow, who was backed up by the AMA publishers, Krupyshev functioned on a purely private basis. Responding to the market, he purged his repertoire of pseudo-classical works.

Still more did the Astoria Kids, a hot combo that performed for over a year at the Astoria Hotel in 1928–29. The Astoria, situated directly across from the former German Embassy on Nikolaevsky (now Isaakievsky) Square, had been an outpost of Berlin fashion until the outbreak of World War I, at which time a new French manager switched its orientation toward Paris.[55] During the 1920s the Astoria was rapidly Americanized and was glad to have the Astoria Kids holding forth on the dining room stage.[56]

Pursuing the same audience, Krupyshev in 1930 organized the group Blue Jazz (*Goluboi dzhaz*), an eight-piece group featuring three recently imported Hawaiian guitars. The new instruments gave a colorful cast to the band's performance of such exotica as the fox-trot "Tahiti," the Russian lyrics of which, incidentally, idealized a society in which there no cars, no laws, and apparently no morals.[57] In addition, the band played adaptations of stock arrangements by American orchestras, and blues, sung in English by Anna Kerner. The Blue Jazz ensemble was briefly successful, but it soon became increasingly difficult for such a free-floating group to function.

The inevitable problem with spontaneously organized groups is that they lack stability. They may give a tremendous boost to the evolution of style, but their autonomy causes considerable anxiety for the person responsible for keeping the band together during lulls between bookings. This causes trouble in America or Western Europe but it is an overwhelming hindrance in the Soviet Union, with its cult of work and official abhorrence of "parasitism." Under the New Economic Policy, workers were free to change employment, small-scale private enterprise was permitted, and a high level of unemployment was officially tolerated. But the rising tide of Communist fundamentalism made the free-floating life of the private combo player a risky one. There was mounting pressure, both cultural and political, toward the large, officially sponsored ensemble. These groups had to be content with performing classical adaptations with only a sprinkling of big-band jazz orchestration.

This was precisely the formula that Boris Krupyshev and his friend Georgi Landsberg had in mind when they established the Leningrad Jazz Orchestra in the winter of 1928–29.[58] Landsberg, a pianist, directed the ten-piece band and was responsible for stocking the "book" with published arrangements by the popular English big bands of Jack Payne and Henry Hall. Landsberg and Krupyshev tried to present their band as a chamber music ensemble, and thus invade the bastions of high culture that had so far been untouched by jazz. They did manage to get a few bookings from the august Society of Friends of Chamber Music and thus to perform in the hallowed hall on Nevsky Prospect in which the classical "greats" had appeared for a century. They also followed Teplitsky to the Capella. But though their performances of Igor Stravinsky's *L'Histoire du soldat* and other serious chamber works drew praise,[59] their execution of "Yes, Sir, That's My Baby" and "My Blue Heaven" failed to endear them to the staid highbrows. Denied patronage, the Leningrad Jazz Orchestra took to the road, touring as far north as Murmansk before members began leaving the group early in 1930. Occasional bookings enabled Landsberg and Krupyshev to keep the ensemble alive for a few years, until it was finally reorganized into the Leningrad Radio Orchestra in 1934. With this stroke, what was left of the Leningrad Jazz Orchestra gained total stability of patronage but gave up all pretense of playing jazz.

From Practice to Theory

Thanks to the efforts of Alexander Tsfasman, Leopold Teplitsky, Boris Krupyshev, and Georgi Landsberg, by 1929 the Soviet Union could claim membership in the ranks of nations infected by the new American music. Following the example of these pioneers, numerous lesser-known groups, most of them purely amateur, sprang up in other parts of the country as well, responding to the public interest aroused by the immense popularity of the fox-trot, two-step, Charleston, shimmy, and black bottom. Soviet officials were later to claim that the high-minded populace had no interest in the decadent music and dancing that was jazz. The years in which the new music and attitudes first penetrated the USSR provide no support for this claim. The popular audience of Moscow may have been exposed to more propaganda and *agitmuzyk* than its counterparts in Berlin, London, or New York, but its response to the new music did not differ from that of urban folk elsewhere. The brisk tempo, spontaneity, physicality, and individualism of the twentieth century, which found their expression in jazz, were quite at home in post-revolutionary Russia.

Nor was Soviet officialdom in those years more outspokenly hostile to the new music and values than their counterparts in Western Europe or North America. An ideological reaction was looming, but there were no thunderclouds visible on the horizon through 1928. The keepers of Russia's musical heritage, the classically trained musicians and critics, showed a surprising openness to jazz before 1929. The chief impediment to the further spread of jazz was Russia's great isolation from the West because of the new regime and its monetary policies. Other potential impediments—hostile propaganda, the claims of "socialist morality," etc.—were either nonexistent or as yet ineffectual.

The very distance that separated Russia from the environment in which jazz was born made the new music a curiosity to be analyzed rather than simply accepted. This the Russians did with a vengeance. Just as Western European musicians and critics were more disposed than their American counterparts to philosophize about jazz, so were Russians quicker than most Western Europeans to seek out the thoughts of others and to elaborate their own views. This was shown clearly in 1926, when the Academy press of Leningrad published a collection of essays titled *The Jazz Band and Contemporary Music*. Issued under official auspices to coincide with the appearance of Sam Wooding's group in Russia, the collection brought together previously published essays by Darius Milhaud, S. Serchinger, Percy Grainger, and Louis Grünberg. The editor, S. Ginzburg, considered the goal of his collection to be "more than modest. . . . If it succeeds in shedding light on the questions raised by broad circles of musicians and nonmusicians regarding the essence and meaning of jazz . . . and if it prods people to think over their relation to one of the most heated questions of musical life today, it will have fully achieved its goal." [60] Unfortunately, neither Grainger's dyspeptic essay nor Serchinger's pompous treatise served this end. Milhaud's contribution was of greater moment, for it attacked frontally the use of classical adaptations and, at the same time, strained to present jazz as an autonomous art form whose proper milieu was the concert stage rather than the dance hall.[61] Milhaud also inveighed against slick performances and praised the more earthy jazz he had heard on Lenox Avenue in New York City.

Poor Milhaud wanted it both ways. He wanted authentic ethnic performance and concert music; he wanted "true jazz" but was incapable of realizing that such music sprang from and was nurtured by a form of liberated urban nightlife that revolved around dancing. Like most spokesmen for elite culture in the twentieth century, Milhaud could wax eloquent over an art that was the musical equivalent of African masks, Scythian gold, or pre-Homeric pottery. But the reality of jazz's true social milieu was too immediate, too threatening. By romanticizing the origins and social function of jazz, Europeans kept it safe, out of reach, antiseptic, and ready for the concert hall. To accept the reality of "fox-trotting Europe" or the Roaring Twenties in America was to admit that jazz involved a way of life, one that might sweep up your own daughter! Darius Milhaud revealed the dilemma faced by all keepers of Europe's high culture who wished to extend a sympathetic hand to the obstreperous new music from across the Atlantic. Before they could accept it, they had to render it as remote and exotic as possible, and transform its perpetrators from modern urban people into Voltaire's Chinese or Diderot's Hindus. Then they could be showered with condescending praise, and their art could be placed safely in a museum case, like a savage's ornamented axe whose beauty can be admired without reference to the fact that its practical function was to lop off heads.

With the publication of Ginsburg's collection, Soviet readers were made *au courant* of some of the most sophisticated European and American views on jazz. Within six months Russians were to find their own homegrown expositor of the virtues of syncopated music, one who would surpass all other European and even American theorists in actual impact on leading jazz musicians. Joseph Schillinger was the featured speaker at the debut concert of Teplitsky's First Concert Jazz Band in April 1927.

A thirty-two-year-old native of Kharkov and an alumnus of the St. Petersburg Conservatory, Schillinger had been among the first Russians to seize on the modern music movement in the 1920s. A member of the board of directors of the Leningrad Association of Modern Music since 1926, he had already won high praise as a composer and pianist.[62] His piano compositions were regularly featured on programs along with works by Stravinsky, Prokofiev, and Hindemith,[63] and his symphonic rhapsody, "October," was judged the best composition by a Soviet composer during the ten years since the Revolution.[64] A mystic and theosophist, Schillinger drew inspiration from both Scriabin and the most ancient musical cultures of the Caucasus, where he conducted ethnographic research. Ever the experimenter, Schillinger was at the same time working on electronic music with Lev Thermin, a collaboration that was to produce the *First Airphonic Suite* in 1929.[65]

Schillinger's path to jazz is unknown, but one can assume that it included exposure to Wooding's band, reading of Ginsburg's book, and extensive discussions with his old Conservatory friend Teplitsky. By the time of the First Concert Jazz Band's debut, Schillinger was armed with an extended lecture on "The Jazz Band and the

Music of the Future."[66] The first part of the lecture reviewed the history of jazz, its instruments and repertoire. Schillinger especially stressed the importance of improvisation and the technical aspects of performance that separate jazz from classical music. He then turned to the role of jazz in Meierhold's *D.E.* and took up arms in defense of "fox-trotting Europe." "Europe wants to grow young again," he declared, siding unequivocally with the losing team in Meierhold's production. Schillinger acknowledged the vulgar aspects of the transatlantic infection that were the result of the American penchant for linking "hearts and dollars." Of course, this is regrettable, he wrote, but it should not blind one to the true essence of jazz: its genuine popularity. Here, finally, was a music worthy of attention by the sophisticates of the Leningrad Association of Modern Music and yet fully in tune with the needs of society at large. According to Schillinger, jazz actually realized the Communist goal of "Music for the masses." It is genuinely *popular*, he argued, and is therefore fully qualified to play a central part in the reorganization of life and work in the USSR.

How was Schillinger's eloquent apologia received by the packed audience that night in the tsar's old choir school? Unfortunately, all but one of the critics ignored it entirely, presumably in their rush to confront Teplitsky's new Concert Jazz Band. The exception was Professor Rimsky-Korsakov, who treated the speaker with the paternal indignation conservative faculty members use in dealing with wayward former students.[67]

Schillinger's disenchantment with the Leningrad musical establishment mounted after the lecture. His unabashed defense of the entire ethos of jazz, not just its musical attributes, marked him as potentially dangerous. The GPU, forerunners of the NKVD and the KGB, interrogated him rather harshly on several occasions in 1928. Schillinger nicknamed them (in English) the "Killer-dillers" and secretly resolved to emigrate at the first opportunity. The arrival of Chicago educator John Dewey in 1928 enabled Schillinger to make his move. At a meeting with Dewey in Leningrad, Schillinger arranged to be issued an invitation to visit America as the authorized representative of the Leningrad Association of Modern Music. By

1929 Joseph Schillinger was in New York. The last telephone call he received before quitting Leningrad had been from the mother of his close friend Dmitri Shostakovich, who had pleaded with Schillinger to do what he could to arrange for her son's emigration to America as well.[68]

Once settled in New York, Schillinger began frequenting the jazz spots, especially the Cotton Club. Between performances with Leopold Stokowski and other major orchestras, he prepared lectures, including "The Rudimentary Analysis of Musical Phenomena," and began writing his magnum opus, *The Mathematical Basis of the Arts*, which was later published in New York in 1949. Schillinger's method of analyzing music was based on rhythm. As Louis Grünberg had written in the first sentence of his contribution to *The Jazz Band and Contemporary Music*, "In the beginning was rhythm."[69] Schillinger accepted this axiom and built his entire theoretical system on it. In terms that were both clear and evocative he explained the interplay of rhythm and other musical elements. Many leading American jazz musicians were drawn to him over the years. Among his avowed disciples were Benny Goodman, Tommy Dorsey, Eubie Blake, and in the 1950s, Gerry Mulligan, Quincy Jones, and John Lewis of the Modern Jazz Quartet. After Schillinger's death, *Down Beat*, the premier American jazz magazine, summarized his system for the benefit of still another generation of jazzmen.[70]

Schillinger also influenced several key figures in the American world of popularized jazz, including Glenn Miller, whose "Moonlight Serenade" was written as a Schillinger exercise, and George Gershwin. Gershwin was drawn to Schillinger in part because of personal links with Russia—his father, who hailed from St. Petersburg, and his doctor, a former secretary to the minister of labor in Alexander Kerensky's Provisional Government.[71] Gershwin began studying with the Russian émigré in 1932 when his own career seemed at a standstill. Schillinger reinvigorated Gershwin's sense of counterpoint and rhythm at precisely the moment when Gershwin was writing *Porgy and Bess*. Working almost daily with Gershwin in the summer of 1935, Schillinger helped to score what was to be Gershwin's most lasting legacy to American music.[72]

Mounting Pressures

Although Schillinger's greatest contributions to jazz were in the United States, the sheer speed with which he came to grips with the new music is emblematic of what was occurring in many fields of Russian culture during the late NEP era. Handicapped by a recent heritage of revolutionary provincialism, educated Russians rushed to make up for lost time. In the process they mastered, and in some fields even surpassed, their Western European counterparts. During the 1920s, at least, this quest was seen as compatible with the building of communism.

The progress of jazz was particularly brisk. By 1928 the new music and dances had conquered large parts of the educated urban middle class and had made inroads among the laboring population of a few centers. Even Moscow's Baptists were dancing the Charleston, complained the author of a 1928 tract called *Against Priests and Sectarians.*[73] Encouraged by the New Economic Policy's laws, fully independent jazz combos had come into being and were fighting for a place in the commercial market. Official patronage of jazz, started tentatively with Parnakh's band in 1922, reached an unexpected height when the Commissariat of Public Enlightenment sent Leopold Teplitsky on his study mission to the bars of Philadelphia. Inspired by direct exposure to leading American jazzmen and to their own homegrown aficionados, several hundred Soviet musicians were valiantly attempting to master the new music. The audience, whether in boisterous private parties in Kharkov, movie-theater foyers in Moscow, or the venerable Capella in Leningrad, responded enthusiastically, while flappers from Odessa to Murmansk loosened their joints to the Charleston beat. There were opponents, to be sure, but they were no more incensed or obstructive in their virtue than their counterparts elsewhere in Europe and America.

Despite this, Soviet society provided limited space in which the twenties could roar. Practically every musician playing jazz sprang from the educated middle or upper middle class, as did the greater part of their public, whether listeners or dancers, and virtually the entire cultural establishment. The student body of the Leningrad Conservatory, for example, was overwhelmingly bourgeois in its composition.[74] Open admissions policies at Soviet educational institutions gradually reversed this situation: fifteen percent of the students at the Leningrad Conservatory in 1925 were peasants, and by 1928 this figure had doubled.[75] The cultural gap between such students and their sophisticated urban colleagues was profound. Scarcely off the farm, the new peasant students were forced to reckon simultaneously with urban noise, city clothes, flush toilets, and the shimmy.

The world of jazz—especially its musicians—tended to seek refuge from the rising tide of indifferent peasants from the countryside by fleeing into the realm of high culture. As we have seen, this also guaranteed more stable patronage. For these reasons, most of the would-be jazz ensembles in Russia in the late twenties added classical and semi-classical numbers to their repertoires. The only band to move in the opposite direction was Teplitsky's, which was never able to establish a truly popular audience after its successful provincial tour. Unfortunately for the jazzmen, many of the highbrows were scarcely more eager than the peasants to receive jazz. In short, the social milieu that was most receptive to jazz occupied a fragile position between the overwhelming peasant majority on the one hand and the Olympian heights of elevated taste on the other. Jazz musicians had good company—large numbers of urban Russians and practically every experimental artist, playwright, filmmaker, or architect whose achievements we now value so highly—but in the end it was a severely restricted world. Acknowledging this, it is important to note that the world of Soviet jazz expanded steadily through the end of 1928. Then, with the suddenness of a sheet of summer lightning, it was overwhelmed by the cataclysm of Cultural Revolution.

5
"The Music of the Gross," 1928–1931

Everything is coming out into the open now . . . the old and the new are going out to battle.

Nikolai Gogol, 1847

For a form of popular culture to flourish and endure it must meet two conditions. First, it must be genuinely well liked. No amount of promotion or hullabaloo can sustain its vitality if it fails to engage the interest of a large number of ordinary people. If a tune is not whistled in private it will never be popular in public. The tyranny of fashion may briefly cow a few, but never the public at large. Second, when a form of popular culture claims the support of part but not all of the public, as often happens, it must be able to protect itself from the hostility or indifference of the rest. Its supporters may choose to withdraw to avoid conflict, like Bohemian painters in nineteenth-century Paris. Or they may sally forth to conquer the opposition, or at least limit the extent of its damage. But if its proponents can neither build a protective barrier around themselves nor limit the harm their critics can impose, the form of popular culture they espouse will die.

All evidence suggests that Soviet jazz in the years 1928–31 had gained general popularity among the educated public of Russia's cities. But the necessary precondition and sustenance for its success was the relative tolerance fostered by the New Economic Policy, which embraced both musicians and audience. With the onslaught

of the First Five-Year Plan, announced in October 1928, this tolerance evaporated. Nor was it possible for the world of jazz to protect itself by seceding into privacy, for the upheaval unleashed by
Josef Stalin impinged on the lives of individuals and groups much
more deeply than had the Bolsheviks' initial revolution in 1917.
Contemporaries called it "The Great Fracture," the dawning of
Russia's "Iron Age"; today it is recognized as the first Communist
cultural revolution, the progenitor of the later upheavals in China,
Cuba, and elsewhere.

Civil War "From Above"

Those who did not live through the turmoil of 1928–31 in Russia
can scarcely imagine its extent. What triggered the awful convul-
sion was the Party's decision to compel peasant farmers—tens of
millions of people—to give up their private land and join their poor
brethren on collective and state farms. The decision was prompted
by the Communists' sustained failure to win over the hostile peasantry by other means, and by what they perceived as their desperate need to gain political control in the countryside.

Its effects were devastating. Stalin later confided to Winston
Churchill that ten million independent farmers had been "dealt with"
in the process, through what was, in effect, a full-scale war in the
countryside.[1] Several million more deaths were directly attributable
to the famine that followed. Millions of survivors, mostly former
peasants, were assigned to labor camps, where they were compelled
to work on many of the major construction projects of the day.[2] So
staggering was the scale of suffering that many people, especially
ideologically sympathetic foreigners, simply disbelieved it. Paul
Robeson, the black American basso who moved among the same
Moscow circles Sam Wooding had touched but who had contact
with politicians as well, flatly denied that the tragedy had occurred
when he returned to America in 1933. Robeson wrote, "This stuff
about starvation is the bunk. What else would you expect Hearst
to say? Wherever I went I saw plenty of food."[3]

Robeson's denial must be attributed more to blinders than to blindness, for the results of the social revolution were amply visible in Russian cities. Tens of thousands of homeless waifs, the offspring of murdered or exiled parents, filled the streets of Moscow. A couple walking out to dance at the Hermitage Gardens could not have avoided these gaunt and resourceful children huddling around campfires in the street or curled up asleep in sections of concrete pipe awaiting burial as part of the new sewer system.[4] Such sights touched the public scarcely less profoundly than the rationing of bread, which was begun in 1929.

Soviet news media did their best to shield the urban populace from knowledge of the rural crisis, but each step of the political revolution within the Kremlin was openly proclaimed. Trotsky and his left-wing supporters were purged from the Communist party in 1928, and in January 1929, the great revolutionary was expelled from the country. Before the end of the year Stalin had turned his wrath against his right-wing opponents, seizing them and extracting from them public recantations of past sins against the Revolution and against himself. Though the process was not complete for several more years, the Georgia-born leader had for all purposes consolidated his hold on the apparatus of power by 1931.

Central to Stalin's method of manipulation was terror. As early as 1927 he had whipped up a fraudulent war scare, which he then used to justify his first assault against critics and "class enemies."[5] No sooner had the scare of Western military intervention died down than Stalin announced that an even more insidious threat of economic counterrevolution was being prepared abroad. This time scores of native Russian engineers in the steel industry were charged with being in collusion with Russian émigré capitalists and foreign intelligence services.[6] The government's legal case was preposterously thin, as anyone who had read the newspaper accounts could readily detect. But therein lay its effectiveness. Soviet citizens quickly perceived that no contact with foreigners could be so innocent as to assure their safety, and no flirtation with alien ways so innocuous as to ensure against retribution. The message was clear. Paranoid xenophobia, far from being a psychological aberration, became for the average Soviet citizen the surest and most rational guide to safe conduct during the Cultural Revolution.

Soviet officials who had served abroad or whose families had foreign connections bent over backward to assert their proletarian loyalties, even to the point of exchanging their well-cut suits for the baggier and more proletarian local products.[7] All manifestations of worldliness were abjured so as not to arouse suspicion that one possessed any basis for independence. The tactic did not always work. Eugene Lyons, the politically radical correspondent for the United Press in Moscow, observed that in the larger cities tens of thousands of men and women were rounded up on the mere suspicion of possessing foreign money, silver, gold, or jewels. Many were never seen again.[8]

Linked with this tide of xenophobia was an aggressive and officially sponsored effort to trumpet the uniqueness of all things Soviet. When the League of Nations dared in 1929 to announce plans to built its "capital" in Geneva, the Soviet government (not yet a member of the League) countered by revealing its intention to build the true world capital, the proletarian capital, in Moscow.[9] The word "Soviet," in its adjectival form, became associated with an infinite number of phenomena that had previously remained outside, or at least peripheral to, the ebb and flow of political controversy. To all appearances, Communist internationalism was appropriating the psychology and policies of nineteenth-century chauvinism.

The Ideology of Cultural Intervention

Cultural matters were thrust to the center stage of national policy by these developments. The carefully delineated compromise of 1925, which had permitted a degree of pluralism in the arts, broke down entirely and was replaced by the slogan "He who is not with us is against us." Ivan Matsa, an insignificant critic whom the tide of Cultural Revolution lifted to national prominence, pointed out the

new directions in his essay, "The Lessons of 'Neutralism' in Art." [10]
In reviewing a show of recent works by a painter named Ivan Bogorodsky, who had just returned from two years' study abroad,
Matsa vilified all foreign influences on Soviet culture. Bogorodsky's
political neutrality may have been simple naiveté, but ingenuous-
ness was now a crime. Why paint German peasants when their
native costumes strike Russian peasants as strange? Bogorodsky's
error, Matsa said, was to play into the hands of Russia's enemies
abroad. Similar assaults were launched in every field of the arts.[11]
Vsevolod Meierhold, whose sins in theater had included the patronage of jazz, found his funding cut by the Main Art Directorate
(*Glaviskusstvo*).

Music in general and popular music in particular were singled
out for high-level scrutiny. The campaign, begun in 1928, was conducted with a greater degree of candor than had existed since 1917.
The journal *Soviet Art*, for example, freely conceded that "Soviet
art still lacks a defined style. . . . the creative forces of the proletariat and peasantry which were called forth by the revolution are still
inadequately formed and have not yet led to anything so celebrated
that it could be defined as the prevailing style of our transitional
Soviet epoch." [12] Admitting that the phrase "Soviet art" had been
bandied about indiscriminately in the past, the journal called for its
careful definition. A 1930 decree on popular culture by the Commissariat of Public Enlightenment made the same admission, pointing out that the so-called revolutionary songs were thoroughly unpopular and largely ignored both by official agencies and by the
public.[13] In spite of eleven years of declarations about Soviet culture, musical programming for workers remained much as it had
been before the Revolution, the Commissariat claimed. "The phrase
'Soviet music for the Soviet variety theater,' which is so natural and
elementary for our circumstances, is not reflected either in the concert bills or in published criticism." [14] Even censorship failed to improve the situation. Glavlit had let the popular music industry do
as it pleased, neither criticizing it nor imposing appropriate Soviet
goals upon it. Scores of local organizations, most of them private,

had perpetuated a chaotic situation which in no way reflected the society's revolutionary objectives. So admitted the Commissariat of Public Enlightenment.[15]

For official organs to admit such failures created a ticklish situation for the regime. Either it had to push forward to create a policy that would revolutionize popular culture or it had to abandon its claims. The pressure of Stalinization made the former course a foregone conclusion. The task at hand was nothing less than "organizing human consciousness," as Commissar Lunacharsky put it.[16]

Curiously, the campaign that was to culminate in 1930 with the call for the suppression of jazz began with an appeal to popular taste. The argument was charming in its simplicity. Soviet popular music had been bad because it reflected the interests of the many small-time, independent profiteers who controlled the booking agencies. If only such people would study public tastes, particularly those of that peasantry, they would change their ways.[17] Whoever proposed such market studies had no way of knowing, of course, that many of the consumers in question—the peasants—would soon be dying by the millions and would scarcely be in a mood to respond to polls on their tastes in popular music.

The consumer-based approach to the music problem was an early fatality of the Cultural Revolution. The discussion did, however, encourage the creation of training programs around the country to develop a new generation of popular artists.[18] But this achievement was trifling in comparison with the success of the alternative approach, which called for the reorientation of all music and art "from above," under the guidance of national organizations of ideologically colorfast "proletarian" artists in every field. Never mind that most of those seeking to cozy up to the new ideological line were not of proletarian origin. Between 1928 and 1932 these grim zealots pursued a crusade of vilification and intimidation in order to rid Russia of all cultural dross from the past and from the decadent West, pernicious influences the Soviet government had foolishly tolerated for a decade. Like Cromwellians lopping off the heads of sculptured saints in Ely Cathedral, they denounced Tchaikovsky as a feudal lord, Rimsky-Korsakov (a former naval officer) as a militarist, and Chopin as a bourgeois aesthete. In 1929, when Ernst Křenek's jazz operetta *Jonny spielt auf* was performed at the Nemirovich-Danchenko Theater in Moscow, the proletarian ideologues succeeded in closing the show and then launched a campaign to ban the saxophone from the Soviet Union.[19] In this, at least, they failed, although a similar campaign twenty years later was to succeed briefly.

These humorless sectarians had been a growing force in Soviet life for some years before 1928. As early as 1925 they had organized into the Association of Proletarian Musicians. From the day of its foundation, the Association served as a kind of semi-official censorship body, regimenting the ranks of Soviet music. For tactical reasons the Association spoke about the need to respond to market demand, but its consumerist argument had a twist. Invoking the Marxist doctrine of "false consciousness," the Association insisted that public taste had been corrupted by bourgeois propaganda and therefore could not automatically serve as a guide for the culture makers. The Association of Proletarian Musicians, so it claimed, understood what the preferences of the proletariat would be if only it were freed from the effects of corrupting influences. Indeed, the Association contended that it alone was capable of defining the true preferences of the proletarian market.

By December 1928, the Central Committee of the Communist party had moved toward accepting the Association's extravagant claim. Henceforth, it announced, only useful and ideologically correct music and literature would be disseminated through the mass media.[20] The new regimentation rigorously excluded private organizations and amateur groups from a place in the cultural scene. As of December 9, 1930, all amateur musicians and artists were subordinated to the control of official organs, lest they be duped by Russia's ever-present "class enemies."[21] With this stroke, the existing basis for popular initiative in the arts, including popular music, was obliterated.

How did the semi-official Association of Proletarian Musicians manage to wield such staggering power in the face of Stalin's efforts to concentrate all political authority in himself? It succeeded because its members claimed to be acting in the name of the Communist party and because their most frequent targets were those government organs which the Party had never succeeded in subordinating. Government agencies had consistently lagged behind the Party in their zeal for the Communist millennium, preferring instead to curry favor with the populace through cultural programs that responded to the universal desire for diversion. For example, government more than Party patronage had stood behind jazz and other forms of popular culture during the NEP era. The zealots understood this, and condemned it. Like Pascal, who argued that "All great diversions are a threat to the Christian life," [22] the Communist party and its fervent believers saw the passion for amusement and levity as an impediment to the attainment of their goals. The Association of Proletarian Musicians seemed to be calling the Party back to itself, to its most revolutionary puritanism, and, for the time being at least, the rising forces within the Party represented by Stalin were pushing in precisely the same direction. As long as the Stalinists saw the Association and similar Proletarian Associations in other fields as promoting their own cause, they gave them free rein.

It was a foregone conclusion that the Association of Proletarian Musicians would eventually attack jazz. Its assault did not occur in isolation, however, for many people in Western Europe and in America had also mounted campaigns against jazz in just these years. The relationship between such campaigns and the continuing spread of jazz is both revealing and relevant to the situation in the USSR. Even in the mid-twenties many Americans and Europeans had convinced themselves that jazz was waning in popularity. "Jazz is transitory," violinist Fritz Kreisler declared to an American reporter in 1925.[23] As early as 1922, *The American Musician* gleefully took the view that jazz "was the voice of the Money-Changer in music. Jazz has ceased to be profitable, and hence we shall soon see no more of it." Jazz, and popular music generally, had received its impetus from the strenuous promotional efforts of phonograph dealers and music publishers. With profits off, jazz must die. "The interment of jazz will not be immediate, but it is inevitable." [24]

The Musical Leader, a Chicago journal, reached similar conclusions two years later. Gone were the "discordant and barbarous" jazz bands of the Original Dixieland Jazz Band era. They had been replaced by orchestras such as Paul Whiteman's, whose music bore no more resemblance to jazz than did the music of Victor Herbert, Johann Strauss, or John Philip Sousa.[25]

Such arguments were patently absurd, more wish than reality, but they were soon being voiced across Europe, and especially in Germany. Some German writers even claimed to see the imminent collapse of jazz, a *"Jazzdämmerung."* [26] The facts belied them. Indeed, the impetus behind the "dying jazz" movement seems to have been the awareness that jazz, in a new form, was spreading more rapidly than ever. The director of the Omaha Symphony Orchestra returned from a European trip in 1929 and reported that jazz was being played in the hamlets of the Continent as well as in its great cities.[27] Having long since conquered the popular music scene in England, Belgium, Germany, and France, jazz was now insinuating itself further afield. Vienna had already fallen. The debut of Emmerich Kalman's operetta *The Duchess of Chicago* had the ancient music capital astir. Viennesse critics asked, "Will American jazz conquer us and force into oblivion our standard operetta forms of decades past, or will some way be found by us to humanize jazz or at least harmonize it with our own musical traditions?" [28] In Turkey the revolutionary government of Kemal Atatürk was licensing jazz bands by 1927, while musicians in Turkey's arch-enemy, Greece, were developing their own style of Hellenic jazz. A Polish dance orchestra scored a dizzying triumph in the same year by performing for thirty-three hours and ten minutes without intermission, a world record.[29]

There was also deepening interest in jazz on the part of the European musical elite. One of the first practical handbooks on jazz for composers and musicians was published in Leipzig in 1929 and included thoughtful essays on rhythm, harmony, improvisation, and jazz aesthetics. *Das neue Jazzbuch* by Alfred Baresel quickly went into a second edition. An even more exhaustive study on jazz, called simply *Jazz*, appeared the same year in Prague, the work of the

Czech bandleader, singer, and musicologist E. S. Burian. By far the most publicized evidence of the deepening hold of jazz in Europe was the decision by Bernard Sekles, director of Frankfurt's Städtisches Konservatorium, to open a class for jazz music in his school. Invective was poured on Sekles, but the Herr Direktor coolly responded: "The teaching of jazz is not only the right but the duty of every up-to-date musical institution."[30] He did not cow his critics. Carl Nielsen, the Danish composer, opined that "If it is of vital importance to humanity that men and women, when dancing, press their knees against one another and gyrate with glassy eyes and empty brains, the picture of nonentity, then jazz has a mission. My opinion is that it spoils the young musician's ear and individuality; it is a nasty and death-like music. . . ."[31]

Such tirades anticipate the polemics over jazz which exploded in Russia with the onset of the Cultural Revolution. While direct evidence of influence is lacking—the Association of Proletarian Musicians could hardly admit to having pirated the arguments of "bourgeois" critics—the tone of the Association's campaign against jazz does not rule out the possibility. Certainly, the Association, like critics of jazz in Western Europe, was fighting a rearguard action, trying to regain the initiative in a battle it seemed to be losing.

The Proletarian Case Against Jazz

Until 1928 the Association of Proletarian Musicians did not deign to recognize jazz even by attacking it, preferring instead to whip the ghost of the tsarist musical past. The only serious attempt at a proletarian analysis of jazz had been included in *The Art of Contemporary Europe*, a small book by Ivan Matsa, in 1926. Matsa at that point had been surprisingly receptive to jazz. He acknowledged that neither strict composition nor harmony in the traditional sense was possible with jazz, but considered the "unexpected internal strength and strict rhythmic unity" of a jazz ensemble to be on a par with works of the nineteenth-century classical masters.[32] Of course, Matsa could not have admitted to lounging about in the cafés of Berlin or Paris, and hence he was careful to distinguish "true jazz" from the corrupted form heard in the nightclubs of the fading West.

The decisive moment in the politicization of jazz in the USSR was April 18, 1928, when *Pravda* published an essay by the novelist Maxim Gorky titled "On the Music of the Gross."[33] Gorky's essay defined the Soviet critique of jazz. The Association of Proletarian Musicians took it as its gospel on the subject, even while recognizing that Gorky himself was quite hostile to their allied Proletarian Association in the field of literature. Long after the Association of Proletarian Musicians had been liquidated and Gorky had died, phrases from the essay appeared time and time again in the press. Over the following half-century, whenever Soviet writers wished to settle scores with this threatening music or simply to contrast the Soviet Union with the degenerate West, they invoked Gorky.[34]

Gorky had lived for many years on the Isle of Capri. Because he was the first Russian novelist to have outsold Tolstoy and because of his earthy style as both man and writer, he had been taken up as an exotic in Western literary circles, a type-cast proletarian from the land of the tsars. After a brief return to Russia at the time of the revolution, he again emigrated in 1919, having discovered that he liked revolution more than revolutionaries. When he wrote "On the Music of the Gross," he was living in a villa near Sorrento. No longer lionized in the West, he found himself increasingly alienated from Western European society. Before the end of 1928 he was to make a return trip to the Soviet Union, and within three more years he would settle there permanently. His bitter ruminations on jazz and modern culture thus have the character of a parting shot at the West that had rejected him. The circumstances could not have been better calculated to produce a tract that would feed Soviet xenophobia.

Gorky wrote from the study in his villa. "It is night," he began, "and the stillness permits the mind to be at rest. . . ." Just then chaos descends.

> In the deep stillness resounds the dry knocking of an idiotic hammer. One, two, three, ten, twenty strokes, and after them, like a mud ball splashing into clear water, a wild whistle screeches;

and then there are rumblings, wails and howls like the smarting of a metal pig, the shriek of a donkey, or the amorous croaking of a monstrous frog. This insulting chaos of insanity pulses to a throbbing rhythm. Listening for a few minutes to these wails, one involuntarily imagines an orchestra of sexually driven madmen conducted by a man-stallion brandishing a huge genital member.[35]

Jazz, in the form of "a new fox-trot executed by a Negro orchestra," had destroyed the fragile chain of thought of this distinguished writer. This, at least, is where Gorky fixes the blame. It apparently did not cross his mind that he should be railing against the proprietor of the hotel next door who permitted his radio to disturb the neighbors. Nor did he strike out against the radio itself, which he instead generously acknowledges to be "one of the greatest discoveries wrested by science from nature." No, the musicians are at fault for creating vile rhythms that sweep through the ether like birds of prey. Jazz, Gorky proclaims, is "the music of grossness," the music of unbridled sexuality. It is both a cause and a symptom of the collapse of Western civilization. "Degenerates gather in all the magnificent cabarets of a so-called 'cultured' continent and, responding to its rhythms with cynical undulations of their hips, simulate the fecundation of woman by man."

Suddenly the radio, the hotel, and even Sorrento are forgotten. To the accompaniment of a jazz band from the land of the Gold Devil, Gorky philosophizes about sex for the benefit of *Pravda*'s readers:

> From time immemorial poets of all nations have lavished their creative power to ennoble this act. They have adorned sex so as to make it worthy of man, so that he should be elevated above the level of the goat, the bull, or the boar. Hundreds, nay thousands of beautiful poems have been composed in praise of love. . . . Through the force of love man has become far more social a being than even the cleverest of animals.

What a contrast to the "gross male" for whom women are not friends but "mere tools of pleasure, unless they are as much birds of prey as he himself . . . ," in which case there can be no mutual life beyond fox-trotting. Eventually, such people become obese and gross. "The man grown porcine is a poor male. Homosexuality becomes an epidemic in the world of the gross." In the end, jazz and fox-trotting lead to total degeneracy.

Gorky then provides a convenient history of jazz, which he represents as the last step in a process of decline that led from Mozart and Beethoven through the waltz to the fox-trot and finally to the convulsions of the Charleston. But how to reckon with the fact that oppressed Negroes were so prominent among the creators of jazz? Gorky has a ready answer. American Negroes "undoubtedly laugh in their sleeves to see how their white masters are evolving toward a savagery which they themselves are leaving behind." The middle class's infatuation with jazz is a sure sign of its moral collapse, while the American Negro's supposed turn away from it is evidence that only the proletariat possesses the values necessary to save mankind. Meanwhile, the music rolls on:

> The monstrous bass belches out English words; a wild horn wails piercingly, calling to mind the cries of a raving camel; a drum pounds monotonously; a nasty little pipe tears at one's ears; a saxophone emits its quacking nasal sound. Fleshy hips sway, and thousands of heavy feet tread and shuffle. The music of the degenerate ends finally with a deafening thud, as though a case of pottery had been flung to earth from the skies. Again limpid stillness reigns around me, and my thoughts return home. . . .

And what is this Russian homeland to which Gorky's thoughts take him? He would have us believe that it is the very embodiment of poetical love, of "active romanticism," and of ennobling relations between the sexes. Strange talk from a man who had written "Twenty-six Men and a Girl," a story based on the widely publicized rape of a young woman by bakers in the south of Russia! Nonetheless, Gorky hit the target where Matsa and most other Russian critics had skirted the main point. Jazz *is* dancing, physicality, emancipation, release. As such, it flew directly in the face of the puritanism of the Cultural Revolution.

Gorky's thoughts on jazz had not come suddenly to the proletarian novelist. Nina Berberova, a young poetess and writer who lived in Gorky's household during these years, remembered a curious event during a Christmas vacation at Marienbad in 1923. Gorky and his entourage of eight émigré Russian artists and writers had descended on the restaurant at the Hotel Minerva near midnight one evening. An eight- or nine-piece jazz band made up of black musicians (probably Louis Mitchell's group) was holding forth. "All of us younger people adored jazz; it was our music," Berberova recalled. "We didn't yet know how to fox-trot or shimmy, but avidly studied all those beautiful girls dancing around us." Gorky loathed it all. After brooding silently for an hour he exploded in rage against jazz, the fox-trot, and modern life generally, and then stomped out of the hall.[36]

Gorky's imprecations fell on receptive soil in Russia. One of the first senior officials of the Soviet state to take up cudgels against jazz was Commissar of Public Enlightenment Lunacharsky, who threw down the gauntlet at the First All-Russian Musical Conference in Leningrad in 1929. Jazz was at the top of the meeting's agenda. Lunacharsky, it will be recalled, had sponsored Teplitsky's jazz sabbatical in America and had bent a receptive ear to the Wooding orchestra during its Russian tour. His wife was an actress who went out of her way to find Hollywood-type roles for herself in the Soviet cinema. But times had changed. Following Gorky, Lunacharsky linked jazz with dancing and with the twentieth century's degradation of sexual mores. The fox-trot, he declared, is nothing less than the "extreme mechanization of rhythm, . . . pounding your will into a cutlet."[37] It symbolized blatant eroticism and was a narcotic to true human feelings. In Lunacharsky's view, the fox-trot was nothing less than a frontal attack on Soviet culture. As such, it had to be countered with distinctly proletarian dances free of the aura of eroticism, mechanization, and narcotic stimulation.

At the heart of both Gorky's and Lunacharsky's theses was the notion that jazz and the way of life associated with it were totally bourgeois. They were the instruments of a deliberate capitalist plot to make man live "through his sexual organs, so that during the intervals between work he will be preoccupied with these sides of his existence."[38] Marx had argued that Christianity was the opiate of the masses. Jazz and the fox-trot were now the dominant religion, manipulated by the new capitalist masters in order to secure and extend their dominion.

Lunacharsky praised the Communist party for taking the initiative in determining the policy of the Soviet Union toward "syncopated music" by convening the meeting. The construction of socialism in Russia had its own "vast rhythm of human movement, which, in the end, comes together in a single enormous symphony of motion and labor." There is no task before Soviet culture more urgent than to launch a counterattack against the aggressive, jazzy syncopations of the fox-trot. In place of individual improvisation will be collective, planned forms of expression.[39]

Gorky and Lunacharsky had set down the new line. Other writers picked up the cue and lambasted Russian composers, bandleaders, and publishers for issuing a "musical fix" (*muzykalnyi durman*).[40] Jazz and the fox-trot were tools in the capitalists' conspiracy to control the true forces of liberation. There was no surer proof of this than their intensive dissemination among black Americans. By this hideous means, Wall Street had converted American Negroes from chattel property to "slaves of capitalism, machines of capitalist production."[41] The word was out. Jazz and jazz dancing constituted a capitalist fifth column in Soviet Russia, a key element in the subtle campaign to destroy the USSR from within. They had to be stopped.

The official attack on jazz followed immediately. Leopold Teplitsky was arrested and exiled, doubtless baffled by his patron Lunacharsky's sudden change of heart. Komsomol units in the schools were instructed to organize discussions on the question "Can a young Communist like jazz?" Several girls in the senior class at the International School in Moscow for children of foreign Communists were expelled for admitting their love of jazz. Other children were forced to confess their errors before the entire class.[42] Similar scenes occurred in secondary schools across the country. Foreign jazz and the popular music of Tin Pan Alley were prohibited, and anyone

caught importing or playing American jazz records was liable to
receive a fine of 100 rubles and imprisonment for six months.[43] The
Small Soviet Encyclopedia, issued in 1930, failed even to mention
the word jazz.

Reverse Gear

It was one thing to spin elaborate arguments against jazz but quite
another to produce an acceptable alternative. Folk songs were ruled
out because they had, as one critic put it, "nothing in common with
the tasks, world view, and psychology of the contemporary industrial proletariat."[44] The Association of Proletarian Musicians tried
desperately to concoct pop tunes for the masses, but their bland
melodies and dogmatic texts held no appeal.[45] In theory, the task
could not have been simpler. What was needed were strong melodies with upbeat, positive lyrics. But having been denied the possibility of borrowing from jazz, songwriters produced little that rose
beyond the most hackneyed traditions of the past. Eloquent testimony to the depth of the problem was the discovery by the State
Publishing House that ideologically acceptable songs accounted for
less than one fifth of all tunes sung even by marchers in the parades
honoring the anniversary of the October Revolution.[46]

In desperation, popular-song writers began asking if it was impossible for jazz to become Soviet. In 1930, the journal *Worker and
Theater* concluded that it was possible, but an entirely new jazz
repertoire would have to be created.[47] Left-wing composers in Germany had already come to the same conclusion. "Why should art
music barricade itself against such an influence?" asked Kurt Weill
in 1929. "It is obvious," he wrote, "that jazz has played a significant role in the rhythmic, harmonic, and formal relaxation that we
have now attained and, above all, in the constantly increasing simplicity and comprehensibility of our music."[48] Schoenberg's student
Hanns Eisler agreed, and was applying elements of jazz in his socialist "struggle songs" (*Kampflieder*).[49] Eisler's technique centered
on simple lyrics sung to march tempos and to the accompaniment
of what he called "Parisian orchestration," which was, in fact, very

close to the classical Dixieland idiom. His instrumentation generally called for two trumpets, two trombones, three reeds, a banjo, drums, piano, and a plucked bass.[50]

The head-on conflict between theory and practice, ideology and popular taste, urgently required resolution. Communist doctrine threatened to paint Soviet musicians into a corner, from which they would have to deny the public's and their own liking for the new music. Paradoxically, the Nazis provided the key to escape from this conundrum by declaring their undying hostility to the music. As early as 1925 Siegfried Wagner, Richard Wagner's son, condemned jazz as the barbaric manifestation of "nigger rhythms." "I cannot understand," he declared, "how German youth can dance to vulgar tunes turned out by half-civilized Negroes. . . ."[51] The Hungarian ruler and Fascist sympathizer Admiral Horthy adroitly exploited jazz in songs extolling his regime, but no parallel existed in Hitler's party.[52] The internationalism of jazz music placed it beyond the pale for Fascists, and by the early 1930s it was coming under attack not only by Hitler but by his co-believers in Japan as well.[53] Pro-jazz revisionists in the Soviet Union realized that if the arch-enemies of communism in Germany and Japan were so adamantly opposed to jazz, it could not be all bad. They set to work.

Russians were impressed by the clever fashion in which Hanns Eisler had combined the forms of jazz with the uplifting message of socialism. At the 1930 "Musical Olympiad" in Leningrad, Eisler was a huge success and even drew praise from the Association of Proletarian Musicians, which presumably cheered the message rather than the medium.[54] But the ban on jazz could not be lifted so easily. There were hundreds of practical battles to be fought. Who was in a position to make the decision to reopen the Leningrad Music Hall, closed since 1928, which had earlier welcomed jazz-type orchestras?[55] Who would lift the ban at the radio stations, which had been closed not only to jazz but to every other form of expression anathematized by the Association of Proletarian Musicians?[56]

These operational problems were minor in comparison with the ideological problem posed by the new music. Gorky had stated it succinctly: jazz was bourgeois, the music of the degenerate. With

Pravda's lead, and egged on by the Association of Proletarian Musicians, this view had gained official status. Unless changed, jazz was doomed to an underground existence in the USSR. Eisler's "solution" may have been clever and even popular, but it was eventually bound to become the victim of the ideologues' wrath, unless the sociological roots of jazz could be redefined in proletarian terms. The very success of jazz in America and Western Europe made this extremely difficult.

Searching for Proletarian Jazz

One American writer observed at the height of the 1930s Depression, "Tin Pan Alley is now paved with profits."[57] And indeed it was: Spencer Williams was doing so well that he could afford to drive a Lincoln; Fats Waller, too, would be buying one in a few years.[58] Swing bands were discovering enthusiastic audiences that were prepared to pay well for their hot music. Sidney Bechet welcomed the prosperity provided by well-heeled clientele. "You hear a lot of folks talk about . . . the way business can't mix with music," he wrote many years later. "But there's no reason for saying a thing like that."[59]

How, then, could jazz be considered a proletarian music? A few American writers had been claiming for some years that jazz was a folk art.[60] Irving Berlin had also argued as much, as had the well-fed and prosperous Paul Whiteman. As Whiteman put it, "Like the folk songs of another age, jazz reflects and satisfies the undeveloped aesthetic and emotional cravings of great masses of people."[61] This notion of jazz as folk art had also been articulated in Western Europe and even in Russia. In 1929, for example, the Leningrad critic Mikhail Druskin argued that "The jazz band has ethnographic roots among those peoples whose music most closely approaches the rhythm of labor."[62]

Such claims, however, did not respond to the overwhelming evidence that the solid burghers of the West had taken jazz into their hearts and that the musicians themselves obviously liked fast cars and clean sheets. If jazz was a proletarian music, how could one account for the blatantly bourgeois aura that surrounded it? The answer revisionist critics proposed was disarmingly simple: there existed not one but two forms of jazz, one proletarian and the other bourgeois. The proletarian variant was rooted in Negro folk life and bore the scars of past oppression. The bourgeois variant derived not from folk blues but from the vulgar commercialism of Tin Pan Alley. Bourgeois jazz was popular culture "from above," devised by capitalist exploiters to lull the masses to sleep and stifle their growing class consciousness.

Elements of this adroit argument had been circulating in Russian jazz criticism for half a decade. After attending a performance by Sam Wooding's polished ensemble in 1926, Marietta Shaginian expounded eloquently on what she believed to be the folk or proletarian origins of jazz.[63] Her conclusions must have been based on sociological rather than musicological research, however, for she was almost completely deaf.[64] Benny Peyton's performance in Moscow moved musicologist Arnold Zukker to extoll the virtues of jazz as folk music.[65] Both writers, as well as Ivan Matsa and Commissar Lunacharsky, devoted far more attention to the corrupted bourgeois "salon jazz" they disliked than to the proletarian "true jazz" they claimed to respect. In cafés and fashionable restaurants jazz had become bourgeois and decadent, for, as Zukker put it, it had no other function there than "to be the acoustical background for those bodily movements which have become almost a symbol of a particular class and a particular epoch."[66]

The argument is clever but absurd. If the problem lay with erotic dancing, then the distinction between true proletarian jazz and bourgeois salon jazz vanishes. After all, some of the sensuous dances to which Bolshevik puritans objected had filtered up to the middle classes from the very unbourgeois world of Negro low life, not down from the Plaza ballroom. The distinction between folk jazz and commercial jazz is equally strained. Closely linked with the unfolkish technologies of radio and phonograph, jazz was commercial from the outset. Had it been otherwise, the emigration of

New Orleans musicians to Chicago, of Chicagoans to New York, of New Yorkers to Europe, and of all of them to the recording studios never would have occurred.

Such sociological distinctions in jazz had been drawn by critics outside the Soviet Union as well, notably in the United States and in France. In these countries, however, attention was fixed on the juxtaposition of "hot" jazz and the "sweet" style essayed by hotel orchestras. The immense popularity of the smoothly lacquered sound of the Whiteman orchestra had forced the issue. The rise of Guy Lombardo's sweet style in the first years after the American stock market crash in 1929 gave further reason to think that true jazz and popular salon orchestras had reached a parting of the ways.

The youthful and mercurial jazz enthusiast, Frenchman Hugues Panassié, wrote a series of articles that led to his important 1934 publication *Hot Jazz*, which for the first time defined the essence of jazz as its capacity to swing. Panassié found this quality principally in the rollicking polyphonic style of the New Orleans and Chicago pioneers, rather than in the more carefully orchestrated groups that came later during the era of Duke Ellington, Fletcher Henderson, and Glen Gray's Casa Loma band. While superficially appealing, Panassié's distinction can now be seen as too simple to fit the facts. Typical of the data that eludes a hot-sweet division is Louis Armstrong's praise for the work of Vic D'Ippolito on first trumpet in Sam Lanin's sweet band, or his enthusiasm for B. A. Rolfe, a trumpeter with Vincent Lopez's orchestra.[67] Obviously, Panassié's preference for primitive simplicity involved far more than purely musical issues. As the British jazz critic Chris Goddard has put it:

> . . . the logic of Panassié's thinking points straight to Arcadia. He seems to have seen the New Orleans era of jazz as an ideal, archaic period, a golden age before the advent of commercialism, peopled by beings of primordial simplicity for whom music was not merely desirable but indispensable.[68]

Much the same could be said of the Russians. For ideological reasons they, too, wanted a jazz that was straight from a proletarian Arcadia. The distinctive feature of their position was that they assigned far more importance to the sociological context of jazz than to its musical identity. However illogically, they searched for a jazz that was uncompromisingly lower class but at the same time purged of all links with eroticism and dancing. It was all but impossible to find. The attempt reveals the heart of the Soviet dilemma: jazz, a genuinely popular form, appealed to the common man precisely because its driving rhythms carried a message of individual and physical liberation that was incompatible with the puritanic morality of communism as it was then defined.

Jewish Jazzmen

Even at the height of the Cultural Revolution, Soviet critics had trouble sustaining their attack on the fox-trot and the other bumptious dances that were so popular in their country. Confronted by public enthusiasm for what they wished to condemn, the puritanic critics quietly backed down, hoping that civic leaders and police would at least manage to keep the dancing within acceptable bounds. Gradually, a more tolerant group of critics came to the fore and placed the jazz debate on a new plane by attempting to prove that jazz was a proletarian music.

In their effort they found powerful backing from several Communist writers in the United States. Charles Edward Smith, then a music critic for *The Daily Worker*, contrasted "hot jazz" with the popular music of Tin Pan Alley, which he characterized as "wish fulfillment music, folk music 'from above.'"[69] Popular music, Smith claimed, was "brought out to hoodwink the masses and divert them from revolutionary class struggles." "True jazz" had the opposite effect. Smith had convinced himself that the music of the New Orleans Rhythm Kings, the Wolverines, and the Mound City Blue Blowers drew attention to the economic plight of the masses and stimulated their growing class consciousness.[70] Smith was forcing jazz into the procrustean bed of Marxist ideology and his American readers knew it, especially those who had Charlestoned to the bands he cited to buttress his argument. Many Soviet critics accepted his theories enthusiastically,[71] although they had little opportunity to test them and despite the fact that Smith never had even half the Russian following of his colleague on *The Daily Worker*, the novelist, poet, and critic, Michael Gold.

Even before the outbreak of the Cultural Revolution, Gold had volunteered to head the American branch of the Association of Proletarian Writers. Because of his initiative, he was invited to participate in the Congress of Proletarian Culture organized in Kharkov in the autumn of 1930. At this meeting, in private discussions with Soviet critics, and in several subsequent essays, Gold expounded his views on the proletarian character of jazz. Unlike Smith, who included white groups such as the New Orleans Rhythm Kings and the Wolverines in his pantheon, Gold insisted that jazz was a Negro music. The exception, according to Gold, were the many Jews who were attracted to the art. Jazz, he argued, had been created by the proletariat of two oppressed ethnic groups, American Negroes and Jews.

Gold had laid the basis for this astonishing argument in a short novel, *Jews Without Money*, published in 1930 and translated into Russian the following year.[72] In it he attacked the notion of America as the land of opportunity, pointing to the many Jews who had been plunged into virtually servitude by their poverty. From this arose the Jew's passionate identification with his fellow sufferer, the Negro. Paraphrasing a character from Theodore Herzl's turn-of-the-century novel *Altneuland*, Gold stated, "Only a Jew can fathom the depths of that problem in all their horror; I mean the Negro problem."[73] He later went on to expound his views on the "Afro-Yiddish" nature of jazz in a series of columns in *The Daily Worker*.[74]

Gold's thesis was not as preposterous as it may seem. Al Jolson's enormously popular film *The Jazz Singer* (1928) dealt with precisely the same issue. It presented the son of a poor Jewish immigrant cantor who assimilates to American life by becoming a jazz singer. At about the same time, many American Jews were entering jazz, most notably Benny Goodman, whose parents hailed from Vilno and the Warsaw ghetto. This was enough to prompt Henry Ford, in signed and unsigned editorials in his *Dearborn Independ-*

dent, to rail against jazz as a Jewish conspiracy to "Negrotize" American culture.[75] Thus, the political Right joined the Left in this curious exercise in the sociology of culture!

The thesis about Jewish involvement in American popular music and jazz did not go unnoticed abroad. German Nazis immediately seized on the point and began denouncing the "Judeo-Negroid" nature of the music.[76] This ensured that Communist writers in Russia would take exactly the opposite position. Thus, V. N. Gorodinsky took up his pen to defend the contribution Jews had made to jazz and to popular music generally. The supposed involvement with jazz of the Jewish poor in America helped to legitimize the activities of the even larger number of Jewish musicians in Russia who had been drawn to the jazz world; Leonid Utesov, Alexander Tsfasman, Valentin Parnakh, Georgi Landsberg, and instrumentalists Simon Kagan, Yakov Rozenfeld, Nikolai Minkh, and Mikhail Frumkin were all Jews. And all now found ideological justification for their infatuation with American jazz music, thanks to the arguments first advanced by Charles Edward Smith and Michael Gold.

Jazz and Foreign Policy

The debates of 1928–32 regarding the sociology of jazz were being held at exactly the same time the Kremlin-sponsored Communist International, or "Comintern," was dramatically revising its policies toward American Negroes. This change of course was to have strongly favorable, if indirect, consequences for the fate of jazz in the USSR. The decisive moment came at the Sixth Congress of the Comintern held in Moscow in the summer of 1928. Prior to this crucial session, the Kremlin had shown scant interest in the racial problem in America or in Negroes generally. The Fourth Congress of the Comintern in 1922 (at which Parnakh had performed) had adopted a "Negro Thesis," which called on black Americans to take up the cause of revolution and spread it back to Africa.[77] This call to arms had had no impact on black Americans or on the American Communist party, which at the end of the twenties still had fewer than one thousand Negro members.[78] Now, in 1928, the need for a bold new policy was fully acknowledged.

The solution proposed by the Sixth Congress of the Comintern was to define the Negro population of the southern Black Belt as an independent nation and to place the Communist party of the United States and the Comintern as a whole at the head of a campaign for their national liberation and political self-determination. This astonishing proposal was embodied in an otherwise turgid document titled "Theses on the Revolutionary Movement in Colonial and Semi-Colonial Countries."[79] Stripped of its sociological claptrap, the new policy called for the establishment of the Black Republic of the South stretching from Virginia to Texas, a kind of Neo-Confederate States of America.

This flabbergasting proposition was the brainchild of Marxist sociologists in Moscow who had been no closer to America than the Lenin Library. None of the four American Negroes who attended the Congress had any knowledge of the South, while the New York-based American Communist party would have been powerless to reverse the policy, even if it had tried to do so.

The proposal was based on the proposition that southern Negroes constituted a distinct nationality. According to Moscow ideologues, these blacks were distinct not only from the white population but also from middle-class Negroes in the northern cities. Since Stalin himself had participated in the commission which had prepared the "Colonial Theses" for the Comintern, it was now necessary to prove the correctness of Comrade Stalin's analysis.[80] The keystone to such proof was to demonstrate the distinctiveness of southern Negro culture in all its aspects.[81]

Enter jazz. If the "Colonial Theses" were to be sustained, it was imperative that jazz be defined as a proletarian music. Equally important, it had to be presented as a genuine folk music indigenous to the southern Black Belt. But what about its undeniably urban character? Kremlin sociologists could not accept this, so it had to be denied. And what about the intimate connection between jazz, modern communication technology, and commercial distribution? This, too, had to be discounted. It is revealing that W. C. Handy, that pioneer businessman-entrepreneur of jazz, emerged as a folk artist steeped in revolutionary consciousness in essays by Michael Gold, Charles Edward Smith, and their Soviet comrades.[82]

Such claims would have seemed even more bizarre had they not been qualified by the doctrine of two jazzes, proletarian and bourgeois. The doctrine itself led to some wild claims, such as Georgi Landsberg's attempt to put forward the urbane Duke Ellington and his sophisticated music as a toiling proletarian struggling in behalf of the political Left.[83] But in the overall defense of jazz in the USSR, the proletarian-bourgeois distinction was a boon. Provided that readers were not too informed on the subject, the juxtaposition enabled Russian apologists to defend the music in terms that were intelligible to the Party and at the same time to sidestep accusations leveled against jazz by its musical and ideological foes.

The proposal to establish the Black Republic of the South was adopted in 1928 as the official policy of the Comintern and hence of the American Communist party. The *volte-face* it required was fully achieved by 1930, notwithstanding the categorical opposition of the Association of Proletarian Musicians and those who had begun the Cultural Revolution believing that jazz was the "music of the gross." But how was the Black Republic to be established? American Communists had little use for what in private they considered a harebrained scheme, and intellectuals condemned it as a kind of "red-winged Jim Crow."[84] But policy was policy, and as a first step toward its implementation the revolutionary consciousness of Negroes clearly had to be raised. Kremlin ideologists proposed producing a film of such power and intensity that it would cause the entire Black Belt to rise in revolt. The story of the Kremlin's abortive race movie *Red and Black* is one of the most bizarre pages in the history of Stalinist attempts to manipulate popular culture.

Red and Black

The decision to produce *Red and Black* was taken in Moscow late in 1931. Its locale was to be Birmingham, Alabama, and it was to portray the bloody results of an attempt by black steelworkers to form a union (to be sure, under white leadership).[85] The project generated scandal practically from the start. The Russian producers had quite reasonably concluded that the actors should be black and in 1931 had arranged through the American Communist party for twenty-two members of the black proletariat to come to Moscow for the filming. But the group that actually sailed from New York on the *Europa* in the late spring of 1932 was scarcely what the Russians expected. The poet Langston Hughes characterized its members as "a band of eager, adventurous young students, teachers, writers and would-be actors" whose sole common denominator was their ability and willingness to pay their own fares in order to travel to Russia to sign contracts they had never seen.[86] Among them was a very pretty young divorcée traveling on alimony, a female swimming instructor, and various clerks and stenographers. Only one member of the group belonged to the Communist party.

The delegation was received at the International Workers Aid film studio upon its arrival in Moscow. An American Negro journalist later described this epochal encounter:

> There were raised eyebrows and puzzled expressions and whispered asides among the Russians. These were the toiling masses of American Negroes?
>
> There before the astonished Russians stood twenty-two men and women ranging in color from dark brown to high yellow. "We need genuine Negroes and they sent us a bunch of *metisi* (mixed bloods)" one disturbed Russian remarked in an undertone. Another puzzled official shook his head after shaking hands with several members of the group. "Their hands, so soft, they don't feel like workers' hands."[87]

There was worse to come. The black "proletarians" nearly staged a strike when their hosts fed them a workers' diet of weak borscht, cabbage, and black bread. More serious, the scenario for the film turned out to be so packed with absurdities that it would have been like a burlesque on the screen. "It is just simply not true to American life," explained Langston Hughes. "But," the Russians countered indignantly, "it's been approved by the Comintern."[88] In the end, the Comintern bureaucrats had no choice but to accept Hughes's criticism.

By mid-summer the young German director Karl Junghans was brought in to set things straight. One of his first acts was to call musical rehearsals at which the ersatz proletarians were expected to belt out lusty field songs, mournful spirituals, and jazzy rhythms. Being northerners, and middle class besides, the Americans had never heard spirituals outside the concert hall, while work songs were totally alien to them. More serious still, only one of the group could carry a tune, let alone accompany the others with a jazzed-up beat.[89] It was a disaster.

The Russians sought to gain time by packing their hired proletarians off on an all-expense-paid tour of South Russia. While the Americans were wining and dining their way from Odessa to the snow-capped Caucasus, the project was dying in Moscow. In the end, President Franklin D. Roosevelt's decision to recognize the Soviet Union killed the effort to create a proletarian Negro extravaganza on film. A sad postscript to the scandalous affair occurred in 1936 when Lovett Forte-Whiteman, a black American who had been dragooned to work on the script, was purged from the Communist party and disappeared in Moscow.[90]

The fiasco of *Red and Black* was a fitting end to Stalin's Cultural Revolution. Begun amid a false war scare and artificially induced xenophobia, the "Great Leap Forward" had at first assumed the character of a full-scale war against those rural and urban elements that refused to yield to Stalinist orthodoxy. As the ideologues prepared to design the new ideals to be proclaimed "from above," they immediately resolved to extirpate from the USSR all bourgeois elements, of which jazz was considered a part. But it proved easier to ban one form of popular culture than to concoct another and get the public to accept it. Some accommodation to jazz was unavoidable by 1930, even without the ideological vindication the Kremlin was forced to mount by the logic of the Comintern's new policy regarding Negroes. The "Colonial Theses" of 1928 were as much a part of the Cultural Revolution as Gorky's fulminations against the degenerate West. In the end, the demands of foreign policy embodied in those theses took precedence over any purge of domestic culture along the lines of Gorky's dyspeptic essay.

The Cultural Revolution had begun by condemning jazz and concluded by rehabilitating it. What remained to be seen was whether Soviet jazz would continue to develop "from below" with a degree of spontaneity, or whether official vindication of jazz would prompt the regime to take it over and shape its further evolution "from above," along lines more compatible with the recent Communist puritanism.

6

The Red Jazz Age, 1932–1936

> In the monarch's presence, the orders he had laid down were obeyed at the Assemblies, but in private life, luxury and abasement took root.
>
> M. M. Shcherbatov, 1768

In the late spring of 1932, after the ice on the Moscow River had thawed, the barge-restaurant Poplavok was towed to its usual position upstream from the Kremlin. Never known for its cuisine, Poplavok attracted a steady clientele of younger people who came there to dance and drink. This season Poplavok boasted a new orchestra, consisting of trumpet, piano, drums, alto saxophone, and violin.[1] Scarcely a hot band, the Poplavok orchestra did pour out many recent Western pop tunes otherwise unknown in Moscow. The crowds loved it, not least because the band's bass drum was emblazoned with the word "JAZZ," painted in large red letters that completely covered the head.

After all Russia had been through, that one word, "jazz," had meaning far beyond the music itself. On March 2, 1930, when masses of small farmers were already dead, Stalin had declared that his underlings were "dizzy with success."[2] That same year it was announced that the First Five-Year Plan had been completed in four and that the country could relax somewhat from its labors. The number of peasant households expropriated annually had declined to a mere twelve thousand. A sense of relief was in the air, which even the discovery of a further plot by old Bolsheviks in January

1933 failed to dispel. A mood of self-congratulation and ease dominated the so-called Congress of Victors with which the Communist
party marked the end of the Cultural Revolution. Nobody could
have known at the time that before the decade ended at least 1,108
of the 1,966 delegates at that Congress would be shot.[3]

The extent and depth of the respite between the end of collectivization and the onslaught of the worst purges in 1936 is easily
underestimated. Cynics have called it "The Great Retreat," the name
of a thoughtful if rather snide émigré publication on the subject.
Others, including most Western Kremlinologists, have seen it as
little more than Stalin's desire for a breathing space during which
to consolidate and regroup his forces before the final assault on
dissent. Even in these years, however, the purge of the Party proceeded quietly but surely, bringing exile and even death to many.
But for the millions not directly affected it was a period of genuine
happiness, a breaking loose, during which, as in America, those
who had survived could sing "Happy Days Are Here Again."

This brief and circumscribed mood of euphoria helps to explain
the unprecedented explosion in the popularity of jazz. Far more
than ever before, the very word "jazz" implied a carefree and exuberant attitude toward life, the very opposite of the grim Cultural
Revolution. In 1929–30 all efforts had been bent on proving that
jazz was proletarian music; now it suddenly emerged in the entirely
different guise of "light genre," which in effect meant popular music. As the sociologists cooled down, the dancers warmed up. Theory
and practice finally came together.

Breaking Loose

There is reason to doubt the regime had much choice but to accept
the situation. So avidly did the public seize on the symbolism of the
word "jazz" that it popped up everywhere, and without control.
There was "theatrical jazz," "cinema-jazz," "extra-jazz," "joy-jazz,"
"tango-jazz," and even "circus-jazz." During the years 1933–34 the
Nemirovich-Danchenko Theater organized a vocal jazz ensemble,
the Bolshoi Theater Orchestra staged Milton Eidger's "King Jazz,"

and the Boris Krupyshev Orchestra mounted the "jazz operetta" *Rose-Marie* and toured with it across the Soviet Union. Reviewing the ubiquity of the word "jazz" in these years, Soviet critic Alexei Batashev concluded it had become a signally successful advertising gimmick.[4] Amid all this jazzomania, few were left to mourn the government's decision to abolish the Association of Proletarian Musicians in 1932.

New jazz bands sprang up everywhere, playing swing arrangements from the West. In Leningrad the Comedy Theater brought together a quartet, while Georgi Landsberg reorganized his group into a big band that became the local radio station's official orchestra. In Kharkov, where in 1926 a music critic had denounced Benny Peyton's group even before hearing it,[5] Boris Rensky now established a popular dance orchestra of ten pieces, which included many jazz numbers in its large and diverse repertoire. Other similar ensembles popped up in Voronezh under the leadership of Evgeni Vinitski and in Odessa under the directorship of pianist Petr Rosenkern. The music of many of these groups is easily forgotten. A *"dzhaz"* (jazz band) organized in remote Sverdlovsk in 1934 was simply the local salon orchestra, rechristened to keep up with the times.[6] But such bands were important symbols of the new mood wherever they existed.

The singer Vera Dmitrievna Dneprova colorfully characterizes the "Red Jazz Age." Trained as a singer of light opera and possessed of an excellent figure and dyed blonde hair, she arrived in Moscow in 1932 in search of the bright lights. While living with two old maiden aunts, Vera Dneprova spent her evenings at the fashionable Metropol Restaurant, where she picked up the latest dances from visiting foreigners. By 1934 she had become the mistress of a young American diplomat, amateur musician, and avid jazz fan, Elbridge Durbrow. Through Durbrow and two other young American diplomats, Charles Bohlen and Charles Thayer, she amassed a respectable collection of American jazz recordings, which she carefully transcribed into sheet music. In musical circles she found other women who shared her infatuation with American popular music, and by 1935 she had organized the Ladies Jazz Orchestra (*Zhenskii dzhaz*) of eight musicians. Dneprova spoke little English but could belt out hits by the Boswell Sisters with conviction and ease. The State Concert Agency (*Goskontsert*) liked the group and signed it up to tour the major Black Sea resorts, including Yalta and Sochi. Durbrow and Bohlen heard a performance at the Ford Tractor Factory in Gorky in 1935 and pronounced Dneprova's band "a pretty damn good jazz orchestra."[7]

All the worst fears about the depravity of dancing expressed by Gorky and Lunacharsky were realized in the restaurants and gardens of Moscow after 1932. Moscow's Savoy (now Berlin) Restaurant, a favorite watering hole during the NEP era, reestablished its credentials with the fast set by featuring a *dzhaz*. The bland salon orchestra holding forth at the second-floor restaurant of the National Hotel was no jazz band but did not hesitate to bill itself as one. The Olivier Gardens survived the Cultural Revolution, as it had earlier muddled through the 1917 upheaval, and once more became a popular dance spot.[8] In the hope of keeping up with the Muscovites, Leningrad's venerable Evropeiskaia Hotel (before 1917 the L'Europe) brought together some of the city's best jazz musicians to play for dances in its restaurant. But in these years Moscow finally established itself as the nocturnal capital of the USSR. At the Metropol Hotel, for example, the band played for dancing until 3:00 A.M., while at the Empire Restaurant (where the Budapest is today) the fox-trotters could carry on to 4:00 A.M.

The *New York Times's* correspondent reported on the situation in 1933:

> Each of the big hotels in Moscow has its own jazz band and dancing floor, presumably for the sake of foreigners and tourists. But many more Russians go there, especially on "Red Saturday," the night before their free day. Foreigners on these nights are decidedly in the minority.
>
> The orchestra of one Moscow hotel has an American Negro tap dancer who nightly brings down the house with dances which the Russians have never seen before. . . .
>
> Jazz music is staging a remarkable comeback in Soviet Russia after years of virtual prohibition. Visitors here looking for the good old Russian folk music of the balalaika and the guitar have

to hunt far and wide. In cafes, restaurants and amusement parks they find orchestras playing their version of American jazz in response to a popular demand.

One visitor scoured Tiflis hoping to find an orchestra playing the old Georgian music, noted for its wild harmony. He heard jazz pieces which were popular only a year and more ago in the United States. He finally bribed an orchestra to play some native pieces.[9]

The new dances gained such popularity that cultural agencies were all but powerless to resist the fad. By 1934 many factories were offering fox-trot lessons free of charge to their workers. One or two days a week workers could stay for an hour after the end of their shift in order to be instructed in the latest Western dances by fashionably dressed women hired by management.[10] So much for Gorky and Lunacharsky!

The "New Class"

The spectacle of Soviet blue collar-workers struggling to master the Lindy Hop poses the question of which social groups participated in the Red Jazz Age. Far more than during the twenties, there were now many workers drawn to the new cultural ideal. After all, as a contemporary Soviet writer observed, "The jazz epidemic is to some degree the natural reaction to the excessively austere puritanism that reigned among us until so recently."[11] Workers, no less than the professional classes, had been bombarded with proletarian sanctimony. They reacted with predictable obstinacy. As we have seen, they stubbornly refused to sing the official proletarian songs that had been created for their betterment. They also rejected much of the highbrow music thrown their way. A well-meaning director at the sprawling Dneprostroi Dam project in the Ukraine announced his intention of inviting a string quartet to bring culture to construction workers at the site in 1929. When his laborers overruled him, he concluded that "our workers don't understand music."[12] Much to the director's disgust, the workers voted to spend the entire cultural fund on popular music and jazz.

But there were practical limits on the workers' enthusiasm for jazz. Workers had slightly more free time at their disposal in the 1930s than they had under NEP, according to the results of time-use surveys.[13] But the same survey data report that workers were compelled to devote more time to ideological and public-affairs concerns than had been necessary earlier. This effectively neutralized any gains from the slightly shortened work week. And if their wages had improved modestly, the workers' living standard had plummeted, due to increases in the cost of living. Real wages in 1932 were only half what they had been in 1928. To make matters worst, many Draconian labor laws were still on the books, and the modest incentives provided by speed-up programs like the Stakhanovite and Shock Workers movements were viewed with widespread cynicism.[14]

The position of managers and officials, however, had dramatically improved. During the Cultural Revolution, engineers and other experts had borne the brunt of attacks by zealots eager to expose the professionals' lack of political commitment. Wages for the professionally competent had been pulled down to the general low standard, and in the schools the advantages that accrued to native intelligence and family upbringing were neutralized through open admissions policies. The cost to manpower training of such radical programs had been enormous. By the winter of 1931–32 the Party leadership came finally to appreciate this. Throughout the following year the official press rang with criticism of "Communist scholasticism," "harebrained scheming," and "proletarian fanaticism." Before year's end, Stalin had rehabilitated the engineers, defended publicly the principle of competitive admissions in the schools, and mounted an ideological attack on the notion that salaries should be set without regard to education or achievement.[15] The path lay open for the establishment of a new class, a managerial and professional elite loyal to the regime that protected its privileges. Every Soviet leader for the next half-century was to be drawn precisely from this Communist upper crust.

The paradoxes in the new elite's position fairly lunged at contemporary observers. To its members was assigned primary responsibility for bringing into being a classless workers' society. To motivate them in their efforts, they were assigned better salaries, fancy apartments decorated in the then-fashionable Empire and Art Deco styles, and access to shops more rigorously exclusive than Bergdorf Goodman or Brooks Brothers could ever hope to be. The new elite was very young, since many of its members had received lightning-quick promotions at the end of the Cultural Revolution, and many were not particularly sophisticated, fully 57 percent in 1933 having no higher or specialized education at all.[16] There did exist a genuine aristocracy of culture and politics, a Soviet high society, during the years 1932–36.[17] Enjoying Kremlin patronage, those at the pinnacle of this establishment could, for example, take Saturdays off to discuss with an American golf-course architect plans for an eighteen-hole course at Serebrianny Bor north of Moscow.[18] On a day-to-day basis, however, the several million men and women who composed the Soviet professional class had more modest tastes. Nice clothes, an evening with friends at a good restaurant, and release through dancing to a "dzhaz" were quite enough. This much the Party could grant them. But through their indulgence in these seemingly innocent pastimes, the Stalinist elite became a kind of Trojan horse for jazz in the 1930s. The result was the creation of an officially sanctioned market and the legitimization of jazz in the eyes of those halfway up the social ladder but aspiring to the top.

The Public's Taste

What music gained popularity among the new urban audiences? Many listeners, particularly those who were older and from established bourgeois families, preferred the dignified and decidedly unjazzy orchestra of Ferdinand Krisch. Krisch's ensemble was the very quintessence of pre-revolutionary decorum. Decked out in white dinner jackets, hair slicked down, and a supercilious half-smile on their lips, members of the Krisch orchestra evoked the good old days of pre-revolutionary St. Petersburg at the Evropeiskaia Hotel, until that establishment succumbed to the big band swing style in 1932–33. Then Krisch added a sax section to keep up with the times. Krisch's renditions of "Romantic Tango," "Rosetta," and

"Magnolias in the Moonlight" won for him a solidly loyal audience that was still buying reissues of his recordings in the 1960s.

Gypsy orchestras also claimed a substantial if rapidly dwindling part of the market. The Prague Restaurant in Moscow stuck with gypsy programming until World War II, while a host of smaller establishments—Rasputin's old haunt, the Yar; the Grelnia; and the Gurzuf—tapped the talents of the still lively gypsy community centered in the area of Zykovskaia Street. By 1935, however, the gypsies were feeling strong pressure from jazz. Simply to mention the word *"dzhaz"* to a member of the gypsy Artomonov family was to invite him to spit in anger and disgust.[19]

A primary reason for the popularity of Russia's aspiring swing bands was their link with the world of dining and dancing. Indeed, two of the most popular bands of the Red Jazz Age gained their livelihood through hotel restaurants patronized by the new elite. Alexander Varlamov and Yakov Skomorovsky represent this era well.

Varlamov was no stranger to popular culture, his great grandfather having composed many of the most widely known salon *Lieder* of the 1830s. Both his mother and grandfather were singers and were well regarded in tsarist musical and social circles. Born in Lenin's hometown of Simbirsk on the Volga, Varlamov came to Moscow in the early twenties and, following a brief flirtation with acting, entered the Gnesin Music School. He studied voice and composition, the latter under Reinhold Glière, one of the finest pedagogues of the era. Varlamov emerged from the Gnesin School just as the Cultural Revolution was ending. He had heard Benny Peyton's band and had seen the Chocolate Kiddies during their 1926 Russian tour. Seizing the moment, he organized a large swing band, which made its debut in the Moscow park theater, the Hermitage, on May 20, 1934.[20] The band was an instant success and issued its first record later that year.

The Varlamov orchestra included a three-man saxophone section, two trumpets, a trombone, and a full rhythm section, with Igor Gladkov, the pianist, doubling on accordion. A violinist was added for good measure, though he is inaudible on the recordings.

Varlamov's band got high marks with the public on account of its singer, Celestina Cole. An American-born Negro, Cole had just arrived in Moscow to study music at the urging of her uncle Robert Robinson, who had emigrated to Russia some years earlier and had been chosen by his fellow workers at a Moscow factory to serve as their deputy to the Soviet. Though it was widely rumored that Cole had sung with Duke Ellington,[21] her 1934 recordings with Varlamov reveal a thin voice more like that of Snow White in the Disney film than a jazz singer. Suffice it to say that Maxim Gorky liked her singing.[22]

Even in his own day, Varlamov was viewed by many Soviet jazz musicians as a dilettante.[23] Certainly, most of his repertoire was schmaltz of the sort that could be heard in any American or European hotel at the time. His 1938 recording of "Sweet Sue" is too fast, while his renditions of "Blue Moon" and Harry Warren's "At the Carnival" are nothing more than vehicles for what in Russia were called the "slow fox" and the "fast fox." At some points, his attempts at jazz are pitiful. Trumpeter Petr Boriskin's solo in "At the Carnival" never strikes out from the melody for more than two measures at a time, indicating he had not yet mastered the art of thinking in chords rather than melodic lines. Clarinetist Mstislav Kaprovich, a veteran from the Parnakh orchestra, plays a howling solo on "Dixie Lee" that is more gimmicks and tricks than music.

Despite these obvious limitations, the Varlamov orchestra at moments seems genuinely to make contact with the swing idiom. Between 1934 and 1938 the sax section evolved into a tight ensemble, capable of playing demanding lines with finesse. Tenor saxophonist Alexander Vasiliev in particular emerges as a driving soloist on tunes such as "Blue Moon" and "Happy Road." Vasiliev's warm and controlled vibrato (which show the direct influence of Coleman Hawkins) and his fluid phrasing indicate a true sympathy for jazz, even though in his early years, as fellow saxophonist Mikhail Lantsman charges, Vasiliev had to have his solos written out for him.

The Varlamov orchestra took a long step beyond the soggy banalities of Ferdinand Krisch, but the limited jazz orientation of its members prevented it from developing into a swinging ensemble. The Yakov Skomorovsky orchestra was far more successful. Skomorovsky was a Leningrader, which in the late twenties meant that he was far more *au courant* with Western musical fashions than the Muscovites. As a trumpeter with the orchestra of the Leningrad Opera Theater, he had attracted the attention of Leonid Utesov and had played with Utesov's Theatrical Jazz Orchestra at its 1929 debut.[24] The classically trained Skomorovsky quickly found Utesov's antics unacceptable. Unwilling to play on one knee and wave his trumpet overhead, he quit and, after a run at the reopened Leningrad Music Hall, introduced his own orchestra in the restaurant of Leningrad's Evropeiskaia Hotel in 1934, cutting Ferdinand Krisch out of the picture. Skomorovsky released his first record in 1932. By late 1934 his fame had reached Moscow, and the orchestra was booked in the restaurant of the newly opened Moskva Hotel. Old-timers report that it was impossible to get a table there when Skomorovsky played.[25]

During the 1930s the Skomorovsky orchestra was invited to perform in a number of successful Soviet films, including *Circus* and *Volga, Volga!* These appearances and the various recordings made by the group reveal it as a competent, Class B swing ensemble fully capable of attracting the livelier young dancers whose tastes had advanced beyond Varlamov.

Far more than any Soviet bandleader considered thus far, Skomorovsky had a gift for identifying musicians whom he could make into jazzmen. Beyond this, he was fortunate to have found an adept arranger in the person of Ilya Jacques (Zhak). Jacques was well aware that Soviet issues of recordings by British salon orchestras of Henry Hall and Bert Ambrose had been extremely popular with the public in the years 1931–33.[26] Hall, who later hired Benny Carter to do arrangements for his BBC Dance Orchestra, was at this time enamoured of the music of Guy Lombardo. Ambrose, in such tunes as "The Continental" and "Lullaby of Broadway," essayed a far livelier and more tightly orchestrated style than Hall.[27] Jacques set out to surpass both Hall and Ambrose.

In Shelton Brooks's "Some of These Days," Jacques scored the best breaks yet produced by a Soviet band, including a gloriously complex phrase by the saxophone section before the final stinger. On "Dinah" Jacques did even better, although he tended to chop up the chorus into so many short solos and breaks that the rhythmic flow was destroyed. Under Skomorovsky's leadership the brasses produced a clean and crisp ensemble. Though beautifully rehearsed, in "The First Kiss" and several other tunes their emphasis on the first beat in each measure prevented any swing feeling.

The band's chief shortcoming, however, was not with the arranged ensembles but with the solos. Ilya Jacques had a good stride left hand, but Skomorovsky himself was a disaster. In his solos on "Dinah" and "Oh Joanna!" he hops around the melody with short doodling notes like a classical ballerina attempting to boogie. His concert tone, partially the result of using an old-fashioned rotary-valve trumpet and the wrong mouthpiece, is scarcely softened by a too-rapid vibrato. Beyond this, the rhythm section pushes the beat so hard that the entire band is rushed. George Kennan, a second secretary in the American Embassy at the time and an enthusiastic jazz guitarist, characterized Skomorovsky's band as "too loud, too fast, and too jerky in its rhythms." [28]

In spite of these problems, Skomorovsky's orchestra was light-years ahead of Bert Ambrose's and, at its best, was thoroughly reputable swing ensemble. The band developed an appreciative following among younger Soviet audiences and, equally important, gained the respect of Moscow's aspiring jazzmen. [29] Skomorovsky's very success with the public indicates that the new audience was becoming more discriminating, and that the more lively the group, the more likely it was to earn the public's endorsement.

Structural Impediments

In evaluating the accomplishment of Alexander Varlamov or Yakov Skomorovsky, it is important to appreciate the formidable hardships under which Soviet jazzmen continued to labor. Instruments

were still virtually unobtainable. The Soviet Union was neither producing saxophones nor importing them. Vasiliev, who played a horn
that lacked the low B key, had to have all his parts scored to avoid
that note.[30] The only drums and cymbals available were those designed for military bands, and modern piston-valve trumpets were
unknown. Older Soviet jazz musicians can regale listeners for hours
with the life history of a single instrument. For example, when David
Gegner, a saxophonist who had emigrated from Berdichev to
Shanghai in 1920, returned from exile in 1935, he created a sensation by offering for sale his Conn alto sax. Bidding on the instrument reached astronomical figures.[31]

The importation of sheet music was equally limited, and nearly
all arrangements had to be patiently transcribed from recordings.
Like medieval copyists who mastered the art of illumination by
copying ancient manuscripts, Soviet arrangers, including Jacques,
gained a close understanding of the orchestration techniques of Ellington or Fletcher Henderson in the process of meticulously reconstructing their scores from recordings.

The Soviet recording industry had been issuing records by local
swing bands since the late twenties. With the end of the Cultural
Revolution and the acquisition of electronic recording equipment
in 1930, the number of Soviet *dzhazes* able to record rapidly increased. Indeed, throughout the 1930s far more popular recordings
were issued than classical ones.[32] But only a handful of recordings
by foreign jazz bands were reissued in Moscow. American, British,
and German jazz records were readily available in nearby Poland,
Latvia, and Estonia, but travel to those countries was virtually impossible for all but officials. Hence, Soviet musicians were almost
entirely dependent on the few records carried into the Soviet Union
by individuals.

Realizing the value of foreign jazz records, Soviet merchant sea-
men imported them illicitly through the ports of Odessa, Leningrad, Murmansk, and Vladivostok. Most of these black marketeers
brought in other items as well, such as English pipe tobacco, and
took huge markups on all goods. Their taste in music was less than

impeccable.[33] A far more reliable source of recordings were those Soviet officials and members of the elite who indulged their own passion for jazz records during sojourns abroad. Some unlikely figures made significant contributions. One of the finest collections of jazz recordings in Leningrad, one that was also accessible to musicians, had been built up by the local NKVD head Ivan Medved.[34] An even bigger Leningrad collector was Sergei Kolbasev, poet, former naval officer, linguist, diplomat, and writer of sea stories. The son of a tsarist bureaucrat and a Maltese immigrant, Kolbasev had served in the Red Navy throughout the Civil War. After being mustered out, he had accepted an assignment as interpreter with the Soviet Embassy in Afghanistan, and then a post in Helsinki. While serving abroad, he began his career as a writer and, simultaneously, began to collect jazz recordings. By the early 1930s he had the most comprehensive collection in the USSR. Not content with merely collecting records, Kolbasev also reproduced them on home-built equipment, and, to expand his collection, undertook to wire-record (again, on home-built equipment) whatever American jazz could be picked up by radio in Leningrad.[35] He also used his homemade apparatus to record jazz from American films that found their way to Leningrad.

Sergei Kolbasev was a collector with a mission. Beginning in 1931, his Leningrad apartment became a Mecca for jazz fans and musicians, an outpost where one could hear the latest records by Benny Goodman, Duke Ellington, Fletcher Henderson, or Benny Carter. To stretch his pedagogical reach further, Kolbasev arranged public soirees in other cities, at which he would play jazz recordings and discuss the music. A typical Kolbasev performance occurred at the Moscow Club for Masters of the Arts in 1933. At this occasion, advertised as "The Musical Culture of America," the tall, bald-headed Kolbasev introduced a capacity audience to recordings of Duke Ellington:

> Duke Ellington has already conquered Europe. Huge crowds met him this summer in England. The left wing of Negro musicians grouped around him is linking up with the radical intelligentsia

of the West. . . . The best jazz bands of the world are unable to avoid the influence of this talented pianist, director, and composer.

Having introduced Ellington's name and protected him against any Association of Proletarian Musicians criticism that might still have lingered, Kolbasev continued:

> Ellington believes strictly in improvisation and almost always plays without written music. He gives his musicians a general sketch of the brief section between separate solos and they then work it out independently. He himself then links the separate sections into a single whole. But even the final work changes from performance to performance, as you can hear in the different recordings of "Mood Indigo.". . .[36]

Kolbasev was not the sole source for American jazz records in the 1930s. Sergei Prokofiev, for example, sought out younger members of the American Embassy in order to keep abreast of the latest hits.[37] But only Kolbasev combined a large collection with an intimate knowledge of the subject. Throughout the early Stalin era, this selfless enthusiast preached his crusade wherever an audience could be assembled. He was to perish in the purge of 1937.

Access to American recordings was the crucial ingredient in the development of Soviet jazz in the 1930s. Scores of aspiring jazzmen from Voronezh to Vladivostok formed their concept of the music by doggedly practicing solo passages with 78 rpm records until they had mastered them, or until the record was worn out. Soviet enthusiasts had no direct access to touring American jazz bands between the departure of Benny Peyton in 1926 and the arrival of the Mitchell-Ruff Duo in 1959. Jelly Roll Morton, who had never traveled abroad, came close to making the trip in 1930, thanks to the recommendations to European promoters by his old New Orleans friend Sidney Bechet. But when members of his Red Hot Peppers discovered they could not send rubles out of Russia to their families, they refused to go. This non-event turned out to be a major turning point in the series of failures that led eventually to Morton's early death.[38] For the Russians it meant further isolation from live American jazzmen.

The International Circuit

Although the Soviet public was cut off from direct contact with American jazz musicians in the thirties, it was not completely isolated from developments abroad. During the years 1934–36 at least seven bands from Western and Central Europe are known to have accepted invitations to perform in the Soviet Union. Among the first to come was the Berlin orchestra of Bobby Astor, whose highly publicized appearance at Leningrad's Park of Rest drew crowds in the summer of 1934. Heaven knows what Astor did, but Georgi Landsberg, the former Leningrad bandleader who had played jazz in the West in the twenties, judged the performances "disgraceful." The Englishman Hale Winn fared little better when he performed in Moscow that same summer. His pickup band was poorly rehearsed, but praise was extended to individual soloists. The following summer Jack Barton brought another British pickup band to Leningrad and Moscow. This group, too, was judged inadequate in its ensemble playing and generally weak.[39]

These were, of course, pronouncements of Soviet musicians and critics rather than the dancing and listening public, which warmly welcomed all the touring British groups. They do, however, reveal the Russian critics' persistent high-culture bias, which assigned greater importance to flashy arrangements and clean, "professional" performance than to raw swing. The ideal European group in Russians' eyes would have been that of Jack Hylton, whose London-based band had been recording since 1921. And in fact Hylton's recordings, with their pretentious if thoroughly musical arrangements, were highly regarded in the Soviet Union, even though the group never got closer to Moscow than Leipzig.[40] Georgi Landsberg gave Hylton the ultimate compliment by identifying his group in print as an "an American *dzhaz*." [41]

The 1934 visit of Macki Berg's small group from Sweden and the tour of a Dutch ensemble later opened new perspectives to the Russians.[42] Far more than previous visitors, the musicians in these two bands sought out their Soviet colleagues and treated them as equals. Berg, who led one of the best swing bands in Scandinavia, had particularly high praise for Alexander Tsfasman's piano playing, while the Dutch band (whose identity is otherwise lost) earned respect and gratitude by hiring more than half a dozen Russian jazzmen for its performances in Moscow and Leningrad. The freewheeling and raucous style of Berg's group, on the stand and off, also endeared them to the Russian musicians. Here, finally, were European jazzmen who played hot and drank hard. Their brief stint at the Metropol in Moscow did much to revitalize the image of jazz musicians as devil-may-care individualists, demanding and getting their freedom from all puritanic conventions.

The 1935 visit of Weintraub's Syncopators to Moscow and Leningrad evoked more disparate reactions. Billed as an "American jazz ensemble,"[43] the Syncopators were in reality the remains of a well-known Berlin cabaret orchestra of the 1920s. The Weintraub band had one major point in its favor in Russia. As Jews driven out of Berlin after the rise of Hitler, its musicians could be praised as victims of fascism. But the Syncopators were also first-class musicians who had developed a polished, highly commercialized show. In their flamboyant showmanship they were what George Simon, the historian of jazz of the swing era, has called a "Mickey Mouse act."[44] The trombonist wound up "Tiger Rag" lying on his back, while in another number he served as a kind of referee in a boxing match of four bar breaks performed by a trumpeter and saxophonist.

For all their clichés and sensational tricks, however, Stefan Weintraub's seven-piece Syncopators were a far hotter band than any that had appeared in Russia since Peyton and Bechet. Soviet musicians and critics were uniformly impressed with the strength the band derived from sheer swing as opposed merely to smooth execution.[45] The band was extremely well received on an initial fifty-day tour in the late spring of 1935 and returned in the autumn for a full year's tour of the USSR. During this time the Syncopators apparently had contact with Soviet jazz musicians and even made several recordings with Russian performers. Unfortunately, no copies of these rare discs are known to have survived.[46] The band's tight ensemble and exuberant rhythm can still be heard on the track to Marlene Dietrich's *The Blue Angel* and on a number of recordings made in Germany, Italy, and Japan during the early 1930s.[47]

Of all the European groups to tour the USSR in the thirties, none achieved a more signal success than Antonin Ziegler's big swing band from Prague.[48] Under various names, this sixteen-piece ensemble toured from one end of the Soviet Union to the other throughout the years 1934–37 and introduced more Soviet citizens to jazz than any foreign group before it.

When Western Europeans and Americans consider Western influences on Russia, they all too often think only of France, Germany, England, and America. From Moscow, however, the West begins in Lithuania and Estonia and has as three of its principal centers Warsaw, Budapest, and Prague. Over the centuries, Western influences from Central European staging areas have penetrated Russia as much as those from the larger centers of Paris, London, and Berlin. Russians' contact with jazz was no exception. Whether it is Alexander Varlamov listening to jazz from Hungarian radio in the 1920s[49] or Soviet bop musicians traveling to Warsaw in the 1960s, Central Europe has more often than not been the mediator between West and East. In jazz, the tour of Ziegler's Jazz Revue began this process in 1934.

The jazz life of the Czech capital rivaled that of any other European city except London, Berlin, Paris, or Brussels. The singer Emil Burian had published his pioneering study *Jazz* there in 1928, and such bands as R. A. Dvorski and His Melody Boys or Ladislav Vachulka's Smiling Boys were regularly featured at the Ace of Hearts and other Prague cafés. Jazz had penetrated the music of several Czech classical composers, and battles of bands were an established feature of the concert and nightclub life of Prague.[50] Independent Czechoslovakia recognized the USSR in June 1934, and almost immediately the Soviet tourist bureau Intourist made contact with a Prague booking agent to engage what was specified as a "representative dance orchestra of modern tendencies" to play at the Metropol Restaurant in Moscow.[51]

Antonin Ziegler had been struggling under a less than lucrative

contract with the Prague coffeehouse Metro and jumped at the possibility of this exotic means of keeping his large swing band together. His musicians saw things differently. Many refused outright
to go to the USSR, and the entire membership of the band turned
over several times before the final contract was signed in September
1934.

Arriving in Moscow on October 1 with twenty crates full of instruments, Ziegler's Jazz Revue began working the midnight to three
A.M. shift at the Metropol. The work was light, so the group added
afternoon performances at a circle of seven Moscow movie theaters
and an evening show at the Moscow Music Hall. Within a week
after its first show at the Metropol, the Jazz Revue sold out performances wherever it appeared.

Knowledgeable Americans who heard Ziegler's band felt that it
played "pretty good jazz but not very up-to-date." Three young
jazz fans associated with the American Embassy took it upon themselves to get Ziegler to use a snappier beat. Ziegler was invited to
perform at the embassy on July 4, 1935. At 8:00 P.M. white-tied
diplomats and their ladies arrived at the Spasso House and filed
into the elegantly columned receiving room for the formal cere-
mony in honor of the United States holiday. The Czech orchestra,
coached by the young Americans, burst into a hot, jazzed-up version of "The Star Spangled Banner." The entire assembly exploded
in laughter and applauded the band's improved, more hard-driving
beat.[52]

Intourist had intended Ziegler's band to play exclusively for foreign tourists. But the Moscow public immediately came to domi-
nate the audience, and clamored for livelier fare than the dated
American popular songs the band had been serving up. "Negro
fox-trots" made their appearance, thanks to printed arrangements
by Fletcher Henderson and other leading American jazzmen, and
Celestina Cole, formerly with the Varlamov orchestra, was engaged
to add authenticity to the band's appearance, if not its sound.[53]

Within a year of Ziegler's debut, word about his Jazz Revue had
reached other cities in the USSR. Intourist, which could now call
on several homegrown groups to work the Metropol, sent Ziegler's

band on a year-long tour that included Kiev, Tblisi, Erevan, Sverdlovsk, Stalingrad, Leningrad, and eastward as far as Chita, near the
Mongolian border in Siberia. Once in the provinces, the group had
to respond to the more conservative tastes of small-town booking
offices and the down-home public. As one of the musicians politely
wrote, "The public here still has its own idea of what jazz is."[54]
Russian folk songs and even a few ideological "mass songs" were
added to the repertoire. At this point, however, Ziegler was accused
of black-marketeering, and suddenly resigned from the band and
left the USSR. In 1938, Ziegler sympathized with the Fascists and
in 1945 left Prague with the retreating Germany army. He was last
seen playing jazz in West Berlin in 1946–47.[55]

The orchestra returned to Moscow without Ziegler, renamed itself Johnson's Band after an earlier Czech group that had been popular in Prague, and settled into a long engagement at the Aurora
coffeehouse. Until its departure from the USSR at the height of the
purges in November 1937, it successfully revived its original repertoire and gained new popularity in the course of another extended tour of the provinces.

Protection in High Places

The success of Ziegler's Jazz Revue in the USSR would have been
impossible without official patronage. The fact that a swing band
from bourgeois Czechoslovakia could have toured from one end of
the country to the other attests to the degree of official acceptance
the new music enjoyed. Any doubts were removed in the presence
of the entire Moscow diplomatic corps on the anniversary of the
October Revolution in 1934.

As was the usual custom, the Soviet government invited all foreign diplomats resident in the capital to a lavish Kremlin reception
to commemorate the event on November 7.[56] As was customary,
too, a brass oom-pah band from the local Red Army garrison provided background music. The 1934 reception was particularly important because the Soviet Union was beginning to court Western
favor as part of a policy later known as the United Front. Stalin,

Kalinin, and the entire Politburo were present, as were such renowned military figures as generals Kliment Voroshilov and Mikhail Tukhachevsky.

At the height of the festivities the army bandsmen suddenly stopped playing, packed up their instruments, and left. For half an hour the elegant assembly in St. Andrew's Hall stood about in perplexity. Then, to the amazement of all, Antonin Ziegler and his Jazz Revue took the bandstand and began pounding out swing music. The foreign diplomats hesitated, uncertain what to do. Only when General Voroshilov and his wife began fox-trotting did the stupified diplomats adjust to the new situation.[57] Jazz, even cabaret jazz from bourgeois Czechoslovakia, was now acceptable, a fact noted with considerable astonishment by Hitler's Moscow embassy in a report to Berlin.[58]

Further evidence that American jazz enjoyed official Soviet patronage began at once to pile up. A reasonably favorable account of jazz had already appeared in the 1931 edition of the *Large Soviet Encyclopedia*. In Leningrad, a City Jazz Commission had been organized in 1933 to upgrade the quality of local ensembles. That composer Dmitri Shostakovich was among those assigned to the task indicates that the local cultural establishment considered it to be of some importance. One of the Commission's few accomplishments was to organize a cycle of lecture-concerts at the end of 1933, called "Jazz in the West and in the USSR." Along with such recorded Western classics as Ray Noble's "By the Fireside" and Shelton Brooks's "Some of These Days," the audience was treated to Isaac Dunaevsky's jazzed-up fantasy based on themes from Tchaikovsky's *Eugene Onegin* and Rimsky-Korsakov's *Sadko*, as well as Anna Zhivotova's newly written "Suite for Jazz Band."[59]

The establishment of the State Variety Agency (*Gosestrada*) in 1935 provided a national body empowered to foster and guide the development of all officially sanctioned jazz and variety orchestras. The following year the Central Committee of the Communist party set up an All-Union Committee on Arts Affairs to channel money for the training and employment of musicians in all the arts, including jazz. Its deputy director was Boris Shumiatsky, a knowl-

edgeable and outspoken jazz fan whose forthright defense of jazz
in the pages of *Pravda* was fated to provoke a genuine crisis within
a year.[60] The attempt to foster the development of popular culture
"from above" may have been naive and inappropriate, but the
original purpose of these two agencies was benign, though rooted
in the tradition of government patronage that had long prevailed
in Russia.

The support for jazz shown by individual officials of the Stalin
regime was just as important as the institutional patronage. A typical patron was General Kliment Voroshilov, a Bolshevik since 1904
and, as head of the Fifth Army in 1918, the organizer of a key Red
Army victory in the Civil War.[61] Voroshilov had little acquaintance
with jazz but was attracted to its jaunty rhythms and had taken
dancing lessons with his wife. In 1937, he went out of his way to
protect Yuli Hait, composer of "Higher and Higher," a jazz march
which celebrated the achievements of Soviet aviation.[62]

Far more conspicuous than Voroshilov's defense was the patronage of jazz by Stalin's sinister aide, First Secretary of the Moscow
Party Committee and purger of the Soviet railways, Lazar Kaganovich. Kaganovich had been introduced to jazz in 1931 by Leonid
Utesov, the Odessa-born bandleader whose "theatrical jazz band"
had achieved phenomenal popularity.[63] No friend of seedy nightclubs and bars, Kaganovich considered jazz to be " . . . above all
the friend of the jolly, the musical organizer of our high-spirited
youth."[64] In a widely distributed brochure published in 1939, Kaganovich and Utesov instructed railroad workers throughout the
USSR on *How To Organize Railway Ensembles of Song and Dance
and Jazz Orchestras*. Their purpose in publishing the handbook
was nothing less than to establish at every railroad station in the
USSR a *dzhaz* to entertain and enliven the local populace. Kaganovich's view of jazz was thoroughly tame, his ideal being the Paul
Whiteman orchestra.[65] Nonetheless, in the booklet, he and Utesov
identified improvisation as a "characteristic stylistic feature of jazz
music" and waxed eloquent on the importance of playing with a
rich, even sensuous, vibrato.

There were small-scale Kaganoviches elsewhere in the Soviet Union who used their authority to patronize jazz. In their zeal on behalf of jazz, few outdid First Secretary of the Ural District Committee of the Communist Party Ivan Dmitrevich Kabakov. Kabakov ruled as virtual tsar of the Urals. All local offices in Sverdlovsk in the early thirties were adorned with two portraits, one of Stalin and one of Kabakov. The regional dictator used his power to patronize jazz at every opportunity. It was the only music heard at his *dacha*. Leaders of the two aspiring swing bands in the city had direct access to Kabakov and could turn to him for help in acquiring instruments or sheet music. Kabakov indulged his passion for jazz from the day of his appointment until his arrest in May 1937.[66]

At a still more modest level were the many low-ranking Party and government officials who by their toleration or support of jazz helped to protect it. Several times a year the staff of the prestigious Vakhtangov Theater in Moscow gave banquets to which were invited musicians, writers, ballerinas from the Bolshoi, and those Party officials who benefited from special freedoms and were not forbidden to associate with dubious artistic elements. The best jazz bands in the city were on hand, and the dancing went on until dawn. The presence of Party members assured the safety of all.[67]

Standoff

French anthropologist Claude Lévi-Strauss observed, " . . . civilization is no longer a fragile flower to be carefully preserved and reared with great difficulty here and there in sheltered corners of the territory. . . . All that is over: humanity has taken to monoculture, once and for all. . . ."[68] This, in effect, was what occurred in Soviet popular culture and music during the late twenties and thirties, except in the USSR two different forms of monoculture were competing for hegemony. First, the Association of Proletarian Musicians had attempted to create a popular music that was absolutely new in form and Communist in ideology. But even at the height of the Cultural Revolution, the Association had brought forth little music, and what they did produce was unpopular. The Association was liquidated in 1932, leaving a vacuum that was quickly filled by the second form of monoculture, jazz. In the few brief years 1932–36, jazz—or what was thought to be jazz—dominated Soviet popular music to a far greater extent than the Association-sponsored works had ever done.

Rationalized in terms of an emerging monoculture for workers, jazz paradoxically appealed most to those who sought relief from Stakhanovite toil and from the oppressive demands of the future. Jazz may not have constituted an alternative to Communist idealism, but it certainly provided respite from it, shelter that enabled the individual to survive in the face of the onerous demands placed upon him. Hence, the position of jazz in these early years of Stalin's rule was highly unstable and shored up principally by the fact that its success was rooted in genuinely popular emotions. Until the end of 1936, jazz held sway in the larger urban centers. It kept at bay not only the ideologues' persistent demands for martial Communist songs, but also the powerful conservative pressures that sought to create a viable popular music on the basis of old Russian folk songs and ballads. So long as this delicate standoff was maintained, the Red Jazz Age continued.

7

Two Jazzmen of the Stalin Era: Tsfasman and Utesov

He [Tsfasman] was the uncrowned king of Russia!
Juri Jelagin, concertmaster,
State Jazz Orchestra of the USSR

Please broadcast all the new tunes by Utesov's wonderful jazz orchestra over the Comintern radio station.
Letter to Radio Comintern from four
Soviet listeners, Nov. 19, 1937

It may seem strange to speak of market forces operating in Stalin's Russia. But when the restaurant manager at the Continental Hotel in Kiev first hired a *dzhaz*, he did so because his clientele demanded it, not because he was commanded to by his superiors. Once on the bandstand, the various orchestras performing at the Continental had to be keenly attentive to the tastes of their audience. If the public wanted to hear "Sweet Sue" or "At the Samovar," they had to be able to play it. Their jobs depended on it.

Genuine popular culture must always be responsive to market forces, and in the Soviet Union during the early 1930s these still differed from region to region, and from city to city. Petr Rozenkern's band in Odessa naturally favored tunes known to the public there, especially the many lusty ballads from that city's Moldovanka quarter. By contrast, urbane Leningraders bent an ear to melodies pirated from the classics, or to current *Schlagers* from Berlin or Paris. Simon Kagan's five-piece Hawaiian Ensemble did well in Moscow, but its repertoire of American pop tunes and jazz would have seemed alien to collective farm peasants from Ivanovo-Voznesensk.

The diversity of the world of Soviet jazz was reinforced by mundane, practical circumstances. The absence of stock arrangements forced each ensemble to be unique, even when modeled after the same prototype. If a particular arranger succeeded in transcribing parts from an American or a Western European recording, the score rarely left his own group, let alone the city. Few groups toured, due to the difficulty of travel on trains bursting with displaced peasants and remnants of the families of liquidated kulaks. Hence, a musician in Kharkov had practically no opportunity to meet his colleagues in Tblisi or Novosibirsk and often did not even know their names. Down to 1934, at least, the sole common elements among the Soviet Union's several score *dzhazes* was their instrumentation (which approximated that of American big bands of the swing era), a bouncing and mildly syncopated rhythm in 2/4 or 4/4 time, and a style of performance on the trumpet, saxophone, and trombone built around the use of vibrato and eccentricities of various sorts.

During the Red Jazz Age that extended to 1936, these highly idiosyncratic jazz ensembles came increasingly to resemble one another. Diversity gradually gave way to uniformity. But against the background of Stalin's massive effort to standardize Soviet economic life in precisely these years, is there anything surprising in this? The argument that the new shift toward uniformity in jazz was a result of the "command economy" gains plausibility in light of Soviet cultural policies. A sweeping decree of May 1932 compelled all architects, writers, painters, and composers to join national unions. Preexisting local, regional, and national associations were liquidated. Henceforth, the organizational aspects of an artist's life were virtually identical, whether he was in Alma-Ata or Minsk. Surely, then, jazz music and popular culture were also standarized "from above"?

But the growth of uniformity among Soviet jazz ensembles owed nothing to state control, which until the mid-thirties had scarcely penetrated the field. There were powerful centralizing influences at work, but these were the product of new market forces, not state action. Specifically, the improvement in communications within the

USSR made possible the rise of jazz "stars" who set styles nationally. These stars operated as independent entrepreneurs, responding to the tastes of specific markets and exercising their leadership through many of the same methods used by their counterparts in the West. The top Soviet jazzmen of the early thirties were capable musicians and even better promoters. The best among them were exceptional personalities as well, trend setters who shaped and crystalized the tastes of their Soviet audiences no less than had Harry James or Cab Calloway in America.

Many bandsmen aspired to stardom. Along with such deliberately jazz-oriented figures as Varlamov, Skomorovsky, and Landsberg, there were the heads of those more conservative but nonetheless successful dance bands that provided fox-trots for so many birthday gatherings, anniversaries, and promotion parties in the Stalin era, men with names like Ginzburg, Heigner, Kemper, and Berezovsky. The list of worthy candidates for the title of star bandsman is long. But by any measure, the top jazzmen of the early Stalin era were Alexander Tsfasman and Leonid Utesov. They were the most famous jazz musicians in Russia, the most recorded, the most frequently filmed, the most often heard on the radio, and the most sought-after for concerts, dances, and parties.

They were also by far the richest. Utesov's wealth was proverbial. A visiting British writer surveyed the Moscow scene in 1940 and pronounced him "Russia's richest man and the king of Soviet jazz."[1] Forty years later, when the image of the starving blues musician gained popularity among Soviet youth, Utesov was embarrassed by his former opulence and went out of his way to minimize it.[2] No one was fooled. Tsfasman never bothered to hide the substantial fortune he had earned as a jazz musician, preferring instead to flaunt it through high living. Such were the fruits of stardom.[3]

Superficially, Tsfasman and Utesov had much in common. Both were Jews from families of modest means, and both had migrated to Moscow from heavily Jewish cities in the south in search of fame and fortune. Like Al Jolson in *The Jazz Singer*, they seized on the new American music as a means of establishing a niche for themselves in the non-Jewish world. The notion that culture should be marshalled to promote a political or social purpose was alien to both these stars of Soviet jazz. Each viewed his art as an end in itself, believing with Montaigne that entertainment and diversion need no special justification. But for all their similarities, Tsfasman and Utesov were fundamentally dissimilar in their relationships both with jazz and with Russian and Soviet culture as a whole. Though their fascination with an alien form of popular music set them both apart from the masses, from that point their ways parted.

An issue which divided many people at the time concerned the best way for the USSR to avail itself on the latest developments abroad. Two schools of thought existed. On one side were those who wanted the Soviet Union to borrow wholesale whatever was necessary to its progress, whether it be machine tools or art forms. Such people were convinced that many aspects of modern life pioneered in the West would be suitable for Communist Russia with little or no modification. On the other side was a much larger group who agreed that Russia must borrow from abroad but insisted that whatever was taken from the West should first be adapted and transformed to render it suitable to the unique conditions and aspirations of the Soviet Union. The dominant concept of the former group was the *adoption* of foreign ways; the guiding ideal of the latter was their *adaptation*.

Tsfasman and Utesov would probably have felt uncomfortable with such philosophizing. Yet through their music and by their actions each of them took a clear stand: Tsfasman was the adopter and the cosmopolitan, Utesov the adapter and the nationalist. Such polarities were by no means new to Russian culture in the 1930s. Early in the nineteenth century the terms "Westernizer" and "Slavophile" had been coined to describe the contrasting positions. While one must wince at describing Utesov, a Jew from Odessa, as a Slavophile, the characterization is nonetheless accurate insofar as it pertains to his attitude toward cultural borrowings from abroad, just as Tsfasman can be categorized as a Westernizer. These traditional characterizations, however, fail to capture the subtle compound of artistic and human elements that combined in the Stalin era to make these men the Soviet Union's first national stars of jazz. To understand this chemistry, we must turn to the jazzmen themselves.

Alexander Tsfasman: Jazz Straight from the Wood

When Tsfasman introduced his first instrumental ensemble to Moscow in 1928, any group in Russia featuring a saxophone and drum set could pass for a jazz band. Within five years the picture had changed dramatically. In the major cities, at least, audiences had become more discriminating. Some groups, like Boris Krupyshev's Blue Jazz, fell by the wayside, while others, notably Georgi Landsberg's big band, retreated from the increasingly competitive free market into secure studio jobs. The general standard of performance rose, but the achievement of most bands remained modest, due to the absence of direct contact with first-rank musicians from America. The extent to which this gap was narrowed at all before 1939 was due almost entirely to the exertions of the pianist, arranger, and bandleader Alexander Tsfasman.

No figure in the history of Soviet jazz can claim more firsts than Tsfasman. He was the first soloist in Soviet jazz and the first Russian to make a profession in the new music. His well-known AMA Jazz Band, founded under the aegis of the Association of Moscow Artists, was the first in the USSR to record, the first to perform live on radio, the first to appear in a sound film, and—significantly— the first to engage in informal jam sessions instead of programmed performances. Beyond this, he was the first Soviet jazz musician to earn sincere praise from a Western European or American jazzman—in this case, the visiting Swede Makki Berg, who heard Tsfasman improvise in 1934.[4] A notoriously cool personality, Tsfasman was nonetheless moved by Berg's compliment.

Throughout his life Tsfasman called on Soviet jazz musicians to strive to attain the level of the best foreign bands. In a 1966 magazine interview titled "Jazz and Jazzomania" he asserted:

It is surely time now to realize that we should have ensembles
and orchestras which stand on a level with the very best foreign
jazz collectives; I have in mind their level of technical execution
and mastery, and not simply the native ability of their participants.[5]

Tsfasman's cosmopolitan perspective on jazz might have been
the fruit of foreign travel, but, unlike Parnakh, Teplitsky, or even
Utesov, Tsfasman did not go abroad until he was nearly sixty, and
then only to Prague and Warsaw. His musical cosmopolitanism was
born in Moscow and nurtured solely on the few pieces of shrapnel
from the Western jazz explosion to reach the Soviet capital. As so
often happened in Soviet cultural life in those years, what began as
a hothouse flower gained strength and perennial vigor when exposed to a hostile climate. With implacable determination, Tsfasman dedicated himself to fostering the new American music
throughout the most gruesome years of Stalin's rule.

There was a pathos in this man's infatuation with America. He
was never permitted to travel to the United States and, in fact, spoke
English poorly. Yet in the depths of the Cultural Revolution in 1930
he defiantly engaged an American Negro tap dancer named Scott
to appear with his band. Among his musicians Tsfasman was known
as "Bob," and in 1936 he even found an American wife, a xylo-
phonist named Gertrude Grandel. The marriage soon fell victim to
the purges, and Gertrude was asked to leave the country.[6] Un-
daunted, Tsfasman continued as before to pack his band's repertoire with American hit tunes like "Some of These Days" and "Smoke
Gets in Your Eyes."

Tsfasman made no attempt to hide his feelings about the U.S.
During the 1934–35 season he was asked to perform "Rhapsody
in Blue" with an orchestra from a Moscow theater. To show the
musicians how the work should be played, he brought Paul Whiteman's recording of the Gershwin classic to a rehearsal. Even with
this guidance, the clarinetist could not manage the two octave glissando with which the work opens. In despair, the poor man turned
to Tsfasman for help. "Don't even try," Tsfasman admonished,

"Nothing would come of it. To play like that you have to be paid in dollars and not in Soviet rubles!"[7]

To the end of his life Tsfasman opposed the notion of "Soviet jazz," which he considered to be a politically inspired form of provincialism. During the purges he was compelled by Party authorities to conduct a political education course for his musicians and brief them on the international situation as recounted in *Pravda*. Tsfasman complied but began his lectures by announcing that "America is not something the cat dragged in! America is . . . Yes! . . . Yes!"[8] None of his surviving friends can recall Tsfasman having ever given vent to his hostility toward the Association of Proletarian Musicians. Yet every aspect of his daily life was a kind of unspoken challenge to the Association's mentality.

A saxophonist with the group judged Tsfasman "unquestionably one of the best dressed men in the Soviet Union."[9] Short and of trim build, Tsfasman had a vast wardrobe of custom-tailored suits in bright colors, especially blues, greens, and maroons. In the summertime he favored whites and light tans, all quite extraordinary in Stalin's Russia. To heighten the effect he assembled a formidable collection of silk cravats, which gave his elegance a decidedly European cast. Just to maintain this extravagant persona must have demanded prodigious expenditures of time and money, not to mention research into underground sources for fine fabrics.

Tsfasman's manner was tailored with equal care. Aloof and even unfriendly, he is recalled as wearing a snobbish mask on his strangely immobile face. He rarely socialized with his musicians. Photographs often show him in white tie and tails, his hair slicked down. Rarely does he look into the camera. And yet this same dandified snob was a social lion in Stalin's Moscow. "He was enormously popular; everyone knew him," recalls the art collector George Costakis.[10] He loved a good party and was sought after for weekends at surburban *dachas*. Evgeni Vakhtangov, founder of Moscow's progressive Vakhtangov Theater, considered him a prize guest at his annual New Year's Eve party. Bob Tsfasman became the darling of the intelligentsia. His independence and his sartorial elegance were like fresh air in a stuffy room, an assertion of autonomy amidst rising conformity.

Tsfasman's meticulous concern for style, musical as well as personal, also shielded him from the persistent charge that jazz was vulgar. In the very years when Soviet citizens were being told that the worst sin was to be "uncultured" (*nekulturnyi*) and when claims concerning the proletarian and earthy nature of jazz still lingered, Tsfasman archly turned his back on the entire debate and continued to play as he liked. This, too, reinforced his stardom.

This paragon of bourgeois stylishness was the son of a Jewish barber in Zaporozhe, then called Elizavetgrad. At the age of twelve, Tsfasman moved with his family to Nizhni Novgorod, where he eventually entered a local music school, majoring in violin and piano. In 1922–23, at the age of sixteen, he wrote "Jimmy," a fox-trot, and also "The Sky Trot" ("Skaitrott") and "The Eccentric Dance." [11] Then came a half-dozen years at the prestigious Moscow Conservatory, where Tsfasman studied piano under one of the finest pedagogues of the twentieth century, Felix Blumenfeld. Throughout his career, Tsfasman boasted of his classical training and fought bitterly to stamp out the rumor that he had quit the Conservatory to take up jazz. Forty years later he took to the pages of *Time* magazine to set the record straight on this point in America.[12] He also argued that jazz should be taught in the conservatories and publicly praised Dizzy Gillespie for defending that proposition. Tsfasman's highbrow emphasis on the "laws of form" gave his music a certain coldness and lack of "soul," but it also led him to attain a technical mastery unmatched in Russian jazz until the 1960s. This same attitude enabled him to form popular tastes rather than follow them. Nor did theorizing close Tsfasman's mind to change: years later he enthusiastically welcomed bop and objected to the Beatles only on the ground that their music was passé.[13]

Tsfasman came into jazz on Benny Peyton's coattails. His AMA Jazz Band consisted of trumpeter, trombonist, drummer, banjo player, clarinetist who doubled on sax, and Tsfasman on piano. Tsfasman rounded out the ensemble with a baritone sax rather than string bass or tuba,[14] an innovation that suggests the influence of recordings by Bix Beiderbecke. As we have seen, the AMA Jazz Band was extraordinarily successful, and within two years of its foundation it not only had appeared on Moscow radio but had issued the first Soviet jazz recording, Harry Warren's "Seminole" and Vincent Youmans's "Hallelujah!" The AMA Jazz Band's last stand before the Cultural Revolution was at the fashionable Casino Restaurant on Triumphal (now Mayakovsky) Square in Moscow. Influenced by Peyton and Bechet, the band pounded away in a style that was both hot and loud. Bacheev's drum solos were especially popular with the young audiences who came to the Casino to dance, drink, and play roulette. A fan recalls the dignified old-school majordomo wincing and holding his ears as he seated his customers.[15]

For the first time, Russian musicians not only were emulating the musical idiom of jazz but were doing so in a way that fully reproduced the uninhibited social environment in which jazz flourished in the West. The musicians associated with Tsfasman were notorious for their freewheeling style of life. They drank hard, even for Russians, and one of their number, saxophonist Alexander Vasiliev, eventually died of alcoholism. Most were devoted gamblers as well. Once, in 1935, the Tsfasman band was scheduled to perform at the Bolshoi Theater. A large backstage room was designated for the musicians to warm up in. Instead of tuning up, they settled down to gamble, first at dominoes, then at cards. Whenever theater personnel opened the door to check on the group, they were stunned at the sight of what appeared to be a dozen professional gamblers hard at their trade. Dumbfounded at this brazen behavior in the atmosphere of fear generated by the first purges, the staff would beat a hasty retreat.[16]

The stakes in the band's games were high, literally as well as figuratively. Israel Robei, a violinist with Tsfasman, pointed out the white-haired baritone sax player to his desk mate, a new member of the band. Robei then explained the presence of this dignified-looking senior citizen in the orchestra. The saxophonist, it seems, was a passionate gambler. One night, playing cards on the bandstand, he lost six thousand rubles. Someone in the audience noticed

the game and reported him. After a night in the local jail, the saxophonist returned the next day, white-haired.[17]

The aura of defiant nonconformity that surrounded the Tsfasman band only increased its popularity. And while the musicians
flaunted their freedom from convention in ways that left them only
millimeters on the safe side of the law, Tsfasman himself gained
fame for his high-handed treatment of Soviet bureaucrats. Only a
star would dare to take the liberties he did. Once, for example, he
got into a scrape with the chief of police in Tblisi, the capital of
Stalin's native Georgia. After knocking the man to the ground,
Tsfasman explained his action by saying, " . . . there are thousands
of idiots like you, but there is only one Tsfasman." Apparently, the
head gendarme agreed, for the next day he delivered a personal
apology to Tsfasman at his hotel, along with a dozen bottles of a
fine old Georgian wine.[18]

Another time, in the summer of 1936, Tsfasman's group was appearing at the Hermitage Gardens under a contract which specified
that the musicians should be paid in advance. It was a grim time in
the Soviet Union, and Moscow's Lubianka Prison was already full
of victims of the purges. The entire high command of the Moscow
musical world turned out for the band's final rehearsal. The head
of the State Committee on Art Affairs was there, as was the entire
censorship board, the notorious Repertory Commission (*Repertkom*). Unfortunately, the management had neglected to bring the
musicians their pay envelopes. With staggering hauteur, Tsfasman
told the band, "Pick up your instruments and let's go home, boys!"
And to the assembled dignitaries he announced, "We'll be back when
you deliver the money to our homes. Good-bye! Hope you have a
nice time." With this, Tsfasman donned his dove-gray Stetson and
departed.[19]

Sociologists would certainly classify Tsfasman and his musicians
as deviants. To the Soviet intelligentsia they were free spirits, whose
nonconformity was the more alluring because they seemed to get
by with it. Let the government introduce prison sentences for vio-
lators of labor discipline, as it did in January 1931, or threaten
anyone absent from work for even a day with dismissal, as it did

in December 1932. These jazzmen stood above it all, wild and free, as long as they survived.

Tsfasman did more than survive. A mood of impending political trouble hung over the band during 1928, but by the following year the official Soviet travel agency Hotel (predecessor to Intourist) concluded that Tsfasman posed no danger and therefore invited him to reorganize and expand his group under its patronage. With the addition of a second trumpet, second trombone, and a third saxophone, and with a tuba replacing the baritone sax, the AMA Jazz Band was reborn as the Moscow Guys (*Moskovskie rebiata*). The group toured to such far-flung spots as Baku, Tashkent, Tblisi, Kislovodsk, and Samarkand and began what came to be annual appearances at the Black Sea resort of Sochi.[20] In 1933 the band was expanded once more, bringing it up to the full complement of saxophones, trumpets, and trombones used by American swing bands of the era. It performed at the Central and Forum movie theaters in Moscow and at the Empire and National restaurants.

Tsfasman's huge popularity was fed by many sources: his personal *savoir-faire*, his disdain for Soviet bureaucracy, and his bandsmen's obstreperous life-styles. Even the fifteen-foot-high saxophone cutouts on either side of his bandstand proclaimed that here was forbidden fruit openly available on the public market. Yet if Tsfasman's music had not been fully up to the mark, he would have had to cede the title "uncrowned king of Russia" to Skomorovsky or Varlamov. As it happened, his greatest successes were achieved not as a colorful personality but as a pianist and arranger.

Surviving recordings make it possible to evaluate the quality of Tsfasman's musicianship with some precision. Because the records are mostly ensemble performances, however, they give only glimpses of his skill at improvisation. Yet they do show that he achieved what no Soviet band before him had attempted: he could swing. In his 1930s recording of "A Shanty in Old Shanty Town,"[21] for example, a polka-like beat predominates during the vocals, but then, suddenly, a much hotter rhythm breaks out—unevenly, perhaps, but definitely swinging.

Tsfasman's band boasted a rhythm section that bore comparison with the better continental groups. At its heart was slap bassist Benek Sklenařik, who had come to Russia from Prague with Ziegler's Jazz Revue, married a Russian, and joined the Tsfasman band. Supporting him was drummer Ivan Bacheev, a well-schooled musician, who later had the misfortune to be arrested at the fighting front in World War II and sent to the Gulag for eight years. The guitarist was Anatoli Wonsowic, a Pole known as "The Prince" on account of his family background. Together, they produced a beat that was respectable even by international standards.

Tenor saxophonist Alexander Vasiliev brought the band a tone and style heavily reminiscent of Benny Carter. And trumpeter Mikhail Frumkin had a wonderful growl à la Bubber Miley of the Ellington orchestra, could use a cup mute to good advantage, and could bend his notes with genuine jazz feeling. But only the core group of musicians could improvise, and even they tended to string together chains of clichés. The clarinetist on several recordings was truly terrible. On the other hand, every member of the band was a good reading musician who, as Jelly Roll Morton advised, could "stick to the little black dots." There was not a prima donna among them, and they willingly submitted to Tsfasman's strong direction.

This may have been due in part to their backgrounds. Three of the group were former army bandsmen and a fourth, trombonist Anatoli Milovidov, had trained in a Red Navy band. Tenor saxophonist Ilya Khazanovsky was a barber who had come up through a fire department band. Most were provincials from such places as Kherson, Rostov-on-Don, or Orel. Only one, violinist Israel Robei, was conservatory trained.[22] In all, they were less highbrow by training, more proletarian in origin, and worked more closely together as a unit than the Soviet jazzmen who had preceded them.

Tsfasman's willingness to change personnel set him apart from rival Soviet bandleaders but linked him with colleagues abroad. In the course of his career he fronted at least six bands, beginning with the AMA Jazz Band and ending with a large Glenn Miller-type orchestra in the years 1945–47. Of these groups, the most significant was the Thirteen Virtuosos of 1933–37. Like territorial bands in the United States, the Thirteen Virtuosos had to keep a diversified repertoire, including "Snowflakes," "A Tyrolean Waltz," and even the "March of the Laboring Reserves" for good measure. Yet the Thirteen Virtuosos avoided fads, such as the mid-thirties passion for tangos imported from Poland, and attempted to emulate the styles of such reputable aggregations as the Jimmy Dorsey orchestra and the Benny Goodman band.

Tsfasman had no access to printed arrangements from the West until the war years,[23] but he was never content merely to copy out scores from American records. Whether in his "The Man I Love" or his wartime fantasy on themes from the film *Sun Valley Serenade*, he produced idiomatic and often interesting arrangements of his own. Alone among early Soviet jazzmen (and a great rarity in Europe as a whole), Tsfasman understood the difference between jazz as a recorded experience and jazz as live music. An improviser, he at least tried to capture that quality in his scores.

He certainly achieved a sense of spontaneity in his piano playing. His recorded solo on "The Sound of Jazz" demonstrates a good command of the Harlem stride style, even achieving the delicate tension between the right hand playing on or slightly behind the beat and the rushing left hand. Tsfasman clearly studied recordings by Harlem pianist James P. Johnson; he learned still more from records by Fats Waller. In his solo on his own tune "I'm Sad Without You" ("Mne grustno bez tebia") he shows an ability to play in an absolutely relaxed mode while keeping strictly to the tempo. In postwar recordings, Tsfasman's style takes another turn, introducing both the sparse style of Count Basie and the bravura sixteenth-note runs of Art Tatum. The evolution of Tsfasman's improvisational style indicates that he was working to free himself from the tyranny of the melodic line and beginning to think in terms of chord structures.

Tsfasman's greatest hits were American numbers like "Blue Skies" and "Chattanooga Choo-Choo." Yet he also composed a few tunes that achieved considerable popularity, most notably "The Sound of Jazz," which recalls the old jamming favorite "Angry." In a period when the Soviet government was punishing negativism and individualism with one-way trips to Siberia, Tsfasman's songs frequently dealt with the themes of private sadness and unhappy love. "An Unsuccessful Meeting" and "I'm Sad Without You" are typical. He was at his best on short ballads, but he also tried his hand at more ambitious compositions. His *Concerto for Piano and Orchestra* is a monument to his lifelong infatuation with the music of George Gershwin. At its worst, the two-movement work sounds like a bad score by Rachmaninoff jazzed up in the Hollywood style of the 1930s.[24] Yet it also contains hot trombone solos, moaning orchestral passages that explode into wild piano improvisations, and dense sections with muted brass and saxophones. The principal theme of the first movement calls to mind Fats Waller's "Ain't Misbehavin' " and that of the final movement is like "On the Atchison, Topeka, and Santa Fe" played to a fast 4/4 rhumba beat. All in all, this derivative but thoroughly engaging tribute to Gershwin reveals Tsfasman as an able pops composer, not unlike Leonard Bernstein with his *West Side Story*.

Tsfasman's musical success far surpassed all other Soviet jazzmen until the 1960s. From the time of his appearance in the 1934 hit film *The Whole World Is Dancing*, he was also a popular star and the jazzmen's jazzman of Stalin's Russia. He did not escape severe difficulties, however. Besides his high-handed treatment of the Soviet bureaucracy, he was guilty of two purely musical sins. First, he persisted in his staunch opposition to the notion that a new form of "Soviet jazz" should replace the wicked American music so popular in the West.[25] Second, his increasing emphasis on free improvisation based on chords flew in the face of the emerging doctrine of socialist realism, which emphasized simple melodies that would be "accessible to the masses." In 1937, official booking agents received word that Tsfasman should be snubbed, and in the following year all the best musicians from his orchestra were pirated by the preposterously named State Jazz Orchestra of the USSR. Defiant and resourceful as ever, Bob Tsfasman managed to negotiate a new recording contract in 1939, for which he assembled an entirely new eleven-piece outfit—the first exclusively recording band in the USSR.

After performing for Red Army troops during the war and intro-

ducing the music of Glenn Miller to Russians in the years 1945–
46, Tsfasman was stripped of his orchestra in 1947. Never again
did he enjoy the favored position he had held prior to the purges.
Following the death of Stalin in 1953 he was rehabilitated, named
an Honored Artist of the Russian Republic and even permitted to
travel to Eastern Europe. But the postwar attacks on jazz and on
him personally had left Tsfasman embittered and cynical. In 1957
a rising Soviet jazzman of the next generation encountered him at
the All-Union Theatrical Society on Pushkin Square. Asked if he
intended to start a new orchestra, Tsfasman replied, "I'm old. I
have a good salary, a *dacha* in the country, a wife, and a car. The
Union of Composers asks only that I submit to it each month a
march, a polka, and a waltz. . . . No hassles." [26]

A sad ending in that Tsfasman's bold musical Americanism and
his close personal ties with the Soviet intelligentsia had turned out
to be vulnerable to attack from puritanical Communist officialdom.
But the young Soviet jazzmen of the 1950s revered Tsfasman as
one of the few uncompromised and genuine artists of the old generation, and so his life work must be judged a success.

Jazz Up from Odessa:
Leonid Utesov

At the height of the postwar tide of chauvinism in the USSR, the
government not only tried to cleanse the country of foreign influences but claimed that Russians had invented many things generally thought to have been devised elsewhere. As a foreign import,
jazz came under assault. Singer and bandleader Leonid Utesov, realizing that the very existence of his *dzhaz* was threatened, coun-
terattacked. He used a comic skit to make the argument that jazz
had been invented not in New Orleans but in rowdy and brawling
Odessa, by street musicians improvising at Jewish weddings. Not
realizing that Utesov's boast was tongue-in-cheek, newspapers around
the world took it as a particularly absurd example of Soviet bombast. [27] Utesov's comic sally did not save Soviet jazz, but it at least

helped to deflate the pressure against it. It characterized Utesov's life-long effort to build a bridge between jazz and what *Pravda* writers still call "our Soviet reality."

Utesov's spoof elicited smiles from Moscow sophisticates and roars of laughter from less highbrow audiences, as he had intended. From the beginning, Utesov focused on a more popular audience than Tsfasman. When he first established his Theatrical Jazz Ensemble in 1929, he immediately took it to Leningrad factories to perform during lunch breaks.[28] Reaching out to a lower-class audience, he was quick to adapt Russian folk songs to his repertoire.[29] His humor, his vocal style, his personal deportment, and his very approach to jazz were calculated to reach the mass public. He succeeded to a greater extent than any Soviet musician who has claimed to play jazz before or since.

Utesov's background had prepared him for this role. In the first of his three autobiographies, written in 1939, he describes his father as ambitious for his son, hoping he might practice law or medicine and "dress in a black suit with gold glasses and a trinket on his waistcoat."[30] A later autobiography, written during Khrushchev's thaw, depicts Utesov, Sr., as a good-humored Jewish tradesman of no great ability, who was sentimental, submissive to his domineering wife, and generally a lovable schlemiel. The black suit and waistcoat had been Utesov's mother's idea. Utesov rejected it and her in 1911 by quitting Geig's Commercial School in Odessa and joining a circus run by a colonel in the local police.[31] Through an orchestra led by Misha Perchikovich, a local barber, he then gained experience on violin and guitar before moving on to another circus company as a clown. The Borodanov Circus took the young Utesov on tour through such heavily Jewish towns as Kremenchug, Tulchin, and Bolshoi Tokmak.[32]

In the years before World War I Leonid Utesov sang in operattas, bars, little theaters, and especially music halls.[33] He would perform anything to please his audience, including tearjerker melodramas like "The Countess Elvira" and titillating sketches like "Secrets of the Harem."[34] Long after the Revolution Utesov was still playing the same old roles. In 1923 he was featured as the "Shimmy Clown"

in a Leningrad revue called "Man and Woman"; Georgi Balanchi-
vadze, later famous as George Balanchine, appeared on the same
bill in an act titled "Plastic Man and Woman."[35]

Given the fact that Utesov could not afford to ignore what his
audience wanted, it is interesting that American themes appeared
so frequently in his theatrical repertoire. As early as 1915 he was
appearing as a black-faced minstrel named John Johnson from Brazil, "Brazil" being the Brazilia Hotel in Odessa. "If a Jew named
Mikelmacher can become a Russian named Muratov, why should
Utesov not become John Johnson?" he reasoned.[36] Utesov also had
in his repertoire a popular farce titled "An American Duel," and
was doing frequent performances of the cakewalk as well. At the
end of World War I he introduced a new act, "Odessa Jazz."[37]

Many of Utesov's Jewish friends were also avidly mining American motifs. Among them was Iza Kramer, who won applause for
his "Black Tom" act at the bar of the House of Artists in Odessa
during the Revolution.[38] Utesov and his fellow Jewish-Russian entertainers were, of course, exploiting the European infatuation with
American exotica that was also sweeping Germany, France, and
England in these years. If there was anything distinctive about Utesov's Americanism, it lies in the extent to which, even during this
early period, he conceived of American music in visual and theatrical terms. The gaudy costume, the grin or grimace, the jaunty
pose—these, as much as the form or timbre of the music itself,
attracted his interest.

The Revolution of February 1917 toppled the tsar and fundamentally changed Leonid Utesov's circumstances by abolishing the
Pale of Settlement in the western and southern regions of Russia,
to which Jews had previously been confined. Free to travel, Utesov
immediately accepted an invitation from Olivier's Hermitage in
Moscow and began assimilating to Russian life. The young musi-
cian-actor soon discovered that the Yiddish ballads of his native
Odessa were too local to win wide acceptance in the Russian capital. To reach the public in the rough-and-tumble dance halls and
public gardens south of the Moscow River, Utesov had to chart a
new path. Eventually, he found it in jazz.

Utesov judged the first live jazz band he encountered—Sam Wooding's Chocolate Kiddies—in terms of its impact on the audience. He acknowledged the musicians' skill but noticed that the public was brought to its feet by the tap dancers, not the instrumentalists.[39] He sensed the intimate link between jazz and dancing and seized on this as the key to the new kind of act he was seeking. From this, he gradually evolved the notion of a theatricalized jazz band, or "*Thea-Jazz*," as he dubbed it in Russian. The concept, which recalls Valentin Parnakh's idea of a mimetic orchestra, served to reinforce Utesov's self-identification as actor rather than musician. He titled his first autobiography *Notes of an Actor* and reiterated his preference for theater over music in subsequent editions down to his death in 1982.[40] No wonder, then, that he welcomed an invitation to join the Free Theater in Leningrad.

When the Free Theater closed in 1927, Utesov sought and received permission to go abroad on a tour to Latvia. Once out of the USSR, he extended his trip to Berlin and Paris, where he had occasion to develop further his notion of theatricalized jazz. In Berlin he was delighted by the clown Grok, a consummate humorist who laced his acts with jazzy performances on the saxophone, piano, and violin.[41] Grok had in effect taken Utesov's old "Shimmy Clown" act and replaced the ragtime accompaniment with a jazz beat. Utesov observed closely.

Paris in 1927 was the city of Mistinguette, Maurice Chevalier, and Josephine Baker. Utesov saw them all. With great astuteness he realized that, for all their differences, these *chanteurs de rhythm* had one thing in common: they all sang in a low, intimate voice that drew the listener into the artist's private orbit rather than propelling some stylized personality outward to a faceless audience.[42] This was later to be a key to Utesov's own success in Soviet jazz and popular music. The Folies Bergère, the Moulin Rouge, and other nightclubs in which he heard the idols of nighttime Paris left Utesov cold; he considered them little different from the pre-revolutionary Odessa music halls in which he had begun his career.

By far the most important discovery Utesov made during his European tour was American bandleader and entertainer Ted ("Is everybody happy?") Lewis. Utesov had heard the English band of Jack Hylton in Berlin and probably several French and American jazz groups at L'Ermitage Muscovite in Paris as well. He heard the excellent band of Claude Hopkins, which backed Josephine Baker's *Revue Nègre*, and the several jazz numbers which Mistinguette included in her show. But the unlikely figure of Ted Lewis was to serve as a model for the most popular entertainer in Stalin's Russia.

Purist historians of jazz brand Lewis's group as another "Mickey Mouse act." They acknowledge his good sense in hiring jazzmen like Muggsy Spanier and George Brunies, but dismiss both his clarinet playing and his band as a whole as hopelessly corny.[43] But in the late 1920s Lewis was considered a legitimate spokesman of jazz; he gave an interview on the subject to the *New York Times* in 1926, and in Paris was hailed as a leading exponent of the art.[44] Certainly, he was a showman. When jazz orchestration had become more complex during the twenties, and after Paul Whiteman had pioneered the use of full brass and reed sections, the flamboyant stage behavior of the small improvising Dixieland bands had become difficult, if not impossible. Lewis helped to reverse this process by requiring his men to memorize their parts, which freed them to move about. He also encouraged his musicians to project their personalities more forcefully. When Gene Krupa, the Czech-American drummer, declared, "Me a showman?—Hell, yes!"[45] he was following Ted Lewis's lead. Utesov did so as well, fully aware that he was using his band to create an ideal model of freedom amidst collectivity, of the individual in society.

> Watching the musicians' free style of behavior, their ability to separate themselves momentarily from the general mass of the orchestra and put forth their individuality, I thought "This is just what I need" ... a free style of performance, where each participant within the bounds of the whole is able to give free expression to his fantasy. ... In such a jazz band (if, of course, it could be transformed and made suitable for our popular stage) my passion for theater and for music could be combined.[46]

Thus, Leonid Andreevich Utesov, a Russian Jew from Odessa, approached American jazz through Ted Lewis, born Theodore Leopold Friedman, a Polish Jew from Circleville, Ohio.

Upon his return to Leningrad late in 1927, Utesov began at once to assemble a jazz band. Except for Teplitsky's group, there were virtually no jazzmen in Leningrad, so he had to raid the Philharmonia and other legitimate orchestras. Eventually he assembled ten musicians from the Marinsky (later Kirov) Theater, the Mikhailovsky Theater, the Theater of Satire, and the lordly Philharmonia. He could not have wished for better-schooled musicians. But his basis for selection was not so much pure musicianship as the willingness of each performer to turn entertainer. Some refused. Joseph Hershkowitz, a trombonist from the Mikhailovsky Theater orchestra, drew the line at playing while crouched on one knee.[47] Yakov Skomorovsky also objected to hamming it up while playing and soon broke off to form his own jazz band. Utesov's group finally made its debut in Leningrad on International Women's Day, March 8, 1929, at the Small Opera Theater. It was the height of the Cultural Revolution and the Proletarian Associations opposed to jazz were in their glory. The curtain opened to a brassy fox-trot played by brightly clad musicians whose individual movements and solos were highlighted by moving spotlights. Taking a leaf from Whiteman's book, Utesov mixed American pop tunes with jazzed-up classics from Rimsky-Korsakov's *Le Coq d'Or* and other well-known works. The crowd was ecstatic.[48]

Critical reaction was mixed. The journal *The Life of Art* (*Zhizn iskusstva*) judged the performance a triumph, but applauded Utesov's cheerful humor more than his music.[49] The Association of Proletarian Musicians lost no time in branding Utesov's band and acts like his "musical rubbish" and "music from the era of the New Economic Policy."[50] The lines were drawn.

Utesov's first response to the Association's criticism was to turn to Dmitri Shostakovich with a request to write the music for a jazz revue to be titled *Conditionally Killed*.[51] Gone were "St. Louis Blues" and the jazzed-up classics of the first show; in their place Shostakovich offered a string of uninteresting fox-trots to which the mu-

sicians acted out an inane comedy. It was a flop, but not enough so
to satisfy the Association. They wanted blood. Utesov's back was
to the wall, and his next show, *Jazz at the Crossroads (Dzhaz na
povorote)* was a sordid concession to the Association zealots. He
turned to his old friend and director of the Leningrad Music Hall,
Isaac Dunaevsky, and commissioned from him four orchestral fan-
tasies based on Russian, Ukrainian, Jewish, and "Soviet" folk songs.[52]
Dunaevsky made only the mildest use of jazz rhythms in these works
of 1931, otherwise presenting the indigenous melodies unadorned.
Utesov, tired of being called "one of our Americans" and "a musical prostitute," capitulated . . . and watched his audience slip away
from him.[53]

Realizing his "adaptations" had gone too far, Utesov turned once
more to jazz in his next show, *The Music Store.* In a characteristic
concession to the prevailing political climates he parodied popular
American jazz, but at the same time used the parody as a cover for
playing precisely what the audience wanted. *The Music Store* was
a jazz revue built around the daily events in a musical instrument
shop. By the time of its debut late in 1930, the Association of Proletarian Musicians was in full retreat. Hence, with each performance Utesov allowed the parody to recede further into the background.[54]

Reviewing Utesov's maneuvers during the Cultural Revolution,
one might readily conclude that he was an opportunist ready to
compromise his professed interest in jazz the moment he felt the
political winds shifting against him. There is much to support this
view. During the Civil War Utesov had entertained White Army
officers one week and then signed up to entertain Red Army troops
the moment they appeared to be ascendent. When it was convenient to attack Duke Ellington in 1939, Utesov did so savagely.[55]
But when Ellington visited Moscow in 1971, he sang his praises
and had himself photographed with the man he had denounced as
a "bourgeois formalist."[56] Utesov publicly sided with Gorky's attack on jazz, and several times in his career used jazz to mount
entire evenings of anti-American propaganda.

Utesov realized he was a hypocrite. In an unguarded moment late in the 1930s he complimented Alexander Varlamov on his jazz band and remarked, "I greatly envy you, for you do what you want."[57] In the early 1960s Utesov was visited by an American interested in Soviet jazz. After the visitor left, Utesov spoke with bitterness and melancholy to a younger Soviet colleague, who later set down his remarks:

> [Utesov] said that for more than thirty-five years he had had to fight for jazz, act diplomatically, maneuver, write articles in which everything was "just the opposite." He recalled his recent meeting with the American. "What I told him was not the truth at all," he said. "I could not tell him the truth, especially now—now that I am a god. A god but a liar. . . ."[58]

If Utesov sometimes disgraced himself by spinelessly capitulating to critics, he more often used humor to mount counterattacks. The epigraph for the chapter "Jazz" in his 1939 autobiography was Marx's line, "For the nonmusical, even the fairest music makes no sense at all."[59] When jazz was virtually banned after World War II, Utesov boldly mounted an entire evening of big band swing music, which he introduced by admonishing his audience about the perils of jazz and advising them on the importance of being able to recognize the dreadful music which threatened the very fabric of Soviet life. He had earlier launched what he called "jazz bombs" against the Association of Proletarian Musicians;[60] he now launched them against the camp of culture boss Andrei Zhdanov.

Russians of the post-Stalin era, familiar only with the Utesov whose every birthday was noted in the official press, are often surprised to learn how combative he was earlier. Once, at the height of the purges, Utesov found himself in conversation with Platon Kerzhentsev, who held the portfolio for the arts in Stalin's government until he too was purged. Kerzhentsev hated popular music and told Utesov so. "But surely you know that Vladimir Ilich [Lenin] looked on popular music differently?" Utesov asked. Kerzhentsev listened while Utesov reminded him that Lenin had frequented nightclubs on Montmartre and had particularly liked the singer

Montegues. Kerzhentsev cynically responded, "Sure, but you are no Montegues." "And you are no Lenin, Platon Mikhailovich," Utesov cheerfully replied.[61]

Utesov fared badly when evaluated as a musician. As we shall see, Stalin and several of his worst henchmen liked Utesov's band, reason enough for serious Russian jazzmen to scoff at him.[62] Most jazzmen denied that he was even interested in playing jazz. Certainly, the Utesov band had formidable shortcomings. Unlike Tsfasman's outfit, the Thea-Jazz had no strong rhythm section; fast tunes tumbled along at a gypsy gait devoid of jazz feeling. Only pianist Nikolai Minkh with his almost too precisely syncopated style saved the day. Beyond this, Utesov had a dreadful repertoire, particularly after a 1936 attack on him as "the personification of the ideological level of popular music in the first period of the New Economic Policy."[63] From then on his repertoire was pure Stalinist kitsch, scored in a style directly imitative of Guy Lombardo's Royal Canadians.[64]

Yet, for all this, the American critic James Lincoln Collier has acknowledged that some of Utesov's light riff numbers "could have been played by a second-line American swing band of the period."[65] Down to 1936, at least, the claim is warranted. Tenor saxophonist Arkadi Kotliarsky had mastered the tone, if not the style, of Bud Freeman. Utesov's principal arranger, Leonid Diederichs, scion of a pre-revolutionary St. Petersburg piano manufacturing family, had picked up a good knowledge of big band scoring by studying records by Duke Ellington, Jack Hylton, and other leading Western groups. For several years Ellington's "Daybreak Express" and "Melancholy" were in the repertoire, as were Cole Porter's "A Little House" Frank Trumbauer's "Sunspots," and hot arrangements of "Over There!" and of popular tunes by Ray Noble, George Gershwin, and Shelton Brooks. It was not mere boastfulness when an embittered Utesov, in his seventieth year, answered a visitor's question with the following statement:

> Do you think we [Soviet musicians] don't know what jazz is? For ourselves, when we're alone, we play in a style that Benny Goodman would envy. Believe me, I'm not bragging; I know what I'm talking about. But for the public we play something

different, something "lively." We are forced to pull our left ear with our right hand and our right ear with our left hand. We work as, in ancient times, Comrade Aesop worked. . . . But what else can we do? What can we do when the censor doesn't allow us to breathe; when a certain Apostolov sits on the Central Committee, a stooge who studied with a military bandmaster; when a certain Vartanov sits in the Ministry of Culture, a creep of a clarinet player; when there is a stone-hearted group of song-hacks and tunesmiths in charge of the Union of Composers? Yes, that is how it is.[66]

There was one point in Utesov's career when his genuine interest in American jazz and his tactical willingness to adapt American prototypes came together in a happy musical union: his extraordinarily successful 1934 film *The Happy Guys* (*Veselye rebiata*). Even though the prestigious *Literary Gazette* branded this jazz-tinged musical a "vulgar mistake" and a host of other critics attacked it as an unsuccessful experiment,[67] the rapidly growing youth audience of the Soviet Union loved the film and saw it in an element of mild protest.[68] Foreign critics pronounced it a resounding success when it was previewed at the 1935 Venice Film Festival.[69] When the polemic threatened to reach beyond *The Happy Guys* to broader matters, the Communist party stepped in. In March 1935 the Central Committee viewed the film at a closed screening in the Kremlin. Stalin apparently liked it, for on March 12, 1935, *Pravda* squelched the debate by offering its blessing to *The Happy Guys* and printing a blistering attack on Utesov's critics.[70] Stalin is said to have later seen the film again several times.

The idea of a Soviet jazz comedy originated late in 1932 with Boris Shumiatsky, deputy president of the State Committee on Art Affairs under Platon Kerzhentsev, who so disliked popular music. Shumiatsky had liked *The Music Store* and thought first of simply filming the jazz revue in its entirety.[71] After conversations with Utesov he saw the possibility of transforming the project into a full-scale and original film. Seizing the initiative, Utesov put Shumiatsky in touch with Grigori Alexandrov, a filmmaker who had returned from an extended sojourn in Hollywood only months before. Even in 1932 Alexandrov had ingratiated himself with Stalin, who also admired Mrs. Alexandrov, the singer Liubov Orlova.[72] Isaac Dunaevsky, Utesov's friend and a member of Alexandrov's circle as well, was brought in to write the music.

The plot of *The Happy Guys* revolves around Kostia Potekhin, a simple singing shepherd from the shores of the Black Sea, whose love of music, especially jazz, triumphs over all impediments as he fights and smiles his way clear to Moscow. During his rise to stardom, he is invited to join a jazz band, the Happy Guys. A wild rehearsal scene shows the jazz band at its best, while a performance at the Moscow Music Hall enabled Alexandrov to stage a full-scale Busby Berkeley spectacular.

Having triumphed at the decidedly middle-brow Music Hall, the Happy Guys decide to invade the Bolshoi. En route they participate in a rain-soaked New Orleans-style funeral, complete with hearse and dirge. With their instruments filled with water, the Happy Guys finally burst onto the stage at the venerable Bolshoi. Chaos ensues, and the musicians, unable to play their sodden horns, bring down the house by rendering the film's theme song in a hot scat vocal style borrowed directly and successfully from 1932 recordings by the Boswell Sisters.

From the first, when Buster Keaton is listed in the credits as someone *not* appearing in the film, *The Happy Guys* is full of Americanisms. Throughout it, the actors and musicians are constantly smiling in the toothy manner Alexandrov had observed in America. A direct model for the film was Hollywood's film of 1931, *The King of Jazz*, starring Paul Whiteman. Even the upbeat title can be traced to Alexandrov's experience in the New World as much as to Stalin's famous dictum, "Life has become better, comrades, more happy."[73]

During Alexandrov's days in Hollywood, blues were on the decline in American popular music and optimistic lyrics ascendant.[74] As a historian of American jazz wrote of the year 1934, "The country, especially the kids, could envision happy, glistening daylight. Joy and excitement, the sort that can be expressed so ideally through swinging music and dancing, lay ahead."[75] Alexandrov sought to capture the mood of an America that was singing "Happy Days Are Here Again" and to translate that mood into a Soviet setting.

As part of his baggage from Hollywood, Alexandrov brought with him the theme song for *The Happy Guys*. A two-part march, the jazz possibilities of which are thoroughly exploited in the film, the theme is attributed to Isaac Dunaevsky in the credits. It is actually a slightly reworked version of the Mexican tune "Adelita," later the favorite song of the dictator "Papa" Somoza of Nicaragua. Whether Alexandrov picked it up in the Mexican districts of Los Angeles or, as one Soviet writer charged, stole it wholesale from the film track of Jack Conway's 1931 film *Pancho Villa*,[76] it had certainly come directly from America. It is arguably the most enduringly popular song in the Soviet Union.

Utesov later claimed that the jazz-playing hero of *The Happy Guys* was intended as a slap in the face of the Association of Proletarian Musicians.[77] The film's light-hearted music and endless slapstick certainly assaulted Soviet puritanism. But a second theme, no less pronounced than the first, sets the world of exuberant youth and anarchic popular culture against the stolid establishment whose members thwart the rise of the jazzman-shepherd Kostia Potekhin. The wild scene of the jazz band on the stage of the Bolshoi symbolizes the triumph of spontaneity over order, youth over age, popular culture over high culture. This, above all, accounts for the film's unprecedented popularity. It also explains why the Communist party, which had sought to align itself with the new generation of the 1930s, could not let the film's critics discredit what had become an icon of Soviet youth.

A paradoxical situation was developing. Jazz, having been cleared of the earlier charges against it, by 1934 had become the musical emblem of the generation of youth designated to become the Builders of Communism. Although Utesov was on the verge of becoming a purveyor of kitsch, a kind of Soviet Lawrence Welk, for the time being, he was, after Stalin, probably the best-known man in the Soviet Union. There was scarcely a classical artist in any field who could boast of a following equal to that of any one of Utesov's sidemen. If Tsfasman had conquered the intelligentsia, Utesov and all he represented had conquered the masses. It was inevitable, given the situation in Russia in the thirties, that their dual victory would eventually call forth a strong reaction.

8

The Purge That Failed, 1936–1941

Plenty of people will try to give the masses, as they call them, an intellectual food prepared and adapted in the way they think proper for the actual condition of the masses.

Matthew Arnold, *Culture and Anarchy*, 1869

In the years after 1936, jazz in the Soviet Union was attacked from many sides and nearly destroyed. Bands were broken up or changed beyond recognition. Leaders were harassed, and arrangers were told to spurn the alien and licentious music in favor of wholesome Soviet songs. A number of jazzmen disappeared into Stalin's forced-labor camps or were shot.

State-sponsored violence against all forms of political and cultural dissent rose sharply with the assassination of the Leningrad Party chief Sergei Kirov, on December 1, 1934. By 1936, the terror had touched virtually the entire urban population, the peasantry having already been brought to heel in 1929–31 through collectivization. According to one recent estimate, more than a million people were executed during the bloody purges of 1937, and many more died in the camps.[1] Is it any wonder that jazz was swept up in this murderous whirlwind? Surely, the attempted purge of jazz was just one more manifestation, and an insignificant one at that, of the mighty political forces that were remolding Soviet life "from above."

If this had been so, there would be little reason to pause on this grim episode. But the purge of jazz was as much a result of forces operating outside of the ruling Communist party as of those within it. Indeed, at one crucial moment the Communist party emerged as the improbable champion of jazz. And, for all the ferocity of its onslaught, the purge was at best a qualified success, an incomplete and flawed effort to mold popular culture at a time when the tools of coercion were sharper than ever before. Had the purges proceeded as uncertainly and ineffectively in other fields, Stalin would have appeared a very maladroit dictator. Was jazz too minor an issue to bother with? Or was genuinely popular culture not so easily shaped?

Soviet jazz in fact fell victim to its own success. The Red Jazz Age had been detonated by the release of public tension after the First Five-Year Plan was declared complete in 1932. Jazzmania continued to gain momentum until the entire urban population threatened to be transformed into so many "Happy Guys." This, at least, was how the opponents of jazz saw it. Professional musicians who played other types of music dominated the critics in their opposition. For four years they had watched their status erode. Hotel restaurants in the big cities had been among the first bastions of traditional taste to fall. Then the strongholds of gypsy music had begun to give way, with only the Restaurant Alin in surburban Moscow keeping a twenty-four-hour schedule of moaning violins by 1935;[2] downtown, the Prague Restaurant alone continued to hire gypsy orchestras. Another redoubt fell when Soviet *dzhazes* invaded the airways through radio, which in turn generated a national market for recordings by swing-style dance bands.

Musicians of the old school observed this steady advance with horror. When Western-type swing bands infiltrated the resort industry and completely took it over, the patience of legitimate musicians was exhausted. And with good reason. The sanatoriums and resort hotels at Sochi, Yalta, Batumi, and similar spas had provided steady work for scores of orchestras. With the rise in popularity of jazz, these musicians lost their audience. They lost their self-respect as well. Miron Poliakin, though by many to be the greatest violinist in Russia after David Oistrakh, managed to sell only forty tickets to his scheduled performance at the spa at Kislovodsk. The Moscow and Leningrad *apparatchiki* vacationing there preferred jazz.[3]

The humiliation suffered by classical musicians caused snickers in jazz quarters. When the film *Anton Ivanovich Gets Angry (Anton Ivanovich serditsia)* was released on the heels of *The Happy Guys,* snickers turned to derisive laughter. Anton Ivanovich was the epitome of the old-school professor of music. His daughter spurns the good professor's world in favor of modern popular music and jazz. In the ultimate humiliation, four human beings-turned-saxophone confront the old man and force him to play the new music. Youth and *dzhaz* are equated and contrasted to a pathetic embodiment of classical music.

The humiliation of legitimate musicians was fully reflected in their level of pay. In 1934 a conservatory instructor might receive 200 to 250 rubles a month and a full professor 400 rubles, only slightly less than a musician in a major Soviet symphony orchestra. A well-known actor seldom earned less than 2000 to 3000 rubles a month in that same year, while a star could earn considerably more. By contrast, a jazzman of the stature of Alexander Tsfasman, Leonid Utesov, or Yakov Skomorovsky might earn tens of thousands of rubles each month, while their sidemen could be receiving monthly salaries of 5000 rubles.[4] The point is not merely that the jazzmen received so much but that the legitimate musicians' salaries imposed absolute hardship upon them. Most exhausted themselves with two or three jobs to make ends meet. When the German conductor Heinz Unger visited Leningrad in the late thirties, he was left wondering, "how [is] it possible to build up an orchestra, or to improve the quality of the playing, when the players are always tired to death?"[5]

Jazzmen were not immediately blamed for the sufferings of legitimate musicians. The climate of *The Happy Guys* optimism was not so easily changed, not even by the Kirov assassination and its grim aftermath. Although the Society of Old Bolsheviks and the Society of Former Political Prisoners were both disbanded in the early summer of 1935, and a harsh sentence was handed down to Stalin's former henchman Lev Kamenev, the illusion of normalcy remained. During this eerie calm before the storm, strong statements on behalf of jazz were issued.

In 1934, the editors of the journal *Soviet Music*, while acknowledging that American music was shot through with formalism and decadence, declared to their readers, "The goal of our journal is to strengthen the ties between the USSR and the USA in musical performance, study, and criticism."[6] In the same issue was published a lengthy review of music in the United States written by Henry Cowell. Some months later appeared the article "Discussion on Jazz," which hailed the virtues of hot jazz and criticized the sweet style. Quoting essays by Charles Edward Smith and Michael Gold in *The Daily Worker*, *Soviet Music* posited that there would never be true revolutionary songs for the modern age unless they were built on a foundation of hot jazz.[7]

The fact that relations between the Soviet Union and the United States had gradually improved since the establishment of diplomatic relations between the two countries in 1933 created a favorable climate for the expression of such a view. The new climate was also reflected in reports on the United States published in the Russian press by Soviet officials who had recently traveled there. Boris Shumiatsky, the cultural official who had helped to mount *The Happy Guys*, returned from a trip to Hollywood full of praise for the most recent films of Cecil B. De Mille as well as for American film techniques, music, and sports.[8]

The most important monument to this official interest was a series of lectures on the history of dance music, delivered in Leningrad by the respected musicologist and critic Mikhail Druskin in the winter of 1935. More than any Soviet writer before him, Druskin acknowledged the rapid evolution of the jazz form. Gorky's nasty barbs may have been appropriate for ragtime music of the teens, he argued, but they were scarcely warranted today. True jazz is far nobler than the pathetic attempts of a few bandleaders to clean it up and Europeanize it. And, Druskin reminded his listeners, Beethoven had never shied away from using syncopation.[9]

By implying that Beethoven might have been sympathetic toward jazz had he known of it, Druskin had gone too far. The Association of Proletarian Musicians, though disbanded in 1932, had not given up, and, beginning in mid-1934, its former members began once more to put forth their ideas. Their organization was not reconstituted, but its ideology of class war and extreme xenophobia began gradually to reappear in public discourse and even gain acceptance in official circles. Of course, the old programs had to be updated so as to buttress the doctrine of socialist realism,[10] which had been set down as a guiding principle for all the arts at the First All-Union Congress of the Union of Soviet Writers in 1934. Once this was accomplished, the new puritans began censoring and approving music with grand abandon and little consistency. One writer, for example, found it acceptable for the Gramophone Trust to issue a record of the upbeat march from *The Happy Guys* but declared that the sentimental ballad "Heart" from the same film should have been banned, despite the fact that at a 1934 meeting of the Supreme Soviet members had spontaneously sung it immediately after the "Internationale."[11] The proletarians' zeal to establish ideological purity in all fields, no matter how minor, also found expression in articles like "What Our Children Are Singing About"[12] and similar titles.

The spirit of narrow nationalism that had appeared in literature and architecture during the Cultural Revolution was no less dangerous to jazz when it came to prominence in the mid-thirties. Suddenly, citizens of the workers' republic were told that the only music acceptable to communism was peasant folk tunes. In its effort to promote folk music, the government in 1936 established "Decades" (*Dekady*), ten-day festivals of national art held in the various republics of the USSR. Jazz, having only recently been redefined as proletarian, was now seen by the new puritans as exclusively a phenomenon of the bourgeois West. The 1936 film *Circus* (*Tsirk*) made this point: the American heroine abandons her country in search of a truly cultured society, which she finds in the Soviet Union. Borrowing heavily from Charlie Chaplin's *Modern Times*, *Circus* used jazz performances by Tsfasman's orchestra to characterize the sinful world the young American leaves behind.[13]

In its emphasis on the upstanding values of the USSR, *Circus* played on the officially sponsored "new moralism," which was also hostile to jazz. Its campaign took many forms. In the autumn of 1935, the newspaper *Izvestiia* reported the arrest of a thousand women who had secretly been selling themselves on the streets of the proletarian capital.[14] New family legislation the following year emphasized the "bliss of motherhood," abolished legal abortions, and—Marx notwithstanding—reinstated the traditional family as the primary unit of Soviet society.[15] The Leningrad Music Hall, where Utesov and Dunaevsky had first experimented with jazz, was purged of its high-kicking chorus line and told to seek new "Soviet forms of popular dance" to replace those that had been borrowed from the Moulin Rouge and the nightclubs of New York.[16] All forms of popular Western music and dance came under suspicion.

To be sure, there were also Americans in these years who warned that jazz posed a threat to Christian civilization.[17] But Soviet moralists commanded incomparable powers of compulsion with which to enforce their views, as composer Dmitri Shostakovich learned. Although Shostakovich had churned out fox-trots to make money, he had more than once used jazz for more serious purposes. In his 1932 score for *Hamlet*, Ophelia sang a turn-of-the-century café song to the accompaniment of hot, spicy jazz.[18] In 1934 he introduced his fateful opera *Lady Macbeth of Mtsensk District* to an astonished but warmly appreciative Leningrad audience. Further productions followed at once in Moscow and in New York. The work is charged with eroticism, and even raised the eyebrows of New York critics, who were not accustomed to seeing operatic scenes performed in bed.[19] It depicts a spirited woman in a spiritually hollow provincial environment who, after falling in love with a handsome young man, murders her husband and father-in-law. She marries her lover, he betrays her, and she commits suicide. The score is as pungent and fierce as the tale of lust and murder it conveys. Its indebtedness to jazz is minimal but was just enough in Soviet eyes to reinforce the identification of jazz with harmonic dissonance and sexual license. When *Pravda* finally swept down against the opera on January 28, 1936, it accused its composer of "borrowing from jazz bands their nervous, convulsive, epileptic music in order to impart 'passion' to his heroine."[20] To the moral watchdogs in Moscow, jazz was the *Gebrauchsmusik* of sin.[21]

Pravda Versus *Izvestiia*:
The Great Jazz Debate of 1936

The revival of a strait-laced and sanctimonious puritanism in 1935–36 provided the final ingredient for an all-out attack on jazz. Legitimate musicians felt humiliated and angered by the advance of jazz-type orchestras; nationalists resented the cosmopolitanism of jazz, not to mention the Jewish origins of many of its proponents; and standard-bearers of a renascent Proletarian Association spirit abhorred the jazzmen's political indifference.

The political climate in 1936 grew steadily more auspicious for a witch hunt. The death (or murder) of Gorky on June 18 and his immediate apotheosis gave renewed currency to his diatribes against jazz; the August 19 trial of followers of Trotsky reinforced the pressures for conformity, while the arrest and interrogation of thousands of Soviet citizens throughout the autumn intensified the general paranoia. Ever since *Pravda* had attacked Shostakovich for exploiting jazz to produce "noise instead of music," Soviet jazzmen had been waiting for the other shoe to fall. This occurred on November 21, when *Izvestiia* published a 700-word letter titled "Jazz or a Symphony?"[22]

The letter, written by two Moscow classical musicians named Berlin and Broun, said nothing that had not been repeated many times before. Its authors began by acknowledging the right of jazz to exist, but then categorically protested that "jazz, . . . thanks to eager but semi-literate administrators, is [being] elevated into an art which is propagandized on the best concert stages at Soviet resorts." Such stages should be the exclusive tribune of "true artistic music," not jazz. The authors, drawing on their recent experiences in the Donbass region, insisted that "the masses love symphonic music, and demand to hear it." All the worse, then, that jazz ensembles have been installed in the vacation spas and that Beethoven and Bizet have been pushed to the sidelines. Symphonic music should not be heard in restaurants, the authors concluded, but neither should jazz be dished out as serious art from the concert stage.

This letter unleashed the most heated and sustained polemic in the entire history of Soviet jazz. For two months, in the very midst of Stalin's gruesome purges, the Soviet public was treated to a ferocious exchange of vituperative articles on jazz published in the nation's two leading newspapers, *Izvestiia* and *Pravda*. *Izvestiia*, representing the Soviet government, led the attack, while *Pravda*, the official organ of the Communist party of the USSR, emerged the unlikely champion of jazz, despite its attack on the music earlier that same year. The nineteen articles devoted to the polemic fully aired the problem of jazz and of popular culture.

The first letter by Messrs. Berlin and Broun was a frontal attack on the "semi-literate administrators" in the Central Music Department, a division of the State Committee on Art Affairs, established by the Central Committee of the Communist party in January 1936.[23] Boris Shumiatsky headed the Music Department and served as deputy president of the Committee on Art Affairs as a whole. Hence, it fell to Shumiatsky to speak out "against bigotry and sanctimoniousness" in an article published by *Pravda* three days later.[24] Shumiatsky's main point was that jazz was "the joy and love of the millions." He then went on to rail against "petty bourgeois moralists" who were using their influence over concert-hall directors to drive jazz and all light music from concert halls across the land.

The aggressive tone of Shumiatsky's reply was a red flag to legitimate musicians, who thundered back a week later in two letters published in *Izvestiia*. After decrying Shumiatsky's "bouquet of insults," Berlin and Broun added the record industry to their list of Soviet institutions infiltrated by jazz. The hack composer Lev Knipper charged in the second letter that Shumiatsky's "twaddle" served no purpose other than to broaden the lexicon of abuse. Both letters, as well as a third published two days later, noted that Shumiatsky had not merely aired his private prejudices but was speaking in his capacity as deputy president of the State Committee on Art Affairs.[25] By now, the debate had expanded beyond resorts and the record industry to the programming policies of the state radio. Confusion reigned. That *Pravda* seemed to have made an abrupt turnabout on jazz since its attack on Shostakovich earlier in the year was particularly vexing. Lev Knipper and others demanded that the Committee on Art Affairs state its position on jazz once and for all.

Goaded by *Izvestiia*, the president of the State Committee spoke up in a long *Pravda* article titled simply "About Music." President Platon Kerzhentsev had already expressed to Leonid Utesov his hostility to popular music. He had also supported orthodoxy in theater by closing down Vsevolod Meierhold's experimental stage, where the bands of Valentin Parnakh and Benny Peyton had first brought jazz to Soviet audiences. Now he was being attacked because his own State Committee on Art Affairs had been patronizing jazz. In spite of the diatribe against Shostakovich, the notion that jazz was a working man's music was still considered valid. True, Americans played a decadent form of jazz in their nightclubs and bars, but this did not prevent Soviet musicians from bringing out the full proletarian potential of the music. Representing the Communist party, Kerzhentsev therefore had to take a stand against the Soviet government's own newspaper or dare single-handedly to redefine Party policy. Kerzhentsev made a stand:[26]

> Jazz orchestras, so popular in the West, still find themselves in a somewhat false position here. Many would like to deny that they play music at all. The Radio Committee went through a bitter struggle in order to broadcast regular programs of the best foreign jazz records. American jazz is decadent, but it is not the music itself that is at fault. And Soviet critics of jazz should also bear in mind that there is much vulgar and formalistic classical music as well.

Kerzhentsev made his points firmly but with moderation. He reminded readers that the State Committee on Art Affairs had already established twenty new symphony orchestras and that it was actively supporting dozens of troupes of folk musicians as well. The Party, he concluded, supports all good music.

Berlin and Broun were not mollified. In a long article in *Izvestiia* the next day, they hailed Kerzhentsev's kind words about classical music but pressed him to state what he intended to do about jazz at the resorts. In passing, they lashed out once more at Shumiatsky and tried to drive a wedge between his position and that of his boss.[27] Shumiatsky had also been at his typewriter. On the same day *Izvestiia* published the third letter from Berlin and Broun, *Pravda* issued Shumiatsky's response to their earlier "filthy accusations." Once more he threw the popularity of jazz in their faces and tried to get them to address themselves not only to Utesov's band, which Berlin and Broun had conceded was acceptable, but to the jazz ensembles of Skomorovsky and several others, of which they had said nothing. Charging his critics with hypocrisy, Shumiatsky confronted them with the fact that administrators in the Commissariat of Public Enlightenment were trying their best to ban jazz and Western popular music from the schools, and in some places had even issued orders against the public singing of the march from *The Happy Guys*. Shumiatsky repeated the old distinction between the jazz played in saloons and "true Negro jazz," of which Skomorovsky was presumably a representative. The Soviet Union should ban saloon jazz, and it should also ban "saloon symphonies," i.e., precisely the watered-down classics Messrs. Berlin and Broun wanted to serve up at the resorts.[28]

Pravda finally gained the upper hand with this blast. Five days passed before the next volley, which came once more from the Party's press. This time, however, the editor himself was drawn into the debate. Reviewing the main points advanced in *Izvestiia*, the editor of *Pravda* concluded that "they were clearly and coarsely erroneous," as had been pointed out by Platon Kerzhentsev. But Berlin and Broun, "instead of honestly recognizing their error or even conducting a decent polemic, used the hospitable support of *Izvestiia*'s editor to insist that jazz be liquidated." With this sally, the polemic shifted away from the two irate instrumentalists to Nikolai Bukharin, the editor of *Izvestiia*. "The editorial board of *Izvestiia* is doing no favor to its clients Berlin and Broun," declared *Pravda*, "and is cultivating bad morals besides. If we are going to argue about taste in music, it's high time to do so honestly."[29]

One might have thought that *Izvestiia*, having had its position declared by *Pravda* to be "clearly and coarsely erroneous," would have retired from the field. Far from it. On the very next day it published another article, "In Favor of Good Music," in which jazz was repeatedly attacked as "fashionable fox-trot music," "a means of relaxation," and "outright hack-work." The author, writing as if he were arguing only with Comrades Kerzhentsev and Shumiatsky and not with the official position of the Communist party, again denounced the supporters of jazz and called for the serious work needed to raise Soviet music to the level of socialist realism.[30]

The confession of error, for centuries established as a principle of Russian law, gained enormous importance in the era of Stalin's purges. Senior cultural watchdogs and the Party's own newspaper had declared *Izvestiia* to have been irresponsible in attacking jazz. Far from recanting, as asked, the editors of *Izvestiia* invoked the authority of Lenin and Stalin in support of their position. To underscore the point, they appended a further note, "From the Editors." "The editorial board believes that citizens of the USSR have the right to express their views on music even when those views are at odds with those of Comrade Shumiatsky," they asserted. The large number of letters flooding into *Izvestiia* offices from all corners of the USSR attested to the huge interest of virtually all professions in discussing the problems of Soviet music. So, instead of meekly retiring from the field, *Izvestiia* declared its intention to press the war on jazz to the limit.

To this end, it launched an *ad hominem* attack against leaders of three of the most popular jazz bands in Moscow, S. Samoilov, B. Rachevsky, and P. Vyshinsky.[31] All were performing between shows at major downtown Moscow movie theaters including the Moscow, the Metropol, and the Union. Samoilov's jazz revue featured the entire orchestra dressed in American Marine uniforms and performing tunes such as "A Sailor's Love," "Naval Rhumba," and "The Storm Blues" to accompany a chorus line of girls "dressed, or undressed," like American sailors. At the Union Cinema, Vyshinsky's *dzhaz* was pounding out "The American Rhumba" and Ellington's "Daybreak Express." "And this is Moscow?!" asked *Izvestiia*. In conclusion, *Izvestiia*'s critic pointed out drily that all Moscow movie theaters were under the direction of the Main Directorate of Cinematography headed by Comrade Shumiatsky, who was responsible directly to Comrade Kerzhentsev. "This is the state of affairs in our music," *Izvestiia* concluded.

Pravda's reply the next day dropped all restraint. Accusing *Izvestiia* of attracting slanderers, gossips, and anti-Soviet elements, the Communist party's newspapers reiterated its support for classical music and then declared categorically that "We need jazz too, and will not allow bourgeois aesthetes and their protectors to drive it from the stage."[32] *Izvestiia* must stop its attacks on jazz and its protection of those who would ban even the production of saxophones and drums in the USSR. After all, thanks to General Voroshilov, even the Red Army had established *dzhazes* in its ranks. "It is time for the editors of *Izvestiia* to understand that they cannot continue forever to open the pages of a newspaper to Philistine twaddle aimed at liquidating jazz."

But *Izvestiia* persisted. It boasted that the repertoire of the jazz bands performing in Moscow theaters had already been purged of the objectionable American numbers in response to *Izvestiia*'s criticism, and went on to remind the public that "Abuse will never constitute a convincing argument in debates on serious questions." *Pravda* should learn that self-criticism is as important in music and jazz as in the consideration of socialist construction as a whole.[33]

On December 15, 1936, *Pravda* played its trump card. What had begun as a purely musical issue had now been elevated to a question of editorial policy, pitting the two main newspapers of the USSR against each other. For nearly two months, the Communist party's press had tried on its own authority to silence the Soviet government's paper. Instead of knuckling under, *Izvestiia* had invoked the authority of Stalin in what had been a successful purge of Moscow theater orchestras. *Pravda* now threw down the glove: "It is hopeless," *Pravda* declared, "to defend positions which are against the line of the Party and of the government."[34] *Izvestiia*'s sins were as much political as musical. Pravda declared that

> In its petty bourgeois fanaticism, *Izvestiia* has demonstrated the correctness of the Communist Party's goals in the arts and also

of the Party's views on self-criticism. The *Izvestiia* editor's latest defeat was therefore a political defeat as well.

With this invocation of the authority of the Party, *Pravda* rested its case. Although each side issued one final broadside,[35] it was vain for *Izvestiia* to press its attack against what had been defined as the Party line.

Izvestiia's outspoken criticism of Party policy was to prove costly. During the same month, Bukharin had expressed his opposition to Stalin's policies in other areas as well. Each time, *Pravda* had invoked the Party line to beat him back.[36] *Izvestiia*'s thrusts and parries were adroit, but on no issue were they sustained with greater tenacity than in the debate on jazz. In the end, *Izvestiia* lost on all fronts. Barely three weeks after the final round in the debate on jazz, the entire editorial board of *Izvestiia* was purged. Most members were never again seen alive, victims of Stalin's Great Terror.

Jazz and the Purges

By any measure, *Pravda* had trounced *Izvestiia* in their epochal debate on jazz. Yet *Pravda*'s victory was less than a resounding endorsement of jazz. Kerzhentsev himself had lashed out at the vulgarity of American jazz, and, as we have seen, his agency had responded quickly to *Izvestiia*'s criticism by purging the repertoire of jazz bands playing in theaters in Moscow. A visiting Argentine band was summarily expelled from the country, and members of a Dutch jazz group who had come on tour some months before were placed under house arrest. In short, *Izvestiia* lost the battle but showed signs of winning the war.

The purge of the Communist party had been acquiring a momentum of its own. Men and women who had dedicated their entire working lives to building up the Party found themselves charged with conspiring against it. Foreign contacts made in line of service to the Party were transformed into plots against its leaders. By March 1937, the purgers themselves were being purged, as 3000 former officers of the secret police were executed. Four months later, the purge reached another bulwark of the regime, the Red Army; before the year was out over 125,000 of its senior officers had been shot. Many institutions abandoned the practice of putting nameplates on office doors because, as a Moscow stenographer explained to the journalist Ilya Ehrenburg, "They're here today, gone tomorrow."[37]

It was inevitable that the purge of the Party would destroy many supporters of jazz. Karl Radek, the expert on German affairs who followed American jazz; Ivan Medved, chief of the secret police in Leningrad and a record collector; Sergei Kolbasev, the lecturer on jazz; and Ivan Kabakov, the regional Party secretary and protector of jazzmen in Sverdlovsk—all disappeared, and were presumably shot.[38] Tens of thousands of more casual jazz fans were doubtless swept into the same net.

Nor did their indifference to politics save the musicians, as some have claimed.[39] The spouse of many a jazz musician turned up at the Inquiry Bureau on the Malaia Bronnaia Boulevard in Moscow and at similar establishments in other cities in search of information on their arrested loved ones. Georgi Landsberg, then leader of the Moscow Radio Jazz Ensemble, was arrested at his home; pianist David Gegner was seized on the bandstand at the Metropol Hotel. Neither was seen again.[40] Valentin Parnakh was also arrested in 1937 and is said to have been among the tens of thousands of prisoners who perished while digging the useless White Sea Canal. Others were more fortunate. Trumpeter Andrei Gorin was imprisoned for insulting a Communist party official but was released after barely a year so he could participate in the newly formed State Jazz Orchestra.[41] Vera Dneprova, leader of the all-girl jazz band in Moscow, was arrested on December 15, 1937, and sentenced to ten years at hard labor but was released after she had spent five years felling trees on the Kola Peninsula.[42]

The most fortunate jazzmen were those who were merely exiled to the remote provinces. One was Alexander Sotnikov, a well-regarded violinist and jazz pianist from Kiev, who had been arrested "for political misbehavior during a concert."[43] Sotnikov was sent to the mining town of Reader (named after an American geologist) on the Chinese border. He had scarcely arrived before he approached the local NKVD, forerunner to the KGB, with a request for permission to form a jazz band to perform at the local Light Metal Workers Club (*Klub tsvetnikov*). The secret police were cautious and grilled Sotnikov on his proposed repertoire. He hummed the tunes for them. When they asked if the music had a political cast, he assured them it did not, and they were satisfied. The orchestra, a twelve-piece swing ensemble, is said to have been far bolder musically that Utesov's Thea-Jazz Ensemble had ever been. Unfortunately, the quality declined as the number of musical exiles wishing to participate grew. Within two years of its founding, the Sotnikov band had swelled to fifty members! Sotnikov then created a small combo within the larger ensemble in order to continue playing the hot classics with correct instrumentation.[44]

What crime had these jazzmen committed? Most of the more visible proponents of jazz had escaped the purges. Tsfasman, Skomorovsky, and even the leaders of the Moscow theater bands *Izvestiia* had criticized remained untouched. The one characteristic common to nearly all Soviet jazz musicians purged in 1937 was their prior travel abroad or their close links with foreigners resident in the USSR. That Utesov and Tsfasman escaped must be attributed to the special protection afforded by fans in high places. In general, the death sentences meted out to various jazz musicians during the purges attest more to the Party's xenophobia than to its judgments of the music.

Indeed, one jazzman—Alexander Varlamov—played more boldly in 1937 than he had earlier and flourished nonetheless. Toward the end of 1937, Varlamov formed a septet to perform hot tunes like "Dixie Lee" and "Sweet Sue." The band also managed to put out several records, all of them rare collector's items today, which show it frantically working to achieve a punchy rhythm and buoyant ensemble sound.

But, with these rare exceptions, jazz barely limped along. Bands continued to rehearse and perform, but they had to be extremely wary. It only took one musician to be picked up on the street after a rehearsal and then disappear without a trace (as actually hap-

pened with the Moscow saxophonist Alexander Lerner) for a state
of constant fear to reign. Utesov led the way in making timely
concessions and found life easier as a result.[45] Most bandleaders
lay low, freezing personnel, repertoires, uniforms, and even the banter
between tunes into whatever form would enable them to muddle
through the terrible year 1937. Soviet jazz endured the Great Terror
the way a bear survives winter: by entering a changeless state of
hibernation. But popular music must constantly change or it will
die. The survival of jazz was bought at the price of its vitality.

Manufacturing Musical Ecstasy

As part of the government's effort to create a distinctly Soviet popular music, newly composed "mass songs" dominated public meetings and airwaves until World War II. Written to simple melodies
which drew on folk songs, marches, and even jazz, the mass songs
were vehicles for light-hearted and enthusiastically affirmative lyrics on the glorious future of socialism. As one of them proclaimed,

> There are no barriers for us on land or sea,
> Neither ice nor clouds can frighten us;
> The flame in our soul, the banner of our country,
> We will carry through the universe and ages . . . [46]

Such potboilers were composed in prodigious numbers. A competition in the winter of 1935–36 brought no fewer than 6575 musical and literary entries.[47] Publishers issued mass songs in immense
quantities, adorning their covers with photographs of faceless hordes
of soldiers, children, peasants, or workers. The government promoted these songs in order to mold popular values. "Whatever you
sing . . . you believe," Alexander Solzhenitsyn once observed.[48] If
tens of millions of Soviet people sang "Nowhere else on earth is
there a country/Where a man so proudly, freely breathes" [49] then at
least some of them were bound to believe it (and if they didn't,
perhaps foreign intellectuals like Sartre and de Beauvoir would).
More than one contemporary has argued that this psychological
conditioning succeeded to some extent. Private fear did not squelch
collective ecstasy. "Yes, we shall force them to work," says the Grand

Inquisitor in Dostoevsky's *The Brothers Karamazov*, "but in their leisure hours we shall make their life like a children's game, with children's songs, in chorus, and with innocent dances."[50] Such was the psychology of the Soviet mass song.

The great weakness of the mass song as popular culture stemmed from its deliberately unfocused marketing. The government producers' desire to create a monoculture led inevitably to the neglect of the tastes of many, if not of most, people. In the USSR this brought about the rapid degradation of the mass song into the most banal form of kitsch, mouthed but not sung, the very antithesis of genuinely popular culture.

Credit must be given to the ability of a few composers of mass songs, notably Isaac Dunaevsky, to write melodies that combined the best qualities of marches, folk songs, and jazz. Dunaevsky possessed true talent, which he had demonstrated first by writing successful popular songs for the Leningrad Music Hall under the NEP. Most of his closest musical contacts were with Soviet jazzmen. He greatly admired Tsfasman's unbending loyalty to American jazz prototypes; he selected Skomorovsky's band to provide music for *Circus, Volga, Volga!* and other hit films of the early thirties; and he worked closely with Utesov on several jazz revues as well as *The Happy Guys*. Born to a Jewish family in the Ukraine, Dunaevsky by 1937 had become a national hero in Russia and received the Order of Lenin. In the late thirties, a story circulated in the Moscow musical underground that Serge Rachmaninoff had suffered an attack of *mania grandiosa* and was seen running up and down Broadway screaming "I am Dunaevsky! I am Dunaevsky!"[51]

In some quarters mass songs were viewed as an antidote to jazz. They were defended in much the same terms American do-gooders in the early twenties had used to try to enlist composers to help crush jazz with better songs.[52] But the most popular mass songs were all, to a greater or lesser degree, tinged with jazz. The strong rhythms, innovative harmonic patterns, and especially the striving for emotional authenticity can be traced to the influence of jazz.

As we have seen, the applicability of these aspects of jazz to the Communist mass song had been persuasively argued in Germany by the left-wing composer and critic Hanns Eisler. Repeated trips to the Soviet Union had given Eisler contacts in the Russian musical world.[53] Eisler's authority had helped Russians to divorce themselves from the lure of folk music and to entertain the possibility of a new and popular light music under socialism.[54] However, Eisler's ideal of grimly militant "songs of struggle," or *Kampflieder*, was leagues away from the lobotomized lightheartedness of the Soviet mass song. If the Russians' saccharine optimism was indebted to any German prototype, it was to Nazi youth songs rather than to Eisler's hymns to struggle.

It goes without saying that the slightest suggestion of Nazi-Soviet interaction in any field would have appalled Russians after 1933. Yet the similarity of Soviet and German diatribes against jazz cannot escape notice. The following, from the pen of Josef Goebbels, Hitler's propaganda chief, could have been drawn from statements by the Association of Proletarian Musicians or the anti-jazz faction at *Izvestiia*:

> Now I shall speak quite openly on the question of whether German radio should broadcast so-called "jazz music." If by jazz we mean music that is based on rhythm and entirely ignores or even shows contempt for melody, music in which rhythm is indicated primarily by the ugly sounds of whining instruments so insulting to the soul, why, then we can only reply in the negative.[55]

The Nazis finally drove jazz from the radio in order to safeguard "the foundations of our entire culture."[56] Swing bands were purged in Berlin, and other groups were commanded to play music that was ideologically more acceptable.[57] Like the *Izvestiia* ideologues, too, Nazi critics branded jazz bourgeois; they differed from the Muscovites only in their racist emphasis on the "Judeo-Negroid" essence of jazz. But for all the Nazis' hostility to jazz music, they were no more effective in suppressing it than were the Russians. Scarcely a month passed in the thirties when Nazi authorities did not thunder against "uncouth and tasteless music."[58] Yet swing fever raged throughout Hitler's Reich, thanks both to its popularity with the listening public and to its protection by Nazi functionaries themselves.[59] Even during the war, German swing bands continued to issue jazz-oriented recordings. Fascist Italy followed a similar policy toward jazz but interpreted it yet more loosely, to the point of permitting Louis Armstrong to make a successful tour of Mussolini's realm in 1934. Jazz everywhere proved far easier to denounce than to eradicate.

Stalin's Jazzmen:
The State Jazz Orchestra of the USSR

The crisis of 1936–37 had left Soviet jazz in a thoroughly ambiguous position. On the one hand, the Communist party had beaten down the attacks on jazz launched by those in the Soviet government with access to *Izvestiia*. On the other hand, the Party had put to death a number of pioneer proponents of the art in Russia and had otherwise made known its opposition to jazz as it existed in the West. And if the ideologues' patronage of mass songs had been intended to provide an alternative to American musical fashions, it also perpetuated them through borrowings from jazz. An updated statement of policy was called for, the more so because further concessions to what had been the *Izvestiia* position would leave the Soviets open to the charge of following the same hostile policy toward what they themselves had defined as a proletarian music as Hitler's National Socialists, who denounced it outright.

The Soviet government's response to the problem was to establish the State Jazz Orchestra of the USSR, a grandiosely named ensemble that could not be accused of kowtowing to decadent Western fashions. In fact, it was safe to the point of tedium. A closed debut concert was held on November 6, 1938, at the Bolshoi Theater. The reaction of the audience of government employees was polite but not warm. Three weeks later, the orchestra made its public debut at the Hall of Columns in the former Noblemen's Assembly in Moscow. Again, the audience seemed indifferent.[60] Finally, a third debut was made before an audience of Moscow theatrical folk and musicians. Juri Jelagin, the group's concertmaster, claims this was "the only real triumph in the history of the State Jazz Orchestra."[61]

Stalin's government cannot be faulted for parsimony in its support for the State Jazz Orchestra. Two million rubles were appropriated to support the musicians, whose salaries were twice as large as those of the best symphony orchestra members. Zhurkevich, supplier of custom-made suits for Moscow's new elite, was commissioned to make afternoon and evening wear for the bandsmen.[62] The men had been assembled in an equally lordly manner. Since Tsfasman's band was known to have the best jazzmen in the country, eleven of its fourteen members were dragooned into the State Jazz Orchestra, like serfs being moved from one estate to another. Two more, including the excellent trumpet man Andrei Gorin, were liberated from prison to ensure the group's quality. These strenuous efforts were amply rewarded, for the State Jazz Orchestra played with a polish and precision any Western pops orchestra might have envied. The five-man saxophone section produced a rich and cohesive sound, while Ivan Bacheev's drumming was up to the standard he had set on the Tsfasman recordings.[63]

For all its precision, the State Jazz Orchestra was a dismal failure. Tsfasman's Americanism and his unpopularity with the bureaucrats had disqualified him for the position of conductor, which went instead to Victor Knushevitsky, a capable musician with absolutely no feeling for jazz. Miffed, Tsfasman then declined the post of second pianist that was offered him, leaving no true jazz player except Bacheev in a position of importance in the State Jazz Orchestra. Knushevitsky's classical background and ignorance of jazz predisposed him to turn the band into a kind of chamber orchestra with saxophones. The results were disastrous. What began as a small group rapidly snowballed into a forty-three piece ensemble, quite enough to stifle any jazz feeling or spontaneity that individual musicians might have spirited into the group.

The same tendency toward elephantine symphonization that had swollen the band's personnel also laid hold on its repertoire. The list of contemporary composers upon whom the State Jazz Orchestra relied most heavily reads like a *Who's Who* of the Stalinist musical establishment, led by the tedious Matvei Blanter.[64] In addition to current potboilers, the orchestra played recycled works by Rachmaninoff, Tchaikovsky, and Fritz Kreisler. The one contemporary "serious" work in its repertoire was Shostakovich's *Suite for Jazz Band*, a commissioned piece in which the composer took little pride of authorship. Aside from these pieces, the repertoire was pure kitsch, elaborately arranged and performed with Hollywood precision but kitsch nonetheless. In its review of the debut concert, the newspaper of the Soviet government boasted ominously that the State Jazz Orchestra had finally rendered jazz truly artistic.[65] Translated, this meant that the only items in the repertoire that could justify the band's invocation of the word "jazz" were a few fox-trots by Tsfasman, a "Fox March" by Dunaevsky, and a watered-down rendition of Duke Ellington's "Caravan." To call this ensemble a jazz group was as cynical as it was ludicrous.

The public quickly discovered this. Billboards advertising a "jazz concert" at the venerable munitions works in Tula attracted a great number of people, who packed the huge auditorium hoping to hear the latest Western popular songs and jazz. Instead, they encountered a band of forty-three solemn musicians who performed little-known works by classical and semiclassical composers. According to Juri Jelagin, "The indignation of the audience was stormy, and the fiasco complete. Knushevitsky's arrangement of "Tea for Two" was singled out for particularly loud booing and hissing. . . ."[66]

A saxophonist in the State Jazz Orchestra recalls an even worse debacle in Yalta. Again, posters announcing an evening of jazz had been plastered everywhere, including the Air Force base near Sevastopol. A large contingent of Red Air Force pilots drove over for the show and were infuriated at the absence of jazz in the State Jazz Orchestra's program. Booing, hissing, and shouting ended in a near riot. The musicians considered themselves lucky to have escaped with their lives.[67]

Public hostility mattered little to a band like the State Jazz Orchestra. It had been created not to please the public but to prove a theory, namely that the word "jazz" could be successfully grafted onto music bearing little or no resemblance to those degenerate howlings that passed for jazz in the capitalist West. The only ones who had to like the music were the people who had created the group in the first place and *their* bosses, not the public. When culture is provided "from above," it is those on top who must like it. In the USSR this meant, finally, Comrade Stalin.

No opportunity to discover whether the Leader of Humanity would like Kerzhentsev's creation arose until the end of 1938. Certainly, the energy and attention Stalin had devoted to destroying much of the Party and most of the officer corps of the Red Army gave no reason to think that he might be a devotee of light music. But there was no way of knowing for sure. So it was all the more unnerving for the musicians of the State Jazz Orchestra when they received orders to report to the Kremlin on New Year's Eve.

The band arrived early at the gate nearest the Moscow River. Since it was forbidden to bring a taxi close to the Leader's domain, the musicians trudged the last part of the way on foot, lugging their instruments and equipment through the snow. It was bitter cold, but they were forced to wait outside nearly an hour before being admitted. By then, horns, fingers, and lips were all but frozen. Hours of waiting in a poorly heated anteroom then followed. The many officers of the secret police hovering about gave a thoroughly somber air to the proceedings and kept the musicians from gawking at their surroundings. They were also prevented from warming up for the performance that would be the most important of their careers.

Suddenly word came down that it was time for the band to perform. The musicians learned that one or two acts would precede theirs, and that they should enter the hall and wait quietly on the bandstand that had been prepared for them. Led by their *cicerones* from the NKVD, the musicians walked into the brightly lit St. George's Hall. The room was laid out with long tables, each of which was piled high with food and bristling with bottles of wine, vodka, and champagne. Stalin and his closest associates—those who had not been purged—sat at a separate table. Everything indicated that the entire assembly had been warmed by drink. There was shouting and laughing. The novelist Alexei Tolstoy, sad and very drunk, was seen standing on a table waving his white napkin.[68] No ladies were present.

Finally, the State Jazz Orchestra's turn to perform came. The first numbers went well. The forty-three musicians observed with relief that Stalin was clapping and nodding his approval. Then the smartly dressed and very Westernized singer Valentina Batysheva sang Matvei Blanter's mass song hit, "Katiusha." Her style was jazzy, and her pretty and intimate voice more like that of Josephine Baker than of Stalin's favorite singer at the Bolshoi, Nedazhda Spiller.[69] The Leader of Humanity was seen to frown and look away. But the brandy and perhaps a calming word from the jazz-loving General Voroshilov, Stalin's neighbor at the table, enabled the crisis to pass. Nonetheless, the signal had been given. Stalin had liked the bland and anemic ensemble numbers performed by the State Jazz Orchestra, but had raised his brow at the sight of a Soviet artist evoking the decadent West. Whatever officials of the All-Union Committee on Art Affairs might wish, this frown further limited the ability of the State Jazz Orchestra of the USSR to respond to popular taste.

In the end, the State Jazz Orchestra satisfied no one. It was too Western for the nationalists and too narrowly Soviet for the cosmopolitans; too hot for the legitimate musicians and too sweet for the jazzmen; too popular for the highbrows and too highbrow for the populace. Thus, the paradoxical result of the attempt to apply totalitarian methods of organization to jazz was a failure caused more by excessive compromise than by rampant dogmatism. *Pravda* had won the debate of 1936, but only after making concessions that emasculated jazz. *Izvestiia* had lost the debate, but only after getting *Pravda* to accept most of its arguments against Western music. If the attempted purge of jazz failed on ideological and political grounds, *Pravda*'s defense of jazz also failed, through lack of conviction.

The campaign to rid the Soviet Union of jazz thus culminated with the nationalization of swing music by the government. This, in effect, legitimized it, just when jazz might otherwise have been on the verge of extinction in the USSR. *Dzhaz* became legally exportable to all parts of the country. No sooner had the State Jazz

Orchestra of the USSR raised its banner in the capital than other state jazz orchestras were established in the various republics. In each case, the local government footed the bill. By 1939 thriving swing ensembles had sprung up with state patronage in the capitals of Armenia, Georgia, Azerbaijan, and other non-Russian republics.

The artistic climate in the republics was far freer than in the capital. Neither Party nor government officials in Tblisi, Baku, or Erevan showed the slightest concern that their local jazz bands conform to a Russian standard of purity. On the contrary, they seem to have gone out of their way to encourage their groups to be more independent and bold. In effect, the establishment of the State Jazz Orchestra of the USSR in Moscow had the unintended consequence of creating laboratories of jazz in the non-Russian capitals. During World War II one of these bands, the Byelorussian State Jazz Orchestra, was to become the most important jazz ensemble in the Soviet Union. And after the death of Stalin in 1953, the products of these jazz laboratories in the Caucasus, the Muslim south, and in the Baltic were to help bring about the rejuvenation of jazz in Russia.

Meanwhile, government power had been able neither to create a "Soviet jazz" the public would accept nor to mold the public's expectations to conform to the rather prissy tastes of the state. All it had succeeded in doing was to capture the word "jazz" for the proletarian cause and embalm it in the dull amber of the State Jazz Orchestra. Yet the Soviet government inadvertently made itself the chief agent keeping jazz before the public. The very travesties committed by the official State Jazz Orchestra ensured that questions regarding the true character of jazz would continue to be raised in diverse forums, and that at least a part of the listening public would continue to pursue its interest in jazz and Western-style popular music.

9
Swinging for the Fatherland: Jazz Militant, 1941–1945

I don't like to see this country get militaristic, but if we have to cope with the situation prevailing throughout the world today, it's a necessity. . . . We musicians will have to pitch right in.

Glen Gray, of the Casa Loma Orchestra, 1940

To many Russians on the eve of World War II, it seemed that jazz was dying. Unfamiliar with the activity of the State Jazz Orchestras in the non-Russian republics, they saw only the muzzling of the independent dance bands that had earlier been responsive to popular taste. The one development in which optimists might have taken satisfaction was the "jazz orchestra" organized by the All-Union Radio Committee in 1938, which performed a few swing arrangements pirated from Ray Noble, Duke Ellington, and Cole Porter. The orchestra had several points in its favor. It was directed first by the experienced jazzman Alexander Varlamov and then, beginning in 1938, by Alexander Tsfasman; it was permitted to perform at the new Moskva Hotel opposite the Kremlin; and its fifteen musicians were talented and well rehearsed. But surviving recordings reveal a group scarcely distinguishable from the State Jazz Orchestra and with a repertoire overburdened with mass songs badly arranged by Matvei Blanter. In short, this orchestra gave lovers of jazz little cause for rejoicing.

Soviet life as a whole was even more bleak. The mass arrest of hundreds of thousands of officials and the deportation of more ordinary mortals had cast a pall of extreme caution over all cultural life. Added to this, the signing of a nonaggression pact between Hitler and Stalin on August 23, 1939, raised fears that the cultural policies of the USSR and Germany would come to resemble each other more closely. Later that year, when the Red Army overran the independent Baltic states of Latvia, Lithuania, and Estonia under the protection of the pact, tens of thousands of the educated and Westward-looking elite of those states were deported to the Soviet Far East. Such were the precautions Stalin was prepared to take to ensure that the Soviet Union would not be infected by the West. Naturally, jazz musicians were among those deported.

The entire issue of jazz and popular culture in the USSR was dramatically transformed by Hitler's invasion of Soviet territory in the predawn hours of June 22, 1941. We now know that Stalin had ample warning of the attack but refused to take the necessary defensive measures. The Soviet populace was caught completely by surprise, and hundreds of thousands in the war zone, including thousands of Red Army soldiers, went over to the German side. Then, as Hitler's armies swept eastward, one of the fastest and most massive mobilizations in history occurred in the Soviet heartland. New army units were formed and cadres filled out. All the professions immediately got behind the war effort. The Central Committee of Art Workers issued a statement committing artists and musicians to front-line duty.[1] In quick order the unions of artists and composers placed their members in the service of the army as well. The journal *Soviet Art* announced that publishing houses would immediately begin issuing anti-Fascist songs and marches specially scored for jazz bands.[2]

While a few instrumentalists volunteered individually for armed service, most of the better-known jazz musicians enlisted with their ensembles. Boris Rensky, for example, the popular Kharkov-based leader, took his entire band to the front within weeks of the start of hostilities.[3] Yakov Skomorovsky and his band also headed for the front, where they accompanied singers in whipping up the troops' fighting spirit with patriotic songs. Leonid Utesov's old sideman, Leonid Diederichs, was among many leaders who quickly organized special wartime programs and presented them to grateful soldiers at army bases. Utesov himself was too old to be drafted, but he immediately placed himself and his orchestra at the service of the fighting forces. Utesov had just been handed the directorship of the State Jazz Orchestra of the USSR and was rehearsing at the Hermitage Gardens in Moscow when the invasion was announced.[4] The show went forward, but within days the band was bouncing to the Kalinin front in two trucks. "Send us Utesov's jazz band to pick up our fighting spirit," a front-line commander had written.[5] (Similar letters reached Captain Glenn Miller three years later, as his band prepared to leave New Haven, Connecticut, for England. Like Utesov, Miller was too old for the draft but had volunteered anyway.) Meanwhile, Alexander Tsfasman and the All-Union Radio Committee Orchestra were preparing to launch a tour of the front lines that eventually extended to one hundred concerts.

Far outnumbering the civilian bands that were called to the colors were the *dzhazes* organized within the various commands of the Red Army and Red Navy. Every military district by now had its swing orchestra, usually an ensemble of fourteen to sixteen musicians supplemented by singing groups and dancers. Their repertoires closely resembled those of the State Jazz Orchestra of the USSR, but their instrumentation permitted them also to play arrangements scored for swing bands, which they did in some number. In a few cases these older divisional ensembles were transformed by the addition of strong civilian jazzmen to their ranks. For example, Skomorovsky's entire band was eventually absorbed into the Naval Song and Dance Ensemble led by Vano Muradeli. But the best military bands were those organized at the outbreak of the war. Among these, none was to distinguish itself more than the Red Flag Baltic Fleet Jazz Orchestra, led by Nikolai Minkh.

Minkh, formerly a pianist with Utesov, had been a charter member of the Leningrad circle of jazzmen headed by Georgi Landsberg and Leonid Diederichs. In 1934 he joined the newly organized Leningrad Radio Orchestra and took over its leadership after Landsberg's arrest. When war broke out, Minkh was mobilized along with the entire Radio Orchestra, and was wounded in quick order. When he recovered early in 1941, he was assigned to the Political

Directorate of the Baltic Fleet and asked to organize an entirely new band. The blockade of Leningrad had already begun and the task was not easy. The drummer Sasha Kozlovsky was dying of hunger when Minkh turned to him. Many of Minkh's other instrumentalists had also suffered under the seige that was to claim 500,000 lives in its first winter alone. Once organized, the Baltic Fleet Jazz Orchestra appeared at halls throughout Leningrad, although concerts within the city were frequently interrupted by artillery bombardments. The band also traveled to towns along the Gulf of Finland and the shores of Lake Ladoga that could be reached from the besieged city. At the island naval base of Kronstadt it performed under the sights of German guns emplaced on the mainland's rolling hills at Oranienbaum. The band persisted amidst the most horrible military siege of the twentieth century. Printed handbills announcing the Baltic Fleet Jazz Orchestra's "Let's Get Acquainted" concert, held during the first summer of the Leningrad blockade, are eloquent testimony to these Russian pop musicians' determination to relieve the public's suffering.[6]

Six months into the war, scores of *dzhazes* had been organized within the Soviet armed services. Minkh recalled,

> there was a huge number of military jazz orchestras. Jazz bands existed in practically every army group and in every fleet, whether the Northern, Black Sea, Caspian Sea, Baltic, or Pacific. And the number of jazz orchestras in the army was beyond count. Many so-called musical platoons were made up of jazz musicians. . . . Such small jazz ensembles, thanks to their mobility, could make their way anywhere. They were in great demand at the front.[7]

There was as much heroism as death on the Russian front, and there were millions who died. The instrumentalists who provided popular music and jazz to the soldiers of the Red Army suffered and died with the rest and provided their share of heroes. For example, the Commissariat of Defense organized a jazz orchestra under the direction of the young arranger Yuri Lavrentiev. After touring the front for a year, members of the band were caught in an ambush and perished as a group. Many other well-known bands, including the State Jazz Orchestra, lost individuals and whole sections. There were also hundreds of amateur musicians who organized bands within their units before perishing in the ranks as soldiers. In light of the harassment jazzmen received only a few years later, such martyrdom should not pass unrecorded.

The musicians fully participated in the everyday suffering behind the lines with both tears and bitter laughter. Alexander Tsfasman's band was invited to perform at the U.S. Embassy in Moscow at the height of the fighting in 1943. Drummer Sergei Sedykh was so starved that he stuffed his shirtfront with hors d'oeuvres, which were served in generous quantities. At the end of the evening Ambassador Averell Harriman rushed to thank the musicians and shook Sedykh's hand so vigorously that the cache of provisions plummeted to the floor.[8]

More than a few Soviet musicians fell into the invaders' hands. Members of one amateur *dzhaz* captured in 1943 were taken to the prison camp Stalag 8-A at Görlitz in Saxony and compelled to work fourteen hours a day in the coal mines. However, the former Soviet musicians managed to persuade the German commandant to allow them to form a combo to perform on the stage of the camp's dining hall. The band, consisting of drums, saxophone, trumpet, accordion, and triangle, played weekly before an international aggregation of inmates down to the summer of 1944.[9] The later fate of its members is unknown, but one can assume it was no better than that of the German Jewish members of the Ghetto Swingers, formed at the Nazis' extermination camp at Theresienstadt in Czechoslovakia, or of members of the jazz band at Buchenwald.

A Touch of Home:
The Wartime Repertoire

What music did the countless *dzhazes* play for the Red Army boys at the front? Surviving photographs show the various bands performing before groups of young men, most of them obviously peasants, seated on the ground in a circle, rifles in their laps. As in any

war, these interludes were times of nostalgia. Glenn Miller's assessment of the mood in the American Army could have been penned
by any Soviet bandleader:

> We didn't come here to set any fashions in music—we came merely
> to bring a much-needed touch of home to some lads who have
> been here for a couple of years. These lads are doing a hell of a
> job. . . . They know and appreciate only those tunes that were
> popular before they left [home]. For their sake, we play only the
> old tunes.[10]

Two thirds of the tunes played by most Soviet bands at the front
were at least three years old.[11] The wartime Soviet repertoire was
particularly strong in the folk songs and sentimental ballads that
symbolized the world back home. Country music rose to national
importance in America at about the same time, and for the same
reason. With their nation imperiled, Americans, too, yearned for
reassurance that their old values were still intact.[12]

Practical circumstances on the Russian front also contributed to
the transformation of many Soviet swing bands into folk groups.
Because pianos were unavailable, scores of accordionists were drawn
into the instrumental ensembles, giving the music a decidedly rustic
sound. In 1944 the journal *Literature and Art* noted that Soviet
popular music groups were creating a new style of "jazz" in the
folk tradition.[13] To some extent, the conservative musical tastes of
postwar Russia were born in this wartime yearning for a peaceful
world of folk life and not merely in the retrograde prejudices of
Stalin's cultural tsars.

Along with the rise of folkish melodies, the war also called forth
a militant nationalism that found expression in music. Works such
as the State Jazz Orchestra's "Slavic Fantasy," or the well-known
"For Our Land, for the Will To Fight to the Death!," were widely
performed to appreciative audiences. Especially after the pivotal
battle at Stalingrad in 1942, which halted the Nazi advance and
opened the way for the Red Army to begin its march toward Berlin,
stirring patriotic marches became the order of the day.[14] Gradually,
the sentimental ballads of 1942 receded into the background; tunes

like "Wait for Me" ("Zhdi menia") gave way to "The Holy War" ("Sviashchennaia voina") and "Song of Wrath" ("Pesnia gneva").

In some quarters, the claims of national mobilization were believed to preclude borrowings from jazz or from other foreign sources. This chauvinistic attitude, which gained strength after Stalingrad, was epitomized in a letter from the front published in *Literature and Art*, in which Boris Rensky was excoriated for vulgarity. Rensky, it seems, was guilty not only of neglecting the patriotic songbook but of trying to play in a genuinely hot and jazzy style, for which he was charged with hysteria, shouting, and "hellish noisemaking." The same article accused members of a certain Red Navy swing band of black-marketeering as well as playing jazz.[15] The spring of 1944 produced a particularly rich harvest of attacks on jazz and jazz musicians at the front. Again, the trail was blazed by *Literature and Art*, issued by the Union of Soviet Writers and the Committee on Art Affairs. Utesov, who had been featuring folk melodies for years, was now attacked for playing too many cheap imports. Another band was criticized for performing a jazzed-up version of "Kreisleriana."[16] The message was simple: as *Literature and Art* put it, "Popular music not only entertains our fighting men and officers; it strengthens in the Soviet people the holy feeling of hatred for the enemy, without which victory is impossible."[17] In the same vein, *Pravda* observed in October 1944, "popular music is called on to fulfill serious social and political tasks, as well as artistic purposes, and hence it would be a mistake to pass over the huge inadequacies in the work of our popular artists."[18]

Such somberly nationalistic feelings are natural to some extent in a military environment during wartime. A U.S. Air Force commandant criticized Glenn Miller for including march-time arrangements of "St. Louis Blues" and "Blues in the Night" in his repertoire of classic American marches.[19] But, as we have observed, in the USSR these were not mere expressions of individual prejudice but had the force of policy; they emanated, as the Russians say, "from the highest level." Combined with the genuine and heartfelt nationalism of the Soviet fighting man, they constituted a solid core of support for the wartime mass song. Never was there closer harmony between the official patronage of mass songs and their popular consumption than during the four years of the War of the Fatherland.

Red, White, and Blue:
The American Tide

The way in which jazz came to function as a counterforce to wartime pressures for nationalistic music provides revealing glimpses into the nature of Soviet popular culture. At the heart of the matter was the ever-present need of army commanders to be sensitive to the fighting man's moods and feelings. No war is won without leadership. But, as Tolstoy observed in his second epilogue to *War and Peace*, it is ultimately the common soldier's will to fight that constitutes the essential ingredient of victory. Folksy patriotic songs can sometimes help to strengthen that will. But twenty years of sporadic exposure to jazz and the popular music of the West had also left their mark on the Soviet Union. No less powerful than the nationalistic urge, and often giving it expression, was the Soviet fighting man's wartime interest in *dzhaz*, to which the Red Army wisely responded.

The interest of the city-bred soldier in jazz was quite understandable. No less than in peacetime, he equated this music with youth, leisure, exuberance, and personal freedom. At the front, he could easily identify it with his aspirations, and with the hope that victory would enable him to pursue them once more.

But what of the peasant? The Red Army was mainly a peasant institution. Why, then, should its leaders have maintained hundreds of *dzhazes*, with their unfamiliar Western-type instrumentation and timbre, when the peasantry had so little familiarity with the music? The answer lies in the nature of modern warfare. Soldiers drawn from the peasantry were called on to handle the most modern weaponry. To enable them to do so, the Red Army had to function as an educational institution, imparting the technological knowledge associated with modern industrial life. Moreover, the massive loss of lives brought rapid promotions to thousands of young men whose previous experience had been limited to the rural backwaters. Eager to fulfill their patriotic duty, these men strove to be worthy of participating in Soviet life at its most modern level. Along with pursuing their education through diligent study on their own at the front and with mastering the principles of Marxism-Leninism, they worked also to acquire what they saw as the accoutrements of Soviet modernity, including its music. From the standpoint of urban man, the war brought the peasant element to the fore, but from the peasant's standpoint, it was a modernizing and urbanizing experience.

This sociological digression might help to explain Leonid Utesov's interesting approach to the problem of dress for his band at the outset of the war. To achieve maximum mobility, each ensemble had to jettison all unnecessary props and encumbrances. But what to do about dress? Should band members perform in army fatigues or somehow keep up their tuxedos and formal wear? "It seemed to me," Utesov later recalled, "that those artists who appeared before the fighting men in the uniforms they usually wore made a mistake. I demanded that the band observe the same smartness in appearance, formality in dress and behavior, and precision in grooming that it observed for the most elegant concert. Even in downpours we performed in dress suits."[20] It is no wonder that the band came to be viewed at the front as an island of urban normalcy.[21]

For peasant and worker alike, there was an element of wholesome escapism in this. A *dzhaz* carried intimations of happier times, of joyful moments of individual release and self-expression. For much the same reason, jazz flourished in practically every country in Europe during World War II. The popularity of Django Reinhardt's jazz performances in occupied Paris (permitted thanks to the benevolence of a jazz fan in the *Luftwaffe*)[22] and the magnetic attraction of the several bands playing in Italy was due partly to this desire for escape.[23]

That jazz was so welcome a release from the bloody drudgery of war also rendered it an ideal vehicle for satire directed against the enemy. Biting anti-Fascist songs had made their appearance with the outbreak of fighting. Initially, the lyrics took the form of traditional Russian couplets (*chastushki*) and were set to simple folk melodies.[24] By 1942 most bandleaders had realized the troops and the public were ready for a more sophisticated satire than the couplets, which too frequently descended to doggerel. The All-Union Radio Orchestra attempted to revive the long-suppressed revolutionary satire of the 1920s.[25] But just as the Blue Blouses of the twenties had had to incorporate jazz in order to survive, so now did the wartime satirists. Leonid Utesov had adopted the motto "laughter can kill"[26] and by 1942 had included a "Jazz Information Bureau" section in his shows. The *Dzhazinformburo* set to jazz hilarious and sometimes off-color ditties, which it dished up in response to queries purportedly received from the audience.

Provided the lyrics were satirical, practically any jazz arrangement became permissible. American swing bands for years had been playing "Bei mir bist du schön," the up-tempo Yiddish pop tune. Utesov reworked it into the satirical "Baron von der Pshik." Beginning the song with a hot cymbal solo, the band swings into a hard-driving chorus interrupted by some of the first convincingly jazzy trumpet breaks to be heard from a Soviet band. The vocal quartet carries the satire, but also copies any number of male ensembles recorded by American swing bands.[27]

The number of American popular tunes imported into the Soviet Union reached an all-time high during the war. "Over There!," "The Marines' Hymn," "Honeysuckle Rose," and many other hits from Tin Pan Alley resurfaced with words supportive of the Red Army's effort. An analogous transference took place in many other countries, including the Axis powers. In Italy, for example, "Exactly Like You" gained popularity as "Ritmando un Ricordo."[28] But the jazz boom the war provoked throughout Europe had a different quality on the two sides of the fighting front. In Germany and Italy it implied a semi-legal dissent with the ideology of fascism and cultural Aryanism. In Great Britain and the USSR it was an expression of national solidarity with the Yanks, and hence could be tolerated and even encouraged. The renaming of American tunes was a political necessity in the Axis countries. In the Soviet Union, if only briefly, it was nothing more than the familiar process of cultural translation or adaptation.

The wartime alliance between the United States and the Soviet Union provided the single most important boost Soviet jazz had ever received. Without rolling back the nationalism in music, it meant that, for the time being, jazziness was no longer a sin. The recording of literally dozens of American tunes by Soviet *dzhazes* caused anxiety among some of the puritans, but most saw it as fully compatible with the national effort. The official hostility to American popular culture that arose in the USSR after 1946 was, in part, a reaction to the breakdown of the wartime alliance.

Soviet-American collaboration between 1941 and 1945 went far beyond the *mariage de convenance* depicted by its later foes on both sides. Suffice it to say that over a billion dollars' worth of American goods and equipment were shipped to the USSR from the United States in 1942 alone, thanks to an interest-free Lend-Lease agreement. Between October 1, 1941, and May 31, 1945, some 2660 ships left American ports for the Soviet Union; they carried half a million army trucks, 13,000 tanks, 35,000 motorcycles, and nearly 2000 railroad engines. The total value of material supplied by the U.S. to the USSR under Lend-Lease approached 11 billion preinflation dollars.[29] Later critics were to point out that some of that American wheat and those Studebaker trucks were used to sustain Stalin's labor camps.[30]

American assistance, however, was of vital importance to the ability of the Soviet fighting man to sustain the Eastern Front. The Red Army soldier knew this better than anyone else, and thus was curious about the United States and receptive to the most trivial information on his far-off comrades in arms. Such information flowed in in some quantity, touching virtually every field of endeavor. In music, word got back that American publishers had issued a collection of Red Army songs with English texts, and that both the Metropolitan Opera Company and the New York Philharmonic had performed programs of Russians' works in honor of the war effort.[31] Soviet readers also learned that American jazzmen were reinforcing the military collaboration through benefit performances by Benny Goodman, Duke Ellington, and others. During this period of goodwill, the physicist Petr Kapitsa did not hesitate to turn to the American Embassy in Moscow for a supply of reeds for Soviet wind players.[32] Others' personal contacts with Americans brought to Russia a number of illegal "fake books," shorthand compilations of melodies and chords beloved by every jazzman and pop musician in the 1940s but despised by ASCAP, for the compilers paid no royalties. These quickly came into the hands of the Soviet *dzhaz* groups at the front. By the autumn of 1942 Utesov's State Jazz Orchestra of the USSR was drawing on American fake books for its performances of the latest tunes from America and Western Europe.[33]

The Soviet government fully approved of the growing impact of American jazz in the USSR. Alexander Troyanovsky, then ambassador to the United States, published a lengthy article in *Soviet Art* on American music. In a thoughtful section devoted to jazz, Troyanovsky affirmed that jazz was rapidly gaining a broader place in the art of music worldwide. Far from dying, jazz was blossoming as never before, Troyanovsky argued, and this was due to the growth of jam sessions in which musicians performed spontaneously and "purely for their own pleasure."[34]

Not all American jazz was readily accessible to Russians. No Soviet citizen, for example, was privileged to hear George Kennan's amateur jazz band, the Kremlin Owls, a group of young American diplomats who confined their performances to private gatherings of foreigners resident in Moscow. For the population at large, the strict ban against private ownership of short-wave radios meant that few civilians, if any, heard the performances of American swing bands beamed across Europe by the U.S. Armed Forces Radio Network. Nonetheless, virtually every Soviet musician active at the front recalls huddling into radio shacks to pick up the daily jazz broadcasts aired for the benefit of American servicemen in Europe. In spite of the difficulties, never before had so much contemporary jazz from America been audible to so many Soviet musicians.

The fruit of this diverse contact was a flood of American-inspired swing music in wartime Russia. Dozens of recordings of hit tunes

"Cake Walk, an Original Salon Dance," published in St. Petersburg, 1911. Other "American" tunes advertised by the Northern Lyre publishing company include "The Creole Girl," "Hiawatha," and "The Brooklyn Cake Walk." (Institute of Modern Russian Culture at Blue Lagoon)

Russian jazz pioneer Valentin Parnakh in sketch by Pablo Picasso. (Dutch journal *De Stijl*, 1926)

Avant-garde artist Alexander Rodchenko's collage of Jazz Age imagery. Illustration for Vladimir Mayakovsky's poem "Pro eto," 1925. (Evelyn Weiss, ed. *Alexi Rodchenko Fotografien, 1920–1938*, 1978)

Poster by Vladimir and Georgi Stenberg advertising a "Negro-Operetta," e.g., Sam Wooding's 1926 appearance at the Moscow Circus.

"The Tahiti Trot," the NEP era's
adaptation of Vincent Youmans's
"Begin the Beguine," 1926.
(Institute of Modern Russian
Culture at Blue Lagoon)

Leopold Teplitsky scouting
American jazz in Philadelphia for
the Commissariat of Public
Enlightenment, 1926.
(Lev Zabeginsky archive)

Leopold Teplitsky's professorial jazz band, 1927.
(Lev Zabeginsky archive)

Image-rich poster advertising Leopold Teplitsky's
First Concert Jazz Band, 1927.

"Shake it, Semenovna!" by the
Leningrad artist Vladimir
Lebedev, 1927.

Russia's first theoretician of jazz,
Joseph Schillinger, in 1927.
(Mrs. Joseph Schillinger)

Superstars of the Soviet dance
mania, Lidia Iver and Arkadi Nelson.
(*Russkaia sovetskaia estrada,
1917–1929*)

Simon Kagan's Hawaiian-style "jazz" band
holds on at the peak of the Cultural
Revolution, 1930.
(Alexei Batashev, *Sovetskii dzhaz*)

Caricature of wayward classical
musicians, 1934: "The Philharmonic Kids,
with Dmitri Shostakovich on banjo and
Sergei Prokofiev on saxophone.

High-kicking chorus line at the Leningrad Music Hall, early 1930s.
(*Russko-sovetskaia estrada, 1930–1945*)

Ted Lewis on the high seas: members of a corny Red Navy jazz band in the mid-1930s. (Sovfoto)

Johnson's band from Prague, on tour in Odessa, 1936. (*Ceska muzika*)

Leonid Utesov spoofs
"His Master's Voice,"
but with an ear cocked to
his other masters.

A courtly Alexander Tsfasman
weathers the proletarian phase of
the Cultural Revolution, 1929.

Leonid Utesov, star of *The Happy Guys*. (Sovfo

The pace-setting Tsfasman orchestra of 1936 poses with American dancer Henry Scott but without Tsfasman himself. (Mikhail Lantsman archive)

Levity in a grim era: saxophonists from the State Jazz Orchestra of the USSR during a break in a 1938 rehearsal. (Mikhail Lantsman archive)

Leonid Utesov's orchestra, complete with machine gun section, after a concert at the front, 1944. (Alexei Batashev)

Alexander Tsfasman, ever dignified, entertains Red Army troops at the fighting front, 1942. (Alexei Batashev)

Unlikely partners in the field of "mass songs": Isaac Dunaevsky, onid Utesov, and Dmitri Shostakovich.

Alexander Varlamov and his septet at the height of the purges, 1937.
(Alexei Batashev, *Sovetskii dzhaz*)

The Stalag 8-A Jazz Band, Görlitz, Germany. Red Army jazz
musicians doing their best with the limited selection of
instruments made available to them by their Nazi captors.
(Vladimir Krushin)

Eddie Rosner brings the Harry James style to the State Jazz Orchestra
of the Byelorussian Republic, 1940.

Power trust of the
Rosner orchestra, in 1943.
Left to right: Louis
Markowitz, guitar;
Eddie Rosner; and
Lothar Lampel, vocalist.
(Ruth Kaminska)

From Shanghai dives to elder statesman of
Soviet jazz: Oleg Lundstrem
in the 1960s.

The Murphy Band of Estonia, one of the first jazz bands in
Eastern Europe, at the Marcelli Restaurant, Tallinn, in 1925.
(Valter Ojakäär)

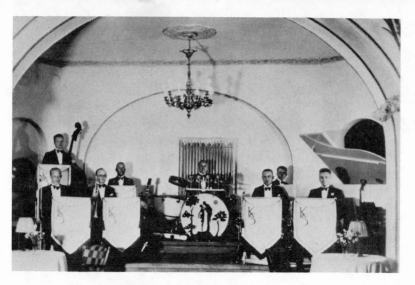

Kurt Strobel's jazz band at the Gloria dance palace,
Tallinn, Estonia, in 1934. (Kurt Strobel)

"The Spirit of Exile," 1946.
The journal *Krokodil*
laments, "How can she
[i.e., classical music] be
considered the 'free child
of the ether' when for two
months she has not been
allowed on the air?"

rokodil depicts a *stiliaga* and his *chuvika* in action in the late Stalin era, 1949. The sign cture Today" has been changed to read "Dance Today."

A meditative Georgi Garanian.

Post-Stalinist innovators: The Eight during a concert at the Lenin Library, Moscow, in 1957. (Igor Berukshtis archive)

German Lukianov at the time of his 1957 move
from Leningrad to Moscow. (Nathan Leites)

Leningrad saxophonist
Gennadi Golstein in 1969.
(Nathan Leites)

Willis Conover at the Voice of America microphone.

Igor Vysotski, alto saxophonist,
at Moscow's fashionable
Molodezhnoe Café, 1965.
(Igor Vysotski archive)

Beyond imitation: Roman Kunsman, alto
saxophonist. (Lev Zabeginsky archive)

Valeri Ponomarev, trumpet, and friends, Moscow, 1960. (Valeri Ponomarev)

Valeri Ponomarev after emigrating from the USSR, with
Art Blakey's Jazz Messengers, New York City. (Valeri Ponomarev)

Vladimir Sermakashev, the hard-driving saxophonist from Baku,
with bassist Yuri Tushinsky. (Vladimir Sermakashev)

Vadim Vyadro, brilliant
free-jazz innovator from
Riga, Latvia, with Austrian
bassist Walter Schtromeier.
(Vadim Vyadro)

Leningrad jazz critic, lecturer
and musical diplomat
Vladimir Feuertag, at
the podium. (Nathan Leites)

Valentina Degtiareva, coquettish and
hot vocalist from Leningrad.
(Nathan Leites)

The Leningrad Dixieland Band leads the parade of musicians at the Tallinn Jazz Festival in Estonia, 1967. (Valter Ojakäär)

George Avakian, Alexei Batashev, Charles Lloyd, and Yuri Vikharev (left to right) demolish language barriers at the Tallinn Jazz Festival, 1967. (George Avakian)

Universal types of the 1970s:
the Aquarium rock band from Leningrad.
(photo by Andrei Usov)

Long-haired and world-wise
Georgi Ordanovsky, leader of the
hard-rock group Rossiane.
(Nathan Leites)

The Scythians bring rock music to Soviet film: rehearsing for
Once More About Love, 1968. (Yuri Valov archive)

Logo for the 1981 rock mus
festival at Tartu, Estonia.

Pioneer Moscow rockers:
the free-spirited
Winds of Change in 1968.
(Yuri Valov archive)

Vladimir Maltsev (right) spins discs at the Metelitsa
discotheque in Moscow, 1978. (Tass from Sovfoto)

Viacheslav Ganelin of Vilnius,
Lithuania, leads his world-class
trio, 1978. (Leo Feigen)

Vladimir Chekasin: ferocity and
sophistication in the Ganelin trio.
(Leo Feigen)

Alexei Kozlov, jazz-rock fusionist, shading Moscow with California. (Alexei Batashev)

Boris Grebenshchikov of Sergei Kuriokhin's free-jazz ensemble, before a poster imploring the audience to "Implement the decisions of the 26th Congress of the Communist Party." (Nathan Leites)

by Cole Porter, Irving Berlin, and other leading American popular-song writers were issued by Soviet bands. Americanization of Soviet popular music reached its peak with the 1944 appearance, in Russian, of the Sonia Henie film *Sun Valley Serenade*, in which Glenn Miller's orchestra performed such favorites as "Moonlight Serenade," "In the Mood," and "Chattanooga Choo-Choo." Practically from the day of its first screening in Russia, this film set the style for many of the best Soviet *dzhazes*. Twenty years later, Soviet bands were still producing their own renditions of the film's famous score.[35]

The availability of published arrangements from the States intensified this influence. Far more important than the melodic borrowings and fake books, these orchestrations introduced Soviet arrangers to the denser scoring and more complex chord structures that had gained currency in the years since the cutoff of direct contact. Tunes such as "Rain" ("Dozhd") by K. Listov or "Song of the War Correspondents" by Matvei Blanter may have been Russian originals but show the clear mark of contemporary American arranging.[36] Similarly, Tsfasman's wartime *Concerto for Piano and Orchestra* is so fulsome a tribute to George Gershwin's style of orchestration that it probably could not have been performed publicly only a few years before.

Musical bureaucrats of the USSR were later to charge that the fashion for American jazz and popular music was the crassest imitation, lacking all originality. The charge is hard to sustain. Alexander Varlamov, from whom nothing of significance had been heard since his 1938 septet recordings, now emerged with the groundbreaking Melody Orchestra, consisting of a string sextet, dual pianos, and rhythm. The unusual instrumentation masked a genuine swing-type orchestra, playing imported and original arrangements by its director. "This was the best orchestra I ever directed," Varlamov later recalled. "It was something of an orchestral innovation: a string group but one that played not salon music but jazz, genuine swing."[37]

These developments would have been unthinkable during the late thirties. They now occurred openly and encountered surprisingly little resistance. To be sure, several Soviet jazz musicians were arrested at the front and sentenced to labor camps, among the victims being saxaphonist Boris Goldberg and drummer Ivan Bacheev. But none seems to have been punished for his involvement with jazz. Alexander Varlamov, for example, was jailed near the end of the war but because he had a German wife, not because he played jazz.

For the overwhelming majority of Soviet pop musicians, jazz was still less of an all-embracing musical form than a series of colorful devices, a hot foreign spice to be added to a preprepared musical soup rather than the stock itself. Yet during the relative freedom of the war years, jazz gained temporary naturalization papers in the USSR. Its adepts had greater contact with the American and Western European pacesetters and assimilated their techniques with fewer compromises than ever before. At no point since 1917 had the USSR participated more fully in contemporary Western popular culture than amidst its majestic struggle for national survival.

On the Eastern Front
with the "White Louis Armstrong"

The need to be responsive to the fighting man's values and the relative openness to American culture created a golden opportunity for the development of jazz in the USSR during World War II. Yet the attempted purge of jazz in the late 1930s, while unsuccessful, had set the music back so far that no native-born Soviet jazzman—not even Tsfasman—was fully capable of exploiting that opportunity. The challenge fell to Eddie Rosner, a bandleader and cornet virtuoso who was almost totally unknown in the Soviet Union before his arrival in 1939 from Poland.

Rosner is a nonperson in the Soviet Union today. His name, known to every Soviet jazz musician and older fan, is scarcely mentioned in books and magazines. His several recordings, exchanged among collectors at astronomical prices, are yet to be reissued. Yet Rosner was the leading jazzman in the USSR from 1939 to 1946. Here, at last, was the genuine article, as musician and as symbol. Driven to the Soviet Union out of necessity and eventually silenced by an anxious Soviet government, he spent seven years in a kind of sustained embrace with the Soviet listening public. With Rosner, swing music in the USSR reached its apogee.

Rosner's thousand performances were a salute to the West, and to America in particular. Whether performing in concert, where he frequently used "Anchors Aweigh!" as his theme song, or jamming after hours on "My Blue Heaven," "All of Me," "On the Sunny Side of the Street," or "I Can't Give You Anything But Love," Eddie Rosner stuck to the standard and by then international jazz repertoire.[38] He loathed the accordion, harmonica, and balalaika[39] as heartily as he loved the blues. A skillful arranger, he himself scored his band's entire "book." His jazzed-up classics, such as Toselli's "Serenade," were complex and sophisticated, while his riff-filled arrangement of "Sweet Sue" was such a hit that at the New Year's Eve party at the Metropol Hotel in Moscow in 1945 he had to play it after every other tune.[40]

What particularly stunned Soviet audiences was the full-blooded and authentic jazz timbre of Rosner's brasses and sax section. In place of the monotonously nasal and quavering tones of most Soviet bands, Rosner's outfit offered a rich, warm sound vitalized with unexpected chord progressions. This quality is amply in evidence in Rosner's 1943 Soviet recording of "St. Louis Blues," a landmark in the history of jazz in Europe.[41] His was a powerful sound as well. Rosner was the first Soviet bandleader to employ his own sound man, who was in charge of a fancy amplification system that had been built to order by the Electrik factory confiscated from occupied Vilno.[42]

Rosner packaged a good act. His band invariably appeared in white tuxedos or double-breasted suits in pastel shades. His use of multicolored lighting surprised even sophisticated audiences of Leningrad intellectuals.[43] And there was just enough hokum—such as the two men costumed as a camel who crossed the stage during performances of Ellington's "Caravan" (a song many older Russians still insist Rosner wrote). Rosner himself was short and dapper, with a closely trimmed mustache à la Harry James, whom he idolized. When standing before his band, his American-made gold Buescher cornet raised high, he was the very image of the Western jazzman. "He made a great impression," recalled the Leningrad novelist Daniil Granin. "Even those of us who were not jazz enthusiasts understood that he was the real thing." [44]

This paragon of contemporary jazz was born Adolf Rosner in Berlin in 1910, son of a Polish-Jewish shoemaker. Identified as a *Wunderkind* on the violin, young Adolf was already concertizing when he entered the Berlin Conservatory at sixteen. While at the conservatory, he became interested in jazz and began sitting in with the Merek Weber and the Rose-Petosy orchestras, both popular dance bands of the Weimar era. Soon he broke off his studies and, after a brief stint with the Rose-Petosy band, signed up with Stefan Weintraub's Syncopators, the most renowned jazz band in Germany and one of the best in Europe at the time. Between 1930 and 1933 Rosner made a number of recordings with the Syncopators that were released in Germany and Italy.[45]

Rosner decided to leave Germany when Hitler rose to power in 1933. He had already been badly beaten by a gang of SA troopers at a bar near the Alexanderplatz in Berlin. He went first to Belgium, but visa problems thwarted his stay there. He then moved on via Zurich and Prague to Poland, where he finally settled.

In light of Poland's perilous position in the mid-thirties, one may wonder why Rosner did not emigrate to America. He had visited New York City briefly in the summer of 1932 with Weintraub's Syncopators, but the band's manager had failed to make the necessary arrangements with the American Federation of Musicians and members of the group were not permitted to leave their ship.[46] Rosner's cocky self-confidence about his future prospects in Europe caused him to reject the possibility of emigration, but he maintained close links with America and American jazz musicians. He learned to speak English "like a New York cab driver," [47] carried on a correspondence with drummer Gene Krupa, and even engaged in a "cutting contest" with Louis Armstrong during the latter's tour of Italy in 1934. "Satchmo" won the event but was sufficiently impressed to give Rosner a photograph of himself signed and dedicated "to the white Louis Armstrong." It is said that Rosner reciprocated Armstrong's gift with a photograph of himself dedicated to "the black Eddie Rosner." [48]

Rosner's choice of Poland under Józef Pilsudski proved to be a happy one, in the short run at least. A talented German-Jewish musician could thrive even without being able to speak Polish, and Warsaw's jazz life scarcely lagged behind that of Berlin or Paris. By early 1936 Rosner had organized a seven-piece outfit that performed successfully in Warsaw, Krakow, and Poland's second city, Lodz. Several members of this group, including Georg "Joe" Schwartzstein, the drummer, and Lothar "Lionel" Lampel, the vocalist, had been with Rosner in Germany.

The new band made its mark in Poland, and Rosner was soon the proprietor of Chez Adi in Lodz. In 1938 the group, now a thirteen-piece swing band, left Poland for engagements in Paris, Monte Carlo, Amsterdam, the Scandinavian countries, and Latvia. The high point of the tour was the three-month booking at the ABC Theatre in Paris, where Rosner shared the bill with Maurice Chevalier, Marie Dubas, and Lucienne Boyer. Evidence of the band's strength can be found in the eight sides it recorded in Paris for Columbia.[49] Among the band's repertoire at this time were a number of tunes—"Caravan," "On the Sentimental Side," "Midnight in Harlem," etc.—that Rosner was later to popularize in the USSR.

Returning to Poland, the Rosner orchestra settled into successful engagements at Warsaw nightclubs such as Gold and Peterburgski's, the Adria, and the Esplanade. On September 1, 1939, when Hitler's army invaded Poland, Rosner's Polish sanctuary was destroyed. Joan Crawford's film *The World is Beautiful* was playing in Warsaw when the bombs began to fall. Rosner's first thought was to escape to the United States in order to hook up with Gene Krupa and other jazzmen there who had befriended him. But the Germans had cut off escape by sea, and the Red Army was fast approaching from the east, claiming its share of Poland in accordance with the secret protocol of the Hitler-Stalin pact. Huddled under the piano of the Esplanade with his nineteen-year-old lover, Yiddish singer Ruth Kaminska, Rosner realized he had no choice but to seek refuge with the Russians. Before making his move he had to take in supplies, which he obtained by striding into Gestapo headquarters, introducing himself as a German whose mother was Italian, and demanding assistance. A German soldier was assigned to accompany Rosner to his lodgings with a motorcycle heaped with provisions.[50] The trip across the lines was harrowing. But Rosner and his party successfully made their way first to Bialystok and then to the former Polish city of Lvov. Within weeks, most of his musicians had regrouped there, including "Joe" Schwartzstein and "Lionel" Lampel, who had made the earlier trek from Berlin to Warsaw.[51]

Ruth Kaminska, now Rosner's wife, had arrived in the USSR full of rosy expectations formed during her youthful involvement with the Communist party in Poland. Rosner's hopes were more modest: he simply wanted to continue his career as a jazz musician. The Russians had not yet put things "in order" in Lvov, so Eddie went straight to the Café Bagatelle and arranged a booking for his band. Valentin Berezhkov, Molotov's interpreter for the Hitler-Stalin pact and later a distinguished Soviet diplomat, recalled Rosner's floor show at the Bagatelle, complete with chorus line and partial strip-tease.[52] Red Army officers filled the tables, some of their ladies stepping out in nightgowns purchased from refugees and mistakenly thought to be ball gowns.[53] The music was unlike anything heard previously in the USSR, a swing band fully as competent as the best European ensembles. Word of Rosner's astonishing group passed briskly from town to town and eventually reached the offices of the first secretary of the Communist party of Byelorussia at Bialystok.

The Byelorussian Republic had lagged behind Armenia, Azerbaijan, and Georgia in establishing its own State Jazz Orchestra. Ample funds for such a venture were at hand, but no qualified director had been found. The first secretary of the Byelorussian party, Comrade Panteleimon Ponomarenko, was a zealous jazz fan and, within Soviet bounds, a *bon vivant*. Arriving with his bodyguards at Rosner's dressing room after a performance in Minsk, he proposed that the newly arrived band be named the State Jazz Orchestra of the Byelorussian Republic.

Rosner set his terms. He insisted on using his own musicians, having a completely free hand with his repertoire, and having a virtually unlimited budget for instruments, dress clothes, amplification, and lights. Rosner spoke no Russian and had to negotiate in German and Yiddish through an interpreter. Ponomarenko acceded to every demand.[54]

And so Eddie Rosner and his musicians escaped the fate of the many thousands of Poles sent to Stalin's camps in the far north in 1939.[55] Instead, he found himself heading the best-financed jazz band in the Soviet Union and bombarded with requests for radio appearances and recordings. He was handsomely rewarded for all this. Aside from receiving the title "Honored Artist of the Byelorussian Republic," he was soon receiving upwards of 100,000 rubles a year, while his wife was earning 500 rubles a concert for a minimum of sixteen concerts a month.[56] A worker at the time could survive on 1500 rubles a year. But that wasn't all. In 1940 Rosner was presented with a four-room apartment in the Moskva Hotel opposite the Kremlin, its salon outfitted with Afghan carpets, silk curtains, and a grand piano. Moreover, he was authorized to sweep by the guards at countless special stores where anything from mink coats to diamond brooches could be purchased. It is doubtful that any jazz musician on earth has ever been recompensed more generously within his society than Eddie Rosner in the Soviet Union during wartime.

Such munificence would have been unthinkable without the protection of Comrade Ponomarenko. Both Ponomarenko and his first assistant Alexei Abrasimov, later Soviet ambassador to East Germany, were fanatical jazz fans. The first secretary was notorious for walking out on operatic performances in order to catch a visiting *dzhaz*, and at his villa had assembled a formidable collection of American movies, including *Alexander's Ragtime Band* and other jazz films. Rosner and his band were frequent guests at the villa, where they basked in the largess of a man who was widely regarded, in Byelorussia at least, as a likely successor to Stalin.[57]

It was probably through Ponomarenko's intervention that Rosner was called on to give a command performance for "The Boss" in the spring of 1941. The great event took place at the Black Sea resort of Sochi. The ubiquitous secret police, the checking of internal passports, the atmosphere of supreme tension—all harken back to the State Jazz Orchestra's New Year's performance for Stalin in 1938. When the curtain finally rose, the musicians stared across the lights into what appeared to be an empty theater. For two hours the band played through its best numbers, leavening them with skits, songs, and banter. After the finale the curtain fell in the silence of what seemed a ghastly joke. Only at six A.M. the following day did a Kremlin *apparatchik* telephone Rosner's manager to inform him that Stalin had liked the performance.[58] That phone call placed an umbrella of safety over Rosner's musical endeavors for the next half-decade.

There is at least some evidence that Rosner's security was purchased at the price of a partial compromise. When the people "upstairs" at the Byelorussian Commissariat of Culture suggested that Rosner include some girls performing Byelorussian folk dances in his show, he agreed.[59] This meant the addition of an accordion for some numbers. When the same people frowned on his inclusion of several Jewish songs in his repertoire, Rosner dropped them. In much the same way, when told that an American diplomat wished to make his acquaintance following a successful concert in Vladivostok, Rosner gave in to his manager's entreaties and shunned the meeting.[60]

With a few such exceptions, the plucky cornetist stood his ground. Wherever possible, he tried to gain his ends through charm. The notorious Repertory Commission (*Repertkom*) claimed the power of censorship over the band's entire act. But "Eddie could twist them around his finger," one of his former musicians recalled, which led the bandsmen to nickname him "the Tsar."[61] But when charm failed, Rosner never groveled. A 1940 delegation of cultural bureaucrats informed him that his jazz arrangements of the classics were blasphemy. Rosner coolly assured the group that Chopin himself would probably be writing jazz if he were still alive, and that under any circumstances the Commissariat had no right to intervene in artistic affairs. When pressed, Rosner could be tougher still.

Shortly after crossing into Russian-occupied Poland in 1939, he and his wife were greeted by anti-Semitic insults yelled by a band of young Polish peasants. Rosner flew at them with both fists and bloodied several noses before the hooligans fled.

Such élan and style endeared Rosner to fellow musicians and the public at large, much as these qualities had earlier won respect for Tsfasman. But Rosner's mastery of jazz far surpassed Tsfasman's, and his personality had none of the chilly aloofness of the Moscow Conservatory graduate. Soviet jazzmen flocked to him in droves. But no opportunity to employ them came until late in 1941, when the Polish general Wladislaw Anders began organizing a fighting force to resist the Germans. Rosner wanted badly to join Anders but thought better of the idea when his wife gave premature birth to a daughter. A group of Soviet musicians joined the band to replace those Poles who departed for the front after Stalingrad and a second group followed.[62]

These replacements were drawn almost entirely from the ranks of musicians from the Caucasus and the newly annexed but then German-occupied Baltic states. As Rosner's wife and his former guitarist agreed, musicians from these outlying republics were far less fettered and hence more advanced in their mastery of jazz than were the Russians. Waldemar Kask, Rosner's new trombonist from Tallinn in Estonia, and Rudi Schenser, a saxophonist from the Latvian capital of Riga, had toured the European jazz circuit until the end of their countries' independence in 1939 and had no patience with the stylistic concessions made by their Russian colleagues.[63] A few of the new recruits, like Pirka Rustambekov, an Azerbaijani saxophonist from Baku, were genuine virtuosos. Whether seasoned pros or tyros, however, the Soviet musicians were fed into the band slowly, enabling each of them to absorb the experience of Rosner's Polish sidemen, many of whom had performed in Brussels, Paris, and other European jazz centers before the war, sometimes with Americans.[64] Thus, the Rosner band became a kind of academy of jazz. Among its most prominent alumni was the arranger Vadim Liudvikovsky, a leading figure in the post-Stalinist jazz revival.

The free and easy manner of Rosner's émigré jazzmen was not

without dangers for the Soviet recruits. Pirka Rustambekov, for example, made the mistake in 1942 of meeting with an American journalist in Vladivostok to listen through his collection of recent jazz recordings. The saxophonist was arrested, accused of spying, and disappeared into the Gulag Archipelago for many years.[65] Counterbalancing this tragedy were the hundreds of musicians and millions of listeners throughout the USSR whose interest in genuine jazz was animated and fortified by contact with Rosner's music. For seven years the Eddie Rosner orchestra functioned like a circuit-riding preacher, proselytizing a music which had become best known through the verbal attacks of its critics.

The cities in which Rosner performed included over forty centers stretching from Lvov in Central Europe to Vladivostok on the Pacific, from Murmansk on the White Sea to Baku on the Caspian. Constantly on the move, the Rosner band crisscrossed many times the sixth of the world's land mass covered by the USSR. It bounced around the war zone on flatbed trucks while under fire and arrived for concerts on remote Sakhalin Island in tanks. It is doubtful that any jazz band in history has ever fulfilled a more demanding travel schedule.

Seeding the Future

For jazz, as for virtually every other area of Soviet cultural life, the war was a period of huge suffering but also a respite between periods of purge and repression. Religion, letters, and the visual arts all blossomed briefly under the call "All Out for Victory." Yet the period of relative freedom was so brief, and the postwar crackdown so severe, that one is tempted to treat the wartime effervescence in culture as an oddity, a rare butterfly that quickly perished when cold days returned.

Far from being a genetic sport leaving no progeny for the future, the cultural freedom of wartime became a crucial element in the dialectic process that first produced the postwar reaction and then, after the death of Stalin in 1953, the great renewal. The war not only gave Soviet jazz greater freedom than it had enjoyed in years, but it did much to certify the legitimacy of the musicians, whose sacrifices on behalf of the fighting men could not be denied. Even Rosner, whose knowledge of the Russian language was still weak in 1945, was widely thought to be not a German Jew but a native son of the Soviet Union.[66] For all its Americanisms, jazz was more nearly acceptable to the ultra-nationalists in wartime than at any other time in the decades preceding and following the fighting. Interspersed on programs with Soviet patriotic songs and sentimental folk ballads, jazz was seen by patron and audience alike as just one more element in the rich firmament of culture for which loyal citizens were laying down their lives. The chauvinists and puritan zealots who were to lead the campaign against jazz after the capture of Berlin had their work cut out for them.

10

The Sonic Backlash,
1945–1953

... he [Tsar Alexei Mikhailovich] ordered the destruction of
any tavern musicians' instruments seen in the streets. Then he
banned instrumental music altogether and ordered the seizure
of musical instruments in the houses.

The Travels of Olearius, 1647

The Red Army's final, merciless drive across East Prussia, Poland,
and Germany in the early months of 1945 was the aggregated set-
tling of millions of individual scores. The spoliation, chillingly described by Alexander Solzhenitsyn in *Prussian Nights*, extended beyond the remnants of Hitler's army to anyone vaguely suspected of
collaboration, and eventually to the German-speaking population
at large.

Beyond the pillaging, devastation, and rape, which was largely
beyond the control of commanders, the Red Army also took seriously its role as liberator. Persons imprisoned by the Nazis were
released, symbols of national socialism destroyed, and local perpetrators of atrocities brought to quick trial and shot. But preceding these activities—and often the first public manifestation of the
Red Army's official presence in a place—was a concert by a Soviet
dzhaz. The pattern had been set early. When the Bessarabian city
of Kishinev was liberated late in 1943, Shiko Aranov's Moldavian
State Jazz Orchestra was on the spot to perform for the local population. As the Second Ukrainian Front moved westward, Aranov's
band moved with it, and was present to lead the celebration after

the capture of Bucharest in 1944. To the north, Nikolai Minkh's Baltic Fleet Jazz Orchestra arrived in Tallinn on the day the Germans were driven out, and gave a concert at the national theater, the Estonia, the following afternoon. Days later Minkh's band was sent across the Gulf of Finland to Helsinki, where it performed before 7000 Finns. So excited was the Finnish public that it seemed to the bandsmen, as Minkh recalled later, that no one in Helsinki had ever heard jazz before.[1] Minkh was wrong, to be sure. When VE Day finally came in Finland, it was marked by a jubilant performance by Jaako Vuormaa's long-established Finnish swing band.[2]

As the Red Army broke through to the major cities of Central Europe, it brought jazz in its wake. In the ancient Polish capital of Krakow a Soviet *dzhaz* delighted the local population with a concert in which Glenn Miller's "Chattanooga Choo-Choo" was performed repeatedly.[3] A Red Army jazz orchestra marked Prague's liberation by performing "Chattanooga Choo-Choo," "In the Mood," and other tunes drawn from the film *Sun Valley Serenade*.[4] Even in Moscow it was deemed appropriate for jazz-type orchestras to take a prominent part in the victory observances. When victory was finally celebrated in the Soviet capital on May 9, 1945, Leonid Utesov and the State Jazz Orchestra of the USSR were mounted on the bandstand in Sverdlovsk Square. On the same day, Eddie Rosner's Byelorussian State Jazz Orchestra serenaded the jubilant populace at Baku.

Euphoric Interlude

The postwar era of repression did not begin on VE Day, although in certain respects it had made its debut in Soviet cultural life as early as 1944. But the man in the street in 1945 had at least some reason to think the euphoria of victory might last. Well into 1946 Soviet popular music seemed to be kicking up its heels. A tour of Moscow restaurants and theaters in the autumn of 1945 would have given the Soviet jazz fan grounds for optimism. Rosner's orchestra was back from Minsk, where it had been playing for the victorious Byelorussian Army. Its stylish renditions of the latest Western pop tunes were so arresting that audiences at the Metropol treated the performances like concerts, without dancing.[5] Utesov and the State Jazz Orchestra were also in town, preparing a new program and even laying plans for a permanent jazz theater.[6] Alexander Tsfasman and the Radio Committee Orchestra were making weekly jazz broadcasts, and Tsfasman himself was entering into discussions that a few months later were to lead him to the directorship of a band at the Hermitage Theater.

These large groups were all but swamped by the many smaller ensembles appearing at Moscow restaurants and theaters. As in America and Western Europe, many musicians who had been demobilized at the end of the war quickly regrouped into small bands that were improvisational in personnel as in style. At the National Hotel restaurant alto saxophonist Leonid Geller fronted precisely such a group, which included the talented and, until then, amateur pianist and arranger Yuri Saulsky. The Artistic Theater (*Khudozhestvennyi*) boasted another such ensemble under the direction of the rotund and genial Hungarian-born drummer, Laszlo Olakh, while a group of veterans from the thirties held forth at the forthrightly named Cocktail Hall (*Kokteil-kholl*) on Gorky Street. This band was led by Nikolai Shmelev, an alumnus of the Varlamov orchestra, but its name, the Syncopators, shows the pervasive influence of Eddie Rosner, former member of the original Weintraub's Syncopators. Rosner's group completed its booking at the Metropol and was followed by Alexander Shulman's swing orchestra. Most of the group's musicians had cut their teeth under Tsfasman's tutelage, but Shulman's repertoire consisted largely of the same Harry James, Jimmy Dorsey, and Duke Ellington hits that Rosner's Byelorussian State Jazz Orchestra had popularized in the last years of the war.

The list could be extended. Suffice it to say that most Moscow restaurants and theaters that had maintained jazz-tinged orchestras before 1936 returned to that policy in 1945. As in the earlier jazz boom, each group had to water down its offerings with waltzes, polkas, and Soviet pop tunes. But Moscow bands like Olakh's and Shulman's saw themselves as principally committed to jazz, the other music being necessary only to appease the more conservative elements of their audiences.

In Leningrad the situation was much the same. Yosif Weinstein had ensconced himself with a small dance band in the Evropeiskaia Hotel, where he played swing arrangements picked up while touring the front during wartime. His musicians wore the same baggy Soviet-style suits which were later to cause titters whenever Soviet officials ventured into sight of Western reporters, but the bass drum around which the band grouped was decorated with a vaguely risqué silhouette of a high-stepping babe from a chorus line. In Armenia and other places where the State Jazz Orchestras had taken hold and policy was more open, restaurants and small clubs often featured "hot" quartets and quintets between sets of the big bands.

After so promising a beginning, everyone was caught off guard by the rapid and deep freeze that set in by the end of 1946 and forced jazz life to a halt. A new militancy appeared in all aspects of Russian cultural life, fortified by a xenophobia more extreme than anything since 1917. The Soviet government withdrew into itself and suppressed all cultural phenomena that could remind its citizens of the world beyond its borders.

Why did this seemingly abrupt reversal take place? Why did a country with good cause to revel in the self-confidence borne of victory and a newfound importance in world affairs instead retreat into suspicion toward the outside world so deep as to exclude even popular music from countries with different political and economic systems?

The simplest and hence most common explanation is that it was due to the chilling impact of rising international tensions on Soviet domestic affairs. As the wartime alliance with the United States disintegrated into the Cold War, the Soviet government set about expunging all traces of American culture with the bitterness of a spurned suitor.

Many Soviet people were, of course, genuinely bewildered by the breakdown of the alliance, and some certainly felt bitter after official relations went sour. But the extent of Stalin's reaction to the breakdown, and especially his repression of all American elements in Soviet culture, cannot be explained merely by his sense of American betrayal, for Stalin and his government had never had as expansive a view of the alliance as some Americans had. The mood of "supreme exultation" that a member of the American delegation at Yalta found in his colleagues was certainly not shared by Stalin,[7] who had for some years been indicating that he saw things differently. Even at the peak of U.S.-Soviet collaboration, in February 1943, Stalin had hinted about the possibility of a separate peace with Germany,[8] and when the Allies were beating back the Germans in North Africa and Italy in 1944, he had referred to their efforts disdainfully as "something resembling a second front."

Against this background, it is not surprising that shortly after VE Day Stalin blamed the war not on national socialism but on the capitalists,[9] and then began planning a Communist Information Bureau (*Cominform*) to spread communism into what was once again conceived as a bipolar world.[10] The pattern of postwar U.S.-Soviet relations had not yet fully jelled, but the prospect of future discord was clearly in Stalin's mind when, standing to deliver a toast at a luncheon for visiting Yugoslav diplomats in April 1945, he hitched up his pants and declared, "We shall recover in fifteen or twenty years, and then we'll have another go at it."[11] In short, Stalin's paranoia, rather than his bitterness over the breakdown in Soviet-American relations, seems to have been the chief cause of the avalanche of vituperation unleashed against all things American, a verbal assault which, as described by George Kennan,

> . . . for viciousness and intensity had no parallel, so far as I know, in the history of international relations. The wartime anti-Allied propaganda of Joseph Goebbels paled, as I can testify, beside it. . . .[12]

Revisionist historians have sought to depict the paranoia of Stalin and his government as a legitimate and defensive response to a series of aggressive American actions in the early postwar years. The argument has surely been overstated, even to the point of distorting the evidence, but the defensive motivation for the Soviet Union's severity rings true with respect to jazz. Soviet cultural officials were certainly convinced that their country was on the verge of being overwhelmed by "Americanization." As they saw it, jazz was in the vanguard of a Yankee assault that had already brought Western Europe to its knees. If a young counselor in the cultural section of the Soviet embassy in Washington, D.C., had been assigned the task of documenting the progress of jazz in Europe and Japan, he would have found articles in the English-language magazine *Jazzfinder* with such provocative titles as "Scandinavia in Ferment," "Britain Bounces," "Emergence of the Australian Style," and "France Rich in Young Musicians." [13] He would have learned that jazz clubs were being formed or revived in practically every country in Europe, and that for the first time they were linking with one another as a kind of federation. A host of new magazines in a dozen countries were devoted to fostering jazz locally, and books on the latest styles were published in Oslo and in neutral Vienna.[14] Our Soviet counselor would surely have learned from the American newspapers that platoons of American jazz musicians had once more begun touring Europe and were expanding their horizon to include Japan, where jazz and swing music were reported "to be sweeping over the country like wild fire since the end of the war." [15]

Soviet officials were in fact well informed on these developments in jazz. What they failed to understand (and the point on which the revisionists' argument breaks down in the cultural sphere) was that the spread of jazz was due far more to the sheer appeal of the music itself and to the peculiarly receptive conditions in the receiving countries than to any deliberate effort by the government of the United States. The vacuum created by the collapse of the Fascist regimes and the relaxation of wartime psychology had opened the floodgates to the forms of popular music and culture that the populace preferred, as opposed to what the more authoritarian governments wanted. But Soviet officials, unable to reckon with a phenomenon of genuine popular culture, could explain this only by conjuring up a sinister plot by the American government to break down local cultural resistance to American imperial expansion. It singled out the Moscow office of the United States Information Service as the agent for this campaign in the USSR[16] and the Voice of America as its mouthpiece from abroad. According to one Soviet writer in 1948,

> Several times each evening propagandists from the Voice of America send us examples of American music, obviously in the full conviction that such musical additions to verbal propaganda on the idea of "Americanism" will attract a large number of listeners. . . .[17]

The Voice of America was beaming live broadcasts from 52nd Street to the USSR. But the directors of "Jazz Club USA," hosted by Leonard Feather, considered their program no more special than the many others that featured American music, whether popular, folk, or light classical. Only in 1955 did the U.S. government begin to treat jazz as a particularly important element of its international communications.[18]

Yet one can readily appreciate the consternation of a zealous Soviet cultural attaché had he come across an article in the West German press called "The International Republic of Jazz."[19] Let the Americans claim jazz was being spread on the mysterious wings of popular taste. To officials of a government committed to forming the cultural values of its citizens, such disclaimers could not help but appear disingenuous, if not outrightly false.

Sounding the Domestic Alarm

Soviet officials were bound to react to what they interpreted as a carefully planned imperialist scheme to insinuate American popular culture into the heart of the USSR. Yet the abject paranoia with which they responded, as well as the manner in which they lashed out at cultural phenomena wholly unrelated to purported American designs against their country, cannot be accounted for simply by invoking the psychology of the Cold War. For the irrational severity of the cultural backlash in the years after 1946 was due as much, and probably more, to purely domestic concerns of the Soviet Union as to any pressures—real or imagined—from beyond its borders. The domestic and international crises, of course, fed on each other; nonetheless, much of the severity of the crackdown on culture must be traced first to problems within the USSR.

Stalin's regime would have faced crushing problems after the war even without a challenge from abroad. The Communist party was now composed largely of new recruits drawn into its ranks in 1944. Quickly initiated into the system during wartime, these fresh recruits were as yet poorly suited to exercise the Party's "leading role" in society, and even less accustomed to following orders from Stalin, rather than from local military and civilian chiefs.[20] For Stalin fully to control the Party, a postwar purge of its unassimilated elements was essential.

Even more serious was the need to gain political control of the population, particularly in the newly acquired territories of Estonia, Latvia, Lithuania, Finnish Karelia, the Western Ukraine, and parts of Moldavia but also in the vast area of the Soviet heartland that had been under enemy occupation. With repatriation, Soviet officials had to deal with masses of their own citizens who had been in more or less regular contact with the Nazis, if only as objects of brutal repression. The ensuing purge naturally blossomed into a campaign to rout the effects of all foreign contacts during the war; what began as a roundup of those who had trafficked with the enemy ended as a general witch hunt directed against all those who had had wartime dealings with foreigners of any description. Paradoxically, Red Army officers who had maintained liaisons with the Allies were particularly suspect, even though such contacts had presumably served the cause of victory.

The Arctic forced-labor camps expanded their operations to swallow the millions of persons who fell afoul of the new standards of loyalty. Estimates on the number of deaths at the camps in the Kolyma region alone in the period 1944–53 range from 600,000 to 1,750,000, and these figures do not include the camps described by Solzhenitsyn.[21] The mass roundups of those accused of subversive activities bred a mood of festering suspicion among the people. Books with such ominous titles as *On the Vigilance of Soviet People* were published in huge printings. They fanned the darkest fears and elevated the slimy act of anonymous denunciation to the status of a national duty of "each flaming patriot of our Socialist Homeland."[22]

It is often said that reform in Russia tends to come on the heel of unsuccessful wars—the Crimean War, the Russo-Japanese War, World War I—while victories lead invariably to periods of domestic reaction, as after the Napoleonic Wars. Never had this maxim seemed more valid than in the years 1946–53.

At the heart of the government's problem was its simultaneous recognition of the economic need to demobilize so soldiers could return to the labor force, and of its own political interest in maintaining the population in a state of wartime discipline and control. Some eight million men were demobilized and sent back to the farms and factories between 1945 and 1948.[23] At the same time, however, the government cracked down hard on civilian slackness: it vigorously prosecuted citizens charged with violating a 1940 law that had made it a criminal act to leave one's place of work; it tried to root out black-marketeering and corruption from urban life; and it severely restricted the conditions for legal divorce in the hope that marital stability would replenish wartime population losses.[24] Everywhere the back-breaking demands of reconstruction were used to justify the maintenance of strict regimentation.

That these changes of policy augured badly for jazz was obvious to some people as early as 1944, when the first round of critical articles appeared. Jazz musicians did not anticipate, however, the extent to which the public's mood was also gradually changing in a direction that, for the first time, left many people less responsive to the siren call of jazz. Victory had brought brief euphoria, but at just the moment when most Soviet citizens wanted a respite, their burden of work increased and leisure time diminished. Craving nothing more than contentment, the populace withdrew into privacy.[25] People were tired, older, and *The Happy Guys* generation had given way to one which placed a higher value on structure and order than on freedom and spontaneity. Hence, much of the population responded to Stalin's postwar crackdown with resigned support.

Jazz Under the Knife

Official patronage, public taste, and the more pressing demands of war had neutralized the 1944 attacks on jazz. The occasion for postwar renewal of the campaign came in August 1946, when a competition for popular entertainers was held in Moscow. Writers for both *Pravda* and *Soviet Art* attended and professed alarm at what they saw.[26] Once these authoritative journals had unlocked the door to puritanical carping, a group of professional critics rushed in to establish themselves as arbiters of public taste. Vladimir Gorodinsky took the first step by putting the widely loved and hilarious Leningrad comic Arkadi Raikin on warning.[27] A few days later the learned literary critic Victor Shklovsky entered the fray with an attack on Leonid Utesov for daring to aspire to the realm of high culture with his "theatricalized jazz."[28] To his credit, Shklovsky then quickly retired from what rapidly became a sordid attack on popular entertainment as a whole.

In these same weeks Elena Grosheva, a staff writer for *Soviet Art*, was making the rounds of the music halls, restaurants, circuses, and other homes of light entertainment. Grosheva was a prig and a pessimist. She held out no hope for existing popular entertainers and called for the development of an entirely new group capable of guiding the workers' "ideological upbringing" (*vospitanie*). Her use of this term, combined with her outrage at the popularity of "partner dancing," signaled the rise of a new paternalism led by a legion of Mrs. Grundys, all deputized by the Party. Within the year, these watchdogs had identified jazz orchestras as "the place where vulgarity and banality flower."[29] Concert organizations and publishing houses were told they would be held responsible for the "upbringing" of the populace, which was now conceived of as no less malleable than the clay from which God first created Adam. A resolution by the Organizational Committee of the Union of Soviet Composers extended this paternalism to classical music, while a series of Central Committee decrees in 1946 and 1947 applied the new standards to specific musical and theatrical productions.[30]

In comparing the post-World War II campaign against jazz with the attempted purge of 1936–37, one essential difference stands out: in the 1930s the arrest of individual jazzmen followed public debate, while in the late 1940s arrests preceded most of the ideological cleansing. Nothing more clearly indicates the direct initiative of Stalin's henchmen in the attack on jazz than the gap of several years between the first arrest of musicians and the appearance of the major diatribes against their music. It was as if the leadership acted and then ordered the music critics to rationalize their deeds.

Eddie Rosner and most of his musicians were arrested during the last months of 1946. Wartime criticism of the great jazzman for playing "cheap salon music"[31] had been passed over at the time but not forgotten. Rosner had been living in the hope that jazz and Western pop music might revive in Russia after the war, but after some months recognized it as a pipe dream. When the Soviet government announced after VE Day that anyone who had been registered as a resident of Lvov before its incorporation into the USSR in 1939 could legally return to Poland, Rosner immediately made plans to emigrate. With the necessary papers in hand, he traveled with his wife and daughter to Lvov in early November 1946. The emigration official assured him there would be no problem if he was paid a handsome bribe. When Rosner complied, he was arrested, on November 27. Ten days later his wife and daughter were taken into custody and charged with conspiracy and insulting the Fatherland. Rosner and his wife were transported separately to Moscow's notorious Lubianka Prison, where they were extensively interrogated and subjected to torture and abuse. Even in prison, Rosner managed to write a tune, "The Big Change" ("Bolshaia peremena"), which later circulated widely in the camps. After sentencing by a three-man panel of the Supreme Soviet, Rosner was exiled to the Kolyma region in Siberia, the most severe outpost of Stalin's prison system.[32]

Other jazz musicians were rounded up in Moscow and other Soviet cities. Leonid Piatigorsky, brother of the famous cellist and leader of a "sweet" orchestra that had recorded various fox-trots in the 1930s, disappeared to serve a decade-long sentence.[33] A. G. Alekseev, who twenty years earlier had run the cabaret *Crooked Jimmy* (*Krivoi Dzhimmi*) and who had subsequently hired many jazz bands for the Moscow Music Hall, was also arrested. Vladimir Sapozhnin and the musicians in his big band from Lvov were hauled off the stage in the Hermitage Theater and banished on the charge of having collaborated with the Germans.[34]

No aspect of the world of popular entertainment was spared. Lidia Ruslanova, for example, the most beloved folk singer of the war years, was arrested and exiled on trumped-up charges of having illegal ties with the United States. Non-Russian musicians were also arrested. Sent to the Gulag at this time were various Azerbaijani, Latvian, Estonian, and Lithuanian musicians. Jewish jazzmen probably suffered most, in part because they were relatively better represented in the field, but also because the rising nativism contained a strong admixture of anti-Semitism.

The fortunate were censured rather than arrested outright. Alexander Tsfasman was stripped of his post as director of the Radio Committee Orchestra late in 1947 but was permitted to make limited solo appearances and to tend his beloved flower garden. Arriving one day at the Union of Soviet Composers with a large bouquet in his arms, he announced bitterly, "This is my profession; the music is just a hobby."[35]

Like the seventeenth-century Zealots of Piety who had harassed Russia's traditional minstrels, the *Skomorokhi*, out of existence, the puritans struck out in every direction against the alien music. Prior to Tsfasman's demise, the State Jazz Orchestra had been ordered not to play jazz. At about the same time Utesov abandoned plans for an elaborate jazz revue.[36] To underscore the point, the government changed the orchestra's name to the State Variety Orchestra. Henceforth, all public use of the word *dzhaz* was strictly forbidden.

Jazz music suffered along with its musicians. A large audience turned out to hear the black American baritone Paul Robeson in concert at Tchaikovsky Hall in 1949. His program, a potpourri of songs from Communist countries, droned along uneventfully until shouts were heard in the upper gallery. Soon a chant was taken up, "St. Louis Blues . . . St. Louis Blues . . . St. Louis Blues." Robeson

tried to ignore it, sensing the danger in the request. He finally silenced the chanters by apologizing that he and his accompanist had
not been able to rehearse the famous W. C. Handy blues.[37]

Specific musical elements connoting jazziness to Soviet audiences
also came under ban. Chords built on flatted fifths, vibrato by brass
players, and the deliberate use of semi-tone "blue notes," were all
judged anathema to good taste and censored. The distinctive timbre
of jazz music grated terribly on the refined ears of the Mrs. Grundys in the Kremlin. The new piston-valve trumpets—long standard
in America and Western Europe—were judged a perversion of art,[38]
and merely to own a Harmon ("Wa-wa") trumpet mute was tan-
tamount to preaching the doctrines of Adam Smith. The charge
"too much rhythm" was hurled at every drummer who owned a
traps set,[39] and plucking the bass viol (instead of bowing it) could
put a bassist under a cloud of suspicion.

The saxophone came in for the most abuse. In 1949–50 all saxophonists in the Radio Committee Orchestra were fired, and composer Dunaevsky ceased scoring for the profane instrument.[40] At
this time most saxophones played in major *dzhazes* had been imported and made available to the musicians by the government.
One day in 1949 every saxophonist in Moscow was told to bring
his instrument and identification card to the office of the State Variety Music Agency. The despicable instruments were confiscated,
and the former saxophonists' identification papers were changed to
remove any indication that they had ever played Adolphe Sax's invention. Tenor saxophonist Yuri Rubanov emerged from the office
as a bassoonist, though he had never so much as held a bassoon;
the official work book of alto saxophonist Thomas Gervarkian indicated that he had been wondrously transformed into an oboist.[41]
The same policy was implemented elsewhere in the Soviet Union.
At the conservatory in Riga, for example, saxophones were banned
as "not ours," and Prokofiev's *Lieutenant Kizhe*, whose score called
for a saxophone, was struck from the repertoire.[42]

To ensure local compliance with the new standards, the Communist youth organization, Komsomol, organized brigades of party
aspirants and music students to check all restaurants, theaters, and

dance halls. One victim of a Latvian brigade recalled meetings at small resorts. Bandleaders were ordered to present lists of the tunes in their repertoires, which were duly checked against a master list of approved melodies. The proscribed tunes even included many of the tangos and rumbas to which Politburo members had danced fifteen years earlier. When the Komsomol brigade finished with the repertoire of the band at the Baltic resort of Gurmala the band-leader was vexed to discover that he had practically nothing left to play.[43]

In the Soviet Union's Eastern European satellites, the censorship work was considered too delicate to entrust to local Komsomol members or any citizens of the countries in question. Accordingly, Tikhon Khrennikov, secretary of the Union of Soviet Composers, organized a kind of traveling inquisition. When this somber band arrived in Budapest in 1949, it passed judgment on classical com-posers, such as Bela Bartok and Zoltan Kodaly, and then proceeded to grade popular musicians. The evaluations determined the in-come and even social standing of these Hungarians for years to come.[44]

An eyewitness of the 1949 inquisition in Prague recalled a con-cert of "model" jazz pieces composed on order for the occasion:

> It was an incredible nightmare. Band-leader Karel Vlach, the greatest among Czech pioneers of swing, sat in the front row, going from crimson to ashen and from ashen to crimson again, probably saying a prayer in his soul to Stan Kenton. Beside him sat an unholy trinity of Soviet advisors on jazz . . . , gloomy, silent, and next to them a senile choirmaster using a hearing aid. And yet not even the emasculated musical monster presented to them satisfied the Soviet advisors.[45]

Shortly afterward, Vlach and his bandsmen, along with their Stan Kenton arrangements, were relegated to a traveling circus. Khren-nikov and his fellow inquisitors headed back to Moscow, after leav-ing instructions that trumpet mutes be banned and saxophones re-placed by cellos wherever possible.

In Moscow, the campaign against jazz was blossoming in ever more fanciful ways. The inseparable link between jazz and the las-

civious modern dances was once more criticized. Since the dances
were impossible without jazz, Soviet composers were ordered to
turn out an entirely new jazz-free dance music. Folk groups were
revived, and the music market flooded with inexpensive balalaikas
and other traditional instruments. But the alien dances retained their
popularity. In a desperate campaign, which was eventually extended to even the provincial workers' clubs, the government ordered Soviet couples to return to the waltz, the polka, the *Krako-
wiak*, the *Pas d'Espagne*, and the *Pas de patineurs*.[46] Great pressure
to comply was applied, including the placement of Komsomol militants on dance floors across the land. But at the Builders Club
(*Klub stroitelei*) in Riga, for example, the young people had not
even heard of the Pas d'Espagne and stood about the dance floor in
dumb amazement as the government's new "popular" dances were
demonstrated for them.[47] Most did not bother to stand around.
Many years later a correspondent for Komsomol's newspaper reported on a club that was still doggedly trying to implement the
decrees of 1949 by banning all dances except the waltz. A group of
three dozen couples danced in the street to their own recorded music, each couple holding an umbrella overhead because it was rain-
ing.[48] Such was the effect of Khrennikov's declaration in Prague
that the Communist party has "too long ignored the accessible genres
of light music, handing them over to the ruinous influence of American jazz." [49]

Decreeing a Cultural Vacuum

While practical measures against jazz were being launched, ideological reorientation was also going forward. As we have observed,
the repression of jazz musicians preceded the theoretical polemics;
punishments were meted out before the cases were tried. The lag
indicates the extent to which Khrennikov and other leaders of the
purge were acting on orders "from above," but also suggests that
ideology in the USSR was no longer a guide to action but simply
an *ex post facto* rationalization for what had already occurred. Be-

cause the most dire consequences of an ideological assault had taken place before the words began to fly, the verbal attacks were curiously stillborn, though no less significant.

Until the beginning of the postwar era, Soviet music had never been fully subjugated to socialist realism. No resolutions of loyalty had been extracted from the musicians, as they had from writers and architects, and no national congress of composers had been held. A series of meetings called in 1947 and 1948 by Andrei Zhdanov, former seminarian and Leningrad city official who was now Stalin's chief aide, corrected this oversight. A preliminary closed conference in January 1947 was followed by a longer airing of opinions in January 1948, which led in turn to the convening of the First All-Union Congress of Soviet Composers in April 1948. On February 10, 1948, the Central Committee of the Communist Party had registered its concern over the state of music by publishing a scathing attack on Georgian composer Vano Muradeli, who had been foolish enough to write an opera about Ordzhonikidze, one of Stalin's former comrades in arms who had been driven to suicide by "The Boss." [50]

The denunciations, warnings, and threats that issued from these meetings are remembered today as part of the "*Zhdanovshchina*," as the general crackdown on culture launched by Stalin's number-two man is called. Many idols fell, including well-known composers Dmitri Kabalevsky, Aram Khachaturian, and Sergei Prokofiev, all of whom had recently received lavish praise from the Party and the government press. What were the sins that caused these recipients of the Stalin Prize to be publicly humiliated? At one level the attack arose from nothing more than the Russian equivalent of "redneck" hostility to what Khrennikov denounced as "the dissonance and disharmonies which are alleged to be signs of 'progress' and 'innovation.'" [51] In the weird coding of Stalinist speech, modernism and "formalism" merged to become the antipode of that wholesome "realism" championed by the Soviet Union. [52]

Beyond this simple instance of Russian nationalism gone mad, two issues were at stake, both of them directly relevant to jazz.

First, the Congress of Soviet Composers had witnessed a general assault on the entire high-culture tradition in twentieth-century music. As one critic put it:

> Our symphonists have put up an iron curtain, indeed, a steel curtain, between the people and themselves. . . . They've done it consciously and deliberately, for to them the [folk] song is something plebeian. They think it is degrading to make use of songs in their work.[53]

Second, the various meetings and conferences sparked a surge of professed interest in popular music as such. With highbrows under attack by their own students, popular composers seized the opportunity to take their case to the Party. While dutifully tipping their hats to folk music, they also made it clear that any new popular music would be the work of professional composers rather than village bards. Agitational mass songs barely figured in the debate. Recognizing the bankruptcy of that genre, Isaac Dunaevsky and his colleagues for the first time were willing to settle simply for an authentically Soviet popular music, something that would fill the same role in Soviet life that the products of Tin Pan Alley did in America.

Underlying the attacks both on the "formalist" highbrows and on the opponents of popular music was a pervasive fear that Russia's musical identity had been lost. Composers of both serious and popular music were exhorted to rebuild this identity by creating uniquely Soviet musical forms. The unacknowledged issue, of course, was the difficulty of accepting the psychological demobilization that had accompanied victory over Hitler. Even in the sphere of music, Stalin's regime wanted desperately to retain in peacetime the unquestioning and hence unnatural unity forged by war. Unable to accept the degree of cultural pluralism unleashed by demobilization, Zhdanov tried to whip up new cohesion by invoking a fresh foreign threat. Hitler's military invasion had been rebuffed, but now, he argued, the Soviet Union faced an equally serious cultural invasion from the United States and Western Europe.

The reasoning of Zhdanov and his followers was ingenious, if paranoid. They claimed that through the Marshall Plan, the United

States was working to absorb other countries into its supra-national empire. To achieve this, the Americans realized that supra-national cultural forms, arts which reflected "the wretched ideology of dying capitalism," were also necessary.[54] The modern music of Virgil Thomson, John Cage, Paul Hindemith, and Igor Stravinsky would fulfill this function. By participating in the modern movement, Soviet composers were unwittingly contributing to the downfall of communism.

Since it was virtually impossible to know what forms of classical music would pass Zhdanov's loyalty test, composers sought refuge in the less exposed world of popular music. But there another devil confronted them, jazz. Because jazz had scarcely been mentioned at the Congress of Soviet Composers, its position as a central target of nativist hysteria has gone unnoticed. No less than modernism, however, jazz was identified as a fundamental threat to Soviet civilization. So rabid was the desire to exterminate it that the ideological fine points concocted in its defense over the past quarter-century were thrown out the window.

The first to go was the notion that jazz was folk music. According to Victor Gorodinsky, music critic for *Komsomolskaia Pravda*, the only "folk" who could claim jazz were the ruling classes of the United States. In his *Music of Spiritual Poverty*, published in 1950, Gorodinsky dredged up lines from Gorky's "The Music of the Gross" to support his view that only a slanderer could assert that jazz was America's folk music.[55] Taking his cue from this argument, a particularly sycophantic Soviet composer, S. Mezhinsky, wrote an intermezzo on the theme, "Music of the Gross."[56]

But what of the old distinction between "hot" and "sweet" jazz? This tidy stylistic delineation had rescued at least some jazz from its critics during the Cultural Revolution. "The diverse forms of jazz, whether 'sweet,' 'hot,' 'swing,' 'boogie-woogie,' or 'be-bop,' . . . cannot be considered styles, as the theoreticians of jazz supposed," wrote Gorodinsky. "One cannot speak of styles in jazz," he continued. "Its ideational and artistic possibilities are too poor for that."[57]

Since jazz's first appearance in Russia, it had been shielded from many attacks because it was seen as a distinctly Negro art form. Particularly in the 1930s, this thesis, supplemented by the claim that jazz was a proletarian music, had prevented opponents of jazz from carrying their campaign to its logical conclusion. Now, however, even this defense collapsed, due in part to the untimely intervention of Paul Robeson. Writing in the journal *Soviet Music* (*Sovetskaia muzyka*) in 1949 (and blatantly feathering his own nest), Robeson argued that the only true Negro music in America was vocal, e.g., spirituals and the blues. Commercial jazz, whether played by whites or debased Negroes, "prostituted and ruthlessly perverted the genuine expressions of folk life." [58] These words, which found their way into the entry on jazz in the *Large Soviet Encyclopedia*[59] buttressed Gorodinsky's argument that the Negro element had completely dropped out of jazz. Wishing to remove any lingering doubts on this point, Gorodinsky sealed his case with learned quotations from the Viennese musicologist Karl Werner and from *The Daily Worker*. "The musical language of American folk music and jazz not only are different," he concluded, "but they are opposed to each other in principle. . . ." [60] The last defense of jazz collapsed. Whether "sweet" or "epileptic hot," [61] jazz was nothing more than a tool of international exploitation manipulated by the "Resident-Führer," Truman.[62]

The fundamental problem for those Soviet officials wishing to cleanse popular taste remained unresolved, as it had for thirty years. With what would Soviet composers resist jazz? It was one thing to decree a new popular music and quite another to create one that the audience would accept, as the failure of Khrennikov's songs attested. Soviet critics had no illusions about this. As one put it, Soviet "popular" songs ". . . are received at the institutions of music, published, and performed on the radio, but elicit no sympathetic reponse from the listeners." [63] The postwar products of the Soviet Tin Pan Alley were hopelessly inane, in part because nobody in the musical world could be sure that a truly popular song would be ideologically acceptable. The market standard of evaluation had been destroyed, but no new standard had been created. Soviet theoreticians lavished praise on Stephen Foster and his nineteenth-century

Russian contemporary Alexander Varlamov (great-grandfather of the jazz musician),[64] but they surely could not have expected popular taste to leap backward a full century!

Yet the official composers offered nothing else. The postwar campaign launched by Zhdanov was eminently successful in the sense that it destroyed the legitimacy of jazz in the USSR. Beyond this, however, it was a creative failure, for it provided nothing with which to fill the musical void. And in culture, as in physics, vacuums do not go long unfilled.

A second and perhaps more surprising dimension of Zhdanov's and Khrennikov's failure was their inability to implement fully the anti-jazz policies they had forced on the musical world. This failure, as much as anything in the previous history of Soviet jazz, reveals the limits of totalitarian control in the realm of popular culture.

Beating the System

From the moment the anti-Western campaigns were announced, Stalin's government demonstrated that it was prepared to use every means at its disposal to stamp out the foreign infection. Borders were closed to all but a few visitors, foreign radio broadcasts were jammed, international mail was searched, and access even to scientific publications from abroad was severely restricted. The campaign against jazz was pursued with equal vigor, both through domestic suppression and through the severance of foreign ties. And yet what Utesov referred to as "long-suffering jazz" survived.[65]

American recordings, for example, though officially banned, were nonetheless purchased in large numbers by Soviet visitors to West Berlin, mostly Red Army officers stationed in East Germany, and brought to Moscow in their luggage. The astronomical prices on the black market for jazz recordings, along with the risk of owning them, meant the larger collections were concentrated in the hands of the well-to-do elite. Writer Nikolai Pogodin was as well known for his up-to-date collection of Ellington recordings as for his anti-American plays.[66] Stalin's daughter Svetlana Alliluyeva went to the

home of a mathematician friend to hear modern jazz records.[67] People
of more modest means also managed to obtain jazz recordings, not-
withstanding their high cost. Harrison Salisbury, who covered the
USSR for the *New York Times* in these years, recalled hearing
American records blaring from the dingiest flats in Moscow's Arbat
Quarter.[68]

A curious feature of the Soviet Union's postwar settlements with
Germany and Austria required those countries to include feature
films among their reparation payments. Some of these were British
or American, and a number in which jazz bands appeared found
their way into Soviet movie houses. A Chaplinesque British film,
shown under the title *George from Dinky Jazz*, recounted the cau-
tionary tale of a bassist-spy who used his rhythmic plucking to
transmit coded messages over the radio. Whether or not this film
strengthened the vigilance of superpatriots, it gave Soviet fans an
opportunity to hear several quite respectably hot performances.[69]

Theaters had to depict the decadent West if they were to denounce it. At the famous Obratsov Puppet Theater in Moscow was
shown a nasty satire on Hollywood titled *Under the Shadow of Her
Eyelashes*. The performance was clever and funny, but many people
went simply to hear the excellent jazz that accompanied it.[70] Utesov, of course, had long since mastered the art of using anti-American
satire as a vehicle for jazz. Like Vsevolod Meierhold in the twenties, Utesov, in performances of such hits as "Brother Can You Spare
a Dime?," elicited more praise for the medium than the message.

Gulag Jazz

Jazz continued to be played to a limited extent because many officials who should have been leading the drive against jazz were
themselves jazz fans. This was a more common phenomenon in
Stalinist Russia than one might suppose and even extended to certain commanders and guards of the concentration camps run by
the State Camp Directorate, the notorious Gulag. Some of the best
jazz of the late Stalin era was played in the same Siberian and
Mordvinian camps where millions of exiles suffered and died.

Eddie Rosner's fate following his 1946 arrest in Lvov exemplifies the freedom that was sometimes available in captivity. Had Rosner remained at liberty in Moscow he would surely have been playing polkas and waltzes. When he arrived in the notorious Kolyma region after a trip of several weeks by boxcar, however, he was immediately called into the main office, equipped with a new cornet, and given help in forming a quartet, which began performing at Kolyma in 1947. The concentration camp's director, it seems, had heard Rosner play during the war and was proud to have so distinguished a musician as his guest. As Rosner's group improved, the commander permitted Rosner to assemble the best jazz musicians from all the camps on the peninsula.[71] Rosner succeeded in reconstructing many of his hottest wartime arrangements from memory, and the group had plenty of time to rehearse. If audience reaction is the measure of talent, this was one of the best swing bands ever to perform in the Soviet Union. By the summer of 1947 it was traveling under guard and in American-made Diamond T trucks to other camps to entertain guards, prison officials, and their ladies. As a reward, the musicians got good food, adequate quarters, and freedom from work on the murderous labor groups.

The fame of Rosner's new ensemble spread. Soon it reached the ears of Alexander Derevenko, director of the entire camp system in the East, and his two-hundred-and-fifty-pound wife Galina. The Derevenkos lived like princes. They had a townhouse in the coastal city of Magadan, they boasted a country seat forty-five miles to the northwest, and they had exclusive use of a large hunting preserve. Like an eighteenth-century *barin*, Derevenko maintained his own court artists, clowns, and so forth.[72] Derevenko and his aide, Captain Ziger, personally selected Rosner to head the Magadan Camp Theater (known as the *Maglag*). They had entrusted the directorship of the Maglag to Maria Gridasova, a formidable lady who "ruled like an empress."[73] Her singers and dancers sported flashy costumes, and she permitted her star performers to wear furs when off stage. Some were big names, including Vadim Kozin, one of the most popular singers of the 1930s, who had been convicted of charges of homosexuality.

The great strength of the Maglag Theater orchestra lay in its excellent musicians, including several from leading Moscow bands and a number of jazzmen repatriated from émigré colonies in Shanghai and Harbin in Manchuria. Their repertoire grew more dated with each passing season, however, in spite of Rosner's arrangements, for they remained in total isolation on the shores of the Sea of Okhotsk. By the early 1950s young people in Magadan found the band old-fashioned, although it continued to delight the Derevenkos and their guests at the Magadan House of Culture, as well as the camp inmates who were brought by convoy to see the show.[74]

For a short while, banishment to provincial cities was halfway between the isolated freedom of Magadan and the repressiveness of Moscow. For the few jazzmen who were exiled from major cities to the provinces, the late Stalin years were a period of great productivity. The bizarre history of the Oleg Lundstrem Orchestra from 1948 to 1953 shows vividly what could be accomplished by exiles under the protection of benevolent or indifferent local officials.

Lundstrem was a third-generation Russian whose father had taught physics at the remote Siberian border town of Chita. After the Civil War the family had emigrated to Harbin, and Oleg was raised in its large and nationalistic Russian colony. In Manchuria young Lundstrem first made contact with jazz through recordings by Duke Ellington and Louis Armstrong. By 1934 the eighteen-year-old had formed a nine-piece band, which promptly cornered the jazz market in Harbin.[75]

Abandoning his studies at the Harbin Polytechnic Institute, Oleg and his younger brother Igor, a saxophonist, took the band in 1936 to Shanghai, which was then entering its final decade as the Orient's most cosmopolitan and open city. At first the Lundstrems starved but heard good jazz, including that of Erskine Tate's old sideman, Teddy Weatherford, and Buck Clayton, whose Californians were just completing a two-year stint at the enormous Canidrome Ballroom. The Russians spent a summer working at the Midnight Café in Tsingtao in order to assimilate all they had heard. When they returned to Shanghai, they were asked to become the house band at the fashionable Paramount ballroom. Members of Shanghai's international audience demanded the latest swing music, and could walk down the street to hear any number of other bands if they did not like what they heard at the Paramount. Under such pressure, the Lundstrem band made rapid strides, consolidating its position in the Shanghai scene over the next decade.

When Mao Zedong's Communists captured Shanghai in 1948, the city's nightlife closed down. The Russian jazzmen faced an impossible situation. The United States, Canada, and most Western European countries would refuse them because of their Chinese or stateless passports. The remaining Russian émigré colonies in the Orient were breaking up. At the same time, news of the wartime relaxation of repressive cultural policies in the USSR had been well received in the nationalistic Russian community in Shanghai. Many decided the day to return to their homeland had finally arrived. Oleg Lundstrem and his Russian jazz musicians arrived in Moscow in late 1948. They headed directly to the Metropol Restaurant.

The restaurant's manager must have been astonished. Here was a group of eager young Russians in their late twenties proposing to play an evening of jazz as if they were in New York or London. Had they not heard by now that the very word "jazz" had been banned? But the risk was theirs, not his, so he allowed the performance to go ahead. A scandal broke out, and within days the entire band was banished to the Volga Tatar town of Zelenedolsk, near Kazan.

The story of the band would have ended there had Lundstrem not possessed the same brassy assertiveness as Alexander Tsfasman and Eddie Rosner. Although full details are lacking, it seems that he managed to negotiate an agreement whereby members of his band were permitted to settle in Kazan, the Tatar capital, on the condition that they enter the Kazan Conservatory and prepare themselves to be useful to Soviet society. By 1950 the *Shanghaitsy*, as they became known, had regrouped in the ancient Volga city and were performing in small groups at the Kazan Restaurant and the Elektra movie theater. Later, the full ensemble reassembled to play big band favorites at the House of Officers. Novelist Vassily Aksyonov, a student in Kazan at the time, recalled visitors from Moscow and Leningrad standing in stunned amazement as they heard the Oleg Lundstrem Orchestra exuberantly playing arrangements by Glenn Miller, Fletcher Henderson, and Duke Ellington that would have led to their instant rearrest in any major Russian city.[76] Paradoxically, the Party's campaigns against foreign and "cosmopolitan" influences were at the same time placing faculty members at the Kazan Conservatory under extreme pressure to conform.[77] Within a short time, Lundstrem's music was also being beamed out from Kazan over Tatar Radio. Most of the radio repertoire was "safe"— Tatar melodies, mass songs, and Gershwin ballads[78]—but fans in Moscow stayed up late to listen to the jazz broadcasts. "They were an amazing and beautiful thing to hear," a young Moscow musician recalled. "These were the sounds of heaven, but coming not from New York or Paris but from Kazan."[79] One wonders if authorities in the Tatar Autonomous Republic were unaware of what they were permitting, or were they themselves jazz fans?[80]

The Baltic Revenge

While a few bold groups continued to play jazz in the shadow of the Kremlin and at favored places of banishment, the popular music center of the USSR in the late Stalin years shifted decisively from Moscow to the non-Russian republics on the periphery of the country. Beginning in 1945–48 and extending to the present, the Russians' price of empire was to see their subject peoples enjoy greater freedom of expression than was available to themselves.

Communications were a factor. The Voice of America and the BBC were jammed, but fans all over the Caucasus and Central Asia could tune into the excellent jazz programs aired by Radio Iran.[81] In the Baltic, jazz programs beamed from Scandinavia, on Radio Luxembourg, or on the Dutch Indonesian service could be heard over shortwave radio. Aware of this, the government tried hard but unsuccessfully to switch the entire country to cable radio, which could be controlled.

While access to foreign broadcasts played a role in stimulating the development of jazz in the non-Russian republics, the most important forces encouraging its growth were purely domestic in origin. In the Baltic republics of Latvia, Lithuania, and Estonia what at first seemed a fresh flowering of jazz was in fact the continuation of an older tradition. Its most solid foundations were in Estonia, where, as we have seen, the Murphy Band had existed since 1918 and had begun performing professionally at a Tallinn café as early as 1925. At the end of the twenties, some dozen orchestras were playing syncopated music in dance halls scattered about the picturesque Estonian capital. Big band jazz had made its debut with the Kurt Strobel Orchestra, whose unissued aluminum recordings of hits such as "Bugle Call Rag" (1934) were on a par with the best sides by continental bands of the day. Indeed, had this fine band been known only two hundred miles to the east, the development of jazz in Leningrad would certainly have proceeded far more swiftly than it did. During the war, a swing band led by Rostislav Merkulov had been organized by professional Estonian musicians evacuated to the Russian city of Yaroslavl, and the Estonian Rifle Corps maintained an ensemble comparable in quality to the better State jazz orchestras in Armenia and elsewhere.[82]

In the last year of Estonia's independence, clarinetist (later architect) Hans Speek organized a first-class big swing band called the Golden Seven (*Kuldne Seitse*), which continued throughout the war and (with different personnel) was among the groups that revived Estonian jazz in 1945. The Golden Seven played tunes from the books of Glenn Miller ("In the Mood," "Tuxedo Junction," "Moonlight Serenade," etc.), Benny Goodman ("The Earl," "Undecided"), and Tommy Dorsey ("Opus No. 1") as well as original compositions by guitarist Vallo Jarvi, trombonist Ülo Randmäe, and clarinetist Valter Ojakäär. Since tape recorders were not yet available and records scarce, the two main arrangers, Randmäe and Erich Kôlar, went to American movies in which the latest tunes were performed and sat through them as many times as necessary to be able to write them out by heart. After 1945 the band played several times a week in Tallinn and Pärnu for school proms, parties, and special concerts at local palaces of culture.

Lithuanian jazz in the interwar years had been concentrated in Kaunas, then the capital. Foreign recordings were readily available and both European and American groups toured there until the Soviet invasion in 1939. Because of this contact, the *Džacas* performed in the thirties by the local Hofmekleris and Ceitelis orchestras at the Metropol and Versalis (Versailles) restaurants was probably less provincial than that of most Moscow groups.[83] The Latvian capital of Riga prided itself on keeping abreast of the latest cultural developments in Paris and Berlin. In addition to its dedicated local musicians like drummer Abels Kalns, Riga was host to many visiting jazzmen from elsewhere in Europe, some of whom were still there at the end of the war.[84]

Nearly all the Lithuanian jazzmen and some of the Latvians were Jews, most of whom perished during the war. Hence, when jazz revived in Lithuania after 1945, it was dominated by younger musicians who used the freedom of the Eden and other movie theaters in Vilnius to develop *de novo*.[85] In Latvia, a core group of older jazz musicians reassembled at the Daile Restaurant under Abels Kalns's leadership and performed jazz openly throughout the late Stalin years. Kalns's generation was rapidly supplemented by new recruits from the Riga Conservatory. One of them, a young violinist named Junnar Kushkis, openly took up the saxophone and managed to gain considerable skill as an improviser in the very years Moscow saxophonists were having their instruments taken from them. The bassist Egil Schwartz was also permitted to organize a big band, on the condition that he play no Western music. Being a capable arranger, Schwartz simply renamed and adapted the latest hits from abroad, including some of the earliest Stan Kenton arrangements heard in the USSR.[86]

Jazz made a healthy comeback in Latvia and Lithuania, but it was the Estonians who used the postwar period of repression to establish themselves as the most active and talented jazzmen in the USSR. Because of the head start they gained in these years, the jazzmen of this tiny Baltic nation, like their co-nationals in so many other fields, unwittingly set the standards of creativity to which Russians were later to aspire in the post-Stalinist era.

The rapid postwar recovery of Estonian jazz was facilitated by the fact that relatively few of the key musicians of the thirties had perished in the Holocaust. Several major figures, including Kurt Strobel and Hans Speek, had left the country by 1947, but there was, in general, far greater continuity in Estonian jazz than in Lithuanian or even Latvian.[87] The reestablishment of the Golden Seven in 1945 symbolized this continuity. Over the next two years the band again recorded arranged works and improvisations in the swing style. Valter Ojakäär, the foremost authority on Estonian jazz, has said only the finest Swedish bands were playing better jazz in northern or Eastern Europe at the time.[88]

On the heels of the Golden Seven came the Rhythmics (*Rütmikud*). At the same time, Felix Mandry organized a new big band with the name the Mickeys. Both groups were organized by musicians of the younger generation. Uno Naissoo, for example, a talented bassist who had been with the Rhythmics, was barely twenty when he broke off to form the Swing Club Quintet. The presence of older jazz musicians in Tallinn raised the general musical standard, while the relative freedom with which groups could be organized encouraged younger men to strike out on their own.

Estonian musicians were not exempt from the anti-jazz policies emanating from Moscow. The Estonian Radio Jazz Orchestra, for example, was renamed the Estonian Radio Variety Orchestra in 1948. Yet Estonia existed apart from Russia proper, particularly in the years before 1949, when a crackdown finally occurred. The contrast with Leningrad is especially striking. Since the thirties, Stalin's government had looked with suspicion at Leningrad as a potential breeding ground for opposition movements in the Party. Following the war, Stalin was determined to remove this threat by bringing the Leningrad Party organization to its knees. Jazz musicians there were caught in the general cleanup. Perhaps Moscow's preoccupation with Leningrad enabled Tallinn to enjoy a period of relative freedom. Whatever the cause, in this atmosphere Uno Naissoo and his friends laid the groundwork for the Tallinn Jazz Festival.

The festival evolved out of the Swing Club of Tallinn, a group of younger musicians interested in playing jazz. Naissoo recalled, "We were simply crazy. We wrote thick essays and argued about them; we tried to play everything, and even attempted to play Stan Kenton's music with a quintet."[89] Informal and tentative, the quintet assembled by the Swing Club was the first purely experimental jazz band in the USSR during the postwar era, and hence the progenitor of the many experimental units of the 1960s in Moscow, Leningrad, and elsewhere. Members of Naissoo's circle soon felt the need to expand their contacts to include other groups as well. Again, Naissoo took the lead, inviting the Mickeys to a joint session at the Palace of Culture in the center of Tallinn's fairy-tale Old Town.

The event, held on May 5, 1948, and repeated on December 23 of the same year, consisted of performances by the two bands. The "festival," which can best be described as a cutting contest, was so successful that it was repeated annually, providing good public exposure for new groups, such as *Metronoom* and the Emil Laansoo Ensemble, when virtually all public jazz was forbidden in Moscow. Estonians are quick to point out that their jazz festival was founded six years before the first Newport Jazz Festival was held. Far more remarkable is the fact that it came into being and survived during the harshest years of Stalin's rule.[90]

Assets and Liabilities

Soviet jazz musicians and their audiences put up an impressive defense to Stalin's all-out campaign to suppress jazz. Never had so much pressure been brought to bear against a form of popular culture, but in the end it failed. Jazz was not killed, its devotees not driven into silence. The most enduring legacy of the Stalinist campaign was entirely unintended: "long-suffering jazz" had been transformed into a martyr, a symbolic rallying point for all those disaffected by the State's heavy-handed attempts to impose a drab conformity "from above." Thus, Stalinists themselves did the most to define the social function of jazz music in the USSR during the decade and a half following the death of "The Boss" in 1953.

Soviet jazz did suffer heavily from the campaigns to suppress it. By 1953, even the best Russian jazz lagged almost a decade behind developments in America. Worse, most jazzmen had made so many accommodations to the demands of "red-neck" ideologues, super-patriots, and Mrs. Grundys that even the "jazz" under criticism was no longer jazz at all but some strange syncopated blend of Western pop music and local sources. Only in Estonia did anything resembling true jazz music continue to be played without interruption. As a Soviet critic candidly observed during the early days of the post-1953 Thaw, in Russia neither "sweet" nor "hot" jazz was to be found in pure form:

> In essence, all light music using any of the diverse elements of the musical language of jazz bears the name "jazz." Most of this is a hybrid blend of pre-revolutionary street music with the simplified rhythms and instrumental sounds of jazz. What we are calling "jazz" lacks both the cynicism of commercial jazz and the hot expressiveness of its improvised prototype.[91]

Such a hiatus was particularly costly in a European country, where there existed no indigenous diapason of gospel singing and the blues to nourish the processes of renewal. When jazz in the Soviet Union revived after 1953, it did so much as it had first developed in the 1920s, through influences from abroad that were subjected to careful study and analysis by Soviet musicians. Their achievement was all the greater because of it.

The heaviest cost extracted by the Stalinists' campaigns was the isolation of talented Soviet jazzmen from the extraordinary ferment in American jazz that produced bop. This complex, demanding, and artistically fertile new movement had been forged behind the scenes in wartime jam sessions in New York. Unknown to the American public because of the American Federation of Musicians' year-long ban on recordings in 1942–43, it had burst on the scene like a bomb, influencing even commercial dance bands by 1946 and overturning the entire American jazz establishment by 1948.[92] If one or two Soviet musicians had essayed a few chord progressions drawn from bop before 1953, Soviet jazz as a whole had yet to learn of, yet alone reckon with, the revolution unleashed by Charlie Parker and Dizzy Gillespie with their 1945 recording of "Groovin' High." The personal intensity and openness to bold experimentation of the young Soviet jazz musicians who emerged after Stalin's death resembles nothing so much as the determination and vigor of youth contending with the effects of amnesia.

11

The Search for Authenticity,
1950–1955

Jazz is only what you are.
Louis Armstrong

My youth passed under the influence of jazz.
Vassily Aksyonov

Stalin died on the evening of March 5, 1953. The Moscow military garrison was placed on alert and Red Army tanks rumbled into the city to form a cordon around the Kremlin. People stood about the streets in tears, some fearful, others expectant. The shock wave radiated throughout the Soviet orbit. In Leipzig, nurses in the children's hospital rushed about the ward crying "*Vaterchen Stahlin ist tod*," "Little Father Stalin is dead."[1] What would follow? A triumvirate of Stalin's henchmen dominated the funeral on March 9. But within nine months, Lavrenti Beria, head of the secret police, had been shot, and Nikita Khrushchev, not one of the original trio, had begun his rapid ascent to power.

The political situation was so fraught with uncertainty that people in most fields became exceedingly cautious. Newspapers that had been criticizing the venality of bureaucrats suddenly fell silent. Public discussion on topics as diverse as coeducation and monumental architecture ceased. The so-called Thaw (*Ottepel*), which took its name from the title of Ilya Ehrenburg's 1954 novel, began with only a few hints of change, far less decisively than the sudden rush of fresh river water with which spring comes to Russia. But the strong-willed Leningrad writer Olga Berggolts did not wait three weeks after Stalin's death to attack the absence of lyricism in contemporary verse and the need for writers to pay more attention to personal feelings. Before the end of the year Ehrenburg had pleaded for more literature that explored the inner world of man. Vladimir Pomerantsev, another writer, attacked wooden didacticism in his landmark essay, "On Sincerity in Literature."[2] Less confidently but very much in the same vein, bandleader Leonid Utesov published an essay defending jazz and the music of Duke Ellington and Jerome Kern in particular.[3] He even called for the rehabilitation of the saxophone, and—most significant for the future—pointed out that Soviet songs and dances were "boring and archaic" and "in no way correspond to the moods of our marvelous youth."

Even these mild demarches called forth opposition, for virtually every Stalinist had remained in office. Champions of socialist realism mounted the barricades in literature, and the foes of jazz continued to demand variety orchestras free of "howling trumpets, moaning saxophones, and convulsive rhythms."[4] The cautious pro-jazz intervention of Isaac Dunaevsky and the more outspoken defenses by Alexander Tsfasman, Oleg Lundstrem, and Nikolai Minkh did not tip the scales against the entrenched opposition.[5]

Clearly, Soviet jazz and popular culture lacked the power to transform themselves from within. Composer Aram Khachaturian made a case against "drab and outworn musical verbiage,"[6] but the old guard maintained the reins of power. The status quo could only be broken by fresh forces, which had already begun to emerge from beneath the immobile crust of Stalinism. Between 1949 and 1953 a new generation of Soviet urban youth came into its own, bringing with it novel ideals, values, and tastes. Members of this generation were closely united on the need for a truly authentic popular culture. These young people laid claim to jazz as their own private musical language and soon produced both a new audience for jazz and a new cadre of musicians.

Stalin's Disinherited:
The *Stiliagi*

During the late fifties and early sixties, Western newspapermen in Moscow became aware of zoot-suited Russian youths who disdained work, hung around foreign tourists, and professed a love for jazz. Periodically, the government would round them up, book them as "parasites," shave their locks, and send them on involuntary vacations to the countryside. Alarmed Stalinists saw these *stiliagi* ("style hunters") as the result of the partial relaxation of controls which followed Khrushchev's "Secret Speech" at the Twentieth Party Congress in 1956.

In fact, the *stiliagi* had been around for seven years before Khrushchev's attack on Stalinism. But, because the Soviet press had not trained its guns on them earlier, they had gone unnoticed in the West. By the time the *stiliagi* were known to foreign observers (and to most Soviets as well), the pioneers of the movement had forsaken it for greener pastures. Yet those forgotten founding fathers of the *stiliagi* had, between 1949 and 1956, defined the new Soviet jazzman and his audience. Before the *stiliagi*, jazz had been absorbed into the cultural establishment and crushed by it. Jazz emerged from the *stiliagi*'s incubator as the centerpiece of a new subculture, cultivated for its own sake and without compromises.

A student at Kazan University described a *stiliaga* classmate: "He combs his hair differently, his clothes are different, and he has a turned-up collar."[7] Certainly, *stiliagi* had a passion for style. Long jackets with broad shoulders, wide-striped shirts or black shirts with white ties, narrow trousers, and thick-soled shoes (preferably foreign but also obtainable from a Soviet factory in Riga) were the *stiliaga*'s uniform. Beards, sideburns, and mustaches were taboo, but long hair was *de rigueur*.[8]

The unlikely prototype for this zoot suit was Tarzan, more specifically Johnny Weissmuller as he appeared in *Tarzan in New York*. This film, which somehow passed the Soviet censorship, was shown widely in 1951–52. An indignant Soviet critic who saw it at the Daile Theater in Riga fumed about the "animalistic-sexual basis of the plot" but ruefully admitted that many youths were infatuated with Weissmuller's "caveman."[9] Even before journalist Semyon Nariniani coined the term "*stiliagi*," "Tarzanians" (*Tarzantsy*) were cropping up throughout Stalin's realm, and in the satellite countries of Eastern Europe as well.

James Cagney's performance in *The Roaring Twenties* provided the second prototype for the *stiliaga*. Strong and ruthlessly inner-directed, Cagney spoke his own language, when he deigned to speak at all. Soon *stiliagi* were talking of "dudes" (*chuvaki*) and "chicks" (*chuviki*); life became "groovy" (*kliovyi*); and food became "grub" (*birlyoz*). Moscow's Gorky Street, which the *stiliagi* had earlier renamed "Peshkov" (Maxim Gorky's real name), was called "Broadway" by 1950. If a *chuvak* was named Boris, he called himself Bob, and Ivan became John. Both Bob and John cultivated a "meaningful taciturnity." [10]

In the absence of Western-style bars, Soviet hotel restaurants served as the *stiliagi*'s native habitat. The test of a true *stiliaga* was to crash successfully a restaurant designated for the exclusive use of foreigners—no mean feat, since contact with foreigners was strictly forbidden. This required snappy new clothes to hoodwink the doormen, but also a command of a foreign language and a lot of cash, preferably in hard currency. In the Stalin era, only the children of the elite had access to these status symbols. Many of the "grand dukes," as they were later known, adopted the upbeat new mode of behavior and dress to flaunt their privileges. Nikita Khrushchev's children were arguably the founders of "style hunting" in 1940,[11] but soon after the war the new cult of youthful assertiveness spread to the Gromykos and other prominent families.

Well before the death of Stalin, *stiliagi* came athwart of the law. Some were gamblers, which was illegal. American-type pool tables being unknown, they played billiards for high stakes. One hustling *stiliaga* pocketed 800 rubles in a single afternoon at the Moskva Hotel's table in 1950.[12] Others flirted on the fringes of the black market, which in Moscow was active near the National Hotel on Stoleshnikov (nicknamed Spekuleshnikov, "Speculators") Alley. It was unknown to most of the population and ignored by Stalin's police. One could obtain Lucky Strikes or Camels, nylons, cocaine, and American jazz recordings. The son of Isaac Dunaevsky fell into this dangerous underworld and is said to have become involved in black-marketeering and then the rape and death of a young girl. Dunaevsky, Sr., committed suicide shortly thereafter.[13]

It took only one such tragedy to sour respectable people on all *stiliagi* and to close their minds to the significance of these young people's studied deviance. Stripped of sensationalism, the early *stiliagi* were the inverse image of the Stalinist society of their fathers' generation. The fathers wore baggy trousers, so the sons had theirs cut narrow; the fathers were careless in dress, so the sons waged a clean-cut protest; the fathers denounced the wicked West, so the sons embraced it; the fathers sacrificed for the future, so the sons indulged in the present. The *stiliagi*, in short, rebelled against the officially sponsored mass culture of the Soviet Union. They represented youth's search for inner-directedness, an escape into privacy from what David Riesman termed "the lonely crowd." [14]

What had begun as a fad among children of the elite well before the death of Stalin had burgeoned into a full-scale revolt by alienated Soviet youths. [15] The Soviet press documented the causes of this development with impressive candor, beginning in 1949. The problem of the low morale of youth first surfaced publicly at the Eleventh Komsomol Congress in 1949, when work quotas were proposed as a means of combatting the spreading idleness. [16] And none too soon. With low fixed costs, a Soviet student not driven by ambition had little reason to work. Each year more students simply dropped out of the rat race. By 1955, fully 17 percent of high school graduates in the Yaroslavl District were "hanging around doing nothing," according to one official report. [17] An even larger group floated through the schools, doing as little as necessary to get by. [18] While the elders thundered against "those who think they can enter the bright palace of Communism without the slightest effort," [19] a significant part of the youth population was beyond hearing, having seceded from Stalinist society in a flush of alcohol and cigarette smoke. [20]

Stalinists, who believed parents should be small-scale duplicates of "The Boss," held the older generation accountable. "Our most widespread type of false [parental] authority," the journal *Soviet Pedagogy* announced in 1949, "is that based on love." [21] Even without this exhortation to tyrannize their children, indulgent Soviet parents knew they had a problem on their hands and bombarded newspaper editors with requests for advice on family life.[22]

Soviet schools were criticized as much as parents, the progressives calling for the expansion of coeducation and the hard-liners demanding sexually segregated boarding schools where Party discipline could be instilled without parental interference.[23] Typical of an atrophying bureaucracy, educational officials reacted with "Olympian calm" to the hundreds of letters they received on the issues.[24]

Above all, however, the Communist Youth Organization, Komsomol, was singled out for blame, and rightly so, since its stagnation had helped to depoliticize the young.[25] In the postwar years, Komsomol was vastly expanded in order to mobilize young people for community projects and the work of reconstruction. It was thoroughly bureaucratized in the process, and its meetings grew "dull and uninteresting," according to its own official paper.[26] Morale collapsed, and cynicism and opportunism rushed in to fill the void.

These factors transformed a handful of nonconforming *stiliagi* in 1949 into a large-scale movement by 1953. Hallmarks of the movement were the utter rejection of public life, which was held to be hollow and Philistine, and the search for an authentic personal life. As one teenager told a *Komsomolskaia pravda* correspondent in 1950, "How I run my private life doesn't concern anyone else. One's way of life is a private matter." [27] The *stiliagi* revolted with the deed, not the word. They shirked work, dressed strangely, and spoke little, withdrawing into rude silence or private argot. In the spirit of classic bohemians, they took delight in the fact that they struck others as deviant. One *stiliaga*, hauled before a court in 1952 and charged with parasitism, defended himself by snatching a fly in his hand and calmly swallowing it. "I'm a mental case," he blandly explained.[28]

The *Stiliagi* Meet Jazz

The early *stiliagi* inevitably found their way to jazz, if only to defy the Stalinist ban against it. When the journal *Soviet Art* published an attack on jazz in February 1952, Ilya Suslov, a nineteen-year-old Komsomol member, was puzzled.[29] As the master of ceremonies for a student band at the Moscow Institute for Publishing and Printing, Suslov had grown to love Glenn Miller's music and had heard favorable reports about the exiled Rosner.[30] He wrote the editor to ask why jazz should not be played openly. *Soviet Art* snapped back indignantly,[31] which, of course, confirmed Suslov as a jazz fan. That same year an amateur band formed at Boys' School Number 59, across from the Canadian Embassy in Moscow. The principal, who knew from the press that jazz was taboo, warned the young musicians, but to no effect. When finally she threatened to call the police if the band played boogie-woogie, she reinforced the entire group's commitment to the world of jazz and *stiliagi*.[32]

The ban on jazz recordings enormously increased their value as a commodity in the *demi-monde* of the *stiliagi*. Besides stimulating the black market, with which a few *stiliagi* were in contact, official repression of jazz created the Soviet Union's first underground publishing network, for bootleg recordings reproduced on X-ray plates. Decades before the works of Solzhenitsyn and Sakharov were circulating in "self-printed" private editions (*samizdat*), *stiliagi* and other fans were disseminating recordings by Bill Haley and the Comets through "X-ray editions" (*Roentgenizdat*).[33]

Dancing pushed the *stiliagi* still further in the direction of jazz. Down to the early fifties, the young male "fashion hunter" danced with his right foot planted firmly on the ground, a cigarette in his lips. X-ray plate recordings by Les Brown, Les and Larry Elgart, and Glenn Miller provided the perfect music for this. In the early fifties, however, the jitterbug made its tentative debut, forcing musicians who played for the *stiliagi*'s dances to explore the hotter tempos of postwar jazz and early rhythm and blues.[34] Student bands at the House of Scholars at Kazan University became avid devotees of the new jazz in order to satisfy the dancers' demands. Disciples of the Lundstrem musicians, these "young Shanghaians" were offering completely banned music to local *stiliagi* by 1951–52.[35]

The most important factor in pushing *stiliagi* toward jazz, however, was the young people's craving for an authentic language of their own. Incessant propaganda had debased the spoken and written word and turned many young people away from language as such. Significantly, when their interest in verbal communication revived in the late fifties, they turned first to poetry and works by their contemporaries, Andrei Voznesensky and Yevgeni Yevtushenko. A decade of mass songs had also debased singing. Not until an entirely new genre of songs filtered back from the Siberian labor camps did the sung word return to Russia. For the time being, the young generation was nonverbal, preferring silence to degraded language in any form. The concept of "hip," of knowing the score without wanting to talk about it, united members of the young vanguard against their elders.

Jazz, with its emphasis on individuality and personal expression, became the *lingua franca* of dissident Soviet youth, the argot of jazz their verbal medium. But not just any jazz. The carefully scored and smoothly synchronized swing bands had succumbed to banal and hollow cheerfulness. By contrast, the emerging bop movement provided Soviet youth with an authentic language, one that permitted real feelings to break through. The complex but earthy musical language forged by Charlie Parker and Dizzy Gillespie demanded the active participation of the listener, who became united with the performer in a quasi-religion of the "hip," unintelligible to the heathen beyond earshot. What David McReynolds said of America's Beat writers in 1960 applies equally to many young *stiliagi* in the 1950s: "Jazz [to them] appears as something of a mass social movement in a society which fears the unconscious. . . ." [36]

What was it about bop or be-bop that so attracted the young Russian? Coinciding with the rise of the long-playing record, bop stressed lengthy unstructured solos in which the individual performer could give vent to his musical emotions and ideas. A harmonic vocabulary expanded by the introduction of diminished sevenths, flatted fifths, and frequent chord substitutions opened new vistas of mood and coloration. Tempos of unheard-of velocity propelled the musician and audience into a delirium of excitement. If the earliest jazz music embodied the anarchists' dream of individual freedom with a minimum of social constraints, bop pushed that freedom to its logical extreme.[37]

In zeroing in on the new bop music, Soviet *stiliagi* discovered exactly what the American Beat writers found, namely the private and uniquely modern ecstasy of social alienation and inner freedom. As American jazz was turning in on itself and becoming more exclusively black, losing for the time being its historic biracial character, the jazz subculture in the USSR, too, turned away from the larger public. Alienated Russians identified with the alienation of America's new generation of bop musicians. Young Russians encountering their first recordings by "Bird" Parker sensed, as Norman Mailer had, they were "white Negroes," "naked angels" keeping at bay an adult society grown cynical and hard.[38] Celebration of this heady psychic state became the central function of the new Soviet jazz. It was an end in itself, with no relationship to dancing or to entertainment.

Moscow's Boppers

The Soviet discovery of bop began during Stalin's lifetime but reached a crescendo in 1955–56, thanks in part to Mr. Willis Conover. For several years American diplomats in Moscow had been observing the *stiliagi* with fascination. They had noted that Leonard Feather's "Jazz Club USA" was attracting many listeners to the Voice of America and sensed that a jazz program designed specifically for Soviet youth would have a large audience. In late 1954 Ambassador Charles E. Bohlen proposed this to Washington, and in 1955 the landmark program "Music USA" made its debut with Willis Conover at the microphone. Over the next quarter-century this unassuming man from Buffalo, New York, was to be the single most influential ambassador of American jazz in the USSR and Eastern Europe. Saxophonist Boris Ludmer and trombonist Sasha Kofman heard Conover in Kiev and turned to jazz.[39] Saxophonist Vladimir Sermakashev followed "Music USA" in Central Asia, and pianist Adam Makowicz picked up Conover in Warsaw;[40] both became converts to jazz. Conover played a decisive role in forming the jazz elite of the entire Soviet orbit.

It goes without saying that the primary motive for establishing "Music USA" was political. The cultural-affairs officer posted at the U.S. Embassy in Moscow in 1956 stated bluntly, "The whole business of jazz was a political question, not cultural." [41] The Kremlin, after all, had long been vilifying jazz as the essence of American life. The U.S. government welcomed a chance to lay its case directly before Soviet young people. Given the climate of confrontation, the evenhanded and responsible manner in which Willis Conover carried out his charge is remarkable. Conover had learned about jazz before the war, while working at a radio station in Cumberland, Maryland. After the war he became a disc jockey at WWDC in Washington, D.C., and organized a few jazz concerts in his spare time. [42] To this day there is something of the amateur enthusiast about him, a complete freedom from jargon and the jaded hauteur of the critic. "*Villis*" is trusted because he grinds no professional axes; he is loved because he can communicate his enthusiasm as a listener. Conover is Conover, preaching no message but that carried by the music itself.

By late 1955 "Music USA" was blaring out of radios across the USSR, the staccato sounds of jazz piercing the shield of Soviet jamming far more successfully than a legato string section could have done. Suddenly, the new Soviet musicians received a flood of fresh material to master.

At the same time, the first generation of *stiliagi* was being overwhelmed by masses of younger teenagers whose sartorial dissent already showed signs of becoming a kind of conformism. Even before the Soviet press began attacking *stiliagi* as hooligans and parasites, the pioneers of the rebellion had progressed beyond it. A few musicians, like pianist Vladimir Vladimirov at the Druzhba Restaurant in Baku, clung to *stiliaga* fashions. Most took a tip from American bop musicians and began dressing in the "cool" style of bankers. But the collective alienation from Soviet philistinism remained, as did the passion for self-expression and individual release. Henceforth, an aura of deliberate deviance was to hang over both the young Soviet jazz musicians and their audiences, imparting to performances a warm and cultish intimacy inaccessible to the older generation and the uninitiated.

Amid the general reaction against the extreme regimentation of the Stalin years in 1955 and 1956, the government's anti-jazz persecution eased up. Literally hundreds of small combos were formed in institutes and universities across the USSR. Few of the musicians could actually play jazz, but most affected what they thought to be the mannerisms of true jazzmen, pouring out their feelings to rapt audiences in search of candor and authenticity. In Riga and a few of the more Europeanized cities, basement clubs à la 52nd Street existed, but the setting for most of these musical soul-barings was more mundane—a workers' club in Kharkov or the House of Culture in Khabarovsk. The performances had the air of counterculture rites.

Of all the new groups formed in 1955–56, The Eight (*Vosmyorka*) broke new ground by being the first Soviet ensemble composed entirely of improvising jazzmen and the first to place the new bop music at the heart of its repertoire. During its brief existence, The Eight crystalized the major musical and social forces emerging among the educated youth of Moscow and gave them their future direction. Several musicians from The Eight still figured prominently in Soviet jazz twenty years later.

The Eight was a product of the post-Stalin thaw. Its leader, bassist Igor Berukshtis, had long dressed in the *stiliaga* mode and later boasted of never having owned a Soviet-made suit.[43] It was Berukshtis's skill as an organizer that enabled the group to exist entirely without official patronage. Even before the Second Congress of Soviet Composers attacked red tape and bureaucracy in March 1957, The Eight refused to have anything to do with the Moscow Variety Agency (*Mosestrada*). The band operated in the twilight world of Soviet private enterprise, accepting only cash in payment and, to calm employers' bookkeepers, passing itself off as a group of accordionists.[44]

The first step toward the formation of The Eight had occurred when Berukshtis joined the house band at the Savoy (now Berlin)

Restaurant in 1956. Although the group was playing kitsch, it included two aspiring jazzmen, Boris Zelchenko, a trumpeter who could transcribe anything from radio, and Konstantin Bakholdin, a nineteen-year-old trombonist of great promise. In the months before Stalin's death, Berukshtis had paid a musical visit to Riga and had returned to Moscow with a manuscript fake book containing lead sheets to hot-off-the-press bop tunes like George Shearing's "Lullaby of Birdland." As these tunes were fed into the Savoy band's repertoire, it began to metamorphose into a bop group, much to the consternation of its leader, a schmaltzy violinist. The addition of the intense dark-haired tenor saxophonist Alexei Zubov and of the well-schooled alto saxophonist Georgi Garanian tipped the scales toward bop. The Eight was born.

The repertoire corresponded almost exactly to the segments of Willis Conover's "Music USA," which all members of the group tuned in to faithfully. Dixieland and swing pieces were interspersed with bop to form a musical smorgasbord. But the banner numbers came directly from recordings by Dizzy Gillespie and emerging second-generation boppers such as Clifford Brown and Max Roach. The more cerebral styles of Miles Davis and Gerry Mulligan were also first heard in Moscow thanks to The Eight.

The Eight included many dedicated modern jazz musicians. Igor Berukshtis reintroduced the plucked bass to Moscow after it had been several years in eclipse. Berukshtis was an ardent and accomplished disciple of Art Blakey's band, and when he moved to the United States some years later, Blakey welcomed him into his Jazz Messengers. The style of tenor saxophonist Zubov defies simple classification, but it has registered every tremor on the American front, from Mulligan to Roland Kirk, Yusuf Lateef, and Joe Henderson to John Coltrane. A hard player and hard drinker, Zubov epitomized the intersection in the 1950s of the early *stiliagi* and jazz.[45]

Three other members of The Eight later distinguished themselves in Soviet jazz: trombonist Bakholdin, also saxophonist Garanian, and pianist Boris Rychkov. Beginning with rather obvious efforts to imitate J. J. Johnson, the young Bakholdin evolved rapidly into a deft instrumentalist, as he later demonstrated in his composition "When There's Not Enough Technique," which he recorded with a quintet headed by Garanian.[46] Garanian, a far less flamboyant saxophonist than Zubov, was slow to plunge into the free jazz of John Coltrane or the oriental atonality which many Soviet jazzmen toyed with in the sixties. But American critic John Hammond appreciated his mastery of the saxophone: "He's phenomenal," Hammond reported, after a concert in 1967, "I'm telling you, I am overwhelmed."[47] A restless musician, Garanian progressed first to the writing of ambitiously scored divertimenti for jazz orchestra and then to jazz-rock fusion with his own Melodiia ensemble.[48] He has never been a great innovator, but his high professionalism as an arranger, his organizational skills, and his good nature later provided a setting for much fine jazz.

Pianist Boris Rychkov represents the best in Soviet and European jazz of the fifties and sixties. He worked tirelessly with taped recordings of Bill Evans and especially Oscar Peterson to learn the elements of their styles, but even his imitations bore the stamp of originality. A musician's musician, Rychkov never received the acclaim in the Soviet Union that was showered on Zubov and Garanian, but his exceptionally clean phrasing, subtle variations in volume, and overall good taste have inspired many horn players.[49]

It is surprising that these young Muscovites attracted an audience, given their avant-garde proclivities. Yet technical institute students, factory clubs, trade unions, and Komsomol groups all begged for their services. Demand reached such a pitch by 1957 that they set up a subgroup, The Five (*Piatyorka*) to take up the overflow bookings. Their jam sessions at the fashionable House of Journalists were packed, and girls followed the musicians like groupies. The band received an unheard-of 120 rubles per appearance, part of which the musicians spent on late-night drinking parties at the Vnukovo Airport bar. What began as the avocation of a few technical institute students burgeoned into a full-time but entirely unofficial profession.

The Watershed, 1957

For all its glitter, the triumph of The Eight was purely local. When Roman Kunsman, a talented Leningrad alto saxophonist exploring some of the same territory as Garanian, visited Moscow at the height of The Eight's popularity, he was surprised to discover that Muscovites were playing jazz at all.[50] Beyond Leningrad, word traveled even more slowly.

What transformed jazz from a local to a national issue and made the new generation of jazzmen from various parts of the USSR conscious of one another's existence was the VI World Youth Festival, held in Moscow in July through August 1957. This gathering brought some 30,000 teenagers and young adults from around the world to Moscow. Its occurrence symbolized the Soviet government's eagerness to break out of the diplomatic and cultural shell in which Stalin had encased the country in his last years. The decision to hold the festival on home territory forced Soviet cultural officials to review their policies on jazz.

This reassessment apparently took place between the Twentieth Party Congress in February 1956 and the following summer. Jazz seemed to pass muster, for the festival organizers announced that the program would include competitions for Soviet variety orchestras (e.g. big bands) and for visiting foreign jazz groups.[51] To show that the shift of policy on jazz was real, Soviet officials immediately invited a Warsaw ensemble, the Polish Blue Jazz Band, to visit the USSR in the summer of 1956.

All these decisions were opposed by the many Stalinists who still retained their old government posts. Orthodox critics attacked the eminently conservative Polish Blue Jazz Band for "duplicating the Voice of America's programming," and faulted its vocalists for singing all their tunes in English and French.[52] Others issued stern warnings to Soviet musicians that they should perform only works from the homegrown repertoire at the festival.[53] The policy of loosening Stalinist controls and limited opening to the West, on which the festival was based, was further jeopardized when Budapest students demonstrated against Soviet domination of their country in the autumn of 1956, which led to the Red Army's invasion of Hungary on October 23. The ensuing war scare played directly into the hands of Soviet ultranationalists. At the Congress of Soviet Composers early in 1957, a former *Pravda* editor railed against the "degrading music of the capitalist world." Alluding to the "Tarzanians" and *stiliagi*, Comrade Shepilov warned that American popular music led to "wild cave-man orgies" and "the explosion of basic instincts and sexual urges." At the very time his government was preparing to welcome about thirty jazz bands from abroad, Shepilov vented his anger against Soviet composers who "aped dreadful jazz music with howling vocal convulsions." [54]

Although challenged by the chauvinists, the policy of opening up to the West remained. Across the Soviet Union, big bands were formed in preparation for the competition. The Central House of Workers in the Arts (*TsDRI*, pronounced "Tsidree") in Moscow was particularly ambitious in this regard. Back in 1954 TsDRI had sponsored a highly successful competition for combos in the Moscow area, with Utesov and Tsfasman among the judges. [55] Naturally, TsDRI's director, Boris Filipov, now wanted to mount a band capable of winning the Youth Festival competition. He therefore turned to Yuri Saulsky, the energetic and youthful bandleader who had trained with Rosner after the latter's return from Magadan. Saulsky in turn hired Vadim Liudvikovsky, former arranger with Rosner's orchestra, who had recently been doing radio work in Moscow. Together, Saulsky and Liudvikovsky assembled the city's best jazz musicians, including nearly all the young players who had transformed the Savoy Restaurant orchestra into The Eight. It was a strong ensemble, capable of playing convincingly even Stan Kenton arrangements such as "Eager Beaver," although Soviet songs constituted the core of its repertoire. Its instrumental offerings were supplemented by a female quartet modeled after the High-Lo's.

Despite its preparation, the TsDRI ensemble had to work to edge out a band from Radio Riga, the Tallinn Metronooms, and the variety orchestras from Leningrad and Tblisi. In the end, Saulsky's ensemble shared first prize with a variety ensemble from Georgia, a compromise, to be sure, but a psychological victory for jazz.

The press had worked hard in the weeks before the festival to prepare for the shock. Soviet participants were instructed on how to explain the housing shortage to foreigners,[56] and were cautioned that hooliganism and parasitism would be vigorously prosecuted. Meanwhile, musicians were issued new Selmer instruments imported from France so they would not be embarrassed before the foreigners.

In the months before the festival, U.S. Secretary of State John Foster Dulles had pressured North Atlantic Treaty Organization (NATO) governments to discourage their young people from attending.[57] He need not have worried, for it was the Soviets who were "corrupted" by the event. An officially approved exhibition of paintings shown at the festival included abstract canvases by young painters from Sweden, Iceland, and Belgium. Through their encounters with these works, a young generation of Soviet artists began their development toward abstractionism and political dissent. Much the same reorientation toward modern Western and American tastes occurred in popular music. Saulsky's TsDRI orchestra impressed foreign visitors, but not nearly as much as Michel Legrand's French big band impressed the Russians, not only in Moscow but on its post-festival tour of the country. "We were astounded," recalled saxophonist Boris Ludmer from Kiev, "and for a while Legrand was our idol."[58] Most impressive were the modernists, including an excellent West German ensemble, Bruce Turner's band from England, Krzysztof Komeda's sextet from Poland with its Miles Davis tunes,[59] and Icelander Gunnar Ormslev's quartet, which played Gerry Mulligan arrangements with great finesse. In public performances and in jam sessions held at the Central House of Workers in the Arts, these bands destroyed the last vestiges of parochialism among young Soviet jazzmen.

Scarcely were the foreign musicians back on the train home than the journal *Soviet Culture* blasted Yuri Saulsky and his medal-winning ensemble for having misrepresented Soviet culture. Plagiarizing shamelessly from Gorky's 1928 essay, the critic charged Saulsky's musicians with playing "coarse, physiological, cheap" jazz—of being, in short, "musical *stiliagi*," also the title of the essay.[60] Much to the editors' chagrin, hundreds of letters defending Saulsky poured into the offices of *Soviet Culture*, along with a few attacking him.[61] By this time, however, the TsDRI band had disbanded, its mission accomplished. For the time being, at least, its work and the unintended consequences of the VI World Youth Festival as a whole could not be undone.

Ground Swell

The spontaneous proliferation of jazz bands in the USSR had begun a full year before Khrushchev's "Secret Speech" at the Twentieth Party Congress in 1956. Most were privately organized and were to remain so, but the government's official booking agency, Variety (*Estrada*), had begun eyeing the market as early as 1955. The post-Stalinist youth culture was becoming big business. In practically any major city one could find a nascent jazz group before the end of 1957. At the Rohte Fahne Park or Nizami Park in Baku, the Café Luna in Riga, or the Tolstoy House of Culture in Novosibirsk, jazz, or something resembling it, was being performed by and for the younger generation. Long before the era of huge public gatherings at which independent-minded young poets declaimed their works, the jazz evening was firmly established as a community rite of the younger generation.

Granting, then, the sociological significance of the multiplication of jazz bands between 1955 and 1958, what was the quality of their music? The point at issue is not merely whether specific individuals and groups were talented—they were. Nor is it to prove or disprove that Soviet jazz remained largely derivative—it did. Rather, it is to discern how rapidly a generation that was nurtured in an environment of Stalinism and socialist realism shook off those blinders and successfully mastered a new aesthetic language.

The main feature of Soviet jazz in the post-Stalin era was its emphasis on improvisation. Heretofore, Soviet musicians had concentrated on mastering the tonal, rhythmic, and coloristic aspects of jazz at the expense of improvisation. There were exceptions, to be sure, such as Uno Naissoo's Studio 8 and Exprompt 4 in Estonia.

But most imitated what could be most easily replicated, doing best at carefully scored big band swing music and worst at informal jam sessions. The pattern had been set early, when Russians had expressed admiration for Sidney Bechet in 1926 but actually copied Sam Wooding.

The new generation, rebelling against overcontrol in all forms, seized upon improvisation and spontaneity as the very essence of jazz. Its members singled out this quality in all music they heard and played, whether bop, post-swing big band jazz, "cool" cerebral jazz, or the Dixieland revival music. Whatever the form, musicians and audience alike placed a higher value on spontaneous improvisation, even if clumsy and maladroit, than on the smooth efficiency of imitation.

This was particularly evident in the many new Dixieland bands, of which there were ten in Leningrad alone. Both the Moscow Jazz Studio band founded by Yuri Kozyrev in 1957[62] and the Seven Dixie Lads founded in 1958 by the Leningrad student Vsevolod Korolev eschewed the elegant if prettified ensemble style of the English "trad" revivalists in favor of freewheeling solos deriving from Eddie Condon's Chicagoans. Only with the creation by Korolev of the Neva ensemble in 1961 did the milder English style gain currency, although even this band seems to have drawn more heavily on the individualistic Wilbur de Paris band than on the British revivalists.[63] Curiously, the hard-stomping ensemble playing of the New Orleans old-timers who were rediscovered in these years never gained a following in the USSR, although later groups, including the Leningrad Dixieland, the Moscow-based amateur band Gamma Jazz, and the Melkonov Ensemble of Moscow, played the revivalist standbys "Ice Cream" and "Just a Closer Walk with Thee."[64]

The Dixielanders were also relatively weak in their rhythm sections, another tendency common to most Soviet jazz in this period. With the exception of Tsfasman's wartime group, this had been an endemic problem, of course, but busy orchestration had somewhat obscured it. With the new emphasis on small bands in the late 1950s the rhythmic weaknesses became more glaring, and were the cause of much concern among musicians and critics alike.[65]

The younger generation failed to produce any first-class rhythm sections, but it more than made up for this in its horn players, particularly trumpeters and saxophonists. Among the Dixie-landers, trumpeters Vsevolod Korolev of the Neva band in Lenin-grad and the leader of a Moscow group, trumpeter Vladislav Grachev,[66] outshone their colleagues. Similarly, among the bop musicians who emerged in the late fifties, the most distinguished were trumpeters German Lukianov, Andrei Tovmasian, and Konstantin Nosov, and the two fine Leningrad saxophonists, Gennadi Golstein and Roman Kunsman.

German Lukianov came to Moscow in 1957 from Leningrad, where he had already begun his formal studies on composition and founded an influential quintet that preceded even The Eight in its turn to bop music.[67] From the moment of his arrival in the capital Lukianov exerted a great influence on the Moscow jazz scene, in which he became a central, if perpetually controversial, figure. Indeed, his refusal to leave town to take the post assigned him upon finishing the Moscow Conservatory cost him his diploma.[68] A composer of considerable skill, Lukianov had begun to play jazz in 1952 and thus had a head start on most of his generation. After The Eight was disbanded in 1958, he joined with Alexei Zubov, Georgi Garanian, and several others from the group to form an excellent new septet, which soon plunged into experiments with polyphony inspired by Gerry Mulligan's recordings. A series of trios followed in the 1960s, each of them recording Lukianov's own composi-tions. His "Useless Conversation" is of particular interest; Luki-anov's trumpet beats a telegraphic rhythm on one note, backed by sparse piano chords and cymbal.[69] There are strong traces of Miles Davis in Lukianov's playing, especially in his use of short phrases placed at the back of the beat. Yet one senses the search for a lan-guage of his own, a quest that would surely have progressed further with the backing of more challenging rhythm sections.

If Lukianov was searching, Andrei Tovmasian found it. A hard-living Muscovite who spent a year and a half in jail on charges of black-marketeering, Tovmasian was the local master of the Clifford Brown–Lee Morgan school of bop for over a decade. Tovmasian

began as an imitator, playing from memory whole passages by Clifford Brown. Yet by 1960 he had acquired the ability to produce
original and dazzling bombardments of articulated notes across his
entire range, which caused his American idol, Don Ellis, in 1963 to
identify him as one of the best trumpeters in Europe.[70] Even though
Tovmasian's tone is somewhat lacking in texture at slow tempos,
he plays with a sure and natural jazz instinct.[71]

Konstantin Nosov, the third Russian trumpet star to appear, made
his career principally in Leningrad, where he played in both big
bands and a quartet. With neither the flamboyance of Tovmasian
nor Lukianov's drive to express himself in original compositions,
Nosov is nonetheless a distinctive voice in the Don Cherry free jazz
idiom of trumpet playing. His phrasing is exceptionally interesting,
and his vibrato, which often wavers down rather than up from the
note, like a New Orleans clarinetist's, imparts a sure blues feeling.[72]
Prevented by his father's official position from touring abroad, Nosov nonetheless enjoys the high regard of virtually every Soviet
jazzman.

Closely linked with Nosov as the leader of modern jazz in Leningrad was alto saxophonist Gennadi Golstein.[73] Born in 1938,
Golstein took up jazz in 1950 and soon abandoned his studies at
the Railroad Technical Institute to play full time. From his first quartet
with pianist David Goloshchekin, Golstein had an ambiguous relationship with jazz. He was nicknamed "Charlie" on account of
his preoccupation with Charlie Parker's music, and had a photo of
Cannonball Adderley on his wall.[74] He soon mastered Parker and
Adderley's innovations and moved on to Roland Kirk and free jazz,
at each stage playing the music convincingly, from within. At the
same time Golstein's strong lyricism exuded true funkiness, both
in his playing of American standard tunes and in such original compositions as "Ritual," "Blue Church Bells," and "Madrigal."[75] Curiously, he seems to have drawn inspiration simultaneously from
the primitivism of the old peasant horn, the *rozhok*, and the vigorous polyphony of the pre-Baroque masters. This tension eventually led him away from jazz entirely, but for a decade and a half

after 1955 he was among the most interesting figures on the Soviet scene, like Lukianov, a genuine experimenter.

Golstein's fellow Leningrader, Roman Kunsman, was beset by fewer of these contradictory tensions. He had studied flute, composition, and piano by the age of sixteen, at which time he asked an uncle in New York to send him an alto saxophone. Within a year of the arrival of that instrument in 1957, this intense young musician had gained a facility in hard bop that would have been the envy of any aspiring musician in the West. His own tunes, such as "A Ray of Darkness," possess a rare aura of authenticity.[76] Like Tovmasian, Kunsman was utterly at home in jazz from the start. Eric Dolphy, Sonny Rollins, George Russell, and later John Coltrane provided him with new vocabulary in what was virtually a native language. As George Avakian, executive at Columbia Records, put it, "He is musically and artistically superb; and as a jazz composer he uses tools far beyond what anyone would expect."[77] Frequent changes of bands and often second-rate sidemen prevented Kunsman's full potential from being tapped in the USSR. Nonetheless, along with Golstein and the trumpeters, he set a standard in bop and post-bop jazz equal to that achieved anywhere else in Europe.

The hegemony of bop in Moscow and Leningrad was complete, but the more academic "cool" school of modern jazz found capable disciples elsewhere in the USSR, especially in the Baltic republics. By 1960 Estonia in particular had established itself as a kind of "West Coast," as opposed to the "East Coast" proclivities of the two major Russian cities. A pleiad of small ensembles took off from the work of Paul Desmond, John Lewis, Lennie Tristano, and other "cool" innovators to form a distinctive school: erudite, full of musical quotations and allusions, preferring a carefully arranged framework to loose improvisation, yet interesting and original. This effervescence of highly intellectualized jazz in Estonia coincided with a period of great activity there by modern classical composers, notably Aarvo Pärt. Alienation from highbrow culture was less pronounced among Estonian youth, and well-trained musicians like

Uno Naissoo, Rein Marvet, and A. Vakhuri borrowed naturally from contemporary avant-garde music. Much the same could be said of Latvia, where an impressive, if small, group of innovators was emerging. Less than a decade after the VI World Youth Festival of 1957, the Riga Conservatory-trained saxophonist Vadim Vyadro was experimenting with twelve-tone jazz, astonishing the Muscovites with his boldness. In his combination of inventiveness, technical sophistication, and sheer intensity Vyadro was years ahead of his colleagues; he bewildered and challenged them. In Riga, as elsewhere on the Baltic, the distinctions between styles were more fluid, less militant, than in Moscow. Latvian pianist Raimonds Pauls, for example, could mix elements of free jazz with Kansas City-style swing in the same number.[78] Eventually, the bop explosion in Moscow and Leningrad ran its course. When that occurred during the 1970s, the Baltic innovators came into their own.

The Big Band Revival

No review of the Soviet jazz scene in the fifties would be complete without mention of the big bands. In America, of course, the genre was in decline in the 1950s. The cost of maintaining large ensembles had become onerous, and young dancers, who had earlier constituted the core of their audiences, had cast their lot with the rock and rollers. Jazzmen themselves wanted the freedom possible in small improvising groups. The changes in dancers' taste and musical style were to some degree paralleled in the USSR as well, but the absence of market mechanisms in the field of Soviet popular culture assured the big bands' continued existence in spite of them. Once budgeted, institutions live on in the USSR, independent of demand. As a result, there were far more big bands playing jazz and American popular music in the 1950s in the USSR than in the United States.

Variety orchestras existed in some profusion. A chain of radio orchestras stretching from Riga to Novosibirsk played bouncy standard tunes à la Utesov, although the presence of dedicated jazzmen in the Estonian and Armenian radio ensembles gave them a more serious orientation toward jazz. Also, the state variety orchestras regained use of the word "jazz" in their name and achieved new vitality in Armenia, Georgia, Azerbaijan, and Byelorussia.

A few older jazz groups had been reconstituted after the death of Stalin, one being Eddie Rosner's. Rosner had been released from prison camp late in 1953 and by early 1954 had reached Moscow, where he quickly obtained permission to organize a new band. Unlike Utesov, Rosner took many younger players into his band, although until he recruited both Golstein and Nosov in 1967, the group had a rather dated and provincial cast.[79] Precisely these qualities probably account for Rosner's great professional success during this period and for the many benefits that were showered on him by those in power. Yet his heart was no longer in his work in the USSR. He submitted no fewer than eighty applications for permission to emigrate, but all were refused. Much later, during President Nixon's 1972 visit to Moscow, a visa was issued, and then only because Rosner entered the U.S. Embassy in Moscow disguised as an American tourist and pleaded for the ambassador to intervene with the Russians on his behalf. Rosner then settled once more in Berlin, where he died in 1976.[80]

Of the dozens of nominal swing bands functioning in the USSR in the fifties, only two stood out in terms of the modernity of their repertoire, the competence of their musicians, and their overall orientation toward jazz: those of Oleg Lundstrem and Yosif Weinstein. Both specialized in American arrangements and original works orchestrated in the current American styles.

The Lundstrem orchestra arrived in Moscow from Kazan in time for the Youth Festival in 1957. Lundstrem's adroitness and tact had earned the group many privileges, including its own apartment building, and he had not sacrificed his musicianship to get them. A steady flow of recordings of works from the Ellington, Miller, and Dorsey repertoires attests to the group's high professionalism. As late as 1976 a poll of Soviet jazz musicians (patterned, of course, on *Down Beat* magazine's polls) gave Lundstrem top place among the country's big bands.[81] The orchestra's variety-show format forced some banal dancers and comedians on the group, but the musicianship was uniformly high. In addition to three former members of The Eight—Georgi Garanian, Alexei Zubov, and Konstantin Bakholdin—Lundstrem attracted a capable jazz arranger in trombonist Arkadi Shabashov.

Like Lundstrem, Yosif Weinstein's Leningrad orchestra began with the American classics of Harry James, Glenn Miller, and Duke Ellington. Over the years, however, Weinstein absorbed "One O'Clock Jump" and other mainstays of Count Basie's repertoire as well as Charlie Barnet's "Skyliner" and other arrangements by Neal Hefti, Buddy Rich, and even Charlie Mingus.[82] Both Gennadi Golstein and Konstantin Nosov made their musical home in this group and, through their adaptations and arrangements as much as through their performances, transformed the Stalinist variety orchestra into a mainstream big band.

Weinstein had been organizing bands in Leningrad since the late thirties, and his Kronstadt District Navy Jazz Orchestra had entertained occupants of the besieged city in the grim year 1943.[83] During the high Stalin era Weinstein had accepted many compromises that would have made it difficult for him to break into the post-Stalin jazz scene in Leningrad had it not been for a competitor's misfortune. A local singer named Valeri Milevsky had fronted a swing band that achieved considerable success through its arrangements pirated from foreign recordings. Unlike the singer with the swing band at the local House of Culture of Industrial Cooperation who purported to sing American jazz by mouthing English-sounding noises,[84] Milevsky sounded like Sinatra himself when he crooned hits by Cole Porter and Jerome Kern. But Milevsky's young bandsmen were early converts to the *stiliaga* world, and, after several skirmishes with the law, members of the group were arrested, charged with parasitism, and ordered to disband as an ensemble. Weinstein picked up the pieces.

With modest musical gifts of his own, Weinstein was at least capable of identifying talent in others and of protecting those he discovered. For a number of years in the late 1950s he entrusted the musical direction of his group to Golstein and Nosov, both twenty years his junior, and gave encouragement to German Lukianov.

The arrangement paid off. The day of the businessman-leader had come to Soviet big band jazz. Weinstein's personal charm and his skill at negotiating with the concert agencies combined with the musicianship of the younger generation to produce a band that had no equal in the USSR in the decade after 1955.[85]

Why Did Jazz Revive?

The Soviet Union had banned jazz, both the music and the word itself, during the last years of Stalin's rule. By the end of the 1950s, the ban had been lifted although most of the officials who had supported it remained in office. Scores of new jazz bands had been formed, many of them exploring bop and the latest modern jazz styles of the day. Dixieland and traditional jazz, which had never really been played earlier, found new proponents, and a number of new big bands were formed, two of them surpassing the achievement of Eddie Rosner in his heyday. Most important, a corps of gifted young performers and composers was on the threshold of an unprecedented accomplishment: the debut of Soviet participation in the international world of jazz.

Should these great strides be credited to the post-Stalinist policy of opening Soviet cultural life to the West? Superficially, they should. Yet there were limits to the new openness. Not one first-rank international jazz star performed in the Soviet Union until 1960, and not one Soviet jazz musician was permitted to travel abroad to hear leading foreign jazzmen. "We didn't even know what jazz musicians looked like," recalled saxophonist Roman Kunsman.[86] Few American arrangements reached Soviet musicians, and the performances picked up on foreign broadcasts were beamed to the USSR precisely because their sponsors understood that the Soviet government wished to keep them out.

Given this, both the new openness of the Soviet government and the efforts by Western governments to break down barriers of communication emerged as no more than supporting elements of the central developments that led to the new jazz: the emergence of a generation of youth alienated from Stalinist society and its search for a mode of expression. The major jazzmen and their audiences were all drawn from this generation in ferment, the educated urban youth born between 1935 and 1952.

The Soviet government's willingness to crack open a small window on the West permitted the popular culture of America and Western Europe to reach these young people. Paradoxically, however, the Kremlin's refusal to swing wide that window and permit free trade in culture actually helped, rather than hindered, the new generation of jazzmen. Those wishing access to Western jazz had to make an effort to hear it. They could not relegate it to background music or otherwise take it for granted. Their engagement with jazz had the intensity of religious belief within the underground church. Without this intensity, modern jazz would never have developed with such impressive rapidity in the USSR.

Beyond this, the Soviet government's refusal to sponsor tours by major foreign jazz bands had the unintended consequence of promoting homegrown jazz. Would Alexei Kozlov or "Charlie" Golstein have bothered to transcribe note for note and carefully analyze the improvisations of Cannonball Adderley or Charlie Parker had they had casual personal contact with these innovators? Would Lundstrem's or Weinstein's young musicians have shown the same eagerness to master arrangements by Stan Kenton and Charlie Mingus had those bands been touring the USSR? Probably not. Yet, this phase of imitation and intense analysis—a process widely criticized in the USSR[87]—provided the environment in which many fine Soviet jazzmen were formed. Relative isolation from the wellsprings of the art encouraged the autonomy of Soviet jazz musicians in the fifties, who studied deeply but at second hand, rather than directly but superficially.

12

Cooptation and Conflict,
1960–1967

Play, play, Dizzy Gillespie,
Gerry Mulligan and Shearing, Shearing
in white clothes, all of you there in white clothes
and in white shirts
on 42nd and 72nd Streets—
there, across the dark ocean . . .

Anonymous poet, Moscow, 1964

From the late fifties through the autumn of 1962, Soviet jazz flourished in a receptive climate. The favorable atmosphere was nurtured by many factors, not the least being the confidence the post-Stalinist leadership gained from the launching of Sputniks I and II in October-November 1957 and the record-breaking grain harvest the following year. The key element, however, was that Khrushchev was intent on following a policy of "peaceful coexistence" with the West as a means of creating circumstances favorable for carrying out domestic reforms.

Khrushchev pursued improved cultural relations with the United States with this end in mind. The new era had opened in 1955 with a Moscow performance of Gershwin's operetta *Porgy and Bess* by a visiting American troupe.[1] In 1957 Khrushchev institutionalized his new policy by establishing at the ministerial level a new State Committee on Cultural Relations with Foreign Countries, whose purpose was to negotiate formal cultural agreements with capitalist countries. It succeeded in doing so with the United States within a year. In 1958 the Tchaikovsky Competitions were set up and attracted entrants from around the world, including American pianist Van Cliburn, who received a gold medal. Cultural exchanges

flourished, although jazz did not figure in them until Benny Goodman's renowned tour in 1962. Exchange performances by the Boston Symphony Orchestra and Bolshoi Ballet, not to mention Isaac
Stern, David Oistrakh, Jan Peerce, and Emil Gilels, fostered good
will and helped wind down the political debates over all music,
including jazz. Surprisingly, neither the Soviet government's forcing
of Boris Pasternak to reject the Nobel Prize for Literature in October 1958 nor the shooting down of an American U-2 surveillance
plane by Soviet rockets on May Day, 1960, clouded the cultural
horizon for long.

The favorable external conditions permitted the internal debate
on jazz to concentrate on the music itself. Vladimir Gorodinsky,
who earlier had tried to purge Stalin's Russia of jazz, now meekly
admitted that some jazz was acceptable to true Leninists.[2] This had
become the official Party line, and was reflected in *Komsomolskaia
pravda*'s 1960 editorial "Soviet Jazz Awaits Its Composers."[3] The
editorial resolved a controversy which had arisen when the newspaper's correspondent in Kiev had objected to the zeal with which
Komsomol's revived "music patrols" were carrying out their mission there. The editors had wisely called on a sympathetic composer, Yuri Miliutin, to calm the waters. Miliutin's measured defense of jazz, published in *Komsomolskaia pravda* on September
22, 1960, had called forth an avalanche of letters, "enough to fill
six issues of this newspaper," the editors observed.[4] His conclusion
that Soviet musicians should play jazz but write their own compositions defused what was left of the Stalinist opposition and was
hailed by musicians and audiences alike as a statesman-like resolution of the problem.[5] For the first time since 1934 Soviet writers
could explore seriously the history of jazz music. The appearance
in 1960 of a thin volume titled *Dzhaz*, written by the dedicated
Leningrad critic Vladimir Feuertag and drummer Vladimir Mysovsky, signaled the revival of jazz studies and also the official acceptance of the jazz terms "bop" and "swinging" (*svingovanie*).[6]

Eating and/or Playing:
The Problem of Patronage

From the earliest days to the present, the most persistent problem facing the jazz musician has been to organize his life in a way that enables him both to play the music he likes and to eat. In the early sixties in the USSR this problem emerged with particular force and was unaffected by the ideological acceptance of jazz. It existed, on the one hand, because the modern jazz preferred by the musicians was less accessible to the public than the Sovietized swing played by the variety orchestras, and, on the other hand, because the young audiences who liked it did not command the resources to pay the musicians. To be sure, Dixieland bands like the Neva group in Leningrad managed to ensconce themselves in secure restaurant engagements, but for the modernists it was more difficult.

The establishment and spread of clubs for jazz fans promised briefly to improve the situation. The first club was born in Leningrad in 1958 under the leadership of the pianist-promoter Yuri Vikharev. In quick order this evolved into a second club at Leningrad University, which worked in tandem with still another club at the local Electro-technical Institute. Two years later a similar club was established in Moscow at the Energy Engineers' House (*Dom energetikov*) under the presidency of the knowledgeable and vigorous Alexei Batashev. Within the next few years other fan clubs were formed in Kalinin, Yaroslavl, Kuibyshev, Gorky, Novosibirsk, Tashkent, Petrozavodsk, and Voronezh, each under the leadership of a local activist. As Yuri Vermenich, the professional engineer who founded the jazz club in Voronezh, put it, these groups were founded " 'from below.' Those persons 'on high' were neither for nor against, not really knowing what a jazz club was."[7] In due course, however, most of these groups gained official recognition, usually through the local Komsomol but often through a house of culture or even a technical school.

The clubs were great propaganda agencies for jazz. In Moscow, for example, jazz club activists organized seminars, discussions, and public lectures attended by some 25,000 persons altogether.[8] But most of the clubs charged no dues and therefore had to ask musicians to perform for free. Of course, no jazzman could resist the blandishments of the knowledgeable and receptive audiences the jazz clubs provided. The inspiration for many innovative ensembles came from avid fans. But for the other essential component of patronage, money, Soviet performers in the popular music field generally resorted to the private market.

For thirty years prior to the mid-fifties, the heart of the private market in popular music had been the local "musicians' exchange," or *birzha*. The exchanges, which had maintained a semi-legal status since the twenties, brought together musicians and patrons in a free-market microeconomy governed by an elaborate but unwritten code of procedures. In Moscow the *birzha* gathered each afternoon at 3:00 P.M. in the street outside the Central House of Workers in the Arts (TsDRI). Sometimes as many as one hundred and fifty musicians would assemble for assignment to dances, restaurants, and parties. Individual musicians could bid for assignments, but organized groups would usually be represented by their manager or *inspektor*.[9] It was a freewheeling, cutthroat gathering, in which a well-connected star could command a high salary and an outsider could be reduced to near penury.

This island of free-market pricing posed a direct threat to the socialist principle of state control. Accordingly, in the mid-fifties the government asked the State Variety Agency (*Gosestrada*) to take over the entire light music industry. But the *birzha*, far from dying, simply moved its headquarters to the street outside the office of the Moscow Variety Agency (*Mosestrada*). Similar switches occurred when local variety agencies were established elsewhere.

Jazz fell nominally under Gosestrada but retained its link with the *birzha* because the State agency quickly proved itself incapable of organizing good jazz bands. The story of Arkadi Babov, the head of the Variety Agency in the resort town of Sochi in the sixties, reveals the reason for the state's incompetence. Babov was a poor musician but true democrat. When saxophonist Vladimir Tkalich presented him the list of members of his new modern jazz ensemble, Babov objected: "We don't want all the best musicians in one

group!" [10] Like many unions elsewhere, Gosestrada replaced a spo-
radically capricious free market with a permanently bureaucratized
system.

Every musician and group wishing to enter the system first had
to be certified and graded by the local Office of Musical Ensembles
(*OMA*), an offshoot of the Union of Soviet Composers. The two-
tiered rankings, still in effect today, distinguish sharply between those
groups authorized to play for restaurants and dances and those
qualified to perform in concert. Jazz bands, quite at home in both
milieus, are usually restricted to restaurants. This crippling limita-
tion embodies the Russians' time-honored bias in favor of high culture as clearly as the creation of Red Seal records fifty years earlier.
The bias is also reflected in the performance test which each individual must pass to be admitted to the system. Sight reading and
classical technique are stressed, while the ability to improvise is
considered of no consequence, a fact which severely impeded the
spread of jazz by relegating many jazzmen to the lowest-pay category.[11] It is interesting to speculate whether the effect was inten-
tional or not.

In addition to being heavily bureaucratized, the system is far from
immune to individual prejudices. When Leningrad saxophonist Roman Kunsman presented himself at the local Office for Musical Ensembles for certification in 1962, the director asked him if he knew
where Comrade Khrushchev was at the moment. When Kunsman
was unable to answer, the director informed him, "We don't need
your type here." Only later did Kunsman learn from a seasoned
colleague that with a timely bribe he could instantly have transformed himself, in the eyes of the director at least, from a *stiliaga*
into a "principled Communist." [12]

As if these impediments to the aspiring jazz musician are not
enough, the variety agencies and offices of musical ensembles continue to exercise strict control over jazz band repertoires through
the notorious repertory commissions (*Repertkom*) and the artistic
councils (*Khudozhestvennye sovety*). Before a new band is certified
for performance, it must present itself for an audition and also submit a list of the tunes it proposes to play.[13] Since all official patron-

age is withheld from groups failing the audition, self-censorship becomes the better part of valor, particularly in those cities where repertory commissions are dominated by foes of jazz. Certification does not settle the matter, however, since revised tune lists, known in slang as *repertishki*, must be submitted and approved on a monthly basis. This, of course, is an open invitation to deceit. One well-known Leningrad jazz ensemble maintained two entirely different repertoires, one to be played for the Repertory Commission and the other for jazz fans.[14] Another group active in Moscow in the 1960s went even further, fabricating long lists of completely non-existent tunes by Soviet composers.[15] In an attempt to halt this widespread practice, the variety agencies began sending members of their artistic councils to dances and concerts to check up on the jazz bands' repertoires. Rationalized as an effort to ensure that composers would receive full copyright payments, this practice has had little effect and has simply forced more of the best jazz into private jam sessions.[16]

Under these circumstances, if a Soviet jazz musician seeking official patronage is exceptionally adroit or willing to compromise, he can live comfortably and enjoy as much job security as his counterpart in the West.[17] If he is neither, two alternatives are open to him. He can take a full-time day job, certainly a time-honored solution for jazzmen. Or he can sign up with a commercial variety orchestra.

All of the big bands working in the fifties continued into the next decade, for the most part serving institutional patrons and older audiences in the provinces. Jazz musicians, with other avenues of work closed to them, flocked into these groups in some numbers. Their impact on the music was minimal, however, since their major commitments as musicians lay elsewhere. Murad Kazhlaev, composer of popular music in the style of the forties, managed for several years in the sixties to hold Georgi Garanian, Konstantin Nosov, and Konstantin Bakholdin in his Baku-based orchestra, although their presence did little to save the band from being tedious.[18] Other big bands of the sixties, such as Vadim Liudvikovsky's Concert Variety Ensemble, which grew out of the old TsDRI orchestra and flourished thanks to a radio contract, attacted larger numbers of jazzmen. Liudvikovsky wisely followed Yosif Weinstein's lead in allowing his young recruits the freedom to develop the band's repertoire. But, as critics had noted with the Weinstein band, the big band medium itself now proved an impediment.[19]

Most of the touring variety orchestras were under the control of the most conservative big-city concert organizations. Realizing this, a few entrepreneurial jazz musicians sought provincial centers in which to organize their own big bands. Pianist Boris Rychkov put together a band under the Georgian Philharmonic organization and filled all but one place with friends from Leningrad and Moscow.[20] In the industrial town of Tula, pianist Anatoli Kroll produced a group capable of playing Thad Jones arrangements with considerably more intensity than Liudvikovsky's band.[21] Yet even Kroll's band was basically a commercial group, with jazz a peripheral element in its repertoire. Its fine jazz musicians played in it mostly for money, maintaining their artistic identity in the jam sessions that invariably sprang up after concerts rather than in the public performances.[22]

Amidst its greatest successes, then, modern Soviet jazz in the sixties remained an elite art, the private possession of the better-educated post-Stalinist youth. Its sole links with established institutions of patronage were quite literally parasitic, arising from the musicians' need to eat. Its inner development remained autonomous, beyond the control of any public agency.

Jazz Cafés:
The Lesser Evil

By the early 1960s, Komsomol faced a serious problem of which jazz was a part. The younger brothers and sisters of the pioneer *stiliagi* had long since abandoned zoot suits and loud makeup to lower-class immigrants from the countryside. Neatly dressed, they nonetheless retained their distance from official Soviet society. Their racy slang and mixture of wry irony and self-dramatization revealed their continuing search for authenticity. These young men and women threw themselves into life, rejecting their parents' do-cility. "It is better to be a tramp and fail than to be a boy all your life, carrying out the decisions of others," observed a character in Vassily Aksyonov's 1961 novel, *Ticket to the Stars*.[23]

These youths found their generational voice in a new first-person-narrative literature and in improvised jazz. A few sought more pub-lic forums, however, and in July 1958 began holding spontaneous outdoor gatherings at the newly unveiled monument to Vladimir Mayakovsky on Moscow's "Broadway" (Gorky Street). Komsomol initially gave its official blessing to these weekly evenings but grew concerned when Mayakovsky Square threatened to become a kind of Soviet Hyde Park. In 1960 Komsomol withdrew its support.[24]

The continued rise of juvenile delinquency in the cities also caused concern in the governments. A 1961 decree, which imposed harsh penalties for parasitism in the Russian Republic, led to roundups and deportations of young people to small towns and the country-side. Other republics quickly followed suit with their own versions of the decree. To all appearances, the situation was getting out of hand, and Komsomol, officially charged with responsibility for youth affairs, had to act.

The organization chose a two-pronged attack. On one side, it staunchly supported the campaigns against delinquency, helping to organize vigilante squads (*druzhinniki*) to patrol the streets; it also came down hard on anything resembling political dissent. On the other, it pursued a more positive program by seeking to accom-modate those writers and jazz musicians who were articulating the yearnings of the rising generation. Komsomol established its own jazz cafés, nightclubs where young Soviet men and women could revel in their private worlds under benign official auspices. Jazz, in short, was to be coopted.

The first hint of this tactic had come in 1957 during The Eight's phenomenal popularity. Comrade Pavel Plastinin of the Moscow branch of Komsomol had warned several members of the group at the time: "You've become too big; the job of organizing youth is Komsomol's task, not yours."[25] Late in 1959 Vasili Trushin, then head of Komsomol in Moscow's Timiriazev District, called in a rising light in the Young Communist organization, Ilya Suslov, to seek his views on the situation. "We're losing the youth," Trushin candidly explained. Suslov, it will be recalled, had defended jazz in the pages of *Soviet Art* at the height of the Stalin era. He now proposed that Komsomol establish jazz cafés to lure the young elite back into the fold and to curb the anarchistic tendencies of jazz music and its followers.

After some months, Trushin returned with word that the proposal had been approved. A long period of negotiation followed, the main issues being, first, whether the cafés should be permitted to serve alcohol, as Suslov wished, and second, whether their budgets should be part of Komsomol's official production plan. "Either you will fulfill your official work plan or you will have a cafe, which means serving liquor," Suslov argued. The cafés were duly withdrawn from the plan and permitted to serve liquor. The first two jazz cafés were established in Moscow in 1961, the *Molodezhnoe* or "Youth Café" just off Gorky Street, and the *Aelita* on Carriage Row (*Karetnyi riad*).[26]

Both cafés were open from five P.M. until midnight, served food as well as drinks, and offered a steady diet of jazz interspersed with standup comedians, poetry readings, and, at the Aelita, dancing. They were a smashing success. Where else could one rub shoulders with fashionable writers like Andrei Voznesensky or Yevgeni Yevtushenko, lazily stir a *kokteil* and nod one's head to the throbbing bass of Andrei Egorov or Igor Vysotski's driving sax? Lines soon stretched around the block for both cafés. The Party was clearly pleased. Instead of hippies huddling furtively around shortwave radios to hear Willis Conover, the cafés brought in clean-cut young Communists to hear jazz by Soviet musicians. They were perfect places to bring visiting foreign dignitaries, too, for they were at once upbeat and controllable. Soon similar nightclubs were established in other cities. The White Nights (*Belye nochi*) in Leningrad, the Allegro in Riga, the Dream Café (*Mriia*) in Kiev, and the Integral at the research town of Akademgorodok outside Novosibirsk were the best known of Komsomol's network of jazz spots.[27] All were refreshing in design, with paintings by young artists (many of them abstractionists) adorning the walls.

To some, the jazz cafés were "very strange, almost like private clubs." [28] To others, they appeared to be more the exclusive domain of the Party's youth hierarchy.[29] From the musicians' standpoint, they were a mixed blessing. They provided audiences and sympathetic environments for more jazzmen than had any institution since the introduction of jazz to Russia. Musicians from Donetsk or Voronezh knew exactly where to go to find fellow enthusiasts in any major city. Thanks to Komsomol's cafés, the after-hours jam session became firmly established as the core event in the jazz world. There is scarcely a Soviet jazz musician today who doesn't look back on the early days of the cafés with longing.

At the same time, pay was miserable, a mere 50 rubles a month for musicians at the Molodezhnoe. At the Integral in Siberia musicians received no pay at all.[30] Even at the Molodezhnoe it was necessary to falsify tune lists to pass the censorship.[31] Worse, the growing number of foreigners in the audiences caused concern in the KGB, which placed the clubs under surveillance. Obviously, the presence of KGB men soured the atmosphere by putting everyone on guard.

The Kremlin's Musicologist: Nikita Khrushchev

Just as Komsomol discovered it was not easy to lure members of the jazz avant-garde into the role of court musicians, Nikita Khrushchev launched an all-out attack on jazz and modern art. "When I hear jazz, it's as if I had gas on the stomach," the Party leader declared on December 1, 1963.[32] In a completely organized society, such comments can easily be translated into national policy. For nearly a year after this announcement, Soviet jazz was again on the defensive.

The first step in the chain of events that led to Khrushchev's announcement was Benny Goodman's triumphal tour of five Soviet cities in June-July 1962. Six years earlier, when the Harlem congressman Adam Clayton Powell had proposed to send Dizzy Gillespie on a tour to Russia,[33] Goodman had begun making personal inquiries at the State Department. Nothing had happened until 1959. In the spring of that year the Yale Russian Chorus planned one of its periodic trips to the Soviet Union. In response to their audiences' desire to hear jazz rather than Russian folk songs, the student chorus brought along two jazz musicians from the Yale School of Music, Dwike Mitchell and Willie Ruff. They were warmly received and their highly cerebral jazz praised by *Soviet Music*.[34] The government's attitude toward jazz was improving, and when Shostakovich and the head of the Union of Soviet Composers visited the United States three months later, Benny Goodman lay in wait for them. There had been talk of bringing Louis Armstrong to Moscow, but the plan had been shelved by the State Concert Agency (*Goskontsert*) for fear the concert would cause pandemonium and broken chairs. But the urbane Goodman posed no such threat, the Soviet officials concluded after hearing him in New York at Basin Street East and talking about chamber music with him over dinner.[35] When the 1958 Soviet-American cultural agreement came up for renewal in 1961, the Soviets accepted the Americans' proposal that Goodman tour the USSR.[36]

The Goodman tour was a great success. The band as a whole struck Russian jazzmen as rather dated, and Goodman's aloofness caused problems, but the American sidemen were greeted as heroes. An all-night jam session at the Astoria Hotel in Leningrad introduced Zoot Sims, Joe Newman, Mel Lewis, and Bill Crow to Gennadi Golstein, Valeri Mysovsky, and other top musicians of that city.[37] Another jam session at the Molodezhnoe in Moscow brought the Americans together with Andrei Tovmasian, German Lukianov, Konstantin Bakholdin, Alexei Zubov, and pianist Vadim Sakun.[38] In Sochi there were arrests of local fans who were seen in public with the Americans, but even intimidation did not cool the public's ardor.[39] Khrushchev himself attended Goodman's Moscow concert and joined the standing ovation at the end. At the Fourth of July celebrations at the U.S. Embassy two days later, Khrushchev had a

chance to meet Goodman, who delivered the Premier an im-
promptu lecture on freedom and creativity.[40]

Khrushchev had surely heard very little jazz. He and his family
had attended Eddie Rosner concerts before the war,[41] he had heard
Goodman's band, and he claimed to have listened to jazz on his
Japanese-made portable radio.[42] One suspects that he formed his
judgment not on the basis of the music but on the company it kept.
And during the summer and autumn of 1962 there was much evidence that this company was not good. Vassily Aksyonov's novels
and short stories extolling youth, jazz, and freedom were at the
height of their popularity. The fashionable young poet Yevgeni Yevtushenko had had the temerity to publish his *Precocious Autobiography* in the Paris *L'Express* without passing it through Soviet
censorship. The thirty-year-old memoirist attacked Party hacks and
"dogmatists" for seeking " . . . to arrest the process of democrati-
zation in our society." He contrasted them with the emerging younger
generation, which " . . . may like jazz music, even dance to rock-
'n'-roll, but this does not in any way prevent them from believing
in the revolution."[43] Yevtushenko also expressed enthusiasm for abstract art.

Igor Moiseev, leader of the popular folk dance ensemble, had
warned in *Izvestiia* that efforts to quell jazz had backfired with young
people and that their "intellectual drive toward independence of
thought and judgment" could not be disregarded.[44] Reversing its
long-term opposition, the government newspaper seemed to have
sided with the thesis that jazz and communism were mutually compatible.[45] Even the Union of Soviet Composers seemed to have backed
down on the issue. In the week of November 12, 1962, it organized
a plenum meeting at the Hall of Columns in Moscow to consider
the entire question of "light music." In an astonishing reversal of
recent policy regarding jazz, the composers were serenaded by jazz
bands, including Vadim Sakun's sextet, Yosif Weinstein's big band,
and The Eight, which had been specially reassembled for the occasion. Dmitri Shostakovich, chairman of the event, had defined the
central problem of the session as " . . . the influence in the Soviet
Union of such contemporary foreign popular music as American

jazz." [46] The plenum tentatively concluded to drop its opposition and attempt to Sovietize jazz by teaching it in the schools and building up a cadre of homegrown musicians.

The Goodman tour, Komsomol's flirtation with jazz, the apparent tie between jazz and political dissent, and now the composers' capitulation—any of these events might have triggered Khrushchev's wrath. But the issue would probably not have become a crisis had not the Chinese government of Mao Zedong begun publicly attacking the Soviet Union in these months. Tension between the two Communist giants had been mounting for several years, and now, after Khrushchev's humiliation during the 1962 Cuban missile crisis, the Chinese declared openly that he had led the USSR away from true communism and into the decadent morass of "revisionism." They ridiculed his soft line on the capitalist West and announced that the center of world revolution had shifted to Beijing. It was downright embarrassing for Khrushchev, not just because he was about to "lose" China, but also because he personally had so little empathy for the tastes and ideals of Soviet young people for which the Chinese were holding him responsible.

Tension grew rapidly. Just as the *People's Daily* was attacking Khrushchev from Beijing, Yevtushenko early in 1962 published his versified slap in the face of the government, *The Heirs of Stalin*. Then, as if to justify the Chinese's darkest suspicions, Moscow painter Eli Beliutin conspicuously mounted a large show of abstract paintings by his students. From the standpoint of Marxist-Leninist hardliners, such art was yet another example of the dangerous slide into heterodoxy. Another show of abstract painting was scheduled to open at the Youth (*Iunost*) Hotel on November 29, 1962, with a jazz band engaged to entertain the guests. When the defenders of orthodoxy managed to have the show postponed "for technical reasons," the jazz musicians, in a show of solidarity, refused to perform without their artist friends. [47] To Khrushchev, it seemed that the entire world of Soviet culture was going out of its way to discredit him.

The showdown came three days later at the opening of still another exhibition of modern art, this one presenting works by Moscow artists from the past thirty years and organized by the Union of Artists. Khrushchev, his political and aesthetic senses tuned for trouble, went to the old imperial equestrian school (*Manège*) to inspect the show. Scarcely inside the door, he flew into a rage. He declared the paintings were unfit to be urinal covers; he attacked the artists as formalists, misfits, and jackasses; and he bawled out the sponsors. As he strode from painting to painting he also announced, "I don't like jazz. . . . I used to think it was static when I heard it on the radio." He referred contemptuously to the jazz ensembles he had recently heard at the Union of Soviet Composers' plenum and commented on the new dances: "Some of them are completely improper. You wiggle a certain section of the anatomy, if you'll pardon the expression." Concluding his survey, Khrushchev declared, "Judging by these experiments, I am entitled to think that you are pederasts, and for that you can get ten years. . . . Gentlemen, we are declaring war on you." [48]

Khrushchev was ready for combat on December 17, when he called a meeting of artists, musicians, and writers to discuss "creative problems." The immediate reason for the meeting was that moderates had just taken over the governing board of the Union of Artists of the Russian Republic. Conservatives, fearing their likely defeat at the forthcoming national congress, had enlisted the aid of orthodox Party leaders. In the process, they had successfully engaged the support of beleaguered Stalinists in fields other than art, including music. Neither Khrushchev nor his ideological chief Leonid Ilichev bothered with specifics in their speeches at the meeting. Ilichev paused to criticize the "infatuation with the outlandish howlings of various foreign—and not only foreign—jazz bands," but his main point was to reassert the old Marxist notion that all art is inherently ideological and that the bourgeois West was using sympathizers within the USSR to wage their battles against socialism in the arts. [49]

To spell out the capitalist menace in each field of the arts, an even larger meeting was called for March 7–8, 1963, in the Kremlin. The dais was packed with Party dignitaries when Premier Khrushchev delivered his 20,000-word oration. All music and art are ideological, he again affirmed, and "peaceful coexistence in the field of ideology is treason to Marxism-Leninism."[50] Avant-garde architecture, abstract painting, and virtually all modern music were linked with the capitalist threat. Khrushchev spoke menacingly about the "obsession with jazz," "so called 'modern' dances," and "dodecaphony." (He carefully excepted the thoroughly tamed Utesov orchestra from his strictures, however.) It was a grim day for modern art and jazz.

Down to the autumn of 1964 Khrushchev's theses on jazz were gospel in the Soviet Union. Komsomol's policy of coopting jazz was suspended, and the Union of Soviet Composers meekly backed off from its effort to accommodate Soviet youth. The Moscow Jazz Club was closed down, the Dream Café in Kiev ceased hiring jazz bands, the manager of the Aelita in Moscow was fired for "disseminating Western influences,"[51] and major touring bands reverted to all-Soviet repertoires. And then, on October 14, 1964, the musicologist in the Kremlin was removed from office. Leonid Brezhnev took his place.

Apogee, 1965–1967

After Khrushchev's fall from power, the embarrassed moderates in the government worked hard to undo the effects of his ham-handed treatment of the cultural elite. *Pravda* hailed diversity and creativity in a lead article,[52] and the Ministry of Culture undertook a series of measures designed to appease the intelligentsia. All this was made easier, of course, by the final split with China by 1963, which had removed the need for the Soviet Union to demonstrate its ideological purity to the world. The post-Khrushchevian thaw was brief, and largely spent before the Soviet invasion of Czechoslovakia in 1968. But 1965–67 was a liberal interlude that witnessed the publication of a major collection of poetry by Boris Pasternak and an effort to implement economic reforms proposed by Professor Yevsei Liberman of Kharkov University, among other things. It was then that Soviet jazz attained its highest level of development.

A series of dramatic measures signaled the end of Khrushchev's siege on jazz. *Izvestiia*, admitting jazz was a "complex, multifaceted, controversial phenomenon whose essence and artistic principles are difficult to contain in a simple formula," conceded that the music was worth developing.[53] Shortly thereafter, Moscow Radio established "The Metronome Club," a weekly half-hour program devoted to the best Soviet jazz, past and present.[54] In early 1966, the State recording firm, Melodiia, for the first time made available records of performances by current Soviet pop and cool jazz bands.[55]

The honeymoon period of Brezhnev's rule enabled a number of talented publicists to speak on modern jazz to mass audiences. In Estonia the clarinetist, composer, and arranger Valter Ojakäär had been lecturing on the history of jazz at the Tallinn Conservatory since 1962. In Leningrad Yuri Vikharev, long an activist with the local jazz club, gained permission to deliver lectures to factory workers during breaks in the working day. Throughout the years 1965–67 he analyzed abstruse works such as Coltrane's solo on "Ev'ry Time We Say . . . ." before crowds of a thousand or more.[56] Vladimir Feuertag, a translator of German literature by profession, carried his erudite lectures on modern jazz to small towns like Petrozavodsk and ancient Novgorod, scouting local jazz talent in the process. Vikharev, Alexei Batashev, and a number of lesser-known personages established themselves as regular correspondents for leading jazz magazines in Poland, Western Europe, and the United States. Thanks to their efforts, the remarkable Polish monthly, *Jazz*, reported regularly on events even in small centers like Uzhgorod and Rostov-on-Don, providing the best documentation of Soviet jazz yet available.

The movement to establish local societies of jazz fans gained new momentum, especially in the provinces. A newly founded jazz club in Petrozavodsk in 1965 celebrated the tenth anniversary of Charlie Parker's death with lectures and discussions organized in cooperation with the local branch of the national Society of Knowledge (*Obshchstvo znanie*).[57] It was not all smooth sailing for jazz in the provinces though. The jazz club in Donetsk, founded in 1967, ar-

ranged through the American Embassy to show a film of Duke Ellington's performance at the White House. When it was learned
that the film depicted blacks receiving medals from the American
President, the film was banned.[58]

New institutional patrons also emerged. The jazz club at Petrozavodsk received support from the Omega Tractor Factory, which
produced tanks and rockets for the Red Army. In Moscow, the highly
sophisticated Jazz Studio was sponsored by the Physical-Technical
Institute, a high-security facility for training atomic physicists and
experts for the defense industry; access to jazz performances was,
and is, limited to those with security clearance.[59] These institutions
attracted some of the brightest and most sophisticated people in the
USSR. Many of these same people also figured as leading patrons
of abstract art in the immediate post-Khrushchev years.

Some of the new jazz enthusiasts approached their subject with
impressive erudition. Leonid Pereverzev, a leading figure in the
Moscow jazz school, penned a series, "Essays on the History of
Jazz," that appeared in the journal *Musical Life* in 1966.[60] Even
more ambitious was the full-length monograph *Jazz Music (Džäss-
muusika)* published in Tallinn in 1966 by Valter Ojakäär. Written
in the Estonian language and drawing on the author's wide reading
in American and European sources, this study presented a balanced
overview of the subject. A far less sophisticated volume, *On Light
Music, Jazz, and Good Taste*, covered the same ground for Russian
readers but was designed specifically to respond to foes of jazz by
means of a catechistic format.[61] Beneath the general studies existed
an impressive substratum of fundamental historical and musicological research that was the more remarkable because it was carried
out entirely by amateurs. In Leningrad, Vladimir Feuertag was preparing an *Encyclopedia of Soviet Jazz*, which regrettably has yet to
appear in print.[62] Beginning in 1965, the Leningrad Jazz Club published an annual volume of essays called *Kvadrat (The Chorus)*. The
typed journal, which is virtually a *samizdat* publication, was officially tolerated for a decade and a half on the condition that its
editors not circulate it beyond the city of Leningrad. Its candid ar-

278 *Red and Hot*

ticles and reviews reveal a high level of critical acumen that is admirable in light of the severe restrictions under which its writers had to work.

In the Don River city of Voronezh, the engineer Yuri Vermenich organized an even more ambitious *samizdat* project in the late sixties with his Jazz Researchers' Group (*Grupa issledovatelei dzhaza*, or *GID*). Wholly unofficially and without a kopek of external support, Vermenich and a handful of collaborators in a half-dozen Soviet cities undertook to translate all the major works on jazz published abroad. Their procedure was simple. When a member of the Jazz Researchers' Group came across a foreign volume of interest to Soviet readers, he would distribute it in sections to translators competent in whatever language was called for, whether English, French, German, Polish, or Czech. Each collaborator would translate his section and then return it to the central office, where five master copies would be made on duplicating machines. These copies were then passed from hand to hand, with scores of additional photocopies being made as necessary.

Vermenich is the single biggest publisher of Soviet *samizdat* in any field and, arguably, one of the major jazz "publishers" in the world. By the late seventies the Jazz Researchers' Group had issued more than thirty-five volumes, the equivalent of approximately 7000 single-spaced pages in translation. Barry Ulanov's *History of Jazz in America*, Bob Reisner's *Jazz Titans*, Sam Charters's *Jazz: A History of the New York Scene*, and Leonard Feather's *Book of Jazz* are just a few of the titles translated in full. The Jazz Researchers' Group also conducts original research: it has done, for example, biographical sketches of five hundred jazz musicians. Thanks to Vermenich's entirely unofficial publishing endeavors, the interested Soviet reader is able to keep fully abreast of the best studies of jazz available.

Few of the Soviet Union's new jazz writers and translators were themselves musicians, with such exceptions as Valter Ojakäär. Nonetheless, their relationship to musicians was extremely close, each group reinforcing the efforts of the other. Evidence of this interaction between performer and critic was the rapid expansion in the late sixties of the range of Western sources from which Soviet jazzmen drew inspiration. Soviets attempted scat singing, for example. Lembit Saarsalu and E. Thomson achieved some fluency in the genre in the sophisticated musical environment of the Estonian capital and formed styles of their own, using Estonian syllabics.[63] Inspired by the wealth of new information, Soviet musicians searched out many unexplored areas of the world of jazz. Leonid Garin showed his fellow countrymen what could be achieved on the vibraphone.[64] Others broke new ground by studying previously unknown musical prototypes heard through the Voice of America. For example, an amateur trombonist with the excellent traditional band at the Moscow "Vibrator" Factory seems to have claimed the Soviet franchise for the Jack Teagarden style of trombone playing.

Performances were judged by increasingly rigorous standards. At the very least, performers were expected to be extremely competent technically. The playing of guitarist Nikolai Gromin, for instance, meets this standard of excellence. While Gromin's many recordings are patently derivative, he uses his sources tastefully and with the confidence that comes from strong technical command of an instrument.[65] Much the same can be said of Yuri Saulsky's excellent vocal-instrumental ensemble VIO-66. Bringing together many of the best instrumentalists of the decade, including pianist Igor Bril, the new Saulsky orchestra achieved a lightness and drive far beyond the skills of big bands of the earlier sixties.[66]

The more rigorous critical standards placed particularly high value on original compositions, especially those embodying indigenous musical ideas. Azerbaijani pianist Rafik Babaev used Central Asian folklore to good advantage in his compositions,[67] while Russian folk themes proliferated in the music written by Alexei Zubov for his quartet Crescendo.[68] Reviewing the rise of folkishness in the music of vibraphonist Leonid Garin, the Medikus quartet from Lvov, the Tallinn ensemble of Arne Vakhuri, and others, the Soviet critic Batashev sees the attainment of an authentically indigenous jazz style.[69] Some folkloristic jazz from the USSR certainly warrants this conclusion. But even so original a work as Andrei Tovmasian's "Lord Novgorod the Great" ("Gospodin Novgorod Velikii") must be seen in an international context. The rise of black nationalism in American jazz had turned jazzmen like Art Blakey, Charlie Mingus, and Sonny Rollins in the direction of inward-looking "soul" music. Soviet musicians studying this current realized that beyond ethnic identity, the essence of "soul" was the sophisticated exploitation of primitive folk motifs and tonalities. By plunging into their own folk sources with this purpose in mind, the jazzmen of the USSR participated in the international current. To be sure, a few were impelled by genuine nationalism, as, for example, guitarist Nikolai Gromin, who experimented with the balalaika. The Soviet government, after all, had been harping for years on the need for a uniquely Soviet jazz based on indigenous traditions. But, for the most part, the turn to ethnicity had none of the ideological content with which the American black nationalists imbued it. Soviet musicians were well informed on the spirit of racial exclusivity in America at the time but rejected it.[70] Tovmasian, an Armenian, pioneered the exploitation of Russian folk themes, while Zubov, a Russian, was, along with Babaev, among the first to explore Central Asian folklore.[71] If there is any ideological content in this quest, it is in the rejection of a blandly technological Soviet monoculture in favor of a richly textured primitive past. In this respect, the jazz musicians were far closer to the Armenian film director Dmitri Paradzhanov, whose 1961 film *Shadows of Forgotten Ancestors* had used Ukrainian folklore to celebrate primitivism, than to the Russian dissident painters whose exploitation of Byzantine iconography sprang from their renewed Orthodox Christian faith.

Standards of performance, composition, and criticism soared in the years following Khrushchev's demise, and a number of unusually talented jazz musicians emerged. The intense young Muscovite Vadim Sakun, for example, cut a wide swath as a bop pianist and a discerning judge of talent in others. After experimenting with various styles, Sakun settled comfortably into the hearty "funk" idiom of Horace Silver and assembled around him a driving bop group. The KM-Quartet had in drummer Valeri Bulanov and bassist Andrei Yegorov two jazzmen who realized what few Russians had understood before: that rhythm players must not only lay down a beat but must play against it at the same time. Valeri Ponomarev, who played trumpet with Sakun, also developed rapidly in the intensified Moscow jazz climate. Ponomarev had not attempted to play jazz until 1961, when he heard Clifford Brown's "Blues Walk" on the Voice of America. Throughout the 1960s Ponomarev was still learning, but he was learning fast. A few years later, after his emigration to America, Art Blakey invited him to join his Jazz Messengers. John Wilson of the *New York Times* described him then as "the most provocative soloist in [Blakey's] group, who combines a bristling attack with dazzling execution and a very neat, compact, controlled development of his solos." [72] Leonard Feather judged him a "surprisingly authentic soloist," while Thomas Albright of the *San Francisco Chronicle* praised "the pinpoint accuracy and logic of his ideas" and his "unwavering heat." [73]

An even more accomplished figure on the Moscow jazz scene in the late sixties was the extraordinarily gifted tenor saxophonist Vladimir Sermakashev. This wiry, black-eyed young man had come to Moscow in 1963 from his native Baku. No city in the Soviet Union was more receptive to the fiercely rhythmic cadences of hard bop than the Turkic capital on the Caspian. The Azerbaijani jazz musicians lived a rougher and more bohemian existence than did the Russians, and their playing showed it. Once in Moscow, Sermakashev was immediately given a place in Sakun's KM-Quartet, which was then the house band at the Molodezhnoe Café. Audiences were swept off their feet by the way Sermakashev concentrated on the rhythm. Even in a relaxed piece like his own "Waltz for Natasha," based on Horace Silver's "The Preacher," he caused the whole band to swing and rock. At times Sermakashev's tone was hard and abrasive, other times full-throated and warm, recalling Lester Young. His phrasing was fluid, and he would often swallow several notes in a run to underscore the rhythmic structure. Whether in his own quartet or with larger groups, Sermakashev

dominates, like a Sidney Bechet of bop. In his combination of grit-
tiness and lyricism, blues feeling and sheer drive, he has few equals,
in Europe certainly and even in America.[74]

Getting Together:
The Festival Craze

In the Soviet Union of the sixties, as in America in the fifties, jazz
became increasingly arcane in its form and elitist in its audience.
Tsfasman and Rosner had played for the masses; Sakun and Sermakashev played for their friends, the *cognoscenti*. The faithful were
many, however, embracing a large percentage of educated youths
and young adults. For them, the jazz performance had the character
of a ritual—Andrei Tovmasian even named a tune "The Rite"
("Obriad"). The public restaurant or dance hall had previously
provided the setting for jazz. But jazz had no native habitat now,
except in the Komsomol cafés. It was a congregation without a
church. And musicians and fans in one city fortunate to have a
locale for their assemblies remained isolated from others. There
were some links. Young jazz musicians in touring variety orchestras
spread the word about good improvisers. Through letters and exchanged tape recordings people learned who played good jazz in
Tblisi or Minsk. The desire for broader contacts had increased,
however, especially after the establishment of local jazz cafés by
Komsomol.

The first intercity gatherings were informal. Members of two or
three different groups might show up at the same time at a summer
resort like Sochi on the Black Sea or Kislovodsk in the Caucasus.
They would organize jam sessions at summer restaurants on the
edge of town and invite any jazz fans who happened to be vacationing there. Soon, however, many bands were planning to arrive
together at the same resort, and enthusiasts were scheduling their
vacations around such happenings.[75] These convocations only
whetted the appetite for more.

Until the fall of Khrushchev, Soviet officialdom had refused to
respond to this growing demand. Nonetheless, meetings of jazz bands

had been taking place regularly in the Estonian capital of Tallinn. In proximity to the more advanced jazz worlds of Poland and Scandinavia, Estonians had steadily built on the foundations laid in 1949. In the wake of the VI World Youth Festival in 1957, the number of participating bands in the Tallinn Jazz Festival had increased from three to twelve and a related festival had been established at nearby Tartu.[76] By 1959, three-day meetings were taking place, and a pair of Russian bands made the trip from Leningrad. The next year four bands traveled to Tallinn from Leningrad, and five groups came from Moscow.[77] The Tallinn Jazz Festival became the single most important event in the Soviet jazz year. Estonian Radio recorded the performances, which were held in a large hall. Fans started coming from as far away as Siberia, seeking the freedom to associate with fellow enthusiasts that was impossible in the more strictly controlled climate of Russia.

Only in 1962 were Russians allowed to imitate the Estonians' example, and then only under severe controls. Pavel Plastinin, the Komsomol official, headed the organizational committee for the First Moscow Festival of Improvised Jazz Music. The "festival" consisted of nothing more than five modern jazz groups getting together for three hours on the evening of October 6, 1962. All of the tunes listed on the typed program[78] had been approved beforehand by the Repertory Commission. "The atmosphere was very serious, academic," one participant recalled. "We were all aware of the consequences if anything untoward were to occur."[79] The mood was only slightly better at the first Leningrad festival, also held in 1962.[80]

The breakthrough came because of the influence of Poland and Czechoslovakia. Since 1958, the Polish Jazz Federation had mounted an annual conclave called the Jazz Jamboree. By 1962, the year Vadim Sakun and his sextet participated, the Jamboree was being held in one of the largest halls in Warsaw. Khrushchev's coolness to jazz kept Soviet musicians at home, but after his fall Russians were permitted in 1965 to appear in both the Warsaw and the Prague festivals. Only musicians with impeccable political credentials were allowed to go. Roman Kunsman's photo had already been printed on the cover of the program for the Prague festival when he was pulled out.[81] But at least the initial selections were based on the results of a rigorous competition. Indeed, Moscow enthusiasts and promoters cleverly used the selection process as an excuse for reviving the Moscow Jazz Festival. The auditions were moved to a large room in the Youth Hotel, stretched over three evenings, and expanded to include sixteen bands and seventy-three musicians. The Union of Soviet Composers and the Moscow Komsomol Committee lent their imprimatur, and a jury of fifteen composers and musicologists presided.[82]

One official was distressed by the undisciplined behavior he witnessed, the "Dilettantism, bad taste, and helpless, pitiful imitation of the ugliest jazz 'fads.'"[83] But most observers considered the festival a success, both musically and politically.[84] The Prague festival was anticlimactic after Moscow, especially since far more Soviet critics and bureaucrats than musicians were permitted to travel to the Czech capital. Nonetheless, four fine bop musicians—Georgi Garanian, Valeri Bulanov, Nikolai Gromin, and Andrei Yegorov—attended and established personal contact with major European and American performers, as well as with their heretofore invisible musical *cicerone*, Willis Conover. The returning Russians reported being shocked by Don Cherry's free jazz, but even critical published reports heightened the mystique of the jazz festival.[85] Henceforth, to appear in a festival, whether foreign or domestic, was to be on the inner track.[86]

Encouraged by the success of its latest experiment in cooptation, Komsomol permitted festivals to take place in Kuibyshev, Riga, Kharkov, and Novosibirsk, as well as Leningrad, Moscow, and Tallinn.[87] The number of festivals continued to mushroom in 1966 and 1967.[88] The Leningrad conclave by 1966 ran over ten days. Its closing concert was held at the Winter Stadium before five thousand people![89] The Moscow festival regularly attracted up to twenty bands, and the perpetuation of the competitive nature of the event ensured their careful preparation, even if it deadened their spontaneity.[90]

By 1967 festival fever was raging among the Soviet jazz community. Multirecord sets of the Moscow Jazz Festival had been issued since 1965, and musicians and fans were eager to make contact with fellow enthusiasts in other cities. Pushing for more and bigger festivals, they became increasingly assertive. They knew that innovators in other fields of the arts, notably modern painters, were holding exhibitions or performances without seeking permission from anyone. They knew, too, that the government had shown some willingness to wink at such independence, although in 1966 the Criminal Code (Article 70) had been supplemented to enable prosecutors to punish political dissent more easily. Also, most jazz activists were aware that in 1966 Andrei Siniavsky and Yuri Daniel had been tried and punished for the crime of writing openly about Stalinism. But it was still possible to dismiss these measures as rearguard actions. Few realized that they heralded the beginning of another tightening of cultural policy. So jazz musicians and promoters forged ahead, eagerly seizing each opportunity for the clan to gather.

The momentum reached its peak in Tallinn during the festival held May 11–14, 1967. This monumental event surpassed all previous Soviet jazz festivals by practically every measure. One hundred seventy-five musicians came from every part of the Soviet Union. The twenty-eight bands hailed from Baku, Khabarovsk, Kalinin, Kuibyshev, Leningrad, Lvov, Moscow, Novosibirsk, Riga, Tblisi, Tula, and Vilnius, as well as from Tallinn.[91] Foreign guests included the Arne Domnerus Sextet from Stockholm, the Kurt Jarnberg Quintet from Gavle, the Erik Lindstrom Quintet and the Heikki Laurila Trio from Helsinki, the Zbigniew Namyslowski Quartet from Warsaw, and the Charles Lloyd's American Jazz Quartet from New York. The event, held at the large sports hall Kalevi, was covered by Reuters, CBS, and BBC. The proceedings were filmed by Estonian television, and recordings of the performances were issued by Melodiia and Atlantic Records.[92]

Tallinn was a festival in the fullest sense. Marching Dixieland bands transformed the ancient cobbled streets into a Baltic version of New Orleans's Vieux Carré. Parties and dances were held nightly, their attendance swelled by people who had attended an international festival of contemporary ballroom dancing that had just closed in Tallinn.[93] Everywhere there were jam sessions, seminars, conversations, meetings. Nothing like it had ever occurred in the USSR.

"The Tallinn Festival liberated us from serfdom," recalled Kiev saxophonist Boris Ludmer. "We played one hundred percent differently after Tallinn." [94]

And understandably so. Although Leningrad's two fine saxophonists Roman Kunsman and Gennadi Golstein were absent,
practically every other star of Soviet jazz was on the program. Several lesser-known groups, like Heinrich Zarkh's vocal-instrumental
group based on the Swingle Singers, caused a stir. But the only band
to receive a ten-minute standing ovation before playing a single
note was not even listed on the printed program. Charles Lloyd's
American Jazz Quartet was the sensation of the festival long before
the last day, when they performed "Love Song to a Baby." The story
of the band's appearance reveals the strivings and limitations of
Soviet jazz at its height.

By the mid-1960s, American performers were frequent guests at
the major jazz festivals in Eastern Europe. Stan Getz, Gerry Mulligan, Ronnie Ross, and other major jazzmen made the trek from the
New World to Prague and Warsaw. European jazz groups moved
easily back and forth across the Iron Curtain, giving jazz life in
Eastern Europe a cosmopolitan flavor. The Soviet Union, however,
remained aloof from most of the developments among her Warsaw
Pact allies. A few European groups were permitted to visit: the accomplished French clarinetist Claude Luter performed at Moscow's
Sokolniki Park in 1961, and Kurt Edelhagen brought his modern
jazz ensembles to Leningrad from Germany. [95] But these visits were
accorded more attention in the Polish magazine *Jazz* than in the
Soviet musical press. No American jazzmen followed in Benny
Goodman's footsteps until Earl Hines's tour in 1966, which was
again followed by a hiatus. The possibility of achieving through the
Tallinn Jazz Festival what had not been accomplished through the
official cultural exchanges was most appealing.

Unofficial promoters in Leningrad and Moscow therefore invited
Charles Lloyd and his quartet to come to Estonia. Members of the
group had to pay their own travel expenses but would be provided
free room and board and tape recordings of their performances.
George Avakian of Columbia Records liked the proposal and of-

fered to assist Lloyd. He soon learned the view of Soviet officialdom on the private invitation to visit their country. "Lloyd won't be welcome," a Soviet diplomat in New York informed Avakian. "Our people don't really like American jazz." [96] The visas were issued nonetheless, and the American Jazz Quartet arrived in the Estonian capital in time for the opening of the festival. Their anxious hosts immediately warned them that they should avoid crowds, for if any demonstrations were to occur the entire festival would be canceled. The KGB had managed to intimidate the organizers, who, their written agreement notwithstanding, now tried to claim that Lloyd's quartet had been invited to attend the festival as spectators, not performers. For the first several days, Lloyd and his three colleagues played basketball, obediently shunning the public. Finally, on the second-to-last day, they were informed that the band would be permitted to appear at the indoor stadium that evening. Both this brief performance and a longer set the next day generated tumultuous applause; Charles Lloyd, Keith Jarrett, Ron McClure, and Jack DeJohnette were the heroes of the hour.

News of these events traveled swiftly to Leningrad, where the band was to perform next. Komsomol had sounded the alarm well before the start of the band's scheduled performance at the House of Culture of the Food Industry on Pravda Street. The hall was filled. But neither the woman who directed the House of Culture nor anyone else on the premises was willing to take responsibility for letting the black musicians perform. So the four Americans sat down on the pavement in protest, in what Russians call a "Polish strike." [97] At 10 P.M. the directoress telephoned the Leningrad office of the KGB, which referred her in turn to the head of the district KGB, who had to be awakened. Without instructions from Moscow, the KGB official had no grounds for taking action. The directoress concluded that she could not allow the concert to proceed. Fortunately, the local jazz café was still open and the bandsmen were able to play one set before their hasty departure on the Red Arrow for Moscow. [98] Although the American jazzmen were followed by the KGB in the capital, they were also received with great warmth at the Molodezhnoe Café, where they jammed with Russian friends far into the night. Warm parties in private homes rounded out their brief visit.

Onslaught

The avant-garde jazz musician was an outsider in the USSR with no steady source of patronage, as he was in most countries, including the United States. Only during the brief period 1965–67 did all the conditions essential for this improvisatory art exist. The results were impressive. Yet an astute observer could have detected evidence of a coming crisis even amidst the jubilation of 1967. The signs—political, social, and musical—were soon to coalesce into a single new force that was to dwarf the jazz establishment of the sixties. The age of rock music was dawning.

13
The Rock Inundation,
1968–1980

In the end . . . the narrow trousers, like cybernetics, were purged of all ideological deviations and recognized officially as corresponding with the ideas of the "ISM." By which time, they had already passed out of fashion.

Alexander Zinoviev

Have you heard the news?
. . . There's good rockin' tonight.

Elvis Presley, 1954

Considering the domestic and international events that occurred at the time of the Tallinn Jazz Festival, it is amazing that the event took place at all. In January 1967, three young political dissidents, Vladimir Bukovsky, Alexander Ginsburg, and Yuri Galanskov, were arrested for slandering the Soviet Union; in spite of the general amnesty proclaimed in honor of the fiftieth anniversary of the Revolution, the trio was made to stand trial. In May, Stalin's daughter, Svetlana Alliluyeva, defected to the West and Moscow's Egyptian client, General Nasser, was defeated by Israel in the humiliating Six Day War. The Tallinn festival went forward, and Soviet jazzmen were permitted to perform again in Prague that year and the next.[1] But a mood of extreme caution prevailed after 1967; the Tallinn festival was first delayed and then suspended for several years, and "the Metronome Club" was withdrawn from Soviet radio.[2] The Moscow Jazz Festival was held once more in June 1968,[3] although it, too, was suspended thereafter for several years. Other recently established festivals suffered similar fates.[4]

It was not surprising. Within a month of the 1968 Moscow festival Andrei Sakharov, a dissident member of the Soviet Academy of Sciences, had send abroad his *Thoughts on Progress, Peaceful Coexistence, and Intellectual Freedom*, which directly challenged Soviet authorities. Meanwhile, Alexander Dubček's Czechoslovakian government had dared to put reformist thoughts into action, so unnerving Brezhnev's government that the Red Army invaded Czechoslovakia to restore Stalinist order. Russian protesters of the takeover were arrested on Red Square, just as young protesters against the war in Vietnam were being arrested in the United States.

There was no formal campaign against jazz. Indeed, Brezhnev applauded a modern jazz quartet that performed at his *dacha* outside Moscow in 1970.[5] But many protectors of Soviet orthodoxy wanted to settle old scores. The jamming of foreign broadcasts, suspended in 1963, was reintroduced in 1968. Fearing unwholesome assemblies of young people, Komsomol abolished jazz evenings at the Dream in Kiev and at similar youth cafés in other cities. The Blue Bird (*Siniaia ptitsa*), which had opened only two years before on Chekhov Street in Moscow, dropped jazz entirely, and the Molodezhnoe Café cut back jazz to two nights a week. The Pechora was opened on Moscow's Kalinin Prospect to replace these dens of iniquity; brightly lit and colorless, the Pechora at least provided a setting for open jam sessions, although it closed early.[6]

Emigration

The reformist days of Leonid Brezhnev's rule ended decisively in 1968, and, with them, the hopes that had sustained many young people collapsed. The expectation of progressive moderation had been particularly prevalent among jazz musicians and their audiences, as they had watched the festival movement thrive so luxuriantly after Khrushchev's fall from power. In their disenchantment, many jazz musicians decided to emigrate. During the years 1971–80, more than sixty well-established Soviet jazz musicians left their native country. Their experiences were in many respects similar to those of the quarter-million other émigrés from the Soviet Union during these years.

They came from everywhere in the USSR, including all the republics in the Baltic and the Caucasus. They ranged in age from the twenty-two-year-old Siberian drummer Mikhail Brantsberg to the seventy-eight-year-old Moscow saxophonist Mikhail Lantsman. Many were Jews, although few practiced their religion. Roman Kunsman, the star Leningrad saxophonist, became devoutly religious only after emigrating. There were also Orthodox Christians, Catholics, and Lutherans among the émigrés, but the non-religious were overwhelmingly in the majority. Many were driven to emigration by a vague but general sense of dissatisfaction. As one saxophonist puts it, "I just needed some change."[7] The most common reason cited by those leaving, however, was the plight of jazz and the arts in the USSR. Saxophonist Boris Midney and bassist Igor Berukshtis, who were the first jazzmen to emigrate in 1964, were blunt: "The arts are censored," Midney explained. "It's very hard to work on your own initiative . . . jazz is suppressed."[8] Trumpeter Valery Ponomarev claimed that the thought of emigration had always been on his mind.[9] "I wanted to live the life of a jazz musician and to be where the jazz musicians lived, and that meant New York."[10]

Despite Soviet propaganda to the contrary, mercenary motives seem to have played no role in the musicians' decisions. They knew they faced double liability in the shaky American economy and the extremely rigorous competition in the American music industry. Ponomarev sold pots and pans at Altman's before Art Blakey took him up, and he was among the fortunate. Vladimir Sermakashev, who had earned practically every prize a jazz saxophonist could win in the USSR, took several years to get on his feet musically. Vadim Vyadro, the uncompromisingly avant-garde saxophonist from Riga, chose to live in great hardship for several years in order to systematize a new music beyond free jazz. Nearly all the émigrés have had to support their music with other careers, ranging from photography to chemical engineering. It is hard to imagine a less mercenary group of people.

If there is one common denominator uniting the émigré jazzmen and distinguishing them from most of the thousands of other émigrés from the Soviet Union in the early 1970s it is the speed with which they have adapted to American life. Most have mastered English, and many revel in the slang and local jargon of their adopted city or region. Vladimir Sermakashev adopted the stage name Wally West. A trio of former Soviet rock singers, Natasha and Sergei Kapustin and Vladimir Schneider, even recorded original lyrics in English under the group name Black Russian. As a group, jazzmen seem to have made the necessary psychological adjustments to a less paternalistic and more individualistic world while still in the USSR. The post-Stalin generation of jazzmen, after all, had been initially attracted to jazz because it symbolized independence and individual expression in a world of staid conformism.

The departure of these and many other leading jazz figures cast a pall over Soviet jazz, particularly in Moscow but also in the provinces. The émigrés became nonpersons, their names and photographs deleted from the chronicles of Soviet jazz history. Even their works ceased to exist. For instance, repertory commissions across the USSR received word that they should prevent bands from playing Yuri Saulsky's "The School Dance" ("Shkolnyi bal") because its lyricist had emigrated.[11] Nonetheless, a large number of capable jazzmen remained to carry on the tradition. Paradoxically, the most immediate problem they faced in Moscow, Donetsk, or Erevan was the one that would have confronted them had they, too, chosen to emigrate: the rise of rock music.

The Big Beat Takeover

In 1973, Moscow jazz critic Arkadi Petrov observed ruefully:

> Unfortunately, during the last couple of years interest in jazz in the Soviet Union has diminished a lot. The generation of old jazz fans has, in a way, lost interest in this music. . . . Rock has invaded the big cities where jazz festivals used to be held, while jazz festivals have moved to small towns. . . . 1968–1970 appear to have been the most stagnant years for jazz in our country.[12]

Rock music had indeed taken over. The throb of electric guitars was heard where avant-garde free jazz had recently reigned. Songs of reckless desire, broken hearts, and broken lives replaced the abstract improvisations of hard bop. Only a few years earlier, block-long lines of keen-eyed youths had waited outside the door of the Molodezhnoe Café to hear Vadim Sakun's sophisticated jazz; the lines in 1973 were for imported clothes and rock music.[13] Within fifteen years, the modern jazz revolution of the late fifties had been swept aside by the music of the Beatles, the Rolling Stones, Stevie Wonder, and the Shadows.

The first hint of this fundamental change in popular taste occurred as early as the VI World Youth Festival in 1957. Many of the visitors shocked Russians with their bizarre dress and offensive music. The journal *Soviet Culture* received more than a few letters complaining about the foreigners' "*stiliagi* jackets, trousers, and wild haircuts" and songs like "Crazy Rhythm" and "Rock-'n'-Roll."[14] No one was quite sure whether rock 'n' roll was a song or a style of music, but it certainly wasn't good. One of the earliest public performances of rock music in the USSR was in a 1958 theatrical scene representing Hell.[15] And when in 1960 the renowned Moiseev folk-dance troupe worked up a satire on American rock music, it was titled "Back to the Monkeys." Poor Moiseev must have been thunderstruck when Moscow audiences burst into applause at the rambunctious music and remained indifferent to the satire as a whole.[16]

Rock music was still in its infancy. Elvis Presley's "Don't Be Cruel" and "Hound Dog" were hit songs in the United States only the year before the Moscow Youth Festival.[17] Yet X-ray plate reissues of these works, not to mention hits by Chubby Checker and Bill Haley, were available even in the Russian provinces within the year. The youth of Khrushchev's Russia soaked up the new music like blotters.

Not all the youth. The pioneer generation of *stiliagi* had abandoned the sartorial manifestations of the movement by 1956–57. As these better educated and upwardly mobile youths embraced modern jazz, working-class Soviet young people took up rock 'n' roll. The long-haired imitators of the Beatles who appeared in the provincial city of Petrozavodsk late in 1964 were proletarian *stiliagi*, failing students and dropouts, for whom "making it" was a futile, and certainly an uninspiring, dream.[18] In the early years, at least, rock music tapped not only a younger but also a lower social stratum than jazz.

If bop and free jazz appealed increasingly to the educated and urbane, rock 'n' roll music in the USSR found an audience principally, though by no means exclusively, among the lower classes. Beyond this, the jazz world also turned its back on dancing in the sixties, while rock audiences embraced it with a passion. The twist did not reach Russia until the early sixties, but it spread immediately to every high school and institute party in the land. Sex had certainly not been expunged from modern jazz, but it had been tamed, disciplined. By contrast, when a hundred couples writhed in unison to "The Yellow Submarine" in 1966, they restored eros to its central place in popular culture. And, too, the rock generation collectivized its rebellion; where the individualistic jazz fan had closed his eyes and silently snapped his fingers, the Soviet rock-'n'-roller wanted his shout to rise with the general chorus.

The minute Komsomol gave its official blessing to modern jazz by establishing youth cafés, it had a vested interest in proving that jazz and rock 'n' roll were polar opposites. What it did not note, and what was only slowly understood in the United States as well, was that the rock rebellion against jazz replicated the upheaval caused by jazz itself a half-century earlier. Musically, of course, modern jazz and rock music are branches of a single tree. But in terms of their social characteristics in the 1970s, rock music rather than modern jazz most fully embodied the "second revolution" of the twentieth century. Rock 'n' roll, in fact, fits precisely F. Scott Fitzgerald's maxim, quoted earlier, that "The word 'jazz,' in its progress toward respectability, has meant first sex, then dancing, then music." [19] Rock music in the USSR, even more than in the United States, represented a return to the quest for an individually liberating and truly popular culture.

The process of assimilating rock music also raised most of the same problems jazz had posed. Access to the new fashion was not a problem after 1967, when the Voice of America devoted a program to rock and soul music.[20] And international radio and the

growth of tourism and student exchanges had opened unprecedented channels for acquiring the latest recordings by Bob Dylan,
Aretha Franklin, and the Jefferson Airplane. But the difficulty of
finding instruments on which to play the new music was no less
vexing than it had been in the 1920s. Electric guitars were not produced in the Soviet Union. They were manufactured in Poland
and East Germany, however, and exchange students from those
countries did a thriving underground business at universities and
technical institutes. Guitars sold for 300 to 400 rubles in the sixties,
and amplifiers for 1000 rubles—provided one was available.[21] The
East German government in 1966 opened in Moscow a store called
Leipzig, which had ten electric guitars for sale on its first business
day. All were sold within minutes to black-marketeers and resold
at a 200 percent markup.

Some guitarists built their own equipment. Yuri Valov, a young
Moscow rock musician, consulted with electrician friends, used
published photographs, and "followed straight logic" to construct
his own guitar and amplifier.[22] Engineering students were especially
adept at the electronic work, which gave rock music a head start at
the Riga Polytechnic Institute and other technical schools. Demand
for equipment was so great that unofficial manufacturers set up
shop in many Soviet cities. Tens of thousands of instruments were
produced on the private "second economy" and distributed through
the black market. Many of the guitars were terrible, but a few were
of exceptionally high quality. Gena Kolmakov, a black-market
manufacturer in Odessa, copied Fender and Marshall instruments
so beautifully, adding improvements in the process, that foreign
musicians visiting Odessa on cruise ships would exchange the genuine articles for his forgeries.

Rock music was banned, and when the Beatles craze hit Russia
in the mid-sixties, efforts to reinforce the ban were strengthened.[23]
As in every previous Soviet attempt to stamp out manifestations of
genuine popular taste, however, this one backfired disastrously. By
reinforcing the sense of generational confinement on which rock
music fed, the prohibition created a vital underground rock culture.
The history of The Eight was relived ten years later by rock groups

such as The Eagle (*Sokol*), the Guys (*Rebiata*), the Little Red Devils (*Krasnye diavoliata*), the Scythians (*Skify*), the Melomanes (*Melomany*), the Vilnius Towers (*Vilniaus Bokstai*), the Dreamers (*Sapnotoji*), and the Winds of Change (*Vetri peremen*). Most of these bands were organized by students to play for dances at technical institutes and universities. Like The Eight before them, they gradually turned professional.

Scores of new rock bands sprouted in the Moscow region every year, but Moscow was by no means the rock capital of the Soviet Union. Baku, where musicians had always gravitated toward the earthiest genres, was several years ahead of Moscow, according to musicians familiar with both cities.[24] Musicians in Riga, Tallinn, and the major cities in the Caucasus were equally quick to take up the latest fashions in rock. All Soviet rock groups in the late sixties reflected the strong influence of British bands. Cliff Richards's Shadows were as popular as the Beatles, and the Dakotas and the Animals followed closely behind. The title of a recording by the latter group provided the name for one of the best Moscow rock bands of the period, the Winds of Change. Sasha Lehrman was an eighteen-year-old cello student at the distinguished Gnesin School of Music in Moscow when he became the group's leader in 1967. He and four other cellists at the school—two of them promising students of Mstislav Rostropovich—had earlier formed so successful a rock group that Lehrman decided to turn professional. Members of the Winds of Change wrote most of their own lyrics. Their subjects were the classic themes of love and loss, sung with an honesty and sincerity long absent from products of the official music industry. "We were political by being unpolitical," recalled Lehrman.[25] Along with solo bards such as Bulat Okudzhava, unofficial rock bands like the Winds of Change for the first time challenged the government's seemingly unshakable monopoly on the Soviet Tin Pan Alley.[26]

Numerous bands, including the Winds of Change, sang many of their lyrics in English. Besides testifying to the Soviet educational system's commendable emphasis on foreign languages, the practice was a deliberate affront to the older generation. Among the young,

English was a cult language, like Latin for the educated of earlier generations. Terms like "*underground*," "*bit grupa*," "*rock bend*," "*grupi*," and "*sashon*" (any rock event) came into general usage. Many Soviet rock groups even wrote their original lyrics in English.

With the rise of modern jazz in the fifties, the cultivation of social deviance as an end in itself had given place to a searching interest in music for its own sake. The world of rock picked up the lost thread of deviance and wove it into the fabric of *demi-monde* life. Marijuana and alcohol were common in the rock underground, although hard drugs were rare outside Moscow. The men sported long hair and pleated bell-bottom trousers ornamented with gold buttons down the outer seams; neckties, required of all male students, were abandoned in favor of gaudy open-necked shirts with strings of beads showing. Women wore miniskirts, loose hair, and heavy eye makeup. Every major city acquired sleazy hangouts for the local rock-'n'-roll set. In Moscow it was the Seasons Café (*Vremena goda*) in Gorky Park, where the Trolls, the Winds of Change, and other bands held forth until 2 or 3 A.M.

The cultivation of purposeful deviance and outright rebellion among Soviet youth reached a new high with the appearance in the late seventies of aggressively anti-social punk and heavy metal bands. Such groups deliberately assaulted respectable society with garish costumes, ferocious volume, and obscene lyrics. Most cities managed to stamp out the more offensive bands, but punk groups appeared with some frequency at dances at Batumi and other Black Sea resorts. The nearby Georgian Republic was far more tolerant toward rock music than were the Russians, and a number of fairly provocative bands like the *Varazi* flourished there, and even enjoyed the protection of the local concert agency.[27]

Leningraders such as Georgi Ordanovsky produced some fierce hard rock music but not punk. The Moscow band that went furthest toward punk was the Minstrels (*Skomorokhi*), led by guitarist Alexander Gradsky. A serious and knowledgeable musician, Gradsky had trained as an operatic tenor. As head of the Minstrels, he specialized in shocking people with flamboyant behavior and rude language. Alexander Burnov, the keyboard player, dyed the hair on

one side of his head gray, leaving the rest natural black. The band
was as good as it was eccentric, and many of Burnov's lyrics were
widely plagiarized by other groups. Over the years, the Minstrels
became such a success that they went soft, growing more respectable and business-like. Long before the band recorded, it had lost
its fire.[28]

Impresarios of Rock
and the Armenian Woodstock

The combination of enormous public demand and ineffectual official opposition enabled rock music to develop a complex and effi-
cient organizational network. At the center stood a group of private
entrepreneurs, the "organizers" (*organizatory*), who formed bands,
booked concerts, and accumulated large bankrolls in the process.
A few of these promoters were themselves musicians, including a
grandson of *Presidium* member Anastas Mikoyan, who founded
the popular and successful band the Flowers (*Tsvety*). Most were
pure impresarios. Typical was Yuri Eisenspitz, the organizer, manager, and financier of the popular Moscow rock band Sokol. Clean-
shaven, conservatively dressed, and entirely conformist in appearance, the young Eisenspitz is said to have made a fortune in the
unofficial market in furs. His real love was putting together rock
events.

Eisenspitz and other organizers took advantage of the opportunity to rent cafés and restaurants. The government made available
cheap rentals for weddings and anniversary parties, but Eisenspitz
used them for his own purposes. The budget for a typical evening
might include the following expenditures: 400 rubles for the rent-
ing of the hall; 300 rubles for the band; and 500 rubles for food
and liquor (purchased on the semi-legal "second economy" at bar-
gain prices). To offset these, an "organizer" might charge ten rubles
a head and expect two hundred people, yielding revenues of 2000
rubles. Net profits then equaled 800 rubles, tax free, or the equivalent of several months' wages for a typical Soviet worker. It is no

wonder that by 1969 Eisenspitz was accompanied on his nocturnal rounds by two burly bodyguards.[29]

To avoid entanglements with the police, promoters like Eisenspitz preferred to stage their events on the outskirts of big cities, at suburban cafés like the Northern (*Severnaia*) near Moscow. There were police raids from time to time, although until the late sixties and early seventies they rarely led to jailings. Indeed, the situation was sufficiently loose and lucrative to attract far more daring impresarios than Eisenspitz. The unquestioned king of Soviet rock entrepreneurs, the Bill Graham of the USSR, was an Armenian, Rafael Mkrtchian. When he burst on the rock scene, "Rafik" Mkrtchian was in his early forties and balding. Temperamental and shrewd, he remains a shadowy figure, even to those who worked for him. "I never asked about him; he never volunteered," recalled guitarist Sasha Lehrman.[30]

Particularly murky are Mkrtchian's dealings with Komsomol in the Armenian capital of Erevan. Presumably, he talked the Young Communist officials into lending their organization's name to the Festival of Rock Music, the first of which he mounted in 1969. For several years the event was an annual Soviet Woodstock, attended by five to eight thousand people daily over several weekends. Each winter Mkrtchian scoured the Soviet Union for the best rock bands and personally invited them to participate in his May festival at the Palace of Sports. The events were well advertised on billboards in Erevan but known to the rest of the Soviet citizenry only by word of mouth. The musicians dealt exclusively with Mkrtchian. If there was an organizing committee, as there were for the jazz festivals, it was unknown to them. Participating bands came from Moscow, Leningrad, Latvia, Estonia, and Georgia. Their performances were completely free of control by the Repertory Commission or other censors. Thanks to Mkrtchian's protection, Armenia became the Mecca of Soviet rock music.

The parallels between Mkrtchian's Armenian rock festivals and the Woodstock festival were deliberate, although the former were infinitely more sedate. Mkrtchian even attempted to produce a film of the Armenian Woodstock in 1972. Four of the biggest rock stars in the Soviet Union formed a new group, Super, for the occasion. Leonid Berger, formerly of the Orpheus band, played piano and sang in the style of his idol, Ray Charles. The bassist and the guitarist came from the Scythians, while Yuri Fokin, soon to enter an Orthodox Christian monastery but for the time being the best rock drummer in Russia, provided rhythm. The film was shot but never released. Rafik Mkrtchian, it seems, had failed to share enough of his profits with Armenian officials. For his oversight, he was arrested and jailed for ten years. Musicians who played in the 1972 festival were also interrogated. Yuri Eisenspitz and other successful promoters were rounded up as well.

Rock music had gotten out of hand. A concert in Kaunas, Lithuania, by the student rock group Kertukai ended in a wild melee of thrown chairs and broken windows. Most attempts to curb such violence were too primitive to be effective. In Leningrad, however, a crisis in 1967 led to a solution that was widely emulated elsewhere. One of the most popular local rock bands, the Argonauts, had been engaged to perform at the Polytechnic Institute. The hall was packed with students and rock fans, among whom word had spread that this was to be a wild evening. The fans drank vodka in the hall, and many got high on marijuana. When the Argonauts performed, a few fans attacked the stage and began shouting and grabbing the musicians. Not even jazz had produced such a scandal. A special session of the City Committee of the Communist Party was held and a decree issued asserting official control over all vocal-guitar bands in Leningrad. Amateur groups were prevented from performing in public until they had passed censorship at the House of Public Creativity (*Dom narodnogo tvorchestva*) on Rubenstein Street. The Leningrad Artistic Council was made directly accountable to the local Party.[31]

The ensuing effort at cooptation drew heavily on the government's earlier experience with modern jazz. This time, however, it penetrated to the high schools. In 1968, some tenth graders at Special English School Number 185 in Leningrad wanted to form a rock band modeled on the Beatles. They were permitted to do so and were even invited to participate in a city-wide competition of rock bands run by the Palace of Pioneers. But periodically a special instructor would arrive at the school to check on the band's repertoire. Not only did he review the entire tune list and select songs that were appropriate for the competition, but he provided succinct critical advice, such as "This is too loud," or "This part is too Western." In spite of all his efforts, the final competition, held in the spring of 1968 at the Palace of Pioneers and open only to Komsomol activists, included many long-haired bands playing pure Western-style rock music.[32]

The Argonauts scuffle in Leningrad had put the Moscow KGB on guard. Concern mounted when rock music, which had at first appealed to a declassé audience, began attracting large numbers of adherents among sons and daughters of the elite. In 1964 a rock group specializing in anti-establishment lyrics was even formed at the highly exclusive Institute for International Economics and Foreign Relations (*IMEMO*) to play at its closed parties.[33] This IMEMO band was suppressed with that special indignation reserved for acts of class treason in a classless society. Nonetheless by 1968 the elite Molodezhnoe Café was splitting its bookings between modern jazz and rock bands; Komsomol's Melody Café (*Melodiia*) was renamed the Melody and Rhythm Café. The house was always packed, and from the standpoint of the KGB there was something dangerously anarchic in its atmosphere. In 1969 it was estimated that there was not a high school, institute, or factory in Moscow without at least one rock band, bringing the total to several thousand and meaning that several thousand private and independent producers were operating in the field of popular culture. No party at Moscow State University was complete without rock music, and even Komsomol was wholly dependent on the private market when it hired music for its dances.

Rock music, like modern jazz, was both more organized and more closely controlled in Moscow than in the provinces. The most serious attempt to exert official control over rock in the capital came with the creation of the Beat Club at the Melody and Rhythm Café in 1969. Komsomol was its nominal sponsor. In reality, it was a

KGB operation from the outset. Many of the best rock musicians in the capital were enticed onto the new club's board, which then announced that it would hold open auditions for members. Promises of concerts, imported instruments and amplifiers, and foreign tours produced a long waiting list of those wishing to register. But registration was no simple matter. It involved filling out a long questionnaire touching on every aspect of the applicant's biography. Yet the applications flowed in. Once registration was completed, however, the club's activities began to dwindle. One band was sent on tour to Africa and the Middle East, but suspicions mounted among the musicians. When the Beat Club was finally disbanded a year later, everyone was disenchanted except the KGB, which now had full dossiers on hundreds of the best rock musicians of greater Moscow.[34]

This devious episode did not quell the underground rock movement, which continued to claim many of the boldest groups throughout the seventies, but it did mark a turning point. Henceforth, rock music became a major concern of Komsomol and the variety agencies. In order to preempt the private market, salary ceilings for officially approved musicians were raised enormously. With most of the "organizers" in jail, the leading stars bought off, and the Armenian Woodstock shut down, rock music appeared to have been neutralized by 1972.

But consumer preferences didn't change simply because producers offered different fare. The better rock musicians understood this and tried to stay close to the public's tastes. The Singing Guitars (*Poiushchie gitary*) of Leningrad, one of the first official rock groups to appear, succeeded by borrowing heavily from the repertoire and styles of the unofficial groups. The Ariel from Novosibirsk also tried to retain as an official group the spontaneity they had possessed during their unofficial days. Not all official rock musicians felt the need to respond to their audiences, however. After all, the State concert agencies, not the public directly, paid their salaries, and therefore it was the bureaucrats above all who had to be pleased. The Blue Guitars (*Golubye gitary*), a commercial outfit under the Moscow Concert Agency, gradually evolved into a bland and old-fashioned variety show that recalled the late Utesov orchestra. Igor Granov, their businessman-organizer, mixed Russian folk tunes and maudlin ballads with the band's other numbers by the Beatles and Jimi Hendrix. Conservative officials liked the act and sent the group on tour to Eastern Europe, the Middle East, and Latin America.[35]

For every polished official group like the Blue Guitars, there were dozens that turned to mush under the combined pressures of commercialism, official prudery, and freedom from competition. The Happy Guys (*Veselye rebiata*) were formed in 1968 to present an image of healthy Soviet youths to young audiences. Taking their name from Utesov's 1934 film, they were a study in officially sponsored prissiness from the start, even though the group boasted several very capable musicians and their eclectic repertoire included many Western tunes.[36] The Balladeers (*Pesniary*) from Minsk were similar, although their use of folk instruments led them down original paths and their greater distance from Moscow permitted them to be slightly bolder in setting their own course.[37]

The government's commitment to detente in the seventies complicated its effort to control rock music. As a sign of improved diplomatic relations with the West, a number of American and European rock bands were permitted to tour the USSR. The Joffrey Ballet of New York brought a small rock group called the Vegetables on their 1975 tour,[38] and the following year the Nitty Gritty Dirt Band performed a foot-stomping blend of rock and country music while on a cross-country tour. In the Soviet Union's rock Mecca of Erevan, six thousand fans clapped and danced inside the hall where they performed, while another fifteen thousand without tickets surged against the outside gates until they were dispersed by a tear gas grenade.[39] British rock star Elton John's 1979 concerts produced frenzy in Leningrad but met a much cooler response in Moscow, where rock music fans among the Party officialdom used their influence to corner most of the tickets.[40] Rhythm-and-blues star B. B. King's 1979 tour received no advance publicity but produced hordes of ticket scalpers in every city, and a near riot in the Georgian capital of Tblisi, where two people sat in each seat in the theater.[41]

By the late seventies the Soviet bureaucracy had accepted rock music as an unavoidable reality. Officially sponsored rock festivals were held in various parts of the country, with the Latvians taking the lead with their Liepaja Amber festival of 1973 and the Estonians following with their *Muusikapäevad* in 1979 and the Tartu Rock Festival in 1980. A few serious articles on rock music began to appear in the press, and the indefatigable Estonian publicist Valter Ojakäär published a thoughtful and comprehensive monograph on Western pop music.[42] But recognition did not loosen official policy toward rock. Lyrics were still closely censored, and anything resembling pornography extirpated; as with jazz in the thirties, the government also tried to foster homegrown tunes drawing on nationalistic subjects. Rock was even exploited for anti-Western propaganda and satire. But is was no easier to mold popular taste "from above" in the seventies than it had been earlier. A few rock stars had been successfully bought off, but at the price of hardening the line between official and unofficial and of confirming underground groups as the standard-bearers of heroic independence. Foreign influences continued to prevail; in 1979 Bob Dylan's record *Blood on the Tracks* was bringing 150 rubles on the black market in Moscow, and more in the provinces.[43] Control was imperfect at best, particularly in the provinces. When the Western rock group Boney M came to Moscow, it was forbidden to play its big hit, "Rah Rah Rasputin, Russia's Greatest Love Machine." Yet only weeks later the house band at the rustic Saisare Restaurant in the remote Siberian city of Yakutsk was using its new synthesizer to perform the tune, over and over again.[44] For all their efforts to guide popular values, Soviet officals were still unable to do more than respond to the vital private market.

After the Fall

Reviewing the 1968 Moscow Jazz Festival, held just before the invasion of Czechoslovakia, critic Leonid Pereverzev took note of the "steadily increasing signs of creative apathy in recent years, which became fully manifest at this year's festival."[45] He ascribed this to the "strict regimentation which ruled out all performances other than those in a concert format." He also noted the absence of many of Moscow's best jazzmen at the festival. And well he might have. Absent was trumpeter German Lukianov. Always a thoughtful critic of his own playing as well as that of others, Lukianov was coming to feel the limitations of the bop school that had long reigned in Moscow.[46] Leningrad saxophonist-arranger "Charlie" Golstein had also stayed away. Introspective and self-critical, Golstein had always had doubts about the validity of his efforts in jazz and was soon to announce that he would abandon jazz in favor of the music of the pre-Baroque classical composers, which, he felt, "manifests greater spirit."[47] Others, like Georgi Garanian and his Melodiia ensemble, fled into the more secure world of commercial music.[48] Of course, Russians were well informed on the deepening isolation of jazz in the United States, which by 1970 had captured only 4.6 percent of the record market, as compared with 73 percent for pop, rock, folk, and country music.[49] But this provided scant consolation.

The great jazz age seemed to have passed. A retrospective mood set in, marked by celebrations commemorating past triumphs. In October 1972, concerts in honor of the fiftieth anniversary of Valentin Parnakh's introduction of jazz to Russia were held in Leningrad and Moscow.[50] The jubilee was also celebrated by the publication of *Soviet Jazz: A Historical Sketch*, written by the physicist and former president of the Moscow Jazz Club, Alexei Batashev. In his foreword to Batashev's study, an official of the Union of Soviet Composers assured readers that the manuscript had been "repeatedly debated" by the Union's Moscow branch.[51] As a result, the manuscript was cut by nearly half. The names and the photographs of all jazzmen who had emigrated were purged from the book, and most controversial points either deleted or stated so elliptically as to be meaningless to all but the initiated. The excisions and cuts assault the informed reader, reminding him that the accomplishments of Soviet jazzmen were made in the face of formidable impediments. A journal titled *Soviet Jazz* that was supposed to have begun publication in 1972 never saw the light of day.

The most interesting product of this mood of retrospection, and in all likelihood its most enduring, is a book by the Leningrad philosopher and jazz enthusiast Efim Barban. Barban had long been interested in bop and free jazz and had contributed several essays to the typescript jazz journal *Kvadrat*. None of these exercises, however, prepared his readers for *Black Music, White Freedom*, which is nothing less than an aesthetic and sociological analysis of modern jazz in the context of the entire history of music in the West. There is indeed a "crisis of perception" in jazz, Barban argues, and it is reflected in the evident unpopularity of avant-gardism. Some writers have claimed that the crisis occurred merely because American black nationalists denied that the new jazz could be played or understood by whites. Barban dismisses this notion as invalid, an exercise in myth-making. The true cause of the public's aversion to all forms of avant-garde jazz is that they constitute a fundamental revolution in music and aesthetics, an upheaval so vast in scope that it can be compared with only two other breakthroughs in Western music in the past one thousand years, namely, the discovery of the principles of key and of dodecaphony. The audience's problem, he explains, is not that its members are white but that avant-garde jazz requires "an extraordinarily broad perceptual culture" in order to be understood.[52]

Bop and free jazz can be appreciated by anyone capable of leaping beyond the formal and perceptual bounds of Western music and embracing aesthetic notions that before were to be found only in Oriental and African art. Once this leap is taken, the listener enters into an entirely new musical realm. Because of its great complexity and formal sophistication, the new jazz is a high art. But since it also gives free rein to "the sensual, spontaneous and ecstatic," it is potentially far more democratic in its appeal than most previous high art in the West.

It is unfair to reduce Barban's analysis to a few general statements. Suffice it to say that he uses the methods of poetics, semantics, and structuralism to place modern jazz in what he considers its appropriate aesthetic context. In the process, he speaks directly to several enduring problems in the history of jazz in the USSR. First, he acknowledges the erotic and Dionysian element in jazz and embraces it as the essence of the music and the vital source of its individualism. Second, he offers a serious response to American black nationalists whose racial exclusivity would place the new music off limits to all whites, including Russians. Third, and most important, he legitimizes bop and free jazz as high art by providing the positive critical framework that had been lacking. Without compromising jazz, he gives it access to the Red Seal world of high culture that had been closed to it for more than a half-century.

Regrettably, Barban's book remains unpublished and is known to Soviet readers only through the numerous typed copies circulated by hand. But his argument has gained acceptance, as evidenced by the fact that today both the Russian Concert Organization (*Roskontsert*) and the Moscow Concert Organization (*Moskontsert*) hire modern jazz groups and support them at the same levels of pay provided to symphonic musicians performing chamber music.

Bop and other forms of jazz gradually recovered from the downturn that followed the invasion of Czechoslovakia in 1968. As if by inertia, the festival movement continued to spread, reaching many provincial towns that had not been touched earlier. Khabarovsk on the Chinese border, Fergana near Afghanistan, Erevan in Armenia, and Kuibyshev on the lower Volga are just a few places where regular festivals were established.[53]

The typical festival of the seventies attracted fifteen or twenty bands from a dozen cities and audiences of five hundred to two thousand persons.[54] The best of these new festivals, notably the annual Rhythms of Summer (*Vasaras Ritmi*) held in Riga, were at least as comprehensive as the more established gatherings and probably more vital. The greatest shortcoming of most of these festivals reflected the dilemma of Soviet jazz as a whole: the most popular performers were the same jazzmen who had dominated the scene ten years earlier. In a jazz poll conducted by *The Square* (*Kvadrat*) in 1976, the winners in practically every category belonged to the same generation that had discovered modern jazz in 1957–60.[55] The revolutionary generation had become the establishment, inhibiting the development of a successor generation.

Jazz stagnated temporarily but it also gained new official support, as shown by the appearance of formalized school ensembles. Following the American practice, institutions like the Gnesin School of Music in Moscow began organizing performing groups, most of which played with great polish but a predictable absence of fire.[56] Worse, few of the senior musicians took younger players into their groups. An impressive exception was German Lukianov, who, after a fallow period, organized a post-bop group, Cadence, in which aspiring jazzmen gained experience with one of the best older players.

The positive results of this tendency toward academism were due largely to the continuing influence and activity of Yuri Saulsky. Since his youthful success with the TsDRI ensemble at the 1957 Moscow Youth Festival and especially through his film scores, Saulsky had gained distinction in several fields of light music and jazz. Unlike many jazz musicians, he was equally respected by the independent-minded avant-gardists, officials of the Union of Soviet Composers, and the various philharmonic societies. When he proposed the establishment of a chain of twenty-one jazz academies around the USSR, his idea found favor. By the mid-seventies, academies were actually being established, the first at Tsaritsyno near Moscow. Their basic courses gave jazz musicians the chance to acquire the formal training that is a prerequisite for higher-paying jobs in the USSR. They also became feeder schools for local concert agencies, thus ensuring that some form of jazz would have a permanent place in the musical establishment. The Ministry of Culture may well have seen Saulsky's schools as a way of bringing jazz firmly under its control. But the consequences of its patronage have been uniformly beneficial both to the music and to the musicians.

Another fruitful manifestation of the new academism was a series of seminars and concerts on "Jazz and Contemporary Music" held at the Scientists' House in the Siberian research city of Akademgorodok outside Novosibirsk in February 1977. The concerts presented examples of virtually every tendency in modern jazz, and the papers were of sufficient quality to warrant their publication, albeit in a limited edition of only fifty copies. Unfortunately, the audience included far more middle-aged scientists than youths.

The jazz audience had aged along with the music. Modern jazz had been linked with the rites of an inquisitive generation of urban youths in the late 1950s and had served as a symbolic rallying point through much of the 1960s. Now those youths were older. They no longer haunted the cafés and institute dances. Their "cool" style of rebellion seemed hopelessly passé, not least because the coolness more often than not now masked the conformity of aspiring organization men and women. They had married, settled down, and started families; what energies they devoted to the public realm were safely channeled through their careers. Earlier, they had been able to isolate themselves from the older generation and thus maintain the spontaneity and the purity of outlook they associated with improvised modern jazz. Now they spent eight hours a day with that older generation, and their individual advancement and well-being often depended directly upon the good opinion of their senior colleagues.

This is not to say that the generation that upended Soviet official culture in 1958–67 sold out. It was far more complicated than that. Many continued to adhere to their earlier values, and a few made great sacrifices for their sake. Others compartmentalized their lives—always a convenient tactic—by separating the authentic ethics and tastes of their private lives from the increasingly compromised values of their workaday existence.

It is not surprising, then, that the most talented new jazz musicians of the seventies communicated best to small, individuated audiences. Big bands were still being formed, and at least one of the new crop, Gunnar Rosenbergs's hard-driving ensemble from Riga, could impart electric excitement to large and youthful audiences. But the main action shifted to soloists in smaller groups. They were not dramatic personalities, but their recorded performances struck just the right note at the private parties of the thirty- to forty-five-year-olds who once filled the cafés. The three most important new figures—Leonid Chizhik, Vagif Mustafa-Zadeh, and Viacheslav Ganelin—were all pianists who moved from large ensembles to small groups during the 1970s. Hailing from Moscow, Baku, and the Bal-

tic, respectively, each built his music on the traditions of those leading centers of Soviet jazz.

Leonid Chizhik came to Moscow from Kharkov, where he was
born in 1947. With conservatory training in composition and mu-
sicology as well as piano, he can absorb the most diverse styles
without apparent conflict. After working with the State Variety Orchestra and Georgi Garanian's commercially successful Melodiia
ensemble, he set out on his own with a trio. Today he performs
principally as a soloist.[57] Chizhik is all polish, combining the fright-
ening speed of Art Tatum with the delicacy of Teddy Wilson. As a
good Moscow jazzman, he uses bop phrasing, but his deepest instincts are more lyrical and romantic. He stands in direct line of
descent from Alexander Tsfasman and, like Tsfasman, has recorded George Gershwin's music.[58] He also performs many of
Tsfasman's old hits, as well as his own pieces, which draw on thirty
years of jazz piano.[59] His proficiently executed allusions to different
periods and styles are perfectly suited to bridging generational lines,
which Chizhik has managed to do with great success.

By contrast, Vagif Mustafa-Zadeh played in the tradition of hard-
driving and complex rhythm that Vladimir Sermakashev first brought
to Moscow from Baku. At the Friendship (*Druzhba*) Café in Baku,
Mustafa-Zadeh worked his way through the music of Frank Ro-
solino, Bill Evans, and Thelonious Monk before meeting Arkadi
Dadashian, a subtle and intense drummer from Tblisi. Dadashian
and the bassist David Koifman successfully blended Near Eastern
counterrhythms with hard bop to provide a steamy setting for
Mustafa-Zadeh's solos—a provocative crossbreed of the music of
Scheherazade and that of Minton's Playhouse in Harlem.[60] At the
time of his untimely death in 1980, Mustafa-Zadeh was just coming to the attention of international audiences.

The Baltic republics have traditionally nurtured strong jazz pianists. Latvian Raimonds Pauls passed quickly through imitations
of Art Tatum and Horace Silver to produce a large body of original
pieces both for trio and for orchestra.[61] In Estonia, a much younger
man, Toñu Naissoo, worked closely with the adept and tasteful

guitarist Tiit Paulus and a group of fine sidemen to keep up his family's commitment to jazz.[62] Another Estonian pianist, Maigus Kappel, brought conservatory training and a background in rock music to his key post in the quartet of tenor saxophonist Lembit Saarsalu. Among its innovations, this stimulating group combined forces with wonderfully evocative folk singers to create a compelling blend of primitivism and modernity.[63]

Far overshadowing other Soviet jazzmen of the 1970s was the third major pianist, Viacheslav Ganelin from Vilnius, the capital of Lithuania. By any measure, he is among the most interesting jazz musicians playing in Europe today. Ganelin was born in a village near Moscow in 1944, though his parents joined the Russian migration to the Baltic in the early fifties. Long before he graduated from the conservatory at Vilnius, he was performing in the local Neringa Café and at the annual jazz festival in Tallinn.[64] A bootleg recording of a Ganelin concert in Berlin caused *Melody Maker*'s reviewer to declare it "one of the most exciting events that 'free music' has ever staged."[65] Ganelin's present trio includes Vladimir Tarasov on drums and Vladimir Chekasin on reeds; the three play fifteen different instruments between them, with Chekasin often playing several horns at once à la Roland Kirk. But even the strummed piano strings and bowed electric guitar are not mere effects.[66] Ganelin has an earthy feel for the blues, and his sidemen can move freely in and around the most withering tempos. The group favors long works with free improvisation interspersed among carefully worked out bridging passages. Regrettably, Ganelin has only recently traveled to the West, and has recorded little in the USSR.[67]

Underexposure

Reviewing the state of jazz in 1977, the leading Soviet jazz critic reported to European readers of *Jazz Forum*, "The press, radio, and TV now dedicate a lot less time and space to jazz than they did in the 'sixties. . . ."[68] In spite of official acceptance, there were fewer concerts to cover, and the aura of newness and forbidden fruit was

gone from those that were held. Although performances at the An-
gara Café and the Medical Workers' Club in Moscow were of genuine musical interest, they no longer attracted the jet set. The old
stars suffered from familiarity while the new generation that would
hold the stage in the early 1980s was only beginning to appear. And
by abandoning dancing and revelry to rock music, modern jazz was
left seeming bloodless, academic, and cold. Only visiting foreign
jazzmen still aroused the old excitement, and these toured the USSR
in unprecedented numbers. From the United States came the University of Illinois Stage Band (1969); Duke Ellington and his orchestra (1971); the Thad Jones-Mel Lewis orchestra (1972); the
New York Jazz Repertory Company (1975); the North Texas State
University Jazz Lab Band (1976); the New England Conservatory
Ragtime Ensemble (1978); and the Preservation Hall Jazz Band
(1979).[69] Jazz bands from Canada, Italy, and other European countries also made successful Soviet tours.[70] As one Soviet writer ruefully observed, "It is a parodox that the foreign groups—both
professional and amateur—gave more concerts in the USSR than
the Soviet ensembles." [71] Recordings by foreign jazz bands also were
issued in far greater numbers than recordings by Soviet groups.

Back to the Roots

Throughout the 1960s, the stylish and judicious Polish journal *Jazz*
had followed closely the rise of rock music. Elvis Presley, the Rolling Stones, and The Who were noted in its pages. The editors' objective was to revitalize and enrich European jazz with an infusion
of the most vital and usable elements of rock music. In Soviet jazz
circles, by contrast, rock was a taboo subject. Its very existence was
an embarrassment to both official and unofficial promoters of jazz.
Rock music was like the visit of a poor country cousin to the man-
sion of a *nouveau riche*; it brought to mind relationships that were
best forgotten. But this ill-bred cousin would not go away. It just
hung around, with its aura of anarchic dancing, sex, and youthful
emancipation. These qualities had been associated with jazz in the

fifties, but times had changed. Especially after the fall of Khrushchev, jazz had gone straight, which is to say, it began to lose its social base and grow irrelevant. With so frail a tie even to alienated youth, jazz lost an important link with popular culture.

This process had reached its culmination by the early 1970s. A few jazz musicians who had come to understand what had taken place separated themselves from the increasingly sectarian world of jazz and ran to catch seats on the train of rock music, which had nearly passed them by. Among the first was Moscow saxophonist Vitali Kleinot, who led the last jazz group to play at the Molodezhnoe Café in 1971.[72] Along with the hard-living trumpeter Andrei Tovmasian and pianist Igor Brill, he began incorporating elements of rock into his music. At about the same time the impressive ensemble Modo was formed in Riga to promote the same linkage of rock music and jazz.

At the very least, fusion was a commercial necessity. The leader of a Moscow big band of the seventies stated it bluntly: "The fusion of jazz and rock music was the only way to reach the public, the only way to get daily work. To play jazz I would have had to sacrifice my family."[73] Leaders of many other groups came to the same conclusion. The Orange (*Apelsin*) in Tallinn, the Anatoli Vapirov band in Leningrad, and Georgi Garanian's Melodiia ensemble were all experimenting with jazz-rock by 1973.[74]

It is easy to dismiss the effort by Soviet jazz musicians to embrace rock music as a concession to commercialism. But their attempts also reveal a new willingness of at least a few sophisticates to take their cues from the genuine preferences of the masses. The work of Moscow saxophonist Alexei Kozlov is a perfect example. Kozlov (no relation of the saxophonist in the twenties by the same name) had come into jazz with the first post-Stalin rebels and had apparently shared the sense of exhilaration of those years. As modern jazz became more arcane and elitist, however, Kozlov moved to the sidelines. Throughout the sixties, he was a secondary figure on the Moscow jazz scene, viewed by his colleagues as an amateur who hedged his bets by maintaining a day job in engineering. His re-

cordings of that decade reveal a competent imitator of Sonny Rollins and Roland Kirk but not a musician with any clear sense of
direction or mission.[75]

Kozlov ascribed the problem wholly to nonmusical issues. As he
saw it, avant-garde jazz had arisen " . . . as a movement of black
extremists. I came to understand that I am not black, and that I
don't share their problems. Why, then, should I play like them?"
Kozlov abandoned modern jazz and threw himself into rock music
with a convert's fervor. "Rock helped me to be born again," he
claimed.[76] The renewed Kozlov formed a band and with it fused
the throbbing beat of rock with the more complex harmonies of
modern jazz. Arsenal, as he named it, was an instant success.

As a jazz-rock fusion musician, Kozlov is no less derivative than
he had been earlier; he simply traded in Coltrane and Rollins for
Chick Corea, Archie Shepp, and Herbie Hancock. Yet somehow
Kozlov is far more convincing as a rock star than he had ever been
as an avant-gardist.[77] And far from being corrupted by his new
status as a culture hero, Kozlov has continued to grow, producing
original works and even a rock opera in 1978, inspired by *Jesus
Christ Superstar*.[78]

Kozlov himself gives several hints on the reasons for the success
of his music. The grandson of an Orthodox Christian priest, he
speaks of "reaching the people," and he defends jazz-rock as a
"democratic" music.[79] Rock music for Kozlov is familiar, "European," while avant-garde jazz has remained alien. By fusing them,
Kozlov had created a new music, capable of becoming the common
cultural property of both the masses and the highbrows of the future.

Kozlov's defense of jazz-rock resembles the old Stalinist defense
of mass songs to a startling degree. Both are based on the belief
that the popular music of the future must be rooted in the living
musical vocabulary of the masses and that that vocabulary can be
enriched by the application of modern musical ideas drawn from
more elitist traditions. Both arguments use populist rhetoric, while
at the same time admitting that the new blend will be produced
through artistic guidance "from above."

There the similarity ends. The Stalinists tried to convince themselves that a dying folk tradition could provide the basis for the new Soviet popular song; the only living musical vocabulary Kozlov detects among the Soviet masses is rock music. The Stalinists thought that traditional orchestral forms could transform folk songs into a modern popular music; Kozlov sees jazz performing that function. Finally, the Communist party under Stalin saw as the purpose of its songs the ideological education of the masses, and hence their economic and political liberation as a group; Kozlov, by contrast, wants his jazz-rock fusion music to liberate the individual psyche through dancing and worldly pleasures. Thus, though beginning with a conservative and even populist line of argument, Kozlov ends by promoting a music which in many ways represents the very antithesis of the older and more austere ideal developed by Lenin's heirs for the New Soviet Man.

14
Coda

Nothing had done more, I think, to discredit cultural analysis than the construction of impeccable depictions of formal order in whose actual existence nobody can quite believe.

Clifford Geertz

When a chronological history of any subject arrives finally in the present, it has gained a dangerous momentum toward reckless predictions about the future. The risk is particularly great when the subject at hand is Russian and Soviet culture, with its abrupt shifts and turns. Far better to confine oneself to conclusions about the past, keeping in mind, of course, the further danger of imposing a false tidiness on the messy rooms of history.

The most obvious conclusion to be drawn from this saga of three-score years is that jazz and Western pop music have always been a factor in Soviet popular culture. Beginning with a few intellectuals in the capital cities and spreading first among the educated classes and then to the urban population as a whole, jazz found sympathetic and devoted adherents in Soviet society. Even in the face of severe repression, jazz continued to be played in the USSR. No amount of force was able to eradicate it as an independent and literally "popular" force.

The existence of jazz forced Soviet officialdom to reckon with the thorny problem of popular culture in a society claiming to be organized according to the precepts of Marxism-Leninism. Nothing approaching a consistent solution has ever been proposed. Even when part of the Communist party has come up with a policy on jazz, it has more often than not been challenged publicly by other factions within the Party or in the Soviet government. Highly visible infighting occurred even at the height of Stalin's purges.

Whether Soviet officials accept or reject jazz, they have always treated it as a serious matter. Indeed, jazz has been the subject of far more official solicitude in the USSR than in the United States, where it was born. This paradoxical situation came about for several reasons. First, the Marxist-Leninist ideal of creating a New Soviet Man has virtually forced the government to monitor the day-to-day behavior of its citizens in order to prove to itself and to the world that the society is making progress toward the ideal Communist state. Second, the Marxist doctrine of the malleability of man and society has encouraged the government to intervene whenever the Soviet public seems to have gone astray. Like parents who refuse to acknowledge that their grown offspring have ideas of their own, Soviet cultural agencies have consistently attempted to assert their paternalistic control, and with predictable results. A third factor arises not from Marxism-Leninism per se but from the bureaucratic system in which it is embodied in the USSR: namely, the urge of *any* powerful bureaucracy to overregulate and overcontrol.

The first decades of Soviet rule witnessed sincere if misguided attempts to create and implant positive alternatives to the public's tastes. Many Western observers, following these efforts at culture-making with fascination, inadvertently adopted the Soviet officials' view that the populace was a passive mass. The idea that this inert mass might actually be capable of asserting its own cultural interests was slow in coming. But the very popularity of American jazz music, even among the official hierarchy, forced Soviet leaders eventually to acknowledge it.

By 1945, official faith in the possibility of forging a new popular culture consistent with the precepts of socialism was weakening. And as confidence in the future declined, Soviet officials came more and more to assert control over cultural life as an end in itself. They did not spare force in this endeavor, but it remained an exercise in frustration. In the end, they were compelled to deal with the public's actual cultural preferences, rather than considering them putty from which a New Soviet Man would be formed. Soviet cultural officials had to face the bitter reality that many of their citizens wished for the same things desired by young men and women elsewhere in the industrialized world: to achieve individual liberation by means of the Dionysian release of erotic energy in music and dance. In the Soviet Union, no less than in other countries, jazz was the bearer of this "second revolution" of the twentieth century.

Although the notion of Party control in popular culture proved quixotic, it still had an enormous impact on the cultural scene, which went far beyond repression. To carry out the Party's cultural programs, a large and complex institutional structure was set up. Its very existence altered Soviet popular culture. But the government proved to be a very conservative patron. Once an idea or program entered the official system, it was never dropped. Thus, the Stalinist campaign to create a purely Soviet popular music was dead by 1950, yet Khrushchev attempted to revive it in 1962–63 and the newspaper *Labor* (*Trud*) was harping on it as late as 1980.[1] Years after rock had outstripped jazz as the main locus of deviance in music, old-fashioned critics were still trying to clean up jazz.

Patronage, too, followed conservative lines. If an ensemble managed to get official recognition, the bureaucratic machine kept it in business, independent of the public's wishes. The survival of big bands over many decades, the perpetuation of music hall ensembles, of turn-of-the-century folk groups reminiscent of the pre-World War I banjo bands in America, and even of official 1960s-style rock groups attest to the powerful, built-in proclivity toward atrophy in the Soviet system of patronage and popular culture.

As a result of this tendency, all transitions and changes are endlessly complicated. As in the Soviet political system, a policy of lifetime employment has been established by default in the popular music field. With its day-to-day evolution retarded by conservatism and bureaucratization, official taste lags further and further behind the public's, until suddenly the pressure is released through a dramatic change. Overnight, the system rushes to coopt the very forms of popular culture which only yesterday it had vehemently resisted. The acceptance of swing music in the 1930s, of modern jazz after 1961, and of rock 'n' roll after 1968–69 followed this pattern. Yet official organs never seem to catch up with public taste. In practically every instance, whenever the government coopted a musical style, that music was already at the point of becoming passé.

Accepting Popular Culture

To the outside observer, the two most striking features of the Soviet government's involvement with popular culture are its ideological commitment to shaping public values and the inertia of its system to carry out that mission. But in reviewing sixty years of jazz in the USSR, three other features are not less striking.

First, for all its purported interest in molding popular tastes, the Soviet government and its cultural bureaucrats have utterly failed to provide any acceptable alternative to the Western-style popular culture they criticize. They have surely tried, and many Soviet musical hacks have dedicated their careers to the effort. But it has never worked. Without exaggeration, one could succinctly describe the Russians' dilemma over American popular music and jazz as the confrontation of a USSR armed with a theory of modern popular culture but little of its reality and a USA possessed of a rich and modern popular culture but without a theoretical basis.

Second, at no point in its entire history has the Soviet Union ever been the successfully organized and standardized monolith depicted by many of its more ardent friends and detractors. It has maintained uniform policies, to be sure, even totalitarian ones, but in the field of popular culture it has proven absolutely impossible to implement those policies effectively. Far from being docile and malleable, Soviet jazz fans have shown themselves to be independent and resourceful. Those who like jazz find ways of playing or hearing it, whatever policy may be. Nor are members of the Party and government immune to public tastes, as the activities of many highly placed jazz fans reveal. It is no wonder that, in the long run, the government had to make its peace with jazz.

Third, the Soviet system has changed. Ideology has seriously withered as a factor in public discourse. The public's interest in Western pop music and jazz in the early thirties forced ideologues to pay heed, but the ensuing *volte-face* took place only after it had been ratified through complex theoretical gymnastics. By the 1960s there were few people left in the government who felt the need to justify their turnabouts with Marxist theory. Sporadic attacks on jazz continued, but they were now devoid of serious ideological content, their chief motive forces being prudery, chauvinism, and professional rivalry. And when, finally, officialdom accepted jazz in the late 1970s, it did so without bothering to justify itself ideologically.

Beyond this, cultural phenomena from abroad are no longer immediately pigeonholed by political or class origin, as was formerly done. The exercise would be pointless today: few people care if a new form of jazz or popular music is labeled bourgeois, and there is no way of keeping jazz out of the USSR anyway, for modern communications have rendered popular culture completely transnational.

The present young adult generation is the first in Soviet history to share fully in European and American popular culture. When, in the future, members of this generation gather together to reminisce about their youth, they will dredge up many of the same "golden oldies" that would come to mind at a similar session in Hamburg, Lyons, Birmingham, or Milwaukee. Many of the old stars whose names they will recall will be foreigners: Duke Ellington, the Beatles, Michel Legrand, the Nitty Gritty Dirt Band, and others. Most will be homegrown jazz musicians, however, like Alexei Kozlov, Vadim Mustafa-Zadeh, and members of rock bands like the Winds of Change and The Time Machine. The young people will feel at home in conversations about music with contemporaries from any other industrial society. The outsiders will be those members of the older generation in the USSR who grew up with the Marxist belief that the Soviet economic system must inevitably produce a unique form of popular culture, remote from the jazz and pop music of the "decadent" West. And even among these people there will probably be at least one collector of jazz records or a devoted fan of the big beat.

Notes

1. The Two Revolutions of 1917

1. See "When European Composers Jazz," *Literary Digest*, Mar. 17, 1929, pp. 25–26.
2. Recalled by R. Dreyfous, New Orleans, Jan. 1981. Miss Dreyfous frequently hired the orchestras of A. J. Piron, J. Oliver, and others in the period 1916–21.
3. See Gerhard Masur, *Prophets of Yesterday: Studies in European Culture, 1890–1914* (New York, 1961), p. 354.
4. See Elizabeth Kridl Valkenier, "AKhRR, Realism and Official Style in the 1920s," *Soviet Union/Union Soviétique*, nos. 1–2 (1980), pp. 197–213.
5. F. Scott Fitzgerald, *The Crackup*, Edmund Wilson, ed. (New York, 1956), p. 16.
6. *Times-Picayune*, June 17, 1917, quoted in Al Rose, *Storyville, New Orleans* (Tuscaloosa, 1974), p. 107.
7. Rose, *Storyville*, p. 155.
8. Quoted and trans. in "German Interpreter of Jazz," *Literary Digest*, Aug. 23, 1919, p. 31.
9. Daniel J. Boorstin, *The Americans: The Democratic Experience* (New York, 1974), pp. 383–84.
10. *Ibid.*, p. 32.
11. For an excellent discussion of the themes of repeatability and spontaneity in American culture see *ibid.*, p. 370.
12. H. O. Brunn, *The Story of the Original Dixieland Jazz Band* (Baton Rouge, 1960), pp. 36–53.
13. *Ibid.*, p. 65. In Jan. 1917, the Original Dixieland Jazz Band recorded "Darktown Strutters' Ball" and "Indiana" for Columbia, but these were not issued until after the Victor record was released.

14. Fitzgerald, *The Crackup*, p. 14.
15. Russell Zguta, *Russian Minstrels: A History of Skhomorokhi* (Camden, 1978), p. 4.
16. Van Wyck Brooks, "Highbrow" and "Lowbrow," *America's Coming of Age* (New York, 1934), pp. 15–35.
17. See Max Laserson, *The American Impact on Russia, 1784–1917* (New York, 1962), and *The United States and Russia: The Beginning of Relations, 1765–1815*, N. N. Bashkina et al., eds. (Washington, D.C., 1980).

2. The "Low Sweet Fever" Under Tsar Nicholas II

1. Maurice Paléologue, *La Russie des tsars pendant la Grande guerre, 20 Juillet 1914–2 Juin 1915* (Paris, 1922), p. 74.
2. Prince Felix Youssoupoff, *Lost Splendour*, Ann Green and Nicholas Katkoff, trans. (London, 1954), p. 223.
3. Boris Schwarz, *Music and Musical Life in Soviet Russia, 1917–1970* (London, 1972), p. 6.
4. Roland Gelatt, *The Fabulous Phonograph, 1877–1977*, 2nd ed. (New York, 1977), p. 101.
5. L. S. Volkov-Lannit, *Iskusstvo zapechatlennogo zvuka* (Moscow, 1964), p. 18.
6. Quoted in A. Gozenpud, *Muzykalnyi teatr v Rossii ot istokov do Glinki* (Leningrad, 1959), p. 580.
7. *Ibid.*, p. 639.
8. Dr. Georg Brandes, *Impressions of Russia* (New York, 1889), p. 26.
9. "Koe-chto o tsygankakh," *Stolitsa i usadba*, May 15, 1915, pp. 14–16. For a vivid description of the gypsy environment see Henri Troyat, *Daily Life in Russia Under the Last Tsar* (Stanford, 1979), pp. 47–49.
10. The lyrics tell of a policeman who found the child and, incidentally, his long-lost wife—a sentimental but appropriate theme in Russia's chaotic urban environment. For the technology of song slides, first applied with this tune, see Isaac Goldberg, *Tin Pan Alley: A Chronicle of American Popular Music* (New York, 1961), p. 128.
11. Volkov-Lannit, *Iskusstvo zapechatlennogo zvuka*, pp. 88–89.
12. Richard Taylor, *The Politics of the Soviet Cinema, 1917–1929* (Cambridge, 1979), p. 95; also Jay Leida, *Kino* (New York, 1966), pp. 163, 172.
13. Volkov-Lannit, *Iskusstvo zapechatlennogo zvuka*, p. 37; Taylor, *Politics of Soviet Cinema*, p. 7.
14. Gregory Guroff and S. Frederick Starr, "A Note on Literacy in Russia, 1890–1914," *Jahrbücher für Geschichte Osteuropas* XIX, no. 4 (Dec. 1971), pp. 520–31.
15. James McClelland, *Autocrats and Academics: Education, Culture and Society in Tsarist Russia* (Chicago, 1979), pp. 52–53.
16. Quoted in Richard Stites, "Women in the Russian Intelligentsia: Three Perspectives," *Women in Russia*, Dorothy Atkinson et al., eds. (Stanford, 1977), p. 60. For the movement as a whole see Richard Stites, *The Women's Liberation Movement in Russia* (Princeton, 1978).

17. Paléologue, *La Russie des tsars . . .* , *19 Août 1916–17 Mai 1917*, p. 70.

18. See G. Wynneken, *Der Kampf für die Jugend* (Jena, 1920); also Masur, *Prophets of Yesterday*, pp. 354ff.

19. See Edward Shorter, "Towards a History of *La Vie Intime*: The Evidence of Cultural Cricitism in Nineteenth-Century Bavaria," *The Emergence of Leisure*, Michael R. Marrus, ed. (New York, 1974), pp. 57ff.

20. Ian Whitcomb, *After the Ball* (London, 1972), p. 99.

21. Leonid Utesov, *Zapiski aktera* (Moscow, Leningrad, 1939), p. 14.

22. "Tantsy Aisedory Dunkan," *Stolitsa i usadba*, May 15, 1914, pp. 25–26.

23. Vl. K., "Tango," *Stolitsa i usadba*, May 15, 1914, pp. 14–15.

24. "Krovavoe tango Vilgelma," Volkov-Lannit, *Iskusstvo zapechatlennogo zvuka*, p. 79.

25. Ivan Ozerov, *Chemu uchit nas Amerika?* (Moscow, 1903), introduction.

26. Edward F. Walker and Steven Walker, *English Ragtime: A Discography, 1898–1920* (Mastin Moor, 1971).

27. Whitcomb, *After the Ball*, p. 155.

28. *Ibid.*, p. 154.

29. Horst Lange, *Jazz in Deutschland: Die deutsche Jazz—Chronik, 1900–1960* (Berlin, 1966), pp. 7–14; see also Peter Czerny and Heinz P. Hofmann, *Der Schlager: Ein Panorama der leichten Musik* (Berlin, 1968), vol. I, pp. 227–34.

30. Interview with Nina Berberova, Oct. 2, 1979.

31. *Ibid.*

32. Alison Blakely, "The Negro in Imperial Russia: A Preliminary Sketch," *Journal of Negro History*, no. 4 (Oct. 1976), pp. 353–61.

33. Langston Hughes, *I Wonder as I Wander* (New York, 1956), pp. 82–85.

34. Batashev and others have claimed that the Fiske Jubilee Singers visited Russia, but this is not supported by J.B.T. Marsh, *The Story of the Jubilee Singers* (Boston, 1881), or by the book's expanded editions of 1884, 1885, 1889, or 1903.

35. Leonid Utesov, *Pesnia po zhizni* (Moscow, 1961), p. 37.

36. Utesov, *Zapiski aktera*, p. 14.

37. Volkov-Lannit, *Iskusstvo zapechatlennogo zvuka*, p. 42.

38. See Morroe Berger, "Jazz: Resistance to the Diffusion of a Culture-Pattern," *Journal of Negro History*, no. 4 (Oct. 1947), pp. 461–94; Neil Leonard, *Jazz and the White Americans: The Acceptance of a New Art Form* (Chicago, 1962), pp. 26–28; Edward A. Berlin, *Ragtime: A Musical and Cultural History* (Berkeley, Los Angeles, 1980), pp. 38–55; Gustav Saenger, "Musical Possibilities of Rag-time," *Metronome*, Mar. 1903, p. 11.

39. Hirsch Sachs-Herbert, in *Musical America*, Sept. 14, 1912, p. 8; and Charles H. Scoggins, in *Musical Progress*, Apr. 1913, pp. 3–4.

40. *Musical America*, Feb. 16, 1913, p. 137.

41. Ivan Narodny, "The Birth Processes of Ragtime," *Musical America*, Mar. 19, 1913, p. 27.

3. Red, But Not Hot, 1917–1924

1. James Lincoln Collier, "The Atlantic Crossing," *The Making of Jazz* (New York,

1978), pp. 314–15; Robert Goffin, *Jazz from the Congo to the Metropolitan* (New York, 1975), pp. 68–70, and his *Aux frontieres du jazz* (Brussels, 1932), pp. 33–38.

2. Goffin, *Jazz*, p. 72.

3. Ernest-Alexandre Ansermet, trans. in Ralph deToledano, ed., *Frontiers of Jazz* (New York, 1947), pp. 115–23.

4. John Willett, *Art and Politics in the Weimar Era* (New York, 1978), p. 90.

5. S. Foster Damon, "American Influence on Modern French Music," *Dial*, Aug. 15, 1918, pp. 93–95.

6. Chris Goddard, *Jazz Away from Home* (New York, London, 1979), pp. 61, 73–75.

7. S. Dreiden, *Muzyka-revoliutsii*, 3rd ed. (Moscow, 1970), pp. 223–37; also see *Ocherki sovetskogo muzykalnogo tvorchestva*, B. V. Asafev et al., eds. (Moscow, Leningrad, 1947), vol. I, pp. 235ff.

8. V. Feiertag and V. Mysovskii, *Dzhaz; kratkii ocherk* (Leningrad, 1960), p. 66.

9. Schwarz, *Music and Musical Life in Soviet Russia*, p. 20.

10. Paléologue, *La Russie des tsars . . . , 3 Juin 1915–19 Août 1916*, p. 285.

11. Whitcomb, *After the Ball*, p. 97; also Robert M. W. Dixon and John Godrich, *Recording the Blues* (New York, 1970), pp. 9–19.

12. *Izvestiia*, Dec. 7, 1919; also *Russkaia sovetskaia estrada, 1917–1929*, (Moscow, 1978) p. 32.

13. *Vestnik teatra*, no. 55 (1920).

14. Aleksei Batashev, *Sovetskii dzhaz; istoricheskii ocherk* (Moscow, 1972), p. 14.

15. Interview with Mikhail Lantsman, Sept. 3, 1979.

16. Interview with Mikhail Brantsberg, Nov. 4, 1979.

17. Communication to the author from Kurt Strobel, Walladale, Australia, Nov. 1, 1981.

18. Aleksandr Bakhrakh, "'*Egipetskaia marka*' i ee geroi," *Novoe russkoe slovo*, Mar. 25, 1975.

19. Berberova interview, 1979. See also Nina Berberova, *The Italics Are Mine* (New York, 1969), pp. 216, 569.

20. Batashev, *Sovetskii dzhaz*, p. 8.

21. "Novye tantsy" and "Dzhaz-Band," *Veshch*, nos. 1–2 (1922), p. 25.

22. Valentin Parnakh, "Novoe ekstsentricheskoe iskusstvo," *Zrelishcha*, no. 1 (1922), p. 5; "Mimicheskii orkestr," *Zrelishcha*, no. 4 (1922), p. 13. It is interesting to note that in his article in the no. 4 (1922) issue of *Zrelishcha*, Parnakh spelled jazz "jass," suggesting that either he or his Moscow editor had come under the sway of the 1917 recordings of the "Original Dixieland Jass Band," as it was identified on the Victor labels.

23. Utesov, *Pesnia po zhizni*, p. 76; *Russkaia sovetskaia estrada, 1917–1929*, pp. 58, 33.

24. On this and related developments see A. A. Ivanov, *Sovetskii elektricheskii muzykalnyi instrument Emiriton (Melodin)* (Moscow, 1953); also "Elektrifikatsiia muzyki," *Sovetskoe iskusstvo*, no. 1 (1928), p. 61.

25. S. Poniatovskii, "Persimfans," *Muzykalnaia zhizn*, 1977, pp. 15ff.; also S. Korev, "Novye metody simfonicheskogo ispolneniia," *Sovetskoe iskusstvo*, No. 2 (1927), pp. 29–31.

26. For a lively review of these developments, see Richard Stites, "Music and Revolution: The Utopian Moment in Russia," MS, Georgetown University, 1979.

27. See E. Gabrilovich's comment in "Rasskazy o tom, chto proshlo," *Iskusstvo kino*, no. 4 (1964), p. 61.

28. "Dzhaz-band i ekstsentricheskie tantsy," *Zrelishcha*, no. 14 (1922), p. 22.

29. Valentin Parnakh, "Dzhaz band—ne 'shumovoi orkestr,'" *Zrelishcha*, no. 15 (1922), p. 11.

30. N. Malko, "Avtor i ispolnitel," *Zrelishcha*, no. 20 (1923), p. 5.

31. "Frank" (pseud. Vladimir Fedorov), "Dzhaz band," *Zrelishcha*, no. 7 (1922), p. 8.

32. Quoted in Donald Drew Egbert, *Social Radicalism and the Arts, Western Europe* (New York, 1970), p. 274; and Reginald H. Wilenski, *Modern French Painters* (New York, 1960), vol. II, p. 73.

33. "Dzhaz-band," *Teatr i muzyka*, no. 5 (1923), p. 581. On contemporary noise orchestras see "Orkestr veshchei," *Zrelishcha*, no. 6 (1922), p. 22.

34. Batashev, *Sovetskii dzhaz*, p. 12–14.

35. The Varpakhovskii ensemble survived to 1928. See Anton Uglov., "Peksa," *Izvestiia*, Jan. 29, 1928.

36. Parnakh, "Dzhaz Band—ne 'shumovoi orkestr,'" p. 11.

37. D. Milhaud, *Notes Without Music* (New York, 1953), p. 189.

38. For role of the international clientele in patronizing jazz in Western Europe see Goddard, *Jazz Away from Home*, p. 186; and Goffin, *Jazz*, p. 75.

39. See Leo Asher's "Ruth," *Glavlit*, no. 15965; Oscar Mintz's "Come to Me," *Glavlit*, no. 54643; etc.

40. "Dzhaz band," *Zrelishcha*, no. 36 (1923).

41. Alfred Rosmer, *Moscow Under Lenin*, Ian H. Birchall, trans. (New York, 1971), p. 167.

42. Quoted in Gordon McVay, *Esenin: A Life* (Ann Arbor, 1976), p. 189. See also Sergei Esenin, *Izbrannoe* (Leningrad, 1970), p. 452.

43. "*Pro eto*," in *Mayakovsky*, Herbert Marshall, trans. (New York, 1965), p. 196. See also Mayakovsky's "Amerika," *Kransnaia nov*, Feb. 1926, p. 174: "The so-called American dance of fox and shimmy."

44. Hans M. Wingler, *The Bauhaus: Weimar; Dessau; Berlin; Chicago* (Cambridge, Mass., 1969), p. 375.

45. Asafev et al., *Ocherki sovetskogo muzykalnogo tvorchestva*, vol. I, p. 246.

46. K. Kowalke, *Kurt Weill in Europe, 1900–1935* (Ann Arbor, 1979), p. 253.

47. In Iu. Elagin (Jelagin), *Temnyi geroi: Vsevolod Meierhold* (New York, 1955), p. 249; also Alma H. Law, "Meierhold's *The Magnanimous Cuckold*," *Drama Review*, Mar. 1982, pp. 166ff.

48. See H. Gil-Marchez, "Back from a Trip to Russia," *The Chesterian* (1926–27), p. 117; "'D.E.' v. teatre im. Meierkholda," *Novyi zritel*, no. 18 (1928), pp. 16–17; Konstatin Miklashevskii, "Po povodu postanovki D.E.," *Zhizn iskusstva*, no. 27 (1924), p. 7; S. Mokulskii, "Novaia postanovka Meierkholda," *Zhizn iskusstva*, no. 27 (1924), p. 11; E. Dr. (Braudo), "Muzyka v 'D.E.,'" *Pravda*, July 10, 1924, (wrongly listed by Batashev, *Sovetskii dzhaz*, as June 10); Fred K. Prieberg, *Musik im der Sowjetunion* (Cologne, 1965), p. 327; James Symons, *Meyerhold's Theatre of the Grotesque* (Coral Gables, 1971), pp. 120–24.

49. K. Rudnitskii, *Rezhisser Meierkhold* (Moscow, 1969), p. 285.
50. B. Romashov, *Izvestiia*, June 18, 1924.
51. Valentin Parnac, "Histoires extraordinaires danses," *De Stijl*, no. 7 (1926), pp. 11–16.
52. Erast Garin, *S Meierkholdom* (Moscow, 1974), pp. 94–95.
53. Elagin, *Temnyi geroi*, p. 271.
54. *Ibid.*, p. 272.
55. "Judge Rails at Jazz and Dance Madness," *New York Times*, Apr. 14, 1926, p. 15; "Wants Legislation To Stop Jazz as an Intoxicant," *New York Times*, Feb. 12, 1922.
56. R. McMahon, "Unspeakable Jazz Must Go!," *Ladies' Home Journal*, Dec. 1921, pp. 115–16; "The Jazz Path of Degradation," *Ladies' Home Journal*, Jan. 1922, pp. 26–71; Jaap Kool, "The Triumph of the Jungle," *Living Age*, Feb. 7, 1925, pp. 338–43.
57. "Welsh Invoke Curfew Law as One Way To Stop Jazz," *New York Times*, Mar. 7, 1926, p. 12. See also "A Cursed Jazz—an English View," *Literary Digest*, Oct. 2, 1926, pp. 28–29; and "British Music Critics Excoriate Jazz," *New York Times*, Sept. 12, 1926, p. 9.
    "French Police Stop Jazz Band at Burial," *New York Times*, Oct. 18, 1923, p. 3; "Italians Sign Petitions Against Jazz," *Musical America*, Sept. 29, 1923, p. 4.
58. "Jazz Is Not Music, Stresemann Asserts," *New York Times*, June 12, 1927, p. 19; "Queen Mary Bars Jazz," *New York Times*, July 18, 1922, p. 3.

4. Russia's Roaring Twenties, 1925–1928

1. Samuel Wooding, "Eight Years Abroad with a Jazz Band," *Étude*, Apr. 1939, p. 234.
2. *Ibid.*
3. "Says Jazz Rules Europe," *New York Times*, Jan. 23, 1925.
4. Wooding, "Eight Years Abroad," p. 234; also Albert Bettonville, "Premier souvenir de jazz: Sam Wooding and His Chocolate Dandies," *Hot Club Magazine*, July 1946, pp. 7–8; also Lubomir Dorůžka, "Sam Wooding—černošský kmotříček sovětského jazzu," *Melodie* (Prague), May, 1977, pp. 338–39.
5. On Wooding's band see Albert McCarthy, *Big Band Jazz* (New York, 1977), pp. 300–311.
6. "Negritianskaia operetta," *Tsirk*, 1926, special edition; E. M. Braudo, "Negro-operetta," *Krasnaia gazeta*, Mar. 17, 1926; S. A. Bugoslavskii, "Spektakli negritianskoi trupy," *Izvestiia*, Mar. 27, 1926; V. G. Chernoiarov, "O dzhaz-bande, o negrakh i o tom, kak my doshli do negrov," *Novyi zritel*, no. 12 (1926); see also Batashev's concise summary of other reviews, *Sovetskii dzhaz*, pp. 20–21.
7. M. E. Koltsov, "Negritianki s opazdaniem," *Krasnaia gazeta*, Apr. 3, 1926.
8. G. G., "Dzhaz-band," *Tsirk*, no. 11 (1926), p. 8, quoted in Batashev, *Sovetskii dzhaz*, p. 21.
9. Wooding, "Eight Years Abroad," p. 233.
10. McCarthy, *Big Band Jazz*, p. 311.
11. Al Rose, Memorandum on Sammy Wooding, 1980, Tulane Jazz Archive, Tulane University, New Orleans, La.

12. *Ibid.*

13. Gil-Marchez, "Back from a Trip to Russia," p. 117. Bugoslavskii, "Spektakli negritianskoi trupy."

14. S. Malashkin, *Luna s pravoi storony* (Moscow, 1926); see also M. Roizman, *Minus shest* (Moscow, 1930), and M. Chumandrin, *Fabrika Rable* (Leningrad, 1929).

15. Ilya Ehrenburg, *Memoirs, 1921–1941*, Tatiana Shebunina, trans. (New York, 1966), pp. 67ff.

16. These surveys are capably reviewed by Jiri Zusanek, *Work and Leisure in the Soviet Union* (New York, 1980), pp. 11–22. Strumilin's data indicate that workers had far less free time than did students.

17. *Za proletarskuiu muzyku,* no. 2 (1926), quoted in *Ocherki sovetskogo muzykalnogo tvorchestva,* vol. I, p. 246.

18. "Muzykalnye nomera v pragramme miuzik-kholla i zritel," *Sovetskoe iskusstvo,* no. 26 (1928), pp. 74–75.

19. I am indebted to Dr. John Bowlt of the Institute of Modern Russian Culture at Blue Lagoon, Texas, for copies of G. Bruni's "Lunnyi svet" and Iurii Grin's "Parizhanka," both issued by *samizdat* in 1926.

20. Solomon Volkov, "Dmitri Shostakovich and 'Tea for Two,'" *Musical Quarterly,* Apr. 1978, pp. 223–28.

21. Klaus Mehnert, *Youth in Soviet Russia* (London, 1933), pp. 203–8.

22. Alfred H. Barr, Jr., "Russian Diary, 1927–28," *October,* Winter 1978, p. 18. For statistics on sexual mores at the time see Sheila Fitzpatrick, "Sex and Revolution: An Examination of Literary and Statistical Data on the Mores of Soviet Students in the 1920s," *Journal of Modern History,* June, 1978, pp. 252–78.

23. Goddard, *Jazz Away from Home,* p. 194.

24. Interview with Ludmila (Mrs. Henry) Shapiro, Oct. 4, 1978.

25. *Russkaia sovetskaia estrada, 1917–1929,* pp. 245–46.

26. On the popular demand for high fashion and clothing that was evocative as well as practical see T. Strizhenova, *Iz istorii sovetskogo kostiuma* (Moscow, 1972), p. 98; also John E. Bowlt, "From Pictures to Textile Prints," *Print Collector's Newsletter,* Mar./Apr. 1976, pp. 16–20.

27. *Russkaia sovetskaia estrada, 1917–1929,* pp. 249–50.

28. Quoted in Kowalke, *Kurt Weill in Europe,* p. 95.

29. From a review by V. I. Avdiev in *Sovetskoe iskusstvo,* no. 2 (1927), p. 77; Anna Zelenko, *Massovye narodnye tantsy* (Moscow, 1927).

30. "Siniaia Bluza," *Novyi zritel,* no. 33, (1924), p. 9; and the periodical *Siniaia Bluza,* issued from 1924 through 1928. This movement is briefly reviewed in *Russkaia sovetskaia estrada, 1917–1929,* pp. 327–44.

31. Barr, "Russian Diary," p. 42; *Russkaia sovetskaia estrada, 1917–1929,* p. 331.

32. *Russkaia sovetskaia estrada, 1917–1929,* p. 336.

33. Quote in Goddard, *Jazz Away from Home,* p. 111.

34. McCarthy, *Big Band Jazz,* 311; also Raymond Mouly, *Sidney Bechet notre ami* (Paris, 1959), pp. 54–55. Other members of the group were Cricket Smith (t.); Fred Coxito (a., b.s.); Dan Parrish (b.); and Dan Kildaire (p.).

35. Sidney Bechet, *Treat It Gentle: An Autobiography* (New York, 1960), pp. 181, p. 147.

36. Chemodanov, "Dzhaz Band," *Vechernaia Moskva*, Mar. 20, 1926.
37. N. A. Malko, "Dzhaz-Band v Moskve," *Zhizn iskusstva*, no. 10 (1926), pp. 12–13, partially quoted in Batashev, *Sovetskii dzhaz*, pp. 18–19.
38. Osip Brik, "Dzhaz-band," *Novyi lef*, no. 6 (1927), p. 11.
39. See Largo, "Dzhas-band," *Izvestiia* (Odessa), May 31, 1926; P. O. Kosicki, "A i spravdi iak zhe z Dzhaz-bandom?" *Nove mistetstvo*, no. 14 (1926). See Batashev, *Sovetskii dzhaz*, pp. 166–67, for a complete listing of reviews.
40. Ludmila Shapiro interview, 1978.
41. Lantsman interview, 1979.
42. Asher's "Ruth" was passed by Glavlit in Moscow, number 77188. "Guiana" passed the Mosgublit censor, number 29238.
43. Interview with Vera S. Dunham, Oct. 17, 1978.
44. Nik. Roslavets, "Muzyka," *Sovetskoe iskusstvo*, no. 5 (1927), p. 72.
45. Batashev, *Sovetskii dzhaz*, pp. 25–26.
46. Interview with Lev Zabeginsky, Nov. 9, 1979. Zabeginsky knew Teplitskii after the pianist settled in Petrozavodsk.
47. See George T. Simon, *The Big Bands* (New York, 1967), pp. 452–53.
48. "American Bandsman in London," *Musical Opinion*, May 1923, pp. 733–34.
49. Zabeginsky interview, 1979.
50. *Ibid.*
51. I am grateful to Lev Zabeginsky of New York for a copy of this review. Unfortunately, the date of the article and the newspaper in which it appeared are unknown.
52. Boris Wohlmann, interview with A. Batashev, in *Sovetskii dzhaz*, p. 28.
53. Posters are preserved in the archive of Lev Zabeginsky, New York.
54. Confirmed by Teplitskii, interview with Lev Zabeginsky, 1966.
55. "Astoriia," *Stolitsa i usadba*, Apr. 15, 1915, p. 26.
56. Batashev claims that this group issued a recording, but no copy is known to this author. *Sovetskii dzhaz*, p. 35.
57. Lyrics by K. N. Podvevskii, published privately (Moscow, 1926). On the "Tahiti-Trot" see Volkov, "Shostakovitch and 'Tea for Two,'" p. 226.
58. "Dzhaz-kapella", *Krasnaia gazeta*, Oct. 13, 1929; see also Batashev, *Sovetskii dzhaz*, pp. 32–33.
59. V. Dr., "Muzyka zhizni," *Leningradskii student*, no. 5 (1929), partially quoted in Batashev, *Sovetskii dzhaz*, p. 34.
60. *Dzhaz-band i sovremennaia muzyka*, S. Ginzburg, ed. (Leningrad, 1926), p. 37.
61. *Ibid.*, pp. 26–27.
62. On Schillinger see Frances Schillinger, *Joseph Schillinger: A Memoir* (New York, 1976), esp. chap. 1; also "Joseph Schillinger," *Pro Musica*, Mar.–June 1929, p. 44; and the bibliography, "Joseph Schillinger, 1895–1943," published privately by his wife (New York, n.d.) Archival materials on Schillinger are preserved at Columbia University; the University of Wyoming; the Museum of Modern Art; and the New York Public Library, which holds the few documents remaining from his Russian period.
63. See programs of Leningrad concerts of Mar.–Apr. 1926, preserved in the Schillinger papers, New York Public Library.
64. This concert was held in Moscow, Nov. 21–28, 1928, at the Conservatory. Cf. program, Schillinger papers, New York Public Library. See also Henry Cowell,

"Joseph Schillinger as Composer," *Music News*, no. 3 (1947), pp. 5–6.

65. Performed with the Cleveland Symphony Orchestra, 1929; see Nicolas Slonimsky, "Schillinger of Russia and the World," *Music News*, no. 3 (1947), pp. 16–17.

66. The following remarks are based on a synopsis of the lecture printed in the concert program preserved in the Schillinger papers, New York Public Library.

67. Rimsky-Korsakov review, Zabeginskii archive, New York.

68. Interview with Mrs. Joseph Schillinger, May 4, 1980.

69. *Dzhaz-band i sovremennaia muzyka*, p. 33.

70. Kenneth MacKillop, "The Schillinger System," *Down Beat*, Sept. 22, 1950, p. 18, Dec. 4, 1950, p. 8.

71. Charles Schwartz, *Gershwin: His Life and Music* (New York, 1979), pp. 4–6, 237.

72. *Ibid.*, pp. 221–22.

73. A. P. Marinskii, *Protiv popov i sektantov* (Moscow, 1929), p. 39, cited in A. Angarov, *Klassovaia borba v sovetskoi derevne* (Moscow, 1929), p. 33.

74. *V pervye gody sovetskogo muzykalnogo stroitelstva* (Leningrad, 1959), p. 170 fn.

75. *100 Let Leningradskoi konservatorii* (Leningrad, 1962), p. 120.

5. "The Music of the Gross," 1928–1931

1. Robert Conquest, *The Great Terror: Stalin's Purge of the Thirties* (New York, 1973), p. 46; Winston S. Churchill, *The Hinge of Fate* (Boston, 1950), p. 498. See also R. W. Davies, *The Industrialization of Soviet Russia, the Socialist Offensive: The Collectivization of Agriculture 1929–1930* (Cambridge, Mass., 1980); Frank Lorimer, *The Population of the Soviet Union: History and Prospects* (Geneva, 1946), pp. 133–37.

2. See Alexander I. Solzhenitsyn, *The Gulag Archipelago*, Thomas P. Whitney, trans. (New York, 1974), vol. I, chap. 2.

3. Paul Robeson, *Paul Robeson Speaks: Writings, Speeches, Interviews, 1918–1974*, Philip S. Foner, ed. (New York, 1978), p. 106.

4. Hans von Herwarth with S. Frederick Starr, *Against Two Evils* (London, 1981), pp. 37–38.

5. Alfred G. Meyer, "The War Scare of 1927," *Soviet Union/Union Sovietique*, no. 1 (1978), pp. 1–25.

6. Sheila Fitzpatrick, "The Foreign Threat During the First Five-Year Plan," *Soviet Union/Union Sovietique*, no. 1 (1978), pp. 26–35.

7. Herwarth, *Against Two Evils*, pp. 53–54.

8. Eugene Lyons, "To Tell or Not To Tell," *Harper's*, June 1935, pp. 100ff.

9. See Anatole Senkevitch, Jr., *Soviet Architecture, 1917–1962: A Bibliographic Guide to Source Material* (Charlottesville, 1974), pp. 166–73.

10. I. Matsa, "Uroki 'neitralizma' v iskusstve," *Literatura i iskusstvo*, nos. 2–3 (1931), pp. 152–57.

11. Sheila Fitzpatrick, "The Emergence of Glaviskusstvo," *Soviet Studies*, Oct. 1971, p. 249.

12. S. Korev, "Sovetskoe iskusstvo i ego potrebitel," *Sovetskoe iskusstvo*, no. 3 (1928), p. 36.

13. Dec. 9, 1930, reprinted in *Sovetskoe iskusstvo za 15 let: Materialy i dokumenty*,

I. Matsa, L. Rempel, and L. Reingardt, eds. (Moscow, Leningrad, 1933), p. 450.

14. Korev, "Sovetskoe iskusstvo," p. 39.

15. S. Voskresenskii, "Organizationnye voprosy estrady," *Sovetskoe iskusstvo*, no. 26 (1928), p. 47.

16. A. Lunacharskii, "Kulturnaia revoliutsiia i iskusstvo," *Sovetskoe iskusstvo*, no. 4 (1928), p. 9.

17. Korev, "Sovetskoe iskusstvo," pp. 37–39.

18. Voskresenskii, "Organizatsionnye voprosy," p. 47.

19. Volkov-Lannit, *Iskusstvo zapechatlennogo zvuka*, pp. 177–78.

20. For the theory of proletarian culture see Edward J. Brown, *The Proletarian Episode in Russian Literature, 1928–1932* (New York, 1953), pp. 64ff.

21. *Sovetskoe iskusstvo za 15 let*, p. 449.

22. Blaise Pascal, *Pensées* (New York, 1931), p. 44. See the interesting discussion of this issue in Leo Lowenthal, *Literature, Popular Culture, and Society* (Englewood Cliffs, N.J., 1961), p. 15.

23. "Fritz Kreisler Returns," *New York Times*, Jan. 11, 1925, p. 31; see also "Says Jazz Will Play Itself Out," *New York Times*, Nov. 11, 1924, p. 16.

24. "The Decline of Jazz," *American Musician*, May 1922, p. 1.

25. "Jazz Not What It Once Was," *Musical Leader*, July 24, 1924, pp. 26–27.

26. Karol Rathaus, "Jazzdammerung?" *Die Musik*, Feb. 1927, pp. 333–36.

27. "Jazz All Over Europe," *New York Times*, Apr. 30, 1929, p. 14.

28. "Vienna Is Alarmed by Inroads of Jazz," *New York Times*, Apr. 15, 1928, see also Ernst Decsey, "Jazz in Vienna," *Living Age*, Mar. 1, 1928, pp. 441–45.

29. "Jazz Bands Popular in Turkey; Kemal Enjoys Western Music," *New York Times*, Oct. 12, 1927, p. 7; H. H. Stuckenschmidt, "Hellenic Jazz," *Modern Music*, Apr.–May 1930, pp. 22–24; "Orchestra Plays Jazz Thirty-three Hours," *New York Times*, Dec. 14, 1927, p. 8.

30. "Jazz Bitterly Opposed in Germany," *New York Times*, Mar. 11, 1928. See also Alfred Einstein, "Some Berlin Novelties," *New York Times*, Feb. 19, 1928; Fritz Stege, "Gibt es eine 'Deutsche Jazzkapelle'?" *Zeitschrift für Instrumentenbau*, July 1929, pp. 410–11; Paul Schwers, "Die Frankfurter Jass-Akademie im Spiegel der Kritik," *Allgemeine Musikzeitung*, Dec. 2, 1927, pp. 1246–48.

31. "Jazz Bitterly Opposed in Germany," p. 10.

32. I. L. Matsa, *Iskusstvo sovremennoi Evropy* (Moscow, Leningrad, 1926), p. 120.

33. M. Gorkii, "O muzyke tolstykh," *Pravda*, Apr. 18, 1928, p. 4. An authorized translation by Marie Budberg, "The Music of the Degenerate," appeared in *Dial*, Dec. 1928, pp. 480–84.

34. Utesov, *Pesnia po zhizni*, p. 129.

35. Gorkii, "O muzyke tolstykh." (All quotations are from this source.)

36. Interview with Nina Berberova, Aug. 19, 1979.

37. A. V. Lunacharskii, "Sotsialnye istoki muzykalnogo iskusstva," *Proletarskii muzykant*, no. 4 (1929), pp. 12–20.

38. *Ibid.*, p. 18.

39. *Ibid.*, p. 19.

40. N. Briusova, "Na borbu s muzykalnym durmanom," *Za proletarskuiu muzyku*, no. 1 (1930), pp. 3–5.

41. L. Lebedinskii, "Nash massovyi muzykalnyi byt," *Literatura i iskusstvo*, no. 1 (1931), pp. 76–77.

42. Interview with Konstantin Simis, May 4, 1979.
43. I. N. "The Soviet Cult," *New York Times*, Jan. 8, 1928.
44. Iu. I. Laane, "Musykalnaia rabota sredi natsmen zapada," *Sovetskoe iskusstvo*, no. 1 (1927), p. 41.
45. *Istoriia russkoi sovetskoi muzyki*, A. D. Alekseev, ed. (Moscow, 1956), vol. I, p. 137.
46. Robert A. Rothstein, "The Quiet Rehabilitation of the Brick Factory: Early Soviet Popular Music," *Slavic Review*, Sept. 1980, p. 374.
47. "Mozhet li dzhaz stat sovetskim?" *Rabochii i teatr*, no. 43 (1930), p. 7.
48. Kurt Weill, "Notiz zum Jazz," trans. in Kowalke, *Kurt Weill in Europe*, p. 477.
49. Hanns Eisler, *Reden und Aufsätze* (Leipzig, 1961).
50. Albrecht Betz, *Hanns Eisler—Musik, eine Zeit die sich eben bildet* (Munich, 1976), p. 87; also Hanns Eisler, "Musik im Klassenkampf," *Sozialistische Zeitschrift für Kunst und Gesellschaft*, Nov. 1973, pp. 93ff.
51. "S. Wagner Attacks Jazz," *New York Times*, Dec. 7, 1925, p. 19.
52. F. Sabo, "Put fashizma v nemetskoi muzyke," *Sovetskaia muzyka*, no. 1 (1934), p. 108.
53. Richard Litterscheid, "Das Ende des Jazz in Deutschland," *Die Musik*, Dec. 1935, pp. 236–37; Ludwig Altmann, "Untergang der Jazzmusik," *Die Musik*, July 1933, pp. 744–49; also "Nazis Reject Jazz," *New York Times*, Mar. 18, 1933, p. 12; and "Hitler Frowns on Jazz," *Literary Digest*, Mar. 24, 1934, p. 24. On Japan see M. S. Druskin, *Ocherki po istorii tantsovalnoi muzyki* (Leningrad, 1936), p. 66.
54. E. Stepanov, *Kulturnaia zhizn Leningrada 20-kh-nachala 30-kh godov* (Leningrad, 1976), p. 259.
55. *Ibid.*, p. 103.
56. In 1932 Association composers got thirty-two radio hours per week in Leningrad; others got only three or four. *Ibid.*, p. 223.
57. Lewis Nichols, "Tin Pan Alley Now Paved with Profits," *New York Times*, Mar. 27, 1932, p. 10.
58. Maurice Waller and Anthony Calabrese, *Fats Waller* (New York, 1977), p. 123.
59. Bechet, *Treat It Gentle*, p. 112.
60. Waldo Frank, "Jazz and Folk Art," *New Republic*, Dec. 1, 1926, pp. 42–43.
61. "Berlin Calls Jazz American Folk Music; Composer Predicts It Will Eventually Be Sung in Metropolitan Opera House," *New York Times*, Jan. 10, 1925, p. 2; Paul Whiteman, "In Defense of Jazz and Its Makers," *New York Times*, Mar. 13, 1927, pp. 4, 22.
62. M. Dr. (Druskin), "Muzyka zhizni," *Leningradskii student*, no. 5 (1929), p. 14.
63. M. S. Shaginian, "Dzhaz-band," *Izvestiia* (Odessa), June 3, 1926.
64. Tatiana Tchernavin, *We Soviet Women* (New York, 1936), p. 172.
65. A. S. Tsukker, "Dzhaz-band," *Novyi zritel*, no. 10 (1926), p. 5.
66. *Ibid.*, p. 5.
67. Richard Hadlock, *Jazz Masters of the '20s* (New York, 1965), pp. 16–17.
68. Goddard, *Jazz Away from Home*, p. 153.
69. Charles Edward Smith, "Class Content of Jazz Music," *The Daily Worker*, Oct. 21, 1933.
70. Similar but less extreme views on the sociology of jazz are developed by Charles Edward Smith and Frederick Ramsey, Jr., eds., in *Jazzmen* (New York, 1939),

and by Wilder Hobson in *American Jazz Music* (New York, 1939).

71. See, for example, "Diskussiia o dzhaze," *Sovetskaia muzyka*, no. 2 (1934), p. 67.

72. N. Ia. "'Evrei bez deneg' M. Golda," *Marksistko—leninskoe iskusstvoznanie*, nos. 5–6 (1932), pp. 173–77; V. Arkhhangelskii, "Maikl Gold. 120 millionov," *Literatura i iskusstvo*, nos. 2–3 (1931), pp. 201–2.

73. Quoted in N. Ia., "'Evrei bez deneg' M. Golda," p. 175.

74. See especially Michael Gold, "What a World!" *The Daily Worker*, Jan. 1, 1934.

75. "Ford Wars on Jazz; Gives Party for Old-time Dances," *New York Times*, July 12, 1925, p. 2.

76. Josef Skvorecky, *The Bass Saxophone* (London, 1978), p. 12.

77. Edward Thomas Wilson, *Russia and Black Africa Before World War II* (New York, London, 1974), pp. 133–34.

78. Wilson Record, *The Negro and the Communist Party* (New York, 1971), p. 62.

79. Wilson, *Russia and Black Africa*, pp. 168–69; Record, *The Negro and the Communist Party*, chap. 3.

80. Adam B. Ulam, *Stalin, the Man and His Era* (New York, 1973), p. 367.

81. Record, *The Negro and the Communist Party*, pp. 67ff.

82. Gold, "What a World!"; Smith, "Class Content of Jazz Music,"; "Diskussiia o dzhaze."

83. Cf. G. Landsberg, "Na putiakh k dzhazovoi kultury," *Rabochii i teatr*, o. 22 (1935), pp. 22–23.

84. Record, *The Negro and the Communist Party*, p. 65.

85. Homer Smith, *Black Man in Red Russia* (Chicago, 1964), pp. 22–24.

86. Hughes, *I Wonder as I Wander*, p. 70.

87. Smith, *Black Man in Red Russia*, p. 25.

88. Hughes, *I Wonder as I Wander*, p. 77.

89. *Ibid.*, p. 80.

90. Smith, *Black Man in Red Russia*, p. 83.

6. The Red Jazz Age, 1932–1936

1. Interview with Mikhail Lantsman, saxophonist of the group, Oct. 16, 1978.

2. *Pravda*, Mar. 2, 1930.

3. Conquest, *The Great Terror*, pp. 55–56, 63.

4. Batashev, *Sovetskii dzhaz*, pp. 57–58. I am indebted to Mr. Batashev for information in this paragraph.

5. P. E. Kozitskii, "A i spravdi, iak zhe z Dzhaz-Bandom?" *Nove mistetstvo*, no. 14 (1962).

6. Interview with Valentin Tsonev, Mar. 4, 1979.

7. Interview with Ambassador Elbridge Durbrow, Apr. 21, 1979.

8. Simis interview, 1979.

9. "Jazz Gains in Popularity as Soviets Lift Ban; Modern Dances Frowned On as Bourgeois," *New York Times*, May 17, 1933, p. 9.

10. Vera Dneprova was among those active in instruction. Durbrow interview, 1979.

11. V. Ia. Shebalin, "Protiv poshlosti," *Sovetskoe iskusstvo*, Nov. 23, 1934, quoted in Batashev, *Sovetskii dzhaz*, p. 58.

12. *Chervone Zaporizhzhia*, Oct. 10, 1929.

13. Zusanek, *Work and Leisure in the Soviet Union*, p. 152.

14. John D. Barber, paper delivered at the Kennan Institute for Advanced Russian Studies, The Wilson Center, Washington, D.C., 1978.

15. Sheila Fitzpatrick, "Culture and Politics Under Stalin: A Reappraisal," *Slavic Review*, June 1976, pp. 217ff.

16. Moshe Lewin, "Society, State, and Ideology During the First Five Year Plan," *The Cultural Revolution in Russia, 1928–1931*, Sheila Fitzpatrick, ed. (Bloomington, 1978), p. 71.

17. Fitzpatrick, "Culture and Politics Under Stalin," pp. 221ff.

18. Durbrow interview, 1979. This project was promoted by the official athletic association until it was killed in the autumn of 1934, following the assassination of Sergei Kirov.

19. Simis interview, 1979.

20. G. Skorokhodov, liner notes to *Dzhaz-orkestr pod upravleniem Aleksandra Varlamova*, Melodiia, 33M60–37647–48.

21. *Ibid.*

22. Another Negro soprano, Coretta Arle, had sung with Peyton's band during its 1926 tour. Arle had come from the West Indies with her father, an engineer, before World War I, married her accompanist, Tietz, and settled into a career as a *Lieder* singer by the time the American jazzmen arrived in Moscow.

23. Lantsman interview, 1979.

24. G. Skorokhodov, liner notes to *Dzhaz-orkestr pod upravleniem Iakova Skomorovskogo*, Melodiia, 33M60–39677–78.

25. Tsonev interview, 1979.

26. These have been reissued in the USSR as *Lunnaia pyl (Moon Dust)* (Henry Hall), Melodiia, 33M60–40367–68, and *Burt Ambrose*, Melodiia, 33M60–39463–64.

27. McCarthy, *Big Band Jazz*, pp. 316, 318.

28. Interview with George F. Kennan, Oct. 12, 1979.

29. Interview with Juri Jelagin, June 1, 1979.

30. Batashev, *Sovetskii dzhaz*, pp. 52–53.

31. Lantsman interview, 1979.

32. Volkov-Lannit, *Iskusstvo zapechatlennogo zvuka*, p. 68.

33. Tsonev interview, 1979.

34. *Ibid.*

35. Volkov-Lannit, *Iskusstvo zapechatlennogo zvuka*, pp. 176–80.

36. *Ibid.*, p. 177.

37. Durbrow interview, 1979, and Kennan interview, 1979.

38. Allan Lomax, *Mr. Jelly Roll*, 2nd ed. (Berkeley, Los Angeles, 1973), p. 212.

39. Georgii Landsberg, "Na putiakh k dzhazovoi kulture," *Rabochii i teatr*, no. 22 (1935), p. 22.

40. For a thorough Continental assessment of Jack Hylton and His Boys see Alfred Baresel, " . . . and His Boys: Das moderne Orchester und seine Musik," *Die Musik*, May 1932, pp. 580–83.

41. Landsberg, "Na putiakh k dzhazovoi kulture," p. 22.

42. Lantsman interview, 1979.

43. M. Druskin, "U istokov dzhaza," *Sovetskoe iskusstvo*, Aug. 1935, p. 38.

44. Simon, *The Big Bands*, pp. 497–98.
45. Landsberg, "Na putiakh k dzhazovoi kulture," p. 23; Druskin, "U istokov dzhaza."
46. Letter to author from H. J. P. Bergmeier, Nov. 28, 1981.
47. For information on this important group, I am indebted to its chronicler, Mr. H. J. P. Bergmeier of Johannesburg, South Africa.
48. Josef Kotek, "Český jazz v SSSR, 1934–1937," *Tanečni hudba a jazz 1966–1967* (Prague, 1967), pp. 37–49.
49. Batashev, *Sovetskii dzhaz*, p. 45.
50. This history is detailed in Lubomir Dorůžka and Ivan Toledňák, *Československý jazz; minulost a přitomnost* (Prague, 1967), pp. 33–40.
51. Kotek, "Český jazz v SSSR, 1934–1937," p. 37.
52. Durbrow interview, 1979.
53. Kotek, "Český jazz v SSSR, 1934–1937," pp. 38–39.
54. *Ibid.*
55. *Ibid.*, p. 40.
56. Held on November 7 due to the change from the Julian to the Gregorian calendar.
57. Durbrow interview, 1979; also interview with Mrs. George F. Kennan, Apr. 2, 1979.
58. Count Werner von der Schulenburg, "Politische Beziehungen Deutschlands mit der Sowjetunion," unpublished MS, 1937, copy in possession of Ambassador Hans von Herwarth, Munich.
59. From the poster preserved in the collection of Lev Zabeginsky, New York.
60. See Chapter 8.
61. On Voroshilov's broader musical interests see Dmitri Shostakovich, *Testimony*, Solomon Volkov, ed. (New York, 1980), p. 100.
62. Leonid Utesov, *Spasibo, serdtse! Vospominaniia, vstrechi, razdumia* (Moscow, 1976), p. 257.
63. See Chapter 7.
64. L. N. Kaganovich and L. O. Utesov, *Kak organizovat zheleznodorozhnye ansambli pesni i pliaski i dzhaz-orkestr* (Moscow, 1939), p. 33.
65. *Ibid.*, p. 36.
66. Tsonev interview, 1979. Tsonev worked at a copper mill 30 kilometers from Sverdlovsk during this period.
67. Juri Jelagin, *The Taming of the Arts*, Nicholas Wreden, trans. (New York, 1951), p. 51.
68. Claude Lévi-Strauss, *Tristes Tropiques: An Anthropological Study of Primitive Societies in Brazil*, John Russell, trans. (New York, 1972), p. 39.

7. Two Jazzmen of the Stalin Era: Tsfasman and Utesov

1. I. D. W. Talmadge, "Communism and Jazz," *Music and Rhythm*, Nov. 1940, p. 27.
2. Utesov, *Spasibo, serdtse!*, p. 69.
3. Jelagin, *Taming of the Arts*, pp. 213–17.

4. Lantsman interview, 1979.
5. I. Ignateva, "Dzhaz i dzhazomaniia: beseda s A. N. Tsfasmanom," *Sovetskaia kultura*, Feb. 1966, p. 19.
6. Jelagin interview, 1979; also interview with George Avakian, June 30, 1981.
7. Jelagin, *Taming of the Arts*, p. 259.
8. *Ibid.*, p. 260.
9. Lantsman interview, 1979.
10. Interview with George D. Costakis, May 4, 1980.
11. Jacket notes to the recording *Aleksandr Tsfasman: kompozitor, pianist, dirizher*, Melodiia, M60–36589–92.
12. *Time*, Apr. 21, 1967, pp. 6–7.
13. Ignateva, "Dzhaz i dzhazomaniia."
14. The personnel were: Andrei Romanenko, trumpet; Anatolii Milovidov, trombone; Nikolai Burov, clarinet/sax; Alexander Trakterov, baritone sax; Vladimir Pechatkin, banjo; Ivan Bacheev, drums; and Tsfasman.
15. Lantsman interview, 1979.
16. Jelagin interview, 1979.
17. *Ibid.*
18. Jelagin, *Taming of the Arts*, p. 258.
19. *Ibid.*, pp. 258–59.
20. Interview with Ludmila (Mrs. Henry) Shapiro, Apr. 4, 1979.
21. This recording and other works by Tsfasman were reissued in the two-record collection *Aleksandr Tsfasman: kompozitor, pianist, dirizher*, Melodiia, 3689–9263–64.
22. Biographical data was provided by Lantsman in interview, 1979.
23. Lantsman interview, 1979.
24. Tsfasman's recording of this work is available on Melodiia, D–026205–6.
25. Jelagin interview, 1979.
26. Interview with Igor Berukshtis, June 12, 1979.
27. See, for example, Hugh A. Mulligan, "Jazz Came Up the Dnieper, Not the Mississippi," *Syracuse Herald-Journal*, Feb. 28, 1961.
28. Leonid Utesov, *S pesnei po zhizni* (Moscow, 1961), p. 151.
29. *Ibid.*, p. 147.
30. Utesov, *Zapiski aktera*, p. 11.
31. Utesov, *S pesnei po zhizni*, p. 36.
32. Utesov, *Zapiski aktera*, p. 15.
33. Utesov, *Spasibo, serdtse!*, p. 213.
34. *Ibid.*, pp. 51ff.
35. *Ibid.*, p. 185.
36. Utesov, *Zapiski aktera*, p. 54.
37. Utesov, *Spasibo, serdtse!*, p. 119.
38. *Ibid.*, p. 62.
39. Utesov, *S pesnei po zhizni*, pp. 130–31.
40. Utesov, *Spasibo, serdtse!* p. 5.
41. *Ibid.*, p. 212; also Utesov, *Zapiski aktera*, pp. 116–17.
42. Utesov, *Zapiski aktera*, pp. 110–12.

43. Simon, *The Big Bands*, pp. 497–98.
44. See "Denies Jazz Is Low Music," *New York Times*, Feb. 14, 1926, p. 10; also Goddard, *Jazz Away from Home*, p. 140.
45. Charles Emge, "Me a Showman?—Hell, Yes!," *Music and Rhythm*, Jan. 1942, p. 20.
46. Utesov, *Spasibo, serdtse!*, pp. 216–17.
47. *Ibid.*, pp. 235, 236.
48. *Ibid.*, p. 237.
49. Simon Dreiden, untitled review, *Zhizn iskusstva*, no. 26 (1929); for another positive assessment see M. V. Verkhovskii, "Estrada za nedeliu," *Krasnaia gazeta*, June 25, 1929.
50. N. Bruisova, "Na borbu s muzykalnym durmanom," *Za proletariskuiu muzyku*, no. 1 (1930), and "Dovesti do kontsa borbu s nepmanskoi muzykoi," *Za proletarskuiu muzyku*, no. 9 (1930).
51. Utesov, *S pesnei po zhizni*, p. 153.
52. *Ibid.*, pp. 154–55.
53. Utesov, *Spasibo, serdtse!*, pp. 144–45.
54. Utesov, *S pesnei po zhizni*, pp. 156–58.
55. Utesov, *Zapiski aktera*, p. 122.
56. Utesov, *Spasibo, serdtse!*, p. 368.
57. Alexander Varlamov, interview with Batashev, in *Sovetskii dzhaz*, p. 76.
58. Yury Krotkov, *I Am from Moscow* (New York, 1967), p. 5.
59. Utesov, *Zapiski aktera*, p. 117.
60. Utesov, *Spasibo, serdtse!*, p. 268.
61. *Ibid.*, p. 256.
62. Even Juri Jelagin dismisses him peremptorily: "[Utesov] never experimented, he never imitated American jazz. . . ." *Taming of the Arts*, p. 266.
63. M. Osipov, "Master sovetskogo dzhaza," *Rabochii i teatr*, Dec. 24, 1936, p. 18.
64. Cf. "Lunnaia rapsodiia" on *Leonid Utesov: Zapisi 30-kh–40-kh godov*, Melodiia, 33D-033307; cf. also the collection *Leonid Utesov: Zapisi, 1929–1946 godov*, Melodiia, D-03307–12.
65. James Lincoln Collier, *The Making of Jazz* (New York, 1978), p. 321.
66. Krotkov, *I Am from Moscow*, pp. 5–6.
67. *Literaturnaia gazeta*, Mar. 15, 1935; see Victor Smirnov, "'Sekretnoe oruzhie'—dzhaz," *Novoe russkoe slovo*, Aug. 27, 1978; See esp. B. Iasenskii, "O dzukh neudachnykh popytkakh," *Literaturnaia gazeta*, Mar. 6, 1935, and M. V. Koval, "Neudavshiisia eksperiment," *Sovetskoe iskusstvo*, Nov. 29, 1934.
68. Tsonev interview, 1979.
69. See I Rod., "Sovetskii film v Venetsii," *Komsomolskaia pravda*, Sept. 4, 1934.
70. "Ob itogakh kinofestivalia i besprintsipnoi polemike," *Pravda*, Mar. 12, 1935. See also B. Shumiatskii, "Muzykalnaia kultura kino," *Pravda*, Apr. 8, 1935.
71. Utesov, *S pesnei po zhizni*, pp. 161ff.
72. Azarii Mariamov, "Liubimtsy tirana," *Novoe russkoe slovo*, May 3, 1981.
73. I. V. Stalin, *Sochineniia*, reprinted by the Hoover Institution (Stanford, Ca., 1967), vol. I, p. 89.
74. Berger, "Jazz: Resistance to the Diffusion of a Culture-Pattern," p. 114.

75. Simon, *The Big Bands*, p. 27.
76. A. Bezymenskii, "Karaul gradiat," *Literaturnaia gazeta*, Dec. 28, 1935.
77. Utesov, *S pesnei po zhizni*, p. 159.

8. The Purge That Failed, 1936–1941

1. Conquest, *The Great Terror*, pp. 699–713.
2. Costakis interview, 1980.
3. Jelagin interview, June 6, 1979. On jazz at the spas see also A. Berlin and A. Broun, "Dzhaz ili simfoniia? *Izvestiia*, Nov. 21, 1936.
4. Jelagin, *Taming of the Arts*, pp. 213–16.
5. Heinz Unger, *Hammer, Sickle, and Baton: The Soviet Memoirs of a Musician* (London, 1939), p. 197.
6. Henry Cowell, "Muzyka v Sodeinennykh Shthtakh Ameriki," *Sovetskaia muzyka*, July 1934, p. 19 fn.
7. "Diskussiia o dzhaze," *Sovetskaia muzyka*, no. 2 (1934), p. 67.
8. B. E. Shumiatskii, "Tri mesiatsa v Amerike i Evrope," *Sovetskoe iskusstvo*, Aug. 23, 1935.
9. Issued as M. S. Druskin, *Ocherki po istorii tantsovalnoi muzyki* (Leningrad, 1936), pp. 70, 74.
10. Z. Bogdanov-Berezovskii, "Mysli o sovetskom simfonizme," *Rabochii i teatr*, no. 15 (1935), pp. 8–9.
11. S. Kulagin, "Novye plastinki," *Sovetskoe iskusstvo*, Sept. 23, 1935.
12. N. Raukhverger, "O chem poiut nashi deti," *Sovetskoe iskusstvo*, July 17, 1935.
13. Cf. the interesting review by N. Malkov, "Charli Chaplin i Dunaevskii," *Rabochii i teatr*, no. 16, (1936), pp. 18–29.
14. Leon Trotsky, *Problems of Everyday Life* (New York, 1973), p. 83.
15. See Gail Warshofsky Lapidus, *Women in Soviet Society: Equality, Development, and Social Change* (Berkeley, Los Angeles, 1978), pp. 112–13.
16. M. Iankovskii, "Neveselye zametki o veselykh zhanrakh," *Rabochii i teatr*, no. 3, (1935), p. 14.
17. "Says Jazz Threatens Christian Civilization," *New York Times*, Dec. 16, 1934, p. 2.
18. Jelagin, *Taming of the Arts*, p. 36.
19. See the excellent critical review in Schwarz, *Music and Musical Life in Soviet Russia*, pp. 119–24.
20. "Sumbur vmeste muzyki," *Pravda*, Jan. 28, 1936, p. 3.
21. See the further discussion "Leningradskie muzykovedy obsuzhdaiut vystupleniia p. o. 'Pravda,' " *Rabochii i teatr*, no. 4, (1936), pp. 8–9.
22. Berlin and Broun, "Dzhaz ili simfoniia?"
23. The legislation of Jan. 17, 1936, is published in *Robochii i teatr*, no. 2, (1936), pp. 2–3.
24. B. Shumiatskii, "Protiv khanzhei i spiatozh," *Pravda*, Nov. 24, 1936.
25. A. Berlin and A. Broun, "Eshche o dzhaze i simfonicheskoi muzyke," *Izvestiia*, Dec. 1, 1936; L. Knipper, "Sumbur u tov. Shumiatsogo," *Izvestiia*, Dec. 1, 1936; S. Korev, "Posporim o vkusakh," *Izvestiia*, Dec. 3, 1936.

26. P. Kerzhentsev, "O muzyke," *Pravda*, Dec. 4, 1936. p. 2.
27. A. Berlin and A. Broun, "'Teorii' tov. Shumiatskogo i raziasneniia tov. Kerzhentseva," *Izvestiia*, Dec. 5, 1936.
28. B. Shumiatskii, "Zaputalis," *Pravda*, Dec. 5, 1936.
29. "Zametaiut sledy," *Pravda*, Dec. 10, 1936.
30. A. Lukatskii, "Za khoroshuiu muzyku," *Izvestiia*, Dec. 11, 1936.
31. D. Kalm, "Dzhaz-reviu ili 'ostav svoi gnev naprasnyi,'" *Izvestiia*, Dec. 11, 1936.
32. G. Berezov, "Obyvatelskaia boltovnia na stranitsakh *Izvestii*," *Pravda*, Dec. 12, 1936.
33. "O brani i muzyke" and also "Dzhaz-reviu," *Izvestiia*, Dec. 14, 1936.
34. "Melkoburzhaznaia razviaznost," *Pravda*, Dec. 15, 1936.
35. "Eshche o brani i muzyke," *Izvestiia*, Dec. 16, 1936; "Obyvatelskii sud," *Pravda*, Dec. 17, 1936.
36. Steven S. Cohen, *Bukharin* (new York, 1971), pp. 366ff.
37. Conquest, *The Great Terror*, pp. 230–319, 386.
38. Batashev, *Sovetskii dzhaz*, p. 38.
39. See Shostakovich, *Testimony*, pp. 120–21.
40. Lantsman interview, 1979.
41. *Time*, Mar. 10, 1961, p. 34.
42. Durbrow interview, 1979.
43. Tsonev interview, 1979.
44. *Ibid.*
45. Utesov, *Spasibo, serdtse!*, p. 257.
46. *Ibid.*, p. 2. This passage draws heavily on the excellent paper by Vladimir Frumkin, "The Cultivation of Mythological Reality: 'Doublethink' in the Soviet Mass Songs of the Thirties," unpublished MS, Oberlin College, 1980.
47. *Ocherki sovetskogo muzykalnogo tvorchestva*, vol. I, p. 255.
48. Alexander I. Solzhenitsyn, *The Gulag Archipelago*, Thomas P. Whitney, trans. (New York, 1975), vols. III–IV, p. 492, quoted in Frumkin, "The Cultivation of Mythological Reality," p. 11.
49. Theme song from the film *Circus*, in *Sovietland*, Nov. 1936, p. 23.
50. Quoted in Frumkin, "The Cultivation of Mythological Reality," p. 3.
51. Jelagin, *Taming of the Arts*, p. 280. On Dunaevsky see L. Danilevich, "Master sovetskoi pesni," *Sovetskaia muzyka*, no. 3, (1950), p. 27.
52. "To War On Jazz with Better Songs," *Playground*, Jan. 1923, pp. 459–60; "War on Jazz Will Enlist Composers," *Musical Digest*, Oct. 31, 1922, p. 11.
53. Druskin, *Ocherki po istorii tantsovalnoi muzyki*, pp. 81–83.
54. See Hanns Eisler, *A Rebel in Music*, Manfred Grabs, ed. (New York, 1978), pp. 95ff; also Hanns Eisler, *Materialen zu einer Dialektik der Musik* (Leipzig, 1976), pp. 112ff.
55. *Týden rozhlasu* (Prague), Mar. 7, 1942, quoted in Skvorecky, *The Bass Saxophone*, p. 11.
56. "Reich Bars Radio Jazz To Safeguard 'Culture,'" *New York Times*, Oct. 13, 1935; also "Nazis Reject Jazz," *New York Times*, Mar. 18, 1933.
57. McCarthy, *Big Band Jazz*, pp. 325–26.
58. "Reich City Bars 'Hot' Music," *New York Times*, Nov. 19, 1938.

59. "Nazi Bans Swing Music as Not Fit for Germans," *New York Times*, Nov. 27, 1938.
60. S. Skredkov, "Kontsert Gosudarstvennogo dzhaza Soiuza SSR," *Izvestiia*, Nov. 29, 1938; also Jelagin, *Taming of the Arts*, pp. 260–62, and Batashev, *Sovetskii dzhaz*, pp. 77–81.
61. Jelagin, *Taming of the Arts*, p. 265.
62. *Ibid.*, pp. 262–63.
63. Recordings of the State Jazz Orchestra are reissued as *Gosudarstvennyi dzhaz-orkestr SSR*, Melodiia, 33N60–39761–62.
64. Blanter, titular director of the State Jazz Orchestra, penned nearly a third of its repertoire, his best-known work being "Katiusha."
65. Skredkov, "Kontsert Gosudavstvennogo dzhaza SSSR."
66. Jelagin, *Taming of the Arts*, p. 265.
67. Lantsman interview, 1980.
68. The sole source for this episode is Jelagin, *Taming of the Arts*, pp. 268–75.
69. Jelagin interview, June 1, 1979. In *Taming of the Arts* Batysheva is identified by her stage name, Nina Donskaia (p. 272).

9. Swinging for the Fatherland, 1941–1945

1. *Ocherki istorii russkogo sovetskogo dramaticheskogo teatra* (Moscow, 1960), vol. II, p. 530.
2. "Izdanie massovykh voennykh pesen," *Sovetskoe iskusstvo*, June 29, 1941.
3. "Boevaia estrada. Artisty u boitsov," *Sovetskoe iskusstvo*, Aug. 7, 1941.
4. Utesov, *Spasibo, serdtse!*, p. 316.
5. *Ibid.*, p. 321.
6. On Nikolai Minkh and his orchestra, see L. Kruts, "Svyshe 600 kontsertov," *Krasnoznamennyi baltiiskii flot*, July 16, 1943.
7. Batashev, *Sovetskii dzhaz*, p. 92.
8. Interview with Mrs. K. Mortimer, Oct. 5, 1978.
9. Interview with Anatolii Krushin, May 12, 1979; also A. N. Krushin, "Teatral-naia gruppa shtalaga 8-A," unpublished MS, n.d., in possession of the author.
10. Quoted in Simon, *The Big Bands*, p. 367.
11. B. K. Ermans, "Leningradskaia estrade v 'Ermitazhe,'" *Literatura i iskusstvo*, Aug. 22, 1942.
12. Bill Malone, *Country Music USA* (Austin, 1968), chap. 6.
13. D. Arsenev, "Smotr sovetskoi estrady," *Literatura i iskusstvo*, Aug. 19, 1944.
14. Utesov, *Pesnia po zhizni*, p. 185.
15. Mark Levin, "U perednego kraia," *Literatura i iskusstvo*, May 10, 1943.
16. "Estrada na fronte i za tylu," *Literatura i iskusstvo*, Apr. 22, 1944; Arsenev, "Smotr sovetskoi estrady."
17. "Estrada na fronte."
18. V. Surin, "Ob iskusstve 'malykh' form," *Pravda*, Oct. 4, 1944. p. 2.
19. Simon, *The Big Bands*, p. 365.
20. Utesov, *Spasibo, serdtse!*, p. 320.
21. M. Korovchenko, "Ostrov Utesova," *Krasnaia zvezda*, Mar. 6, 1974.

22. Michael Zwerin, "The German Officer Who Loved Jazz," *International Herald Tribune*, Nov. 2, 1979, p. 72.
23. Collier, *The Making of Jazz*, pp. 328–29.
24. "Iskusstvo-frontu," *Sovetskoe iskusstvo*, Sept. 4, 1941.
25. A. Tsfasman, interview with Batashev, in *Sovetskii dzhaz*, p. 89.
26. Utesov, *Spasibo, serdtse!*, p. 317.
27. *Leonid Utesov: Zapisi 30-kh–40-kh godov*; see also Utesov, *Pesnia po zhizni*, p. 180.
28. Collier, *The Making of Jazz*, pp. 326–29.
29. Werner Keller, *East Minus West Equals Zero: Russia's Debt to the Western World, 1862–1962* (New York, 1962), p. 241.
30. Varlam Shalamov, *Kolyma Tales*, John Glad, trans. (New York, London, 1980), p. 173.
31. "Muzyka v SShA," *Literatura i iskusstvo*, Aug. 22, 1941.
33. Mrs. K. Mortimer interview, 1978.
33. F. Spiridonov, "Leonid Utesov," *Literatura i iskusstvo*, Oct. 17, 1942.
34. A. Troianovskii, "Muzyka v Soedinennykh shtatakh," *Sovetskoe iskusstvo*, Sept. 18, 1941.
35. Oleg Lundstrem, *Serenada solnechnoi doliny*, Melodiia, 33s–60–07077–B.
36. *Leonid Utesov: Zapisi 30-kh–40-kh godov.*
37. Batashev, *Sovetskii dzhaz*, p. 96; also Lantsman interview, 1979, and interview with Louis Markowitz, Nov. 9, 1979.
38. Markowitz interview, 1979.
39. Interview with Ruth Turkow Kaminska (Mrs. Adolf Rosner), May 30, 1979.
40. Durbrow interview, 1979.
41. Eddie Rosner, "St. Louis Blues," USSR, 9214; USSR, 1221509.
42. Ruth Turkow Kaminska, *I Don't Want To Be Brave Any More* (Washington, D.C., 1978), pp. 17–18.
43. Interview with Daniil Granin, Aug. 5, 1979.
44. *Ibid.*
45. The most authoritative information on this period of Rosner's life is to be found in H. J. P. Bergmeier's unpublished chronologies of Rosner's career and that of S. Weintraub, MS, Johannesburg, South Africa.
46. *Ibid.*
47. Interview with Willis Conover, Oct. 15, 1979.
48. Markowitz interview, 1979, and Kaminska interview, 1979. Kaminska, however, states that Armstrong's photo was signed "to the white Louis Armstrong from the black Eddie Rosner." *I Don't Want To Be Brave Any More*, pp. 7–8.
49. For full discography, see Bergmeier, "Rosner Chronology."
50. Kaminska, *I Don't Want To Be Brave Any More*, p. 7.
51. Markowitz interview, 1979.
52. Interview with V. Berezhkov, May 4, 1979.
53. Kaminska, *I Don't Want To Be Brave Any More*, p. 11.
54. Markowitz interview, 1979.
55. Iu. B. Margolin, *Puteshestvie v stranu ZE-Ka.* (New York, 1952), p. 47.
56. Kaminska, *I Don't Want To Be Brave Any More*, pp. 17, 64.

57. Markowitz interview, 1979.
58. Kaminska, *I Don't Want To Be Brave Any More*, pp. 36–39.
59. *Ibid.*, p. 27.
60. *Ibid.*, p. 58.
61. Markowitz interview, 1979.
62. Kaminska, *I Don't Want To Be Brave Any More*, pp. 52, 63.
63. Markowitz interview, 1979.
64. Three members of the group, drummer Georg Schwartzstein, singer Lothar Lampel, and clarinetist Harry Wohlfeiler, had been with Rosner in Germany as well.
65. Kaminska interview, 1979.
66. Granin interview, 1979.

10. The Sonic Backlash, 1945–1953

1. N. Minkh, interview with Batashev in *Sovetskii dzhaz*, p. 95.
2. McCarthy, *Big Band Jazz*, p. 326.
3. Interview with Dr. Maurice Friedberg, Oct. 5, 1979.
4. Interview with Josef Skvorecky, May 12, 1978.
5. Interview with Thomas Whitney, Oct. 26, 1979.
6. *Ibid.*; also Utesov, *Spasibo, serdtse!*, p. 346.
7. Committee on Foreign Affairs, *Soviet Diplomacy and Negotiating Behavior: Emerging New Context for U.S. Diplomacy* (Washington, D.C., 1979), pp. 200–201.
8. William O. McCagg, Jr., *Stalin Embattled, 1943–1948* (Detroit, 1978), p. 38.
9. Speech of Feb. 9, 1946; I. V. Stalin, *Sochineiia* (Stanford, 1946), vol. III, pp. 1–22.
10. Marshall D. Shulman, *Stalin's Foreign Policy Reappraised* (New York, 1969), p. 15.
11. Milovan Djilas, *Conversations with Stalin*, Michael B. Petrovich, trans. (New York, 1962), pp. 114–15.
12. George F. Kennan, *Memoirs* (New York, 1967), p. 122.
13. *Jazzfinder*, 1949.
14. Andy Gurwitch, "What Europeans Write About Jazz," *Down Beat*, Aug. 13, 1947, p. 10; Divind Bergh, *Moderne Dansemusikk* (Oslo, 1945); Johannes Fehring and Walter Heidrich, *Der neue Jazz-Stil* (Vienna, 1948).
15. Tatakoshi Kyogoku, "Jazz with a Classical Tint Rules Japan," *Down Beat*, Dec. 1, 1948, p. 15; see also "Satchmo in Sweden, Italian Tour Mapped," *Variety*, Oct. 19, 1949, and "Armstrong To Make Another Europe Trip," *Down Beat*, Nov. 3, 1950, p. 3.
16. Annabelle Bucar, *The Truth About American Diplomats* (Moscow, 1949), p. 107. Bucar was a former embassy staffer who defected to the USSR.
17. G. Shneerson, "Vrednyi surrogat iskusstva," *Sovetskaia muzyka*, no. 7, (1948), p. 87.
18. See Chapter 10, pp. 243–44.
19. "Die internationale Republik des Jazz," *Die Melodie*, June 1949, pp. 14–15.

20. McCagg, *Stalin Embattled*, pp. 44, 82.

21. Robert Conquest, *Kolyma: The Arctic Death Camps* (New York, Oxford, 1979), pp. 226–27.

22. K. Semenev, *O bditelnosti sovetskikh liudei* (Moscow, 1949), pp. 64–66.

23. Walter C. Clemens, Jr., "Soviet Disarmament Proposals and the Cadre--Territorial Army," *Orbis*, Winter 1964, pp. 778–79.

24. Lapidus, *Women in Soviet Society*, p. 117.

25. Zusanek, *Work and Leisure in the Soviet Union*, pp. 152–53; Vera S. Dunham, *In Stalin's Time: Middle-Class Values in Soviet Fiction* (Cambridge, London, 1976), pp. 16–17.

26. "Konkurs artistov estrady," *Sovetsoe iskusstvo*, Aug. 9, 1946; I. Lvov, "Uspekhi i nedostatki sovetskoi estrady," *Pravda*, Aug. 10, 1946.

27. V. Gorodinskii, "Prikhodite, pobeseduem," *Sovetskoe iskusstvo*, Aug. 16, 1946.

28. V. Shklovskii, "O dzhaze Utesova," *Sovetskoe iskusstvo*, Sept. 6, 1946.

29. B. Iarustovskii, "O bytovoi muzyke," *Izvestiia*, June 5, 1947.

30. Academy of Sciences of the USSR, Institute of the History of Arts, *Istoriia russkoi sovetskoi muzyki* (Moscow, 1963), vol. III, pt. I, pp. 12–13.

31. Arsenev, "Smotr sovetskoi estrady."

32. Kaminska interview, 1979, and Markowitz interview, 1979; Ruth Kaminska's life in Siberia is described in her autobiography, *I Don't Want To Be Brave Any More*, chaps. 20–25.

33. Lantsman interview, 1979.

34. Interview with Ilia Suslov, Apr. 20, 1979.

35. Interview with Herbert Marshall, Nov. 7, 1979.

36. Whitney interview, 1979.

37. Harrison E. Salisbury, *America in Russia* (New York, 1955), pp. 257–58.

38. Utesov, *Spasibo, serdtse!*, p. 351.

39. Andrei Zhdanov, quoted in Alexander Werth, *Musical Uproar in Moscow* (London, 1949), p. 82.

40. Lantsman interview, 1979.

41. *Ibid.*

42. Interview with Ilkhonon Yoffe, Jan. 4, 1979.

43. *Ibid.*

44. Tamas Aczel and Tibor Meray, *The Revolt of the Mind* (Westport, 1959), p. 131.

45. Skvorecky, *The Bass Saxophone*, p. 22.

46. Compare with "Ford Wars on Jazz; Gives Party for Old-time Dances," *New York Times*, July 12, 1925, p. 2.

47. Yoffe interview, 1979.

48. *Komsomolskaia pravda*, Apr. 6, 1962, p. 2.

49. G. Shneerson, "Vrednyi surrogat iskusstva," *Sovetskaia muzyka*, no. 7 (1948), p. 93.

50. The affair of Vano Muradeli's opera, *The Great Friendship*, as well as the event leading to the Apr. 1948 congress are thoroughly recounted by Werth, *Musical Uproar in Moscow*, and Schwarz, *Music and Musical Life in Soviet Russia*, pp. 213–68; transcripts of the Jan. 1948 meetings are in *Sovetskaia muzyka*, Jan. 1948, pp. 3–102.

51. Werth, *Musical Uproar in Moscow*, p. 29.
52. I. Nestev, "Realisticheskoe napravlenie v muzyke," in Union of Soviet Composers of the USSR, *Sovetskaia muzyka na podeme* (Moscow, Leningrad, 1950), pp. 60–85.
53. Vladimir Zakharov, quoted in Werth, *Musical Uproar in Moscow*, p. 55.
54. G. Shneerson, *Muzyka na sluzhbe reaktsii* (Moscow, 1950), p. 3.
55. V. Gorodinskii, *Muzyka dukhovnoi nishchity* (Moscow, Leningrad, 1950), pp. 80, 85.
56. Utesov, *Pesnia po zhizni*, p. 195.
57. Gorodinskii, *Muzyka dukhovnoi nishchity*, p. 81.
58. P. Robeson, "Pesni moego naroda," *Sovetskaia muzyka*, July 1949, p. 104; trans. in *Paul Robeson Speaks*, p. 117.
59. *Bolshaia sovetskaia entsiklopediia*, 2nd ed. (Moscow, 1952), vol. XIV, p. 200.
60. Gorodinskii, *Muzyka dukhovnoi nishchity*, pp. 95 fn., 100–101.
61. Shneerson, "Vrednyi surrogat iskusstva," p. 88.
62. Shneerson, *Muzyka na sluzhbe reaktsii*, p. 95.
63. E. Kolmanovskii, "Trudnoe polozhenie v legkom zhenre," *Sovetskaia muzyka*, no. 1 (1953), p. 31.
64. Shneerson, "Vrednyi surrogat iskusstva," p. 91.
65. Utesov, *Pesnia po zhizni*, p. 196.
66. Berukshtis interview, 1979.
67. Svetlana Alliluyeva, *Only One Year*, Paul Chavchavadze, trans. (London, 1969), p. 256.
68. Salisbury, *America in Russia*, p. 112.
69. Berukshtis interview, 1979.
70. Interview with Harrison E. Salisbury, Feb. 26, 1979.
71. Kaminska, *I Don't Want To Be Brave Any More*, p. 132.
72. Conquest, *Kolyma*, pp. 69–70.
73. Interview with Vassily Aksyonov, Nov. 12, 1980.
74. *Ibid.*
75. Igor Lundstrem, "Orchestra Conducted by Oleg Lundstrem: A Brief History," unpublished MS, courtesy of its author.
76. Aksyonov interview, 1980.
77. Interview with Leonid Khotin, Sept. 21, 1981.
78. Interview with Arkadii Shabashov, July 29, 1981.
79. Berukshtis interview, 1979.
80. No recordings of the Lundstrem Orchestra before 1956 are known to exist. Numerous tunes fron the band's repertoire at this time, including many in American arrangements, were recorded on *Orkestr Olega Lundstrema*, Melodiia, Sm–04293–4; *Estradnyi orkestr pod upravleniem Olega Lundstrema*, Melodiia, 33S–01333–34, and *Serenada solnechnoi doliny*, Melodiia, 33–S–07077–B.
81. Interview with V. Sermakashev, Feb. 18, 1980.
82. Information courtesy of Valter Ojakäär (Tallinn), and Kurt Strobel (Warradale, Australia); see also Valter Ojakäär, *Džassmuusika* (Tallinn, 1966), p. 209. A taped copy of recordings by the Kurt Strobel Orchestra is in the collection of the author.

83. Interview with Jurgis Blekaitis, Oct. 25, 1979; and with Bronis Raila, Oct. 26, 1979.

84. Yoffe interview, 1979.

85. Interview with Felix Rovin, Oct. 23, 1979.

86. Yoffe interview, 1979.

87. Kurt Strobel is now living in Australia, and Hans Speek in Sweden.

88. Valter Ojakäär, letter to the author, Feb. 18, 1981.

89. Ojakäär letter. Members of the Swing Club included several persons who later gained prominence as scientists as well as musicians, among them A. Riabov, U. Agur, U. Loop, U. Vinter, H. Yurisalu, P. Saul, and Naissoo. See *Uno Naissoo*, Melodiia, S60–09439–40.

90. For information on the Tallinn Jazz Festival I am indebted to Valter Ojakäär.

91. V. Konen, "Legenda i pravda o dzhaze," *Sovetskaia muzyka*, no. 9, (1955), p. 31.

92. Ira Gitler, *Jazzmasters of the '40s* (New York, London, 1966), p. 12.

11. The Search for Authenticity, 1950–1955

1. Interview with Christina Mentzschel Starr, May 16, 1980.

2. This episode is capably reviewed by Deming Brown in *Soviet Russian Literature Since Stalin* (Cambridge, 1978), pp. 3ff.

3. Leonid Utesov, "O pesne i legkoi muzyke," *Sovetskaia muzyka*, Nov. 1953, p. 40.

4. S. Egin, "O legkoi muzyke i pesne," *Sovetskaia muzyka*, Feb. 1954, p. 106.

5. I. Dunaevskii, "Nazrevshie voprosy legkoi muzyki," *Sovetskaia muzyka*, no. 6 (1955), pp. 19–25; A. Medvedev, "Chto vy dumaete o dzhaze i legkoi muzyke?" *Sovetskaia muzyka*, no. 11 (1956), pp. 98–109.

6. A. Khachaturian, "O tvorcheskoi smelosti i vdokhnovlenii," *Sovetskaia muzyka*, Nov. 1953, p. 7.

7. Quoted in E. Rusakova, *Komsomolskaia pravda*, Aug. 11, 1956, p. 2, in *Current Digest of the Soviet Press* (hereafter *CDSP*) III, no. 33, p. 9.

8. Aksyonov interview, 1980; Berukshtis interview, 1979; and Suslov interview, 1979.

9. *CDSP* IV, no. 23, p. 37.

10. Rusakova in *CDSP*.

11. Kaminska, *I Don't Want To Be Brave Any More*, p. 42.

12. Berukshtis interview, 1979.

13. Utesov, *Spasibo, serdtse!*, p. 63.

14. David Riesman, *The Lonely Crowd: A Study of the Changing American Character* (New York, 1953), pp. 184ff.

15. The best study of this phenomenon remains Allen Kassof, *The Soviet Youth Program: Regimentation and Rebellion* (Cambridge, 1964), pp. 154ff. Kassof concentrates on the post-1954 era.

16. "XI-yi sezd Komsomola," *Izvestiia*, Apr. 1, 1949, pp. 1–2; *Pravda*, Apr. 1, 1949, p. 1.

17. Kassof, *The Soviet Youth Program*, p. 145.

18. "O 'vechnykh' studentakh," *Komsomolskaia pravda*, June 22, 1952, p. 2.

19. E. Strogova, "Mif legkoi raboty," *Literaturnaia gazeta*, Dec. 11, 1952, p. 2.
20. Letter by A. Kuznetsov, *Komsomolskaia pravda*, June 23, 1949, p. 3; also Mark G. Field, "Drink and Delinquency in the USSR," *Problems of Communism*, May–June 1955, pp. 29–38.
21. Supplement to *Sovetskaia pedagogiia*, 1949, trans. in *CDSP*, June 28, 1949, p. 5.
22. I. Peretnikova, "Semeinoe vospitanie," *Izvestiia*, June 19, 1949, p. 2.
23. On boarding schools see N. Maleev, *Izvestiia*, July 30, 1952, p. 2, in *CDSP* IV, no. 31, p. 49. On coeducation see *Literaturnaia gazeta*, July 15, 1949, p. 1, in *CDSP* II, no. 29, p. 53.
24. *Ibid.*, *Literaturnaia gazeta*.
25. Kassof, *The Soviet Youth Program*, chaps. 4, 6.
26. G. Petrov, "Bez kritiki net progressa," *Komsomolskaia pravda*, Nov. 25, 1949, p. 2.
27. A. Bekhterev and M. Aleksandrov, "Otvet komsomoltsam," *Komsomolskaia pravda*, Sept. 20, 1950, p. 3.
28. Semen Nariniani, *Komsomolskaia pravda*, Sept. 19, 1952, in *CDSP* IX, no. 38, p. 20.
29. "O dzhaze" *Sovetskoe iskusstvo*, Feb. 16, 1952, p. 3.
30. Interview with Ilya Suslov, Aug. 29, 1981.
31. Eshche o dzhaze," *Sovetskoe iskusstvo*, Mar. 12, 1952, p. 3.
32. Berukshtis interview, 1979.
33. Aksyonov interview, 1980; for similar movements in other countries see "Disc Bootleggers Are Waxing Fat on Stolen Goods," *Down Beat*, June 16, 1950, p. 10.
34. Berukshtis interview, 1979.
35. Aksyonov interview, 1980.
36. David McReynolds, "Hipsters Unleashed," *The Beats*, Seymour Krim, ed. (New York, 1960), p. 208.
37. Cf. William Bruce Cameron, "Sociological Notes on the Jam Session," *Social Forces*, Dec. 1954, pp. 177–82.
38. See John Tytell's thoughtful discussion of this point in *Naked Angels* (New York, 1976), pp. 6ff.
39. Interview with Sasha Kofman, Oct. 16, 1978; interview with Boris Ludmer, Feb. 12, 1979.
40. Sermakashev interview, 1980; *Washington Post*, Sept. 15, 1978, p. 8; also Willis Conover, liner notes to *Adam Makowicz*, Columbia LP, 35320.
41. Interview with Hans A. Tuch, Apr. 14, 1979. See also Felix Helair, Jr., "United States Has Secret Sonic Weapon—Jazz," *New York Times*, Aug. 6, 1955, p. 1; and John A. Kouwenhoven, "Stones, Steel and Jazz," in *Made in America* (New York, 1958) pp. 21–49.
42. Conover interview, 1979.
43. Berukshtis interview, 1979.
44. *Ibid.*
45. Zubov's Kreshchendo quintet of the mid-sixties is recorded on *Dzhaz-67*, Melodiia, 33S–01885–6.
46. "Kogda ne khvataet tekhniki," *Dzhaz-66*, Melodiia, S–01159–60.

47. Quoted in Alexei Batashev, "K.O.! Soviet Combo at International Jazz Festival," *Soviet Life*, Mar. 1967, p. 15.

48. "Divertimento in Three Movements for Orchestra" *Dzhaz-67*, Melodiia, 33–D–020987–8 (A) R3; *Ansambl "Melodiia,"* Melodiia, S60–05277–8.

49. His trio is recorded on *Dzhaz-66*, Melodiia, 33D–018193; and *Dzhaz-67*, Melodiia, SO 1887–8; on Rychkov see also V. Petrov, "Virtuoz roialia," *Molodost Sibiri*, Nov. 2, 1966.

50. Interview with Roman Kunsman, Oct. 2, 1979.

51. Berukshtis interview, 1979, Suslov interview, 1981.

52. V. Ardamatskii, "Dozhd i dzhaz," *Komsomolskaia pravda*, Aug. 22, 1956, p. 3.

53. Boris Chirkov, "Repertuar i natsionalnye traditsii," *Komsomolskaia pravda*, Apr. 26, 1957, p. 4.

54. Shepilov's speech is in *CDSP* IX, May 8, 1957, pp. 15ff; see also *New York Herald Tribune*, Apr. 4, 1957, p. 4; and John Gunther, *Inside Russia Today* (New York, 1958), p. 313.

55. Suslov interview, 1981.

56. *Molodoi kommunist*, in *CDSP* IX, no. 22 (1957), p. 19.

57. K. Efimov and G. Maksimov, "Chem boitsia Mister Dulles?" *Komsomolskaia pravda*, Mar. 14, 1957, p. 3.

58. Ludmer interview, 1979.

59. See "Krzysztof Komeda," *Jazz* (Warsaw), Jan. 1963, pp. 15ff; A. Batashev, "Slovo o Komede," *Kvadrat* (Leningrad), no. 14 (1978), pp. 52–56.

60. M. Ignateva, "Muzykalnye stiliagi," *Sovetskaia kultura*, Aug. 8, 1957. Cf. response by N. Minkh, "Razmyshleniia o dzhaze," *Sovetskaia muzyka*, Feb. 1958, pp. 42–47.

61. "Eshche raz o dzhaze," *Sovetskaia kultura*, Oct. 1, 1957.

62. *Studiia, 1967–1977* (Moscow, 1977), p. 3.

63. *Neva*, Melodiia, 33D–0020453. Details on Leningrad Dixieland bands were kindly provided by Nathan Leites.

64. *Leningradskii diksilend*, Melodiia, 33D–21486; for A. Melkonov cf. *Po stranitsam VI Moskovskogo festivalia sovetskoi dzhazovoi muzyki*, Melodiia, S60–12815–16.

65. Elena Koronevskaya, "Soviet 'Djaz' Scene," *Morning Star*, Sept. 19, 1967.

66. *Dzhaz-67*, Melodiia, 33D–02098.

67. German Lukianov, trumpet; Valerii Mysovskii, drums; Taimuras Kuchalev, piano; Oleg Mashkovich, bass; and Slava Bashlakov, tenor saxophone; cf. Yuri Vikharieff, "A Short History of Jazz in Russia," *Down Beat*, Feb. 28, 1963, p. 21.

68. Biographical information on Lukianov is to be found in *Kvadrat* (Leningrad), no. 13 (1976), p. 34; see also G. Lukianov, "Nadeius sozdat svoi sobstvennyi stil," *Kvadrat*, no. 6 (1969).

69. *Dzhaz-66*, Melodiia, 33D–018193.

70. Don Ellis, "Pamietnik warszawski," *Jazz* (Warsaw), Mar. 1963.

71. Cf. especially with Vitalii Kleinot's quintet, *Dzhaz-67*, Melodiia, 33D–020987–8.

72. Cf. *Dzhaz-67*, Melodiia, S–01887–8.

73. For biographical information see *Kvadrat* (Leningrad), no. 13 (1976), pp. 23ff;

Josef Balcerak and Jan Borkowski, "Turysci jazzowi na trasie: Moskwa-Leningrad-Warszawa," *Jazz* (Warsaw), Nov. 1960, p. 6; "Gennadi-Charlie," *Jazz* (Warsaw), no. 3 (1967); and V. Snitkin, "Gennadi Golstein," *Melodie und Rhythmus*, no. 17 (1968).

74. Leonard Feather, liner notes to *Soviet Jazz Themes*, AVA Records.
75. *Ibid.*, for recordings of these songs by Nat Adderley, Victor Feldman, etc; also *Leningrad Jazz Festival 1964*, Vee Jay Records, VJS–2504; and *Dzhaz-67*, Melodiia, SO–1887–8.
76. Recorded by Mikhail Kull's quintet, *Dzhaz-67*, Melodiia, 33S–01885–6. For Kunsman's performances with the Oleg Lundstrem Orchestra cf. *Dzhaz-67*, Melodiia, 33S–01885–6.
77. Interview with George Avakian, Sept. 17, 1981.
78. For a late example of this see "Reo dzeza ritma," Melodiia, 33SM02045–6.
79. Berukshtis interview, 1979.
80. Bergmeier, "Rosner Chronology."
81. *Kvadrat*, (Leningrad), no. 13 (1976), p. 4. See also Henryk Terpilowskij, "Przedstawiam orkiestre O. Lundstrema," *Jazz* (Warsaw), Apr. 1961, p. 5; and "10 let molodosti," *Molodost Sibiri*, Aug. 20, 1967.
82. In the absence of a complete discography, one might consult *Dzhaz orkestr Iosifa Wainshteina*, Melodiia, 1–8791; also *Leningradskii dzhaz-orkestr*, Melodiia, SM–03841–2; *Dzhaz orkestr Vainshteina*, Melodiia, SM–02823–4.
83. *Dzhaz orkestr pod rukovodstvom Iosifa Vainshteina* (Leningrad, 1979), n.p.
84. Kunsman interview, 1979.
85. Leonard Feather's assessment of this band can be found in "Inside Soviet Jazz," *Down Beat*, Aug. 6, 1962, p. 15.
86. Kunsman interview, 1979.
87. See Dm. Kabalevskii, "Poiski i zabluzhdeniia," *Sovetskaia muzyka*, Feb. 1962, p. 13.

12. Cooptation and Conflict, 1960–1967

1. The tour, proposed by the USSR's ambassador to the United Nations, Andrei Vyshinsky, was heavily underwritten by the producers, Robert Breen and Blevins Davis, even though the Soviets spent 600,000 rubles on the project. Cf. Egbert, *Social Radicalism and the Arts*, vol. V: *Russia*, pp. 463–64.
2. V. Gorodinskii, "Razgovor o dzhaze," *Komsomolskaia pravda*, June 13, 1959.
3. "Sovetskii dzhaz zhdet svoikh kompozitorov," *Komsomolskaia pravda*, Dec. 25, 1960.
4. *Komsomolskaia pravda*, Sept. 22, 1960, p. 4. The entire polemic is translated in *Soviet Review* Mar. 1961, pp. 3–10.
5. Cf. L. O. Utesov, "Mysli o dzhaze," *Sovetskaia kultura*, Feb. 25, 1961.
6. V. Mysovskii and V. Feiertag, *Dzhaz* (Leningrad, 1960), pp. 99, 124ff; see also A. A. Pen-Chernov's historical reflections in "K sporam o dzhaze," *Muzykalnaia zhizn*, no. 17 (1959), pp. 17–18, and no. 18 (1960), pp. 18–19. See also the chapter on American jazz in V. Konen's *Puti amerikanskoi muzyki* (Moscow, 1961).

7. Iurii Vermenich, "Desiat let spustia," *Kvadrat* (Leningrad), no. 13 (1976), pp. 45–51.
8. *Studio, 1958–1978* (Moscow, 1978); also Batashev, *Sovetskii dzhaz*, p. 122.
9. Berukshtis interview, 1979.
10. Interview with Vladimir Tkalich, 1979.
11. Zabeginsky interview, 1979; Brantsberg interview, 1979; interview with Igor Vysotski, Oct. 8, 1979.
12. Kunsman interview, 1979.
13. This system is also used for Soviet classical music. Cf. Rudolf Th. Jurrjens, *The Free Flow: People, Ideas, and Information in Soviet Ideology and Politics* (Alphen, Rijn, 1979), p. 334.
14. Interview, name withheld.
15. Zabeginsky interview, 1979.
16. Tkalich interview, 1979.
17. See interviews in Ted Hallock, "Jazz in Russia," *Down Beat*, Oct. 3, 1956, p. 14.
18. *Murad Kazhlaev: Dzazovye ansambli*, Melodiia, 33–D–19346; also *Krutye povoroty*, Melodiia, ST33S–04535–6.
19. *Vadim Liudvikovskii*, Melodiia, 33–D–19367–7, also L–S01725–6.
20. Interview with Anatole Gerasimov, Oct. 26, 1979.
21. Lev Zabeginskii, "Tulskii dzhaz," *Komsomolets* (Petrozavodsk), Apr. 15, 1967; *Orkestr "Sovremennik"; Dirizher Anatolii Kroll*, Melodiia, 33S60–05279–80.
22. Interview with Arkadii Shabashov, July 30, 1981; also Kunsman interview, 1979.
23. Cited in Brown, *Soviet Russian Literature*, p. 180.
24. These events are capably reviewed by Alfred E. Friendly, Jr., MS on Soviet dissent, Washington, D.C., 1977, pp. 62–107.
25. Berukshtis interviews, 1979.
26. The name "Aelita" was borrowed from a Martian beauty in a story by Aleksei Tolstoy to signify fantasy and romance.
27. For details see "Dzhaz klubu-odin god," *Leningradskii universitet*, Apr. 24, 1962; interviews with Yoffe, Kofman, Ludmer, Zabeginsky, Vysotski, and others; also interview with Vadim Vyadro, Dec. 6, 1979.
28. The reference is to Aelita; Gerasimov interview, 1979. See "The 'Liberal' Life," *Time*, Feb. 16, 1962, p. 26.
29. Kofman interview, 1978.
30. Brantsberg interview, 1979.
31. Zabeginsky interview, 1979.
32. "Khrushchev on Modern Art," *Encounter*, Apr. 1963, pp. 101–3.
33. Dizzy Gillespie with Al Fraser, *To Be or Not . . . To Bop: Memoirs* (New York, 1979(, p. 413.
34. Willie Ruff, "Jazz Mission to Moscow," *Down Beat*, Jan. 1960, pp. 16–20; L. Pereverzev, "Negritianskie artisty v SSSR," *Sovetskaia muzyka*, Sept. 1959, pp. 135–36.
35. Interview with Kenneth Kerst, Nov. 3, 1979.
36. For details on the negotiations see Marguerite Higgins, "Soviet-U.S. Agree, Culture with Jazz," *New York Herald Tribune*, Mar. 9, 1962, p. 1.
37. Smirnov, " 'Sekretnoe oruzhie.' "

38. Batashev, *Sovetskii dzhaz*, p. 126.
39. Interview with Terrence Catherman, Nov. 27, 1979.
40. *Ibid*. For further information on the tour see Yuri Vikharieff, "Waitin' for Benny: A Report from Russia," *Down Beat*, July 5, 1962; Yefim Galanter, "Benny Goodman in Moscow," *Soviet Life Today*, Sept. 1962, p. 64; also *New York Times*, May 31, June 3, 1962.
41. Kaminska, *I Don't Want To Be Brave Any More*, p. 42.
42. Khrushchev on Modern Art," pp. 102–3.
43. Yevgeny Yevtushenko, *Precocious Autobiography*, Andrew R. MacAndrew, trans. New York, 1963, pp. 122–23, 99.
44. Igor Moiseev, *Izvestiia*, Apr. 29, 1962.
45. Cf. A. N. Tsfasman, "Kogda igraet dzhaz," *Izvestiia*, Aug. 24, 1962.
46. D. D. Shostakovich, "Sereznye problemy legkikh zhanrov," *Sovetskaia kultura*, Nov. 15, 1962.
47. *New York Herald Tribune*, Nov. 30, 1962, p. 7. *New York Times*, Dec. 2, 1962, p. 9.
48. "Khrushchev on Modern Art," *Encounter*, pp. 101–3; also *Khrushchev and the Arts*, Priscilla Johnson and Leopold Labedz, eds. (Cambridge, 1965), pp. 100ff.
49. *Pravda*, Dec. 22, 1962, reprinted in *Khrushchev and the Arts*, pp. 105ff. See also *Newsweek*, Jan. 7, 1963, p. 33; *Time*, Jan. 18, 1963, p. 26.
50. *Pravda*, Mar. 10, 1963; *Khrushchev and the Arts*, pp. 147ff.
51. Ludmer interview, 1979, and Suslov interview, 1981.
52. A. Rumiantsev, "Partiia i intelligentsiia," Feb. 21, 1963.
53. A. Medvedev, "Dzhaz na povorote," *Nedelia* (supplement to *Izvestiia*), May 16, 1965.
54. Batashev, *Sovetskii dzhaz*, pp. 135–36.
55. *Dzhaz-65*, Melodiia, 33D–17010.
56. Zabeginsky interview, 1979.
57. *Ibid*.
58. Interview, name withheld.
59. Interview with Mikhail Oleinikov, Oct. 5, 1979.
60. L. Pereverzev, "Ocherki po istorii dzhaza," *Muzykalnaia zhizn*, nos. 3, 5, 9, 12 (1966). See also Iu. Fedorenko, "Ocherki po istorii dzhaza," *Za inzhenernye kadry* (Leningrad), nos. 31, 32, 34, 35, 36, 43 (1977).
61. A. Chernov and N. Bialik, *O legkoi muzyke, o dzhaze, o khoroshem vkuse* (Moscow, Leningrad, 1965).
62. See reference to this or a similar project in *Jazz* (Warsaw), May 1966, p. 14; the only relevant biographical guide in print is S. Bolotin, *Biograficheskii slovar muzykantov-ispolnitelei na dukhovykh instrumentakh* (Leningrad, 1969).
63. *Vakhuri's Ensemble "Collage"*, Melodiia 38D I–028231.
64. L. Garin, *Dzhazovye kompozitsii*, Melodiia, 33S–60–05397–8; also *Dzhaz-65*, Melodiia 33D–17010; *Dzhaz-67*, Melodiia, S–01887–8. The earliest known Soviet use of the vibraphone was by Yosif Weinstein's 1946 Leningrad orchestra.
65. *Dzhango: dzhazovye kompozitsii*, Melodiia, 33–S60–11247–48; *Moskovskii kvartet "gitara,'"* Melodiia, 33D–00034063–4; *Dzhaz-78*, Melodiia, 33660–11425–26.

66. *Vio–66*, Melodiia, D–26097–8; *Dzhaz-67*, Melodiia, SO 1887–8; A. Batashev, "Pervaia polgoda," *Sovetskaia kultura*, Aug. 25, 1966.
67. *Rafik Babaev: Kvartet*, Melodiia, 33D–0001747–8.
68. *Dzhaz-68*, Melodiia, 33D–024284.
69. Batashev, *Sovetskii dzhaz*, pp. 149–51; see also Iu. Vermenich, "Natsionalnoe i internatsionalnoe v dzhaze," *Kvadrat* no. 9 (1970).
70. "Muki 'novogo dzhaza'" *Za rubezhom*, no. 11 (1967).
71. Andrzej Zarebski, "Russian Jazz," *Jazz Forum*, Jan. 1969, pp. 59ff.
72. John S. Wilson, "Jazz: Art Blakey and Messengers," *New York Times*, Dec. 29, 1977.
73. Leonard Feather, "Art Blakey: Jazz at Parisian Room," *Los Angeles Times* Apr. 27, 1978; Thomas Albright, "Jazz Festival," *San Francisco Chronicle*, Sept. 20, 1977. See also *L'eco di Bergamo* (Italy), July 21, 1980; *Smålandsposten* (Sweden) Oct. 17, 1979; *Stuttgarter Nachrichten* (Germany), July 15, 1980.
74. Cf. *Dzhaz-66*, Melodiia, 33D–018194; *Dzhaz-68*, Melodiia, 33D–024295–6 (a); *Tallinn-67*, Melodiia, D–020845–6; *Instrumentalnyi ansembl p/u Vladimira Sermakasheva*, Melodiia, D–00031948–9.
75. Tkalich interview, 1979; also Henryk Terpilowski, "Jam Session na Poludniu," *Jazz* (Warsaw), Sept. 1964, p. 6.
76. Aleksy Bataszew, "III Festival w Tartu," *Jazz* (Warsaw), Apr. 1960, p. 14.
77. Siergiej Lawrowski, "List z ZSSR," *Jazz* (Warsaw), June 1961, p. 2.
78. "Dzhaz-62" (Moscow, 1962); A. Batashev, who organized the event, claims fifteen bands performed, a figure which is not reflected in the published program (*Sovetskii dzhaz*, p. 128.)
79. Interview, name withheld.
80. Serge Lawrowski, "I Leningradzki Festiwal Jazzowy," *Jazz* (Warsaw), nos. 7–8 (1962), pp. 8–9.
81. Kunsman interview, 1979.
82. Union of Soviet Composers, Moscow, and Moscow City Komsomol Committee, "Dzhaz-65" (Moscow, 1965), p. 3.
83. Medvedev, "Dzhaz na povorte."
84. L. Pereverzev, "Molodezhnye dzhazy Moskvy," *Muzykalnaia zhizn*, no. 14 (1965).
85. A. Medvedev, Iu. Saulskii, "Dzhaz 65," *Muzykalnaia zhizn*, no. 2 (1966), pp. 18–20. Willis Conover, "Jazz Festival in Prague," *Down Beat*, Jan. 13, 1966, pp. 15–17.
86. In the following year V. Sermakashev and the Molodezhnoe Café (KM) Quartet appeared in Prague, and Georgi Garanian's quartet was sent to Warsaw. Arkadii Petrov and Aleksei Batashev, "Na mezhdunarodnoi arene—dzhaz," *Sovetskaia kultura*, Dec. 15, 1966.
87. A. Batashev, "Organizatsionnye problemy zhanra," *Sovetskaia kultura*, Oct. 9, 1965.
88. A. Batashev, "Leningradskii festival dzhazovoi muzyki," *Muzykalnaia zhizn*, no. 13 (1966); also memoir by N. Leites, 1982, in possession of the author.
89. Yuri Vikhareff, "Jazz Festivals in Russia: 1966," *Jazz* (Warsaw), Sept. 1966, pp. 10–12; also Batashev, "Leningradskii festival dzhazovoi muzyki."
90. L. Pereverzev, "III Moskovskii festival dzhaza," *Muzykalnaia zhizn*, no. 15 (1966).
91. *Džässifestival "Tallinn 67": Programm-programma* (Tallinn, 1967); see also V.

Zimianin, "Tallinn 67," *Sovetskaia kultura*, May 11, 1967; L. Martinkenas, "K okonchaniiu festivalia dzhazovoi muzyki v Talline," *Komsomolskaia pravda*, May 26, 1967; Valter Ojakäär, "Tarykalvomme Tallinnassa," *Rytmi* (Helsinki) no. 1 (1967), p. 18; H. P. Hofmann, "Tallinn 1967," *Melodie und Rhythmus*, June/July 1967, pp. 7–10; also Batashev, *Sovetskii dzhaz*, pp. 138–39.

92. *Džässfestival "Tallinn-67,"* Melodiia, D–020845–6; *Charles Lloyd in the Soviet Union*, Atlantic Recording Corp., 1970.

93. L. Rannamets, "Tallinn: dzhaz i tantsy," *Komsomolskaia pravda*, May 26, 1967.

94. Ludmer interview, 1979. See also L. Zabeginskii, "Prazdnik dzhaza v Tallinne," *Kolsomolets* (Petrozavodsk), June 1, 1967.

95. Wadim Jurczenkow, "Claude Luter w Moskwie," *Jazz* (Warsaw), Nov. 1961, p. 6; Michal Birzakow, "Edelhagen w Leningradzie," *Jazz* (Warsaw), Sept. 1964, p. 6.

96. Interview with George Avakian, Nov. 27, 1979.

97. Interview with Vladimir Frumkin, Mar. 5, 1981; also Smirnov, " 'Sekretnoe oruzhie.' "

98. *Ibid.*; also Avakian interview, 1979.

13. The Rock Inundation, 1968–1980

1. N. Minkh, "Otlichnyi dzhaz-no etot raz s vostoka," *Sovetskaia kultura*, Dec. 21, 1967; N. Minkh, "Praga: festival dzhaza," *Muzykalnaia zhizn*, no. 2 (1968).

2. Alexey Batashev, "Soviet Union," *Jazz Forum*, Mar. 1968, p. 28.

3. V. Muradeli, " 'Dzhaz 68'—talant, masterstvo, samobytnost," *Sovetskaia kultura*, June 11, 1968; see also L. Gerasimova, "Jazz 68," *Jazz Forum*, Mar. 1968, p. 29; and "O dzhaz festivale v Moskve," *Sovetskaia estrada i tsirk*, no. 9 (1968).

4. On Tashkent see V. Savranskii, "Muzykanty nastoiashchie!" *Pravda vostoka*, May 8, 1968; on Erevan see G. Zhukovets, "Ritm 68," *Komsomolets* (Erevan), May 12, 1968.

5. The group included L. Zabeginskii, Mikhail Kovalevskii, Vitalii Zharkov, and Vitalii Prudovskii.

6. M. Sinitsyn, "Dzhaz i 'Pechora,' " *Smena*, no. 15 (1969).

7. Interview, name withheld.

8. Don DeMicheal, "A Day in the New Lives of Two Russian Defector–Jazz Musicians," *Down Beat* XXXI, no. 31 (1964), pp. 12–14; "Far-Out Dzhaz," *Time*, Aug. 28, 1964, p. 30.

9. Interview with Valery Ponomarev, July 29, 1981.

10. Michael Zwerin, "Blakey's 'Messenger' from Moscow," *International Herald Tribune*, Apr. 29, 1980.

11. Tkalich interview, 1979.

12. Arkadi Petrov, "1972—a Year of Assimilation?" *Jazz Forum*, Feb. 1973, p. 52.

13. Zabeginsky interview, 1979.

14. "Eshche raz o dzhaze."

15. Used by Rodion Shchedrin in his revival of Mayakovsky's satire, *Mystery-Bouffe*. *New York Times*, Apr. 20, 1958, sec. 6, p. 56.

16. *New York Times*, Mar. 7, 1961, p. 39.

17. *The Rolling Stone's Illustrated History of Rock-'n'-Roll*, John Miller, ed. (New York, 1980), pp. 10–12.
18. Presley recordings existed in Voskresensk near Moscow by the winter of 1956–57; Zabeginsky interview, 1979.
19. Fitzgerald, *The Crackup*, p. 16.
20. Interview with Francis Ronalds, Oct. 4, 1979.
21. Interview with Yuri Valov, Nov. 8, 1980. On Valov see Chapin Day III, "Decadence Direct from Russia," *San Francisco Chronicle*, July 7, 1976; also Walter Blum, "The Iron Curtain Rockers," *San Francisco Sunday Examiner*, Mar. 13, 1977.
22. Valov interview, 1980.
23. Shabashov interview, July 29, 1981.
24. Vysotski interview, 1979; and Sermakashev interview, 1980.
25. Interview with Sasha Lehrman, Nov. 10, 1980. On Lehrman see Bill Bronstein, "Playing the Government's Tune," *San Francisco Jewish Bulletin*, June 25, 1976.
26. Cf. *Bulat Okudzhava, 60 Pesen*, Vladimir Frumkin, ed. (Ann Arbor, 1980), p. 15.
27. Lehrman interview, 1980.
28. Valov interview, 1980, and Lehrman interview, 1980.
29. Multiple interviews, names withheld.
30. Lehrman interview, 1980.
31. Frumkin interview, 1981.
32. Interview with Vladimir Brovkin, Nov. 27, 1979.
33. Vysotski interview, 1979.
34. Valov interview, 1980; Lehrman interview, 1980; and other interviews, names withheld.
35. Valvov interview, 1980.
36. Interview with Andre Rusanoff, Sept. 17, 1981; also Lehrman interview, 1980.
37. *Pesniary*, Melodiia, ST33S–04655–56.
38. Thomas Gambino, *NYET: An American Rock Musician Encounters the Soviet Union* (Englewood Cliffs, N.J., 1976).
39. Seth Mydans, "Dirt Band Storms Moscow," *Associated Press*, June 7, 1977.
40. Michael Binyon, "Elton John: In Russia with Love," *Washington Post*, May 30, 1979, Craig R. Whitney, "Moscow Hails Elton John Coolly," *New York Times*, May 29, 1979; "Elton John Rocks Russia," *Washington Post*, May 23, 1979.
41. "The Blues Abroad," *The New Yorker*, June 25, 1979, pp. 23–24.
42. Valter Ojakäär, *Popmuusikast* (Tallinn, 1978).
43. Barney Cohen, "R & R in the USSR," *Saturday Review*, June 23, 1979, p. 29.
44. Craig R. Whitney, "Unorthodoxy Swings onto Soviet Music Scene," *New York Times*, Aug. 14, 1979.
45. L. Pereverzev, "Prazdniki i budni nashego dzhaza," *Muzykalnaia zhizn*, no. 16 (1968), p. 22.
46. G. Lukianov, "Razvitie dzhaza poshlo po nevernomu puti," *Kvadrat*, no. 13 (1976), pp. 34–42.
47. G. Golstein, "Muzyka dolzhna byt proiavleniem dukha," *Kvadrat*, no. 13 (1976), pp. 23–28.

48. Ansambl "Melodiia," Melodiia, S60–13217–18; *Vashi liubimye pesni*, Melodiia, SM04345–6.

49. Efim Barban, "Novyi dzhaz: vtoroe dykhanie," *Kvadrat* (1976), pp. 77ff.

50. "Soviet Union," *Jazz Forum*, Feb. 1973, p. 18.

51. A. Medvedev, in Batashev, *Sovetskii dzhaz*, p. 5.

52. Efim Barban, *Black Music, White Freedom*, unpublished MS, 1977, p. 6. The author wishes to thank Mr. Leo Feigin for making a copy of the manuscript available to him.

53. L. Malinovskaia, "Dzhaz-eto tvorchestvo," *Tikhookeanskaia zvezda*, Dec. 19, 1968; A. Batashev, "Kogda zanaves opushchen . . . ," *Volzhskii komsomolets*, Apr. 16, 1969; V. Malov, "U nas v gorode dzhaz," *Molodoi leninets* (Stavropol), May 22, 1970; "Jazz Festival in Tblisi," *Moscow News*, no. 18 (1978).

54. *Koda* (organ of the III Voronezh Jazz Festival), May 16, 1971; John Jack, "Raising the Curtain," *Jazz Journal*, Jan. 1974, pp. 12–13.

55. *Kvadrat* (1976), pp. 48ff.

56. *Po stranitsam VI moskovskogo festivalia sovetskoi dzhazovoi muzyki*, Melodiia, S60–12813–4; *Dzhaz-78*, Melodiia, 33S60–11425–6.

57. Arkadii Petrov, "Leonid Chizik," *Kvadrat* (1978), pp. 43–51.

58. *Dzhordzh Gershvin—trio Leonida Chizika*, Melodiia, 33S60–08625–6.

59. *Instrumentalnoe trio Leonida Chizika*, Melodiia, S60–05777–8.

60. *Dzhazovye kompozitsii Vagifa Mustafa-Zade*, Melodiia, 33S–04593–4; *Vagif Mustafa-Zade*, Melodiia, 33S60–06407–8; *Dzhazovye kompozitsii*, Melodiia, 33D–030777–78; *Vagif Mustafa-Zade*, Melodiia, 33S60–12277–80.

61. *Raimonds Pauls*, Melodiia, 33DO–25939–40 and 33SM–03669–70.

62. *Tiit Paulus ja sobrad*, Melodiia, S60–15457–8.

63. *Lembit Saarsalu Quartet*, Melodiia, S60–13563–4.

64. "Ganelin-Tarasov-Chekasin: sintez," *Kvadrat* (1975), pp. 14–16; Alexey Batashev, "Vyacheslav Ganelin," *Jazz Forum*, Oct. 1973, pp. 41–42. For an early assessment of Ganelin see Ludas Szaltenis, "Jazz w Wilénskim konservatorium," *Jazz* (Warsaw), Mar. 1964, p. 14.

65. *Melody Maker*, Mar. 21, 1981, p. 22. See also Craig R. Whitney, "Lithuania is Home for Hottest Soviet Jazz Combo," *New York Times*, Aug. 12, 1979, p. 8.

66. On Chekasin see V. Kolman, "Lider sovetskogo dzhaza," *Sovetskaia molodezh*, Apr. 29, 1981.

67. The best recording of Ganelin was issued in Great Britain: *Ganelin/Tarasov/Chekasin Live in East Germany*, LEO, LR-102.

68. Alexey Batashev, "USSR—Jazz in the Seventies," *Jazz Forum*, Feb. 1977, p. 46.

69. On Ellington see Stanley Dance, "Duke's Grand Tour," *Down Beat*, Feb. 3, 1972, pp. 33–34; on the Preservation Hall Jazz Band see "Notes on Trip to USSR," *The Second Line* (New Orleans), Winter 1980, pp. 29–38. On the New England Conservatory tour see "An Interview With Gunther Schiller," *Annual Review of Jazz Studies*, (New Brunswick, N.J., 1982), pp. 126ff.

70. A. Evreinov, "Kontsert ansamblia iz Turina," *Volgogradskaia pravda*, Oct. 20, 1977; on Oscar Peterson's interrupted tour see Vadim Yurchenkov, "Oscar Peterson in the Soviet Union," *Jazz Forum*, Jan. 1975, pp. 47–49.

71. Batashev, "USSR—Jazz in the Seventies," p. 47.

72. Vadim Yurchenko, "From Leningrad and Moscow," *Jazz Forum*, Feb. 1973, p. 19.
73. Interview with Mikhail Oleinikov, Mar. 5, 1979.
74. *Leningradskii dzhaz ansambl p/upr. A. Vapirova*, Melodiia, S60–07915–16; *Ansambl "Melodiia,"* Melodiia, S60–05277–8.
75. *Dzhaz-65*, Melodiia, 33D–017009; *Dzhaz-67*, Melodiia, 33D–02987–88(a).
76. Aleksei Kozlov, "Dzhaz-rok i dzhazovyi renessans," *Kvadrat* (1978), p. 25.
77. *Po stranitsam VI Moskovskogo festivalia sovetskoi dzhazovoi muzyki*, Melodiia, 33D–02987–8(a).
78. *Jesus Christ Superstar* was first performed in the USSR in English at the Vilnius Conservatory in 1971, two months before it opened in London. A second and musically more ambitious rock opera, *Iunona i Avos* by Aleksei Rybnikov with lyrics by Andrei Voznesenskii, made its torrid debut in 1981 at the Lenin Komsomol Theater in Moscow. Cf. Serge Schmemann, "Bold Rock Musical Opens in Moscow," *New York Times*, July 11, 1981; Patricia Blake, "Lenin's Rockers," *Time*, July 20, 1981, p. 65; I. Meyer, "Sovetskaia rok opera," *Novoe russkoe slovo*, Aug. 11, 1981, p. 8.
79. *Ibid.*, pp. 28–30; also interview by W. Conover with Kozlov, 1967 (Conover interview, 1979).

14. Coda

1. "Sovetskaia pesnia," *Trud*, Mar. 15, 1980.

Index

357